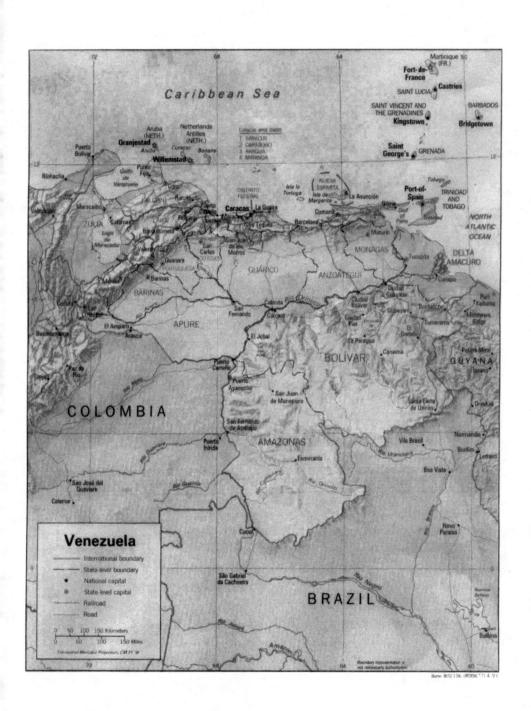

Caribbean Sea

Martinique 60
(FR.)
Fort-de-
France
SAINT LUCIA ★ Castries

SAINT VINCENT AND
THE GRENADINES
Kingstown ★

BARBADOS

Bridgetown

Saint
George's ★ GRENADA

Aruba
(NETH.)
Oranjestad
Aruba

Netherlands
Antilles
(NETH.)

Caracas area states
1 YARACUY
2 CARABOBO
3 ARAGUA
4 MIRANDA

Willemstad

Bonaire

Curaçao

Puerto
Bolívar

Ríohacha

Punto
Fijo

Golfo
de
Venezuela

Coro

Tobago

Port-of-
Spain
TRINIDAD
AND
TOBAGO

NORTH
ATLANTIC
OCEAN

DISTRITO
FEDERAL

Isla la
Tortuga

NUEVA
ESPARTA

Isla de
Margarita

La Asunción

Puerto
Cabello

Caracas
Maracay

La Guaira

Cumaná

FALCON

Maracaibo

Cabimas

Barquisimeto

Puerto
La Cruz

Los Teques

Barcelona

Maturín

ZULIA

Valencia

MONAGAS

Lago de
Maracaibo

Valera

Guanare

San
Carlos

San Juan
de los
Morros

Tucupita

DELTA
AMACURO

Curiapo

Port
Kaituma

Guasipati

Matthews
Ridge

PORTUGUESA

GUÁRICO

ANZOÁTEGUI

Barinas

Ciudad
Guayana

Mérida

BARINAS

San
Fernando

Cabruta

Ciudad
Bolívar

Bochinche

Cristóbal

San
Cristóbal

El Amparo

Arauca

Caicara

Ciudad
Piar

Tumeremo

El
Dorado

GUYANA

APURE

Bucaramanga

Peters Mine

El Johal

La Paragua

Paz de
Río

Puerto
Carreño

BOLÍVAR

Canaima

Tunja

Puerto
Ayacucho

San Juan
de Manapiare

Santa Elena
de Uairén

Oronua

COLOMBIA

San Fernando
de Atabapo

Puerto
Inírida

AMAZONAS

Esmeralda

Vila Brasil

Bonfim

Normandia

Letten

San José del
Guaviare

Boa Vista

Calamar

Cucuí

Novo
Paraíso

Venezuela

International boundary
State-level boundary
★ National capital
⊙ State-level capital
    Railroad
    Road

São Gabriel
da Cachoeira

Río Negro

BRAZIL

Balbina

0 50 100 150 Kilometers
0   100   150 Miles

Transverse Mercator Projection, CM 71 W

Boundary representation is
not necessarily authoritative.

Base 802106 (R006 7?) 4 91

HUGO CHÁVEZ

NIKOLAS KOZLOFF

HUGO

OIL, POLITICS, AND THE CHALLENGE TO THE UNITED STATES

CHÁVEZ

First published in 2006 by
PALGRAVE MACMILLAN™
175 Fifth Avenue, New York, N.Y. 10010 and
Houndmills, Basingstoke, Hampshire, England RG21 6XS.
Companies and representatives throughout the world.

PALGRAVE MACMILLAN is the global academic imprint of the Palgrave
Macmillan division of St. Martin's Press, LLC and of Palgrave Macmillan Ltd.
Macmillan® is a registered trademark in the United States, United Kingdom
and other countries. Palgrave is a registered trademark in the European Union
and other countries.

ISBN-13: 978-1-4039-7315-3
ISBN-10: 1-4039-7315-6

Library of Congress Cataloging-in-Publication Data is available from the
Library of Congress.

A catalogue record of the book is available from the British Library.

Design by Letra Libre

First edition: August 2006
10 9 8 7 6 5 4 3 2 1
Printed in the United States of America.

CONTENTS

Introduction   1

1. "Oil Is a Geopolitical Weapon"   7

2. The Battle for Control over Oil   23

3. TINA—"There Is No Alternative"   37

4. Chávez and His Fight against Neoliberalism   53

5. Chávez's Civil–Military Alliance   77

6. The Test of Chávez's Civil-Military Alliance   91

7. Chávez's South American Oil Diplomacy   105

8. Chávez and the Information War against
   the Bush Administration   119

9. In the Andes, Turning the Tide against
   the United States   133

10. The Chávez-Morales Axis   153

    Epilogue   173

Notes   179
Index   257

INTRODUCTION

On August 22, 2005, American evangelical minister Pat Robertson made national headlines by claiming on his TV show the *700 Club* that if Venezuelan president Hugo Chávez "thinks we're trying to assassinate him, I think that we really ought to go ahead and do it." Robertson went on to say that Chávez was a "terrific danger" to the United States and intended to become "the launching pad for communist infiltration and Muslim extremism." Robertson added: "It's a whole lot cheaper than starting a war. And I don't think any oil shipments will stop." Robertson's comments inflamed public opinion in Venezuela and led to strong statements from Venezuelan officials. Defense Secretary Donald Rumsfeld offered a mild rebuke to Robertson's comments, declaring "Certainly it's against the law. Our department doesn't do that type of thing." Both Rumsfeld and State Department spokesman Sean McCormack were careful to state that the remarks came from a private citizen and did not represent official U.S. policy. "Private citizens say all kinds of things all the time," Rumsfeld remarked. McCormack did not condemn Robertson's statements, although he stated that the minister's comments were "inappropriate." "This is not the policy of the United States government. We do not share his views," McCormack said.[1]

Rumsfeld and McCormack's statements notwithstanding, the Bush administration's response lacks credibility, and there is some indication that Robertson does not diverge so significantly from official U.S. policy. Venezuelan chancellor Alí Rodríguez suggested that McCormack criticized Robertson for being imprudent. "It would appear that in their subconscious what they are condemning is imprudence and not the call for assassination," Rodríguez remarked. What is more, the Venezuelan president has charged that he has been targeted for assassination by the White House. In an interview with Ted Koppel on ABC's *Nightline*, Chávez remarked, "We have been subjected—Venezuela has been subjected—to permanent aggression against us and against me personally." In March 2005, the State Department retorted that Chávez's accusations were "wild." However, serious doubts emerged about that claim when Felix Rodríguez, a former Central Intelligence Agency (CIA) operative and influential Bush supporter in south Florida, claimed in an interview with Miami's Channel 22 that the administration has "contingency plans." When pressed to explain, Rodríguez said the plans "could be economic measures and even at some point military measures." Rodríguez and his views must be taken seriously. As the *Washington Post* has noted, Rodríguez "is well known in Latin America for his role advising a Bolivian military unit that captured and executed Cuban revolutionary Che Guevara in 1967. He was well-connected with President Bush's father during his tenure both as president and vice president." Clearly, Chávez is not taking any chances: he recently beefed up his security detail.[2]

While the veracity of such reports are unclear, it is not as if the Venezuelan leader is unjustified in feeling paranoid. In the run-up to the April 2002 coup d'état against the Chávez regime, the Bush administration funneled U.S. taxpayer money to the Venezuelan opposition through the National Endowment for Democracy. Speaking on *Nightline*, Chávez remarked, "Now this administration has truly broken with all protocols of democracy and respect for people. The coup d'état against Venezuela was manufactured in Washington. My death was ordered. And it was ordered recently." During the coup, Chávez was taken prisoner by elements within the military. The coup regime spread the lie on television that he had willingly resigned. As he watched the announcement from inside the military headquarters of Fort Tiuna, Chávez thought, "Now they are going to kill me." An officer lent Chávez a phone and he called his wife, bidding her farewell. Fortuitously, Chávez narrowly escaped death. "The order to kill me had been given," he remarked later. "What happened was that the generals that were up in arms did not have true leadership and some generals, but above all the young officers that were taking care of me, neutralized that order." Since the April 2002 coup, Hugo Chávez has consolidated his position in Venezuela and seems to be riding high. According to recent opinion polls, he has a 71.5 percent approval rating, and he is South America's most popular and charismatic leader. Having consolidated his position, Chávez is poised to become a hemispheric leader with real clout. With reelection to a second six-year term very likely in December 2006, the Venezuelan leader is certain to continue to be an irritant to the Bush administration and his successor in the White House.[3]

Many Americans might wonder why Bush and his fundamentalist allies seem so intent on getting rid of Chávez in the first place. This book seeks to elucidate the political significance of Chávez for Venezuela and indeed for the entire hemisphere. Since his election in 1998, Chávez has challenged U.S.-led trade initiatives, the war in Iraq, and the drug war in Latin America. As if that were not enough, he also has developed warm ties with the island nation of Cuba, selling oil to the country in exchange for delegations of foreign doctors. Domestically, he has increased taxes on U.S. oil firms doing business in the country in an effort to "sow the petroleum" to Venezuela's neediest. Chávez has used this increased oil revenue to carry out an array of ambitious social programs in education, housing, health, and, perhaps more controversially, land reform. Such reforms naturally align Chávez with communist Cuba. More significant still, Chávez has sought to increase economic and political ties to other South American nations in an effort to counteract U.S. influence in the area. Particularly threatening to the White House is Chávez's new South American oil company, Petrosur, which the Venezuelan leader envisions as a kind of Organization of Petroleum Exporting Countries (OPEC) for the region. Chávez has even launched his own hemispheric satellite channel, Telesur. It is undeniable that Chávez, a rural man of mixed racial background, has become a symbol of the revolt against U.S. political and economic interests throughout the hemisphere.

I was prompted to write this book about Venezuela owing to my recent involvement with the country. My interest in Hugo Chávez goes back some five years or so. The firebrand politician first piqued my attention while I was pursuing research for my dissertation in Caracas. Watching Chávez deliver speeches on TV from my hotel suite, I was struck by his offhand manner, which stood in stark contrast to many wooden U.S. politicians. Typically, Chávez would deliver his speeches before a great painting of Simon Bolivar, the great hero who fought for independence against Spain. In seeking to compare himself with Bolivar, Chávez seemed to be pitching himself to the Venezuelan people as a revolutionary fighting against an imperialist power, in this case the United States. Chávez rambled on diverse subjects, such as Venezuelan history and the oil industry, occasionally interrupting his speeches by breaking out a tiny pocket copy of the new constitution. Later I watched Chávez take calls from all over the country on his TV show *Aló, Presidente*; he frequently burst into song or played the xylophone. While I found these presentations entertaining, I wondered whether Chávez was more hot air than the real thing. Traveling around the country,

I saw little evidence of serious social transformation, although highway banners proclaiming the so-called Bolivarian Revolution were always in abundant supply. What is more, while I agreed with Chávez's criticism of U.S. foreign policy, his origins in the army gave me pause. I have a deep and abiding suspicion of authority and men in uniform, and Chávez's constant harking on military symbolism through parades and regalia struck me as vulgar and crass. Meanwhile, although I had no illusions about the opposition media and their scurrilous attacks against the president, Chávez's constant attacks on the press and his singling out of individual journalists made me wonder whether he really had dictatorial intentions. That was certainly the concern of some students and faculty I met at the Central University in Caracas. They were on the left, not the right, but were wary of Chávez and his long-term intentions. I had similar ambivalent feelings about the man's moves to do away with the old, corrupt labor unions. While I was in Caracas, Chávez tried to enforce state-monitored elections within labor unions by putting a referendum measure on the ballot. Since then, a pro-Chávez labor union has grown in importance and seeks to supplant the older confederation which received funding from the Solidarity Center of the AFL-CIO. The center had in turn been supported by the U.S. State Department, the United States Agency for International Development (U.S. AID), and the U.S. funded National Endowment for Democracy. Though I did not attach much importance to Chávez's labor policy at the time, clearly it was a first move to assert his control against traditional U.S. influence.[4]

I left Venezuela in August of 2000 and returned to the United Kingdom. Although I continued to pay attention to developments in Venezuela, I put more stock in other social movements in South America, such as the landless tenant movement in Brazil, the Movimento dos Trabalhadores Rurais Sem Terra (MST), and the indigenous movement in Ecuador. But then, watching the coup d'état unfold against Chávez in 2002, I was frankly moved by the outpouring of support from the poor people of Caracas. Flowing down from the poor barrios, they surrounded the presidential palace until the coup government was forced to disband. As Chávez quickened the pace of social programs in the wake of the coup, there was no denying that something big was afoot in Venezuela. Intrigued, I started to take a second look at Chávez and wrote a series of reports about Venezuelan political developments for the Council on Hemispheric Affairs (COHA) in Washington, D.C. Today Chávez is making near daily headlines and the time seemed right to write a book that would provide readers with information to make sense of and come to their own conclusions about the Venezuelan leader, independent of the U.S. media establishment which assumes that Chávez is a feared enemy of the United States.

Throughout the book, I seek to make the case for why Chávez is important to Americans. The Venezuelan leader has cashed in his country's energy resources to achieve important political capital. In reversing Venezuela's traditional oil policy, Chávez became an important enemy of the Bush administration. I have devoted two chapters to Chávez's oil challenge to the United States and its political dimensions. The Venezuelan leader has also challenged U.S.-led trade initiatives and the drive towards globalization. In later pages I discuss in detail Chávez's ideological challenge to the White House and the impact which he has had on Venezuela and the wider region. For corporate America and the advocates of unfettered free-market capitalism, Chávez's emergence has come as something of a wakeup call. The Venezuelan leader, however, has challenged not only U.S. economic orthodoxy but America's historic control over the military. This book provides the reader with an inside look into the Venezuelan military and its turn away from the U.S. Pentagon. Americans would also do well to consider Chávez's economic and political impact on the hemisphere as a whole. Indeed, Chávez has done much to unite other South American countries against traditional U.S influence. This book gives the reader a sense of the social ferment spreading across South America and illustrates Chávez's place in this wider transformation. If current trends continue, Chávez only stands to further consolidate his status as a hemispheric leader. Clearly he will be a figure to be reckoned with by the United States.

CHAPTER ONE
"OIL IS A GEOPOLITICAL WEAPON"

Oil looms large in the realm of U.S.-Venezuelan relations. Venezuela is the fifth largest oil exporter in the world and the fourth largest supplier of oil to the United States after Canada, Mexico, and Saudi Arabia. In 2004, Venezuela's state-owned oil company, Petróleos de Venezuela Sociedad Anónima (PdVSA), accounted for 11.8 percent (1.52 million barrels a day) of U.S. imports. In the event of a wider war in the Middle East, Venezuela could become a critical energy supplier.[1]

Even before Hugo Chávez was first elected president in 1998, he was explicit in describing his views about petroleum. "Oil is a geopolitical weapon," he declared, "and these imbeciles who govern us don't realize the power they have, as an oil-producing country." Chávez had no need to be modest about his country's economic leverage. Consider: Venezuela is home to the western hemisphere's largest conventional oil reserves, estimated in 2004 at 77.8 billion barrels. That figure dwarfs the United States, which only has 22 billion in reserves. What is more, Venezuela has trillions of cubic feet of natural gas. In addition to its proved reserves, Venezuela has an estimated 260 billion barrels of heavy crude, more or less equal to Saudi Arabia's reserves, in the Orinoco belt lying in the center of the country. By 2020, analysts predict that Venezuela could outstrip Mexico as an oil exporter to the United States—if relations do not sour beforehand. Through bargaining and maneuvering Chávez has worked to achieve a higher price for oil through the Organization of Petroleum Exporting Countries (OPEC), the oil cartel of which Venezuela was a founding member. With oil prices hovering at about $59 a barrel in 2005, Chávez is awash in cash and wields considerable economic and political influence throughout his country and Latin America.[2]

The evidence suggests that Chávez may try to follow through on his inflammatory electoral rhetoric. Ever since April 2002, when Chávez was

briefly removed from power in a coup, he has accused the United States—
not without merit—of sponsoring his attempted overthrow as well as supporting a devastating oil lockout in 2002–03. Never one to soften his
language, Chávez bluntly refers to the United States as "an imperialist
power." What is more, according to Chávez, Bush had plans to see him assassinated. In a further barb, Chávez declared that if he were killed, the
United States would not receive a drop of oil for another thousand years.[3]

To understand the power struggle over oil which is played out between
the United States and Venezuela, it's essential to see how Chávez's position
is a 360 degree turn away from the U.S.-friendly policies of earlier regimes.
Those governments, according to Chávez, were unpatriotic and unduly sub-
servient to U.S. interests, and failed to secure oil wealth for the good of
Venezuelan society.

Perhaps no figure was more closely allied to U.S. oil interests than Luis
Giusti, PdVSA's head from 1994 to 1999. The dashing Giusti, who has fair
hair and a light complexion, was born in an oil field camp in 1944. Although
Giusti came of age during the 1960s, a time of political ferment, student activism, and even communist insurgency in Venezuela, he seems to have
steered clear of such rabble rousing. Pursuing his studies as a petroleum engineer, he graduated from the University of Zulia, located in the oil-rich
city of Maracaibo, in 1966. He later earned a petroleum engineering degree
from the University of Tulsa and worked for years in the scorching hot oil
fields and refineries.[4]

Today Maracaibo is a sprawling city of 1.5 million people. The city rests
on a lake, the largest in South America, which measures 200 kilometers
north to south.[5] I have visited the area twice, first in the early 1990s and
later in 2000 as a graduate student conducting field research on the environmental history of oil. What I was immediately struck by in Maracaibo is the
insufferable heat; to the north lies desert. A slight breeze from the lake
brings some slight relief, but not much. On my first trip, I vividly recall exit-
ing my hotel on the Plaza Baralt after breakfast. Walking in the downtown, I
found sweat pouring off my wrist within minutes. Someone later remarked
to me that one might fry an egg on the pavement in Maracaibo on a typical
day, and I have no reason to disbelieve it.

The oil infrastructure dotting Lake Maracaibo is living testament to
the engineering feats of a bygone age. On my first trip I was taken aback by
the thousands of rusty oil derricks built by the Americans who were trying

to get rich on petroleum decades ago, embedded in the waters of the lake. Visiting oil boom towns is hardly the most popular tourist itinerary, but I had developed a considerable curiosity about the area. To get to the other side of the lake from Maracaibo, I took a dilapidated taxicab across a long causeway. The terrain is barren and desolate, with desert shrubs peeking up from the ground. In Ciudad Ojeda, the streets were cluttered with vendors and useless junk. I retreated to a luxury hotel that was air conditioned, probably for visiting oil executives, as no one else would likely be able to afford it. Touring around, I saw old company towns, which had been inherited by the state-run Maraven, a PdVSA affiliate. Pristine and protected compounds are surrounded by tall iron fences. From the outside they look like orderly American company towns with streets, stores, hospitals, and pharmacies.

Although many Venezuelans working for American oil companies achieved much higher wages than they would have made in the countryside, not everyone in the oil boom towns benefited. During my trip, I saw the result of the long-standing neglect. I rode to an area known only as R-10. There I spotted wells spewing oil into people's backyards. Most of the houses were made of concrete or aluminum. At one house I spotted a pool of green toxic waste at the front door. Nearby, oil leaked onto the ground where children were playing. Meanwhile, flames spewed from a pipeline.

In a small country where U.S. political and economic influence has been pervasive, being too closely identified with foreign petroleum interests can prove politically costly. Luis Giusti's 'crime,' according to nationalists such as Chávez, was that he identified too closely with foreign oil men as opposed to looking out for Venezuelan interests. Giusti came of age at a time when the country sought to exert greater control over oil resources. Although some oil wealth had filtered down to the poorest and successive regimes were able to carry out important works in health and education, the nation still suffered from persistent poverty and unequal distribution of wealth. Nationalization of the foreign oil companies in 1975–76, designed to "sow the petroleum" more equitably, was supposed to change all that.[6] With the creation of PdVSA, Venezuelans gained a sense of national pride. In the same year that nationalization was carried out, Giusti was working with Shell Oil. Under the nationalization, Shell then became Maraven, a PdVSA subsidiary. The ambitious young man quickly ascended the corporate ladder at Maraven, gaining valuable experience in exploration, production, refining, corporate planning, and marketing. Giusti's hard work and determination paid off; in 1994 he became PdVSA's chairman and chief executive officer.

But Giusti's tenure at PdVSA proved controversial. According to Chávez, who later sought to bring the state oil company under greater government control, Giusti and others pursued an oil policy that was closely allied to the interests of Washington and foreign oil companies, a policy that was antithetical to Venezuelan interests. Specifically, under his direction, PdVSA started to open up to private participation and to increase production. In a country where oil was seen as a symbol of national independence and sovereignty, Giusti's "apertura," or opening of the oil sector, proved particularly divisive and created hostility toward PdVSA executives. Reportedly, Giusti questioned the traditional economic orientation of the country. "Here [in Venezuela]," he remarked, "people brandish the terms 'sovereignty' and 'patriotism'. Enough of that." According to Giusti, there is no greater loss of sovereignty than poverty, which is how he justifies his strategy to develop Venezuela's natural resources.[7]

Giusti, however, must have been aware that many Venezuelans did not share his business views, and he did his best to sell his vision to the country. "Garrulous and candid," remarked *Business Week*, "Giusti mobilized support with a campaign of talking to ministers and politicians, lobbying congressional committees, making speeches, and writing articles." Giusti's impact on Venezuelan oil policy was remarkable, and fiercely criticized. According to government officials, between 1976 and 1993, out of every dollar of oil exports, 66 cents on average wound up in government coffers. However, this was reversed dramatically from 1993 to 2002. Government figures have said that during this period, government revenue from oil fell dramatically, from 66 cents to 33 cents on the dollar. According to energy minister Rafael Ramírez, "apertura amounted to a veritable assault on Venezuelan oil.[8]

The government's own Ministry of Energy and Mines was increasingly losing power over PdVSA. Bernard Mommer, a respected German-born oil analyst who himself has worked at PdVSA, writes that the Venezuelan company's board of directors was dominated by former executives of the foreign oil companies. It was they, charges Mommer, who actually took over oil policy.[9] Having become a political actor in its own right, PdVSA, in line with Giusti's new emphasis, started to concentrate more on the development of the oil industry as opposed to fiscal revenues. "To put it differently," adds Mommer, "the policy issue was no longer prices but volumes."[10] Giusti increased oil output by 1 million barrels a day to 3.6 million by 1997.[11] The new PdVSA head also announced that the state-run petrochemicals company Pequiven would be privatized following a legal reform.[12] Meanwhile, the country was opened up to foreign competition in the petroleum sector and joint ventures.[13] Not surprisingly, complying with OPEC quotas was not a high priority within PdVSA. Giusti himself remarked that OPEC's quota system was "an obsolete subject "that was "no longer relevant in today's market."[14] In 1994, Venezuela went over its OPEC production quota.[15]

By 1998, Giusti's PdVSA was producing about 800,000 barrels over its OPEC quota.[16] What is more, Giusti was becoming a household name in Venezuela. His most vocal cheerleader was the American press: in 1998, *Business Week* gushed, "He denies any national political ambitions, although his name has been mentioned as a future presidential candidate"; *Time* magazine even named Giusti "Manager of the Year."[17] Meanwhile company executives enjoyed large expense accounts and, according to Chávez, earned up to $180,000 a year. Giusti himself made $315,000 a year.[18] In the words of Chávez, PdVSA executives were living it up in "luxury chalets where they perform orgies drinking whisky."[19] A social divide was developing between PdVSA's staff, which employed only 40,000 workers (less than 1 percent of the working population), and the rest of the country.[20] Indeed, the company "was viewed as a den of arrogant, pampered technocrats—and a cookie jar for Venezuela's elite, whose corruption has left two-thirds of the population in poverty."[21]

Even more damning from Chávez's point of view, in 1996 PdVSA entered into a joint venture with a San Diego-based company called SAIC (Science Applications International Corporation).[22] SAIC is a corporate behemoth: in 2005 the company earned $7.5 billion and it holds a lucrative contract with the U.S. Army to develop the next generation of combat vehicles.[23] SAIC moreover "provides high-technology physics and engineering services to support Defense Department research."[24] The company, according to the World Policy Institute, a New-York based organization concerned with domestic and international policy, works on everything from intelligence gathering to missile defense to Iraqi reconstruction for the Pentagon.[25] What is more, SAIC had contracts with oil companies to handle information technology (IT).[26] The joint venture between SAIC and PdVSA, known as INTESA (Informática, Negocios y Tecnología), was in charge of managing PdVSA's IT operations.[27] But SAIC, according to Chávez, had ties to the U.S. Central Intelligence Agency (CIA) and was using INTESA to conduct espionage and sabotage in Venezuela.[28] The development of IN-TESA, according to current energy minister Rafael Ramirez, was a terrible blow for PdVSA. "There is nothing more valuable for an oil-producing country nor for any enterprise than the information about its deposits, its production, its capacity," he remarked. "That is, this information is worth very much and also has a strategic geopolitical value."[29] The list of SAIC executives reads like a who's who of Washington insiders. Former NSA director Bobby Ray Inman, former Defense Secretary Melvin Laird, and ex-CIA director Robert Gates all served on SAIC's board of directors at one time or another.[30]

In 2000 I conducted research at the historical archive of the government's own Ministry of Energy and Mines. Located in a depressing concrete high-rise in the area of Bellas Artes, the ministry's offices were ramshackle. At one point, however, I had to obtain permission to review materials from the Creole Petroleum Corporation, a U.S. oil company that had done business in the Lake Maracaibo region for many decades. Through some contacts, I was able to obtain a letter from a high executive at the ministry. I traveled across town to PdVSA offices and presented my credentials to the oil company archivist. I was allowed to look at some company records from the 1930s, hardly sensitive information. But returning from lunch, I noticed that the bound volumes I had been consulting were no longer on the table. Irritated, I approached the archivist. Defending herself, she remarked that a PdVSA executive had given her conflicting orders and that I would not be allowed to continue my research. I had been overruled, and no amount of lobbying could reverse the decision. The incident perhaps demonstrates the kind of corporate culture that pervades much of PdVSA.

When one visits PdVSA facilities, it is not difficult to see why many Venezuelans had grown distrustful of the company. At one point during my stay in Caracas, I went to interview a high-up company official. This time I was told to go far outside the city to another set of offices. To get there, I had to travel by subway and bus. Located in a beautiful pastoral setting, the facilities provided a strong contrast with the grimy, polluted downtown. Inside, company staff members dressed in expensive business suits ate in a splendid dining room.

Bristling at the corporate independence of PdVSA and its privileged executives, Chávez actively campaigned against the privatization of the company during the presidential election of 1998. The presidential hopeful promised to fire Giusti and to "review" oil deals with foreign companies.[31] Provocatively, Chávez challenged vested interests at PdVSA by seeking to reestablish a predominant role for the presidency in the design and implementation of an oil strategy through the Ministry of Energy and Mining.[32] This shrewd move no doubt secured more political support for the aspiring politician. Chávez cruised to victory in December of 1998, winning the presidential election with 56.2 percent of the vote.[33]

Following through on his promise, Chávez promptly fired Giusti who became an energy advisor to U.S. president George Bush.[34] Giusti became affiliated with the Baker Institute for Public Policy, a think tank headed by James Baker, secretary of state under George Bush Sr. There the former PdVSA head contributed to the U.S. drive to invade Iraq. In the days before 9/11, Giusti participated in laying the groundwork for an invasion. In a report entitled "Strategic Energy Policy Challenges for the 21st Century," Giusti and other members of a Baker Institute Task Force argued that "Iraq remains a destabilizing influence to . . . the flow of oil to international markets from the Middle East." The report adds that the United States should conduct a policy review towards Iraq, "including military, energy, economic, and political/diplomatic assessments." Baker submitted the report to Vice President Dick Cheney, the former head of Texas oil firm Halliburton. At the time Cheney was chair of the White House Energy Policy Development Group. In addition to Giusti, Baker also relied on other advisers for his report including Kenneth Lay, the disgraced former CEO of Enron, which went bankrupt following a massive accounting fraud.[35]

Giusti also took a job as senior adviser to the Washington-based Center for Strategic and International Studies, a group that counts such figures as Henry Kissinger, Brent Scowcroft, Zbigniew Brzezinski, and William Cohen as counselors.[36] Giusti also continued his relationship with Shell, becoming the company's nonexecutive director, and served as a member of the advisory board at the Riverstone Group, the energy branch of the Carlyle Group.[37] The investment company is infamous for its ties to insider politicians. After losing to Bill Clinton in the election of 1992, former president George Bush became an advisor to Carlyle, helping to strengthen the company's ties to the Saudi royal family. Current U.S. president George W.

Bush was appointed to the board of directors of Caterair, an airline food business acquired by Carlyle, in 1990.[38]

From his well-connected perch in Washington, Giusti lambasted Chávez and the firebrand politician's energy policy, saying "They have a foolish ideology about sovereignty in oil," no doubt to sympathetic and influential ears in Washington.[39] In July 2000, Cuban leader Castro, speaking live on Venezuela's state TV station, made an inflammatory accusation about Giusti. The ex-PdVSA chief, he claimed, had links with Cuban exiles in Miami interested in unseating Chávez from power. Castro urged reporters to ask Giusti how much money he had received in the past few months from Miami-based groups. Giusti vehemently denied the accusations. "It is a gigantic slander," he remarked.[40]

To understand why oil arouses such intense political passions in Venezuela, one must consider the history of U.S. oil companies doing business in the country. Braving bats, bears, jaguar, rattlesnakes, and lizards, oilmen ventured deep into the jungle in search of black gold in the early twentieth century. Prospectors put up with the difficult terrain along the east bank of Lake Maracaibo, which included jungle, marshes, and savannah.[41] Early oil pioneers also had to contend with deadly tropical disease such as malaria as well as ferocious Motilón Indians who resisted oil encroachment.[42]

After World War I, "Venezuela fairly swarmed with curious and ambitious Americans" looking for oil.[43] Jersey Standard, realizing that its largest competitor, Shell, was investing heavily in exploration and development in Venezuela, entered the Andean nation.[44] Jersey Standard would eventually grow in Venezuela, buying a majority stake in the Creole corporation in 1928; the company eventually acquired Lago Petroleum Corporation. Standard was joined in Venezuela by Gulf.[45] Speculators and oil company representatives bid for concessions and offered handsome sums and bribes to Juan Vicente Gómez, a U.S.-supported military dictator.[46] Nevertheless, in December 1921, Gómez received a shock when he was apprised of a plot to invade Venezuela. The plan was foiled when the Dutch authorities stopped a ship from setting forth from Holland. The ship had been chartered to travel to Venezuela and engage in a "filibustering expedition." Another ship was prevented from setting sail from England.

Both ships, it was believed, had been funded to the tune of $400,000 by "oil interests of the United States," which "had been pulling every possible string" so as to block the advancement of British oil interests.[47] British reports, based on information supplied by Gómez authorities, stated that "a person named Bollorpholl of New York representing himself to be connected with State Department has handled the money."[48] Diplomats hinted that Standard Oil, which had been disappointed with legal decisions that favored British companies, "would like to see Gómez's downfall and may have contributed to this expedition."[49] Apparently oil interests had been conspiring with Venezuelan military officers.[50] What is more, the Venezuelan minister for foreign affairs, Esteban Gil Borges, had been "practically in the pockets" of American oil companies.[51] Although the plots never came to fruition, local officials worried that oil workers could be subverted for political ends.[52]

Although the economic conditions of migrants arriving in the oil zone were better than conditions in the countryside, workers were subjected to virulent racism on the job and wages failed to keep up with rising prices. Workers faced other dangers, including tropical disease and accidents. Excluded from many of the amenities that foreigners enjoyed, Venezuelan workers were ripe recruits for radical ideologies and movements. In 1925, workers struck for shorter hours and higher pay which alarmed U.S. diplomats.[53] As the U.S. consul remarked, "the outlook for peace and tranquility does not seem bright in the oil district . . . the lack of disturbance and the protection of company property may not characterize . . . future labor troubles."[54]

Also problematic was the threat oil development posed to the local ecology and many traditional villages along the lake. The famous Los Barrosos–2 blow-out, which occurred in the Cabimas area of La Rosa on the east side of Lake Maracaibo, set an ominous environmental precedent in December 1922. The gusher began when the well (which later came to known as R-2 of the Venezuela Oil Concessions) blew out.[55] For more than a week, oil spewed into the air at the astonishing rate of 100,000 barrels of oil per day. The blow-out continued for nine days, sending a total of some 900,000 barrels of oil into the lake.[56] According to Henri Pittier, who witnessed the blow-out, the diameter of the column of oil was only 30 centimeters, but it reached a height of more than 100 meters. A river of oil immediately formed, which reached as far as the city of Maracaibo, 35 kilometers away. Pittier claimed he saw this gusher from the opposite side of the lake and that one could discern the plume of oil from the roofs of Maracaibo.[57]

Compounding the situation, offshore oil operations were vulnerable to fire, as boiler stations with boardwalks connected the oil wells. Each well was flanked by other kinds of oil infrastructure, including platforms holding pumps, mud tanks, pipe racks, manifolds, flow stations, and separator or transformer tanks.[58] Obviously, such infrastructure and derricks posed an enormous environmental threat. One lakeshore village built on stilts, Lagunillas, was located directly within the most important oil zone in Venezuela during the Gómez era.[59] In 1928, the entire community paid the price for oil company pollution when a major fire occurred, destroying hundreds of houses and engulfing the town in flames. Local officials claimed the fire had been started by a spark from an open-hearth fire that ignited oil spilled by a leaky drill near the town.[60] The fire lasted for more than two hours and left only 125 of 700 houses standing.[61] After another fire in 1939, residents were evacuated inland to Ciudad Ojeda, about 15 miles to the north.[62]

In Maracaibo, one may still see relics of the bygone era before the onset of oil development; especially in the historic district of Santa Lucía, where charming, brightly painted wood houses stand. I was told that there had once been many more of these structures. But in the rush to modernize, many had been bulldozed. Before the demolitions, there had been folkloric *gaita* competitions between the various Maracaibo neighborhoods. Gaita (lilting songs that are performed to the accompaniment of drums and other string instruments) are unique to Maracaibo.

At night, I would return to my hotel in Bellavista, a wealthy city district where the architecture was rather crass and vulgar. The *maracuchos*, or natives of Maracaibo, had seemingly started anew: with the onset of oil development, the city had done its best to erase its past and appear modern. But had the effort been entirely successful? Even in Bellavista, I sometimes had the sense that time had stood still. In my hotel room, I had a black rotary telephone dating perhaps to the 1940s. Eating in the hotel restaurant, I was intrigued to find an elderly American sitting at the next table speaking Spanish with his friends. It is not every day that I would bump into Americans in Maracaibo, and tourists are a rarity. A hotel employee told me that the man was a regular fixture in the restaurant. He was in his nineties and had been an early oil pioneer in the area. Unlike many of his counterparts, he had married a Venezuelan woman and decided to stay.

Maracuchos and Americans have long worked together. The U.S. oilmen befriended and taught Venezuelan workers, who eventually learned the inner workings of the oil industry. Nevertheless Creole, which had grown rapidly during the 1930s, would have to redo its public image if it wanted to maintain its privileged position in Venezuela. By World War II, with Gómez dead and the more nationalist Medina Angarita government in power, Venezuela moved to increase taxation on foreign oil companies.[63] Creole set about an ambitious public relations campaign designed to ingratiate itself with the government and the public at large. The company started a so-called indoctrination school to hire Berlitz instructors to teach Spanish on the fields. Creole constructed schools and stores, provided medical services for workers and their families, operated extensive transportation systems to get workers from their homes to the work sites and back, and took care of sanitation, water supply, and electricity.[64]

Creole's public relations efforts notwithstanding, the company's political problems continued. A couple of years ago I made a Freedom of Information Act request to find out more about Creole's inner workings. After a long wait, the Federal Bureau of Investigation (FBI) sent me some documents dated from the early 1960s. A. Lewis Russell, an industrial security administrator with Creole, wrote to J. Edgar Hoover at the FBI, requesting information about anticommunist groups in the United States. Russell was looking for materials for use in an educational program entitled "Democracy vs. Communism."[65] Why, I wondered, would Creole be so concerned about waging a war for hearts and minds? I got my answer in the next pages, which revealed juicy details about the company's fears. Acts of sabotage had been committed against Creole. The company did not even trust crew members serving on one of its own tankers, the *Esso Caripito*. Company officials were concerned that there might be an uprising on the ship and that the crew was working with the Venezuelan Armed Forces of National Liberation.[66] Clearly, long after the initial oil boom period, U.S. petroleum companies like Creole had plenty of political worries while doing business in Venezuela.

What is remarkable to consider is that Chávez's pick to head the Ministry of Energy was a former communist rebel, Alí Rodríguez. Born in 1937 in the town of Ejido, in the Andean state of Mérida, Rodríguez cuts a stern figure[67]. Sporting wirerimmed glasses, a hard-edged smile, and now balding, he is physically quite distinct from his rough contemporary Giusti.[68] Born into poverty, his parents were farmers.[69] Growing up in Ejido, Rodríguez learned to put food on the table by hunting ducks.[70] Rodríguez was able to escape rural poverty, however, and studied law and economics at the Central University in Caracas.[71] There, he fell under the influence of German-born Marxist economist Bernard Mommer.[72] Rodríguez graduated in 1961 and, inspired by the example of Fidel Castro in Cuba, became known as Commander Fausto.[73] He went back to the Andes and became a guerrilla fighter, surviving on canned sardines, oatmeal, wild turkey, and arepas (small cakes made out of corn or wheat flour).[74] Although Rodríguez worked as a bomb specialist, he came to be known as a sensible, even-tempered man.[75] He became something of an expert in oil-related matters. "In the mountains, I organized seminars on oil administration," he has said. Although communist rebels ultimately were not successful in toppling successive democratic regimes in Venezuela, Rodríguez continued to work as a guerrilla into the 1970s.[76] In all, Rodríguez had a 15-year career as an insurgent.[77]

How does one explain the fact that Rodríguez and others took up arms to overthrow regimes in the 1960s and 1970s? The ongoing social unrest, on the surface at least, seems to be somewhat surprising. From 1958 to 1998, Venezuela earned $300 billion from oil, the equivalent of 20 Marshall Plans.[78] Yet, despite the influx of oil wealth, in the late 1970s more than a third of the population still made less than the minimum wage.[79] Oil wealth moreover was not spread uniformly across the country; city residents and those living in the petroleum zones enjoyed higher incomes than rural inhabitants. A damning United Nations report in the early 1960s concluded that Venezuela had one of the most unequal income distributions in the world.[80]

One of the casualties of this unequal oil development was the Chávez family. Hugo Chávez Frías was born in July 1954 in the town of Sabaneta, a sleepy rural settlement where local inhabitants ride bicycles to get around.[81] Growing up in Sabaneta, the young Chávez was surrounded by herds of Zebu cattle, royal palms, and mango trees.[82] Sabaneta lies within the western provincial state of Barinas, the most elevated part of the Venezuelan *llano* (plain).[83]

Like many other Venezuelans of mixed race, Chávez grew up in poverty.[84] One of six children, he was born in extremely humbling conditions.[85] "I was a farm kid from the plains of South Venezuela," he remarked to Ted Koppel of ABC. "I grew up in a palm tree house with an earthen floor.[86] Chávez added that the physical conditions were difficult in Sabaneta, and there was no electricity.[87] Sabaneta, located along the banks of a river, had only three earthen streets.[88] Chávez's father brought his wife to the city of Barinas to give birth in his mother's house. It was only much later that Chávez's parents returned there, and his father built a house. "It was a block house," Chávez said, "a rural house . . .made out of asbestos with a cement floor."[89]

Since there was no school in Sabaneta, Chávez went to Barinas.[90] Living with his grandmother Rosa Inés, Chávez experienced rough economic conditions from an early age. "Poverty," Chávez recounted, "obliged us to look for resources."[91] Chávez learned to plant corn and clean the back yard. Rosa Ines made coconut sweets, which the young boy would sell in little bags.[92] In addition to selling his sweets at school, Chávez also hawked his candy at the special *llanero bolo* (bowling hall) and sold oranges to the local ice cream store. He would also climb trees with Nacho, his brother, to gather fruit to sell. Chávez would throw the oranges to him, and load up the wheelbarrow with fruit.[93]

For Chávez and other children growing up in the llano, the challenge was how to break free of grinding poverty. Fortunately, the young boy came of age during a time of great political and social ferment when educational opportunities were expanding. In 1958, the corrupt Pérez Jiménez military dictatorship fell from power and it seemed that at long last conditions might improve in the countryside.[94] The leading opposition party, Acción Democrática (AD) had long emphasized educational improvements.[95] In January 1958 universal suffrage and electoral politics were again allowed to flourish.[96] In the presidential election held the same year, the AD candidate Rómulo Betancourt polled poorly in Caracas and the central cities but received impressive rural support which enabled him to win the election.[97] Appeasing this rural constituency would be one of Betancourt's primary tasks.[98] Not surprisingly, education received a boost under the new regime and the literacy level increased.[99] Nevertheless, change was slow to take effect in many areas of the countryside. In 1971, the illiteracy rate in Venezuela was 23 percent and even reached 40 percent in some areas of the country.[100] Although public education was guaranteed to all, in practice the system was skewed toward the privileged few while the rural population was left behind.[101]

Unlike many of his peers, Chávez held an advantage from an early age through his family. Though Chávez's father had scarcely passed sixth grade, both his parents were primary school teachers and fortunately "they [my parents] inculcated to us the importance of studies.[102] But out of every 100 children from my town, 99 didn't get to study."[103] Once in Barinas, Chávez benefited from his grandmother, who taught him to read and write, and attended the only school in Barinas, the O'Leary School.[104] Chávez, then, was relatively fortunate. However, Chávez's formative years living in poverty would later have a profound impact on the young man. After serving in the army and becoming a political figure on the national stage, Chávez would seek to bring the oil companies under greater state control and to fulfill the promise of economic prosperity for Venezuelans who had not shared in the oil bonanza.

Though the Chávez family moved to Barinas, almost half the Venezuelan population still resided in the countryside in 1957.[105] In 1959 a new government run by the left-wing nationalist party Acción Democrática (AD) proclaimed agrarian reform.[106] Over the next ten years 95,000 Venezuelan rural families were settled.[107] The reform quickly yielded tangible result: farmers saw their per-capita income increase substantially.[108] In addition, many peasants settling in the new agrarian communities became literate and also underwent a dramatic psychological shift, becoming more politically conscious and trusting of others than their traditional counterparts.[109] Yet AD president Betancourt was no radical—he sought reform and political reconciliation.[110] The agrarian reform itself was the product of a commission that included large landowning and business groups.[111] Additionally, only about one-quarter of those who had sought access to land benefited from agrarian reform.[112] When the government did expropriate private lands, these were mostly properties belonging to former dictator Pérez Jiménez, who fell from power in 1958. Even then, former owners were compensated generously.[113] Although the government provided housing, medical facilities, water and sanitation systems, roads, and a credit program and price support program, these measures only affected a few of the settled agricultural communities.[114] Bureaucratic incompetence further hampered the land reform process.[115] Not surprisingly, one-third of resettled families abandoned their land by 1970.[116] AD headed off any dissent to its policies by tying peasant groups to the party.[117] When AD opposed illegal takeovers of private land by peasant groups and Betancourt accused radical peasants of being communists, the president of the Venezuelan Peasants Federations, Ramón Quijada, broke with the government in disgust.[118] The government's short-comings came as a disappointment to Alí Rodríguez. For him and other Venezuelan radicals, the persistence of rural poverty and the inability of the government to eradicate age-old, historic inequities must have seemed inexplicable.

CHAPTER TWO
THE BATTLE FOR CONTROL OVER OIL

I have been to Rodríguez's home region of the Andes twice, the second time for some months. A charming colonial town in the mountains, Mérida is also home to one of the largest universities in the country. Unlike larger, crime-ridden cities, such as Maracaibo and Caracas, Mérida seemed relatively safe at night, and I would take long walks. Mérida, at an elevation of 5,384 feet, has benefited from the tourist industry and the city hosts many hotels and restaurants.[1] During my hikes in the surrounding mountains, however, I was struck by the rural poverty. Those few farms that I saw were rudimentary and simple. The roads were unpaved, and at one point I had to make a detour due to a landslide. As one ascends, one encounters a forbidding and desolate tundra landscape. At this altitude, the sunlight is piercing. I hiked to the small town of Nevados, the last way station for backpackers intent on continuing farther up the mountains. The town has tiny white houses and a small church. I checked into the local *posada* (or inn) and waited for dinner to be served. Below me I saw the valley, but before long I had difficulty making out the scenery; it seemed as if I was in the middle of a cloud. The next day, hiking down into Mérida, I did not see any farms; the area seemed depopulated. I finally came to an isolated peasant hovel, where I stopped for the night. Sitting around a fire, their faces illuminated by the flickering firelight, were a couple of *campesino* (peasant) men in tall cowboy hats. The señora meanwhile was slaving over the counter, pounding the wheat arepas before setting them to bake. She remarked that while she had been born in Nevados, she had spent the last 26 years of her life on this farm.

The government finally pardoned Rodríguez, and he came down from the Andes. Shortly thereafter he became a well known figure in Venezuelan politics. He was elected to Congress, where he took a particular interest in oil and energy. The former rebel served for many years as a member of left-wing parties such as La Causa R (the Radical Cause) and later Patria Para Todos (PPT or Fatherland for All) which split from Causa R in 1997. While working with PPT, Rodríguez was the party's spokesman on oil policy. He rose to prominence, becoming president of the Committee for Energy and Mines in the House of Representatives. During Giusti's tenure at PdVSA, Rodríguez became particularly incensed by the turn toward foreign investment in the oil sector and as a legislator even went to the Supreme Court to challenge the legality and constitutionality of various PdVSA clauses contained in company contracts awarded in 1996. In 1998, the savvy political operator supported Chávez's successful presidential bid.[2]

Rodríguez was ideally situated to become Chávez's point man on oil policy. During the 1998 presidential election, Chávez had excoriated PdVSA as a "state within a state." When he came into office, world oil prices were at their lowest point in many years, a mere $8.43 a barrel. The Organization of Petroleum of Exporting Countries (OPEC), responsible for 40 percent of world oil production, was tearing itself apart bickering over quota violations. Determined to reverse this sorry state of affairs, Chávez decreased production. Indeed, from 1997 to 2003 Venezuelan production went down to approximately 2.7 billion barrels a day. The country's share of OPEC exports fell to 10 percent, down from 12 percent during Giusti's reign. The price of crude skyrocketed, reaching its highest level since the 1991 Gulf War.[3]

Seeking to solidify his new stature within OPEC, Chávez hosted a meeting of the body's heads of state in Caracas in September 2000. In a TV broadcast, he declared that the upcoming meeting was not just about oil. The summit, he continued, would discuss global poverty, foreign debts, and unfair terms of trade for poor nations. In a move that hardly could have pleased Washington, the Venezuelan president called for greater unity among OPEC's 11 member nations. He also advocated for greater restraint in crude output in order to keep oil prices high. Industrialized nations were not amused. Amid protests and long gasoline lines in Europe, they demanded that OPEC stabilize the oil market. In seeking to rally the OPEC nations, Chávez seemed to be taking up the mantle of Juan Pablo Pérez Alfonzo, a Venezuelan energy minister and founding father of OPEC, who helped to loosen the grip of foreign oil companies on petroleum-producing nations. "And now," Chávez remarked, "OPEC has arisen again." In a further slap to Washington, Venezuela agreed to ship 53,000 barrels of oil per day to Cuba under preferential rates. The shipments surely must have come as a relief to cash-strapped Fidel Castro. Although the island nation produced the equivalent of 75,000 to 80,000 barrels per day of oil and gas, it imported 100,000 barrels per day.[4]

In line with international efforts, Chávez also launched an assault on PdVSA at home. The president submitted a new constitution to the public, which was later approved by popular vote. One of the key provisions of the constitution forbade the privatization of PdVSA. Under the 2001 Hydrocarbons Law, the government increased royalties paid by private corporations to 30 percent, from the earlier 16.6 percent, and guaranteed PdVSA at least a 51 percent share in new oil production and exploration. Predictably, opposition was not long in coming. Interviewed for the *Latin Business Chronicle* in 2002, Giusti remarked that the Hydrocarbons Law was a return to the day of the petro-state, which first started in 1975. Under the new terms, Giusti warned, no oil company was likely to enter into joint ventures with the state.

Undeterred, Chávez reestablished a predominant role for the presidency in the design and implementation of an oil strategy through the Ministry of Energy and Mining. For support, Chávez turned to Rodríguez, who became minister of energy and mines. Assisting Rodríguez at the ministry was Bernard Mommer, Rodríguez's earlier mentor. Rodríguez's appointment was a clear sign that Chávez intended to comply with OPEC production quotas and slow the country's crude output.

Rodríguez was ideally situated to continue his meteoric rise on the international stage. In January 2001, the once-obscure Marxist rebel from the Andes was elected to be secretary general of OPEC, where he served until mid-2002. Traveling to Vienna, Rodríguez once again brought Mommer, who served this time as the former guerrilla's adviser. Analysts interpreted Rodríguez's appointment as an attempt to reward Venezuela for changing its long-standing policy of busting OPEC quotas. Reacting with shock, the *Financial Times* remarked, "It is quite a rare occurrence for an ex-guerrilla to get his hands on the levers of the world economy, but that's what Alí Rodríguez has done." Rodríguez quickly set to work at OPEC, where he was held in high esteem by his colleagues. He became the chief architect behind the cartel's policy of shoring up rock-bottom oil prices by linking production cuts to a U.S. $22 to $28 a barrel price band. Rodríguez's policy quickly won over non-OPEC producers—Angola, Mexico,

Norway, Oman, and Russia—which also agreed to lower supplies in an effort to drive up prices.[5]

The United States was clearly concerned about OPEC's revitalized role on the world stage under Rodríguez. President Bill Clinton called for lower oil prices in 2000, an appeal that Chávez dismissed, remarking that oil prices were fair for developing nations of OPEC. Later that year U.S. energy secretary Bill Richardson traveled to Caracas, where he met with Rodríguez. Richardson was the highest-ranking U.S. official to visit Venezuela since Chávez took over the presidency. With high fuel prices stoking fears of a slowdown in the U.S. presidential election pitting George Bush versus Al Gore, Richardson remarked that "clearly the price of oil is still much too high." Tensions between the United States and Venezuela were ratcheted up further under the presidency of George Bush. Already oil prices had nearly doubled, to over $20 a barrel. According to experts, however, oil prices were not a significant source of friction between the two men. After all, oil interests were well represented at the White House, and the companies were unlikely to protest high prices at the pump. What Washington could not countenance was the renewed international profile of OPEC, largely the result of Chávez's efforts.[6]

Meanwhile, Chávez's long-standing feud with PdVSA had escalated. In December 2001, business leaders opposed to the Hydrocarbons Law initiated a work stoppage. Adding to Chávez's problems, dissident PdVSA executives joined in.[7] Chávez sacked company president Guaicaipuro Lameda because of his resistance to the Hydrocarbons Law and his persistent criticism of overall energy policy.[8] For Chávez, executives such as Lameda had been little better than Giusti. Chávez appointed five new members to the board, leading Lameda to charge that Chávez was politicizing the company. Management was also unhappy about staff reductions and payroll reductions. Certainly, Chávez's confrontational style in firing PdVSA staff did not assuage the opposition much either. Speaking on his show *Aló, Presidente*, Chávez, using a bullhorn and naming individual company officials by name, exclaimed to his audience, "You're out mister, thank you for your services, you're fired." Chávez's behavior offended the Venezuelan middle class, and the president has admitted that his combative attitude was "one of the most serious mistakes I have made." Chávez has defended himself by saying that he had become so fed up that he let his temper get the better of him.

The work stoppages and unrest continued into early 2002, creating an impossible climate for the president. PdVSA executives demanded that

Chávez change the company's board of directors. Chávez refused to back down. PdVSA's board was supported by ex-director Giusti, who remarked that Chávez was trying to put "a bomb inside the company to implode the whole thing." The company, he added, had gone from being a firm that people could trust to a governmental entity. Fedepetrol, a union representing more than half of all oil workers, pledged its support to the managers. The situation escalated as the Venezuelan Workers Confederation (CTV) and Fedecámeras, the Chamber of Commerce Federation, moved to support PdVSA management by calling a strike. CTV, the major trade union, was allied to Acción Democrática, which Rodríguez had fought against long ago as a guerrilla fighter.[9] Both the CTV and Fedecámaras were clearly linked to the United States and George Bush: each had received money from the U.S.-taxpayer-funded National Endowment for Democracy.[10]

In Vienna, the guerrilla from the Andes fretted over developments back in Venezuela and grew concerned about the fate of his former boss. Rodríguez had heard that Iraq and Libya, upset over U.S. support for Israel, were planning an oil embargo. What is more, Rodríguez learned, the United States was planning to prod a coup into action in Venezuela to head off any threat of embargo. Rodríguez immediately called Chávez, alerting him to the imminent coup, scheduled for April 11. In a desperate attempt to stave off revolt, Chávez stated that he would not join or tolerate an oil embargo. Secretly, however, he hid several hundred pro-government troops in underground corridors beneath Miraflores, the presidential palace, so as to head off an uprising.[11]

Before traveling to Venezuela in 1999, I had to secure institutional backing so as to acquire my visa. Through one of my professors, I was able to make valuable contacts with IESA (the Instituto de Estudios Superiores de Administración, or Institute of Upper Administration Studies). IESA not only made my research trip possible but generously offered me office space and computer access. When I got to Caracas, the IESA secretary set me up in a nearby apartment. IESA was only a few blocks away from my home in San Bernardino, a pleasant tree-lined neighborhood. Tranquil and surrounded by tropical green vegetation, IESA was a relief from chaotic and polluted downtown Caracas. After working in the archive, I would spend many hours there at the computer. Occasionally I would strike up conversations with the business students, who tended to be well dressed and light complexioned. Some of them seemed obsessed with Chávez—to them, he was a demon intent on ruining their country. While I personally was a bit leery about Chávez and his long-standing ties to the military, the students' comments struck me as exaggerated and somewhat extreme.

Historically, IESA has been a bastion of the Caracas elite and its influential and powerful business interests. Giusti himself spoke there in the 1990s concerning the oil apertura. One of IESA's most powerful members was Pedro Carmona Estanga, who sat on the school's board. Born in 1941 in the city of Barquisimeto, he became an economist. At the very time that Rodríguez was heading into the Andes to fight for revolution, Carmona was attending the conservative Universidad Católica Andrés Bello, from which he graduated in 1964. He went on to do postgraduate work abroad in Brussels. During the 1990s, he defended Luis Giusti's reign at PdVSA. Writing in the conservative Caracas paper *El Universal*, Carmona remarked that the company required autonomy from the government. "The petroleum internationalization," he wrote, "has been successful. Luis Giusti deserves praise, as he has carried out honest work and counts on national and international recognition." Later, after Chávez had fired Giusti and sought to bring PdVSA under control, Carmona took to the pages of *El Universal* once again writing, "The crisis in PdVSA can be traced to the government's decision to create a managing board with political ends, shattering moreover the meritocracy in high management." When Carmona wrote his column, he was president of Fedecámaras, a main focus of opposition to Chávez. Chávez struck back against Carmona, calling the businessman an "oligarch" and "scrawny."[12]

Carmona was an important figure in Venezuela. He managed important Venezuelan petrochemical companies in the 1980s and 1990s, such as Aditivos Venoco (1989–93), Química Venoco (1989–2000), and Industrias Venoco (1990–2000). At Venoco, Carmona was moving in powerful circles. One of its founders was Isaac Pérez Alfonzo, whose family had also built two shopping malls. Pérez Alfonzo was the father of Isaac Rafael Pérez Recao, a figure who the Chávez authorities later claimed was tied to the attempted coup against the Venezuelan president. Pérez Recao has downplayed his relationship with Carmona. "I don't know him very well," he remarked, "but I know that he is a principled man of integrity." Pérez Recao had an enormous fortune and was one of the shareholders at Química Venoco. He had numerous investments in Coral Gables, Florida, and was also involved in the arms business. An implacable enemy of Chávez, Pérez Recao reportedly paid large sums of money to military figures who had criticized the president and been fired. Pérez Recao apparently frequented South Florida, home to thousands of affluent and middle-class Venezuelans who had fled the country after Chávez's election in 1998. Reportedly, Pérez Recao "had openly bragged that he was plotting to remove the president from power, by force if necessary, and told friends on April 8 in Miami Beach that a coup was imminent." In summing up Pérez Recao, *Tal Cual*, a Venezuelan newspaper that had been critical of Chávez, was withering. The impetuous young man, one columnist noted, had grown up in the yuppie era, but "his trajectory indicates that he didn't even have the shrewdness of the movie *Wall Street*." The youth, the paper suggested, seemed to have a Rambo-like fondness for weapons. Pérez Recao has admitted that he was an opponent of the Chávez regime, but denies any involvement in the planning of a coup d'état or military rebellion.[13]

The battle of wills came to a head on April 11, 2005, when the opposition organized a huge demonstration. Between 100,000 and 200,000 people marched to the PdVSA headquarters and from there to the presidential palace. The march was peaceful, and the government did not interfere, even though protesters blocked a large Caracas freeway for several hours. Things turned ugly, however, when anti-Chávez snipers fired at pro-Chávez supporters, who in turn returned fire in self-defense. Seventeen people died during the shootings. In the midst of the violence and confusion, a group of high military officers, arguing that it was time to avoid further loss of human life, rejected Chávez's governing authority. The head of the armed forces announced that Chávez had resigned, a claim subsequently denied by Chávez. In a stunning development, the military named Pedro Carmona as head of a transitional government.[14] A full-fledged coup had taken place, and, according to the *Miami Herald*, Pérez Recao was "a prime mover behind interim President Pedro Carmona's brief regime, shoehorning friends into his Cabinet, providing him with bodyguards and joining him in meetings April 12–13 with leaders of the military rebellion." Pérez Recao, however, denies playing any role in helping to set up the coup regime.

Under the new coup government, PdVSA policy underwent a dramatic shift. Carmona, for example, reinstated PdVSA president Guaicaipuro Lameda. PdVSA's managers also announced that there would be "not one more barrel of oil for Cuba." In other words, PdVSA was again claiming that the company, not the government, had the right to set oil policy. On the day after the coup, a euphoric Edgar Paredes, a top PdVSA executive, announced the end of oil exports to Cuba and declared that the company would now undertake increases in production, which necessarily implied an end to Chávez's policy of cooperation within OPEC.[15]

Although Chávez's political future was now endangered, Carmona and his associates failed to take the president's greatest asset into account: Alí Rodríguez. As it turns out, the intelligence provided by the OPEC head proved crucial. A paratroop division loyal to Chávez waited in an underground bunker as the coup took place. José Baduel, chief of the division, phoned Carmona in the palace to inform him that troops were "virtually under his chair, [and that] he was as much a hostage as Mr. Chávez." Baduel instructed Carmona to return Chávez alive within 24 hours. Meanwhile, even if he had willed it, Carmona could not have escaped. Hundreds of thousands of pro-Chávez supporters had marched down from poor barrios and were surrounding the building.

On April 14, Chávez was restored to power and Carmona was placed under house arrest, accused of rebellion and seizing the presidency. When a court ordered him transferred to prison, he fled to the Colombian embassy where he requested and was granted asylum. Analysts reported that Carmona escaped "by taking advantage of a massive anti-Chávez protest march that drew away the security detail assigned to guard his home." Meanwhile, Pérez Recao fled to Florida, where he took refuge in a condo in Key Biscayne. Investigators for the Chávez regime raided his home in Caracas, where they found boxes of ammunition. The authorities additionally claim to have uncovered National Guard uniforms, bulletproof vests, projectiles, telephoto lenses, sharpshooter rifles, night-vision devices, gas masks, police shields, and motorcycles.[16] Pérez Recao claims that the Chávez regime is trying to incriminate him. In a letter sent to the Caracas newspaper *El Universal*, Pérez Recao admits to owning weapons but adds that he was obliged to secure arms because his family was subjected to kidnapping threats.[17]

Having narrowly escaped political disaster and even death, Chávez was more determined than ever to consolidate his hold over oil policy. The firebrand president resumed oil shipments to Cuba, resulting in even greater friction with Washington. In May 2004, the U.S. State Department's Commission for Assistance to a Free Cuba—the administration's propaganda office on Cuban issues—issued a report stating that Venezuelan oil shipments to Cuba had to be halted if political change on the island was to occur—which was tantamount to calling for a de facto embargo against the Castro regime. In a recent interview on Al Jazeera, the Qatar-based Arabic news network, Chávez cited Venezuela's controversial energy alliance with Cuba as an example of how "we use oil in our war against neoliberalism."[18]

Meanwhile, Chávez eyed PdVSA warily. In an effort to reconcile with the company's meritocracy, Chávez reinstated some executives who had been dismissed.[19] But he was also intent on bringing PdVSA under control. That would necessarily imply raising government revenue through high taxes, reducing operating and labor costs, and having the company abide the oil output policy set by OPEC. But PdVSA and the country were in disarray. Due to the April disturbances, exports, refining, and production operations were drastically curtailed. There had been five company presidents in just three years. For help, Chávez turned to an old friend.

Back in Vienna, the man who had perhaps single-handedly saved Chávez from political death was working hard to achieve a greater international profile for OPEC. But Chávez, having come under fire from the United States and the opposition, needed Alí Rodríguez back at home. The old guerrilla fighter was the only man who commanded enough clout to take charge of PdVSA. What is more, his down-to-earth personality would provide a welcome contrast to Chávez, known for his uncontrolled, spontaneous outbursts. After repeated pressure, Rodríguez agreed to resign his post and return to Caracas to head up the state-run oil company. The decision to leave, he related, was not easy. But, he said, "It's a gesture from my part to give something in return to the country in difficult times, it's a tremendous responsibility given to me by the president."[20] Rodríguez's new position as head of PdVSA came as a boon to his own leftist party in Venezuela, PPT, in the government coalition. Members of Rodríguez's party already held the education and labor ministries. The politically experienced PPT members had more skill than those of Chávez's own party, MVR (Movimiento Quinta República or Fifth Republic Movement).[21] Taking up his new responsibilities, Rodríguez faced a stark reality: although he had valuable diplomatic and negotiating experience, he had never run a large company.[22] In a country where 80 percent of the population lived in some degree of poverty, Rodríguez was determined to make PdVSA, whose sales amounted to $50 billion, an instrument in fighting social inequality.[23]

Scarcely four months into his new job, however, Rodríguez confronted a political firestorm. In November, the opposition announced a strike designed to dislodge Chávez from the presidency once again.[24] Chávez rejected the label of "strike," remarking that "striking is a right of workers that we reclaimed, we come from those struggles, it is a mechanism so that the workers may reclaim their violated rights from the boss."[25] Some observers have referred to the labor disturbances of 2002–03 as a lockout.[26] The tenacious meritocracy at PdVSA, including 30,000 managers and technicians, observed the lockout.[27] Chávez bluntly referred to the group launching the lockout as saboteurs.[28]

The charge, as it turned out, might not have been unwarranted. Sitting in a government office with his ministers, Chávez was surprised to witness an electronic bombardment of the company's computer system. The system went crazy, Chávez says, and suddenly "a boy arrives, a hacker, with a little gizmo, and I told him, 'You're a witch?' (laughs), because he came with a gizmo and said 'there's an electronic war here.'" What followed, Chávez explains, was a veritable hacker war.[29] According to Wilpert, a sociologist and journalist, the lock-out was basically staged by managers and white-collar technicians who shut down computer controls.[30] "I didn't know anything about that [computer hackers]," Chávez joked, "but I am learning a lot now." Speaking seriously, Chávez said the opposition was able to cause oil spills in Lake Maracaibo by remote control.[31] In the long term, PdVSA sustained serious damage to its IT system. The government claims INTESA was spying on Venezuela and was involved in the sabotage.[32] Chávez later claimed that SAIC (Science Applications International Corporation) shared PdVSA information with the CIA.[33] Rodríguez, a longtime friend of Cuba's Castro, compared the oil strike with the U.S. economic embargo on the island nation.[34] Chávez could ill afford economic disruption in the oil sector: the country relied on petroleum for 80 percent of export revenues and more than half its tax earnings.[35] Fearing the worst, Rodríguez sought to boost loyal technicians' morale by traveling to the Puerto La Cruz oil refinery in the east of the country. The plant was the only operational refinery that the opposition had not shut down. "Armed guerrilla action is one form of combat I've left behind," he remarked, "but this is a war to save democracy." By now 65, frail and using a cane, Rodríguez stepped into the control room at the plant, to the cheers and applause of exhausted workers. Rallying the night shift, Rodríguez exclaimed, "The striking managers thought they were the only ones who can run this industry. But you are showing the world that they have failed. The workers are winning the battle now." The workers must have derived solace from the veteran guerrilla, but overall the situation facing Rodríguez was bleak: all over the country, oil terminals, derricks, and pipelines were paralyzed, and oil exports had been nearly cut off by the beginning of December. Daily crude output was down below 200,000 barrels and output of refined products had plunged. Even the plant at Puerto La Cruz was refining only one-third of its normal capacity. The situation had become so serious that Venezuela even took the unheard-of step of importing fuel from Brazil.[36] The lockout caused disruption at gas stations, where Venezuelans had to wait in long lines.[37] Nevertheless, Rodríguez was confident that he and Chávez would triumph. He did, however, acknowledge that it was an error not to have disciplined PdVSA managers after the April 2002 coup d'état.[38]

The Chávez administration apparently agreed. This time the government took a no holds barred approach by firing upper management and 18,000 of the 33,000 full-time PdVSA workers.[39] The government justified its decision by claiming that the workers had not shown up for work for months and had caused economic damage to PdVSA.[40] Ultimately, Chávez prevailed; the lockout withered away by February 2003.[41] However, Rodríguez has noted how PdVSA had trouble putting the company back on line. The staff members who had been let go had been in charge of virtually every aspect of the company's operation, including exploration, production, transport, refining, commerce, supply, and finances. PdVSA had to play a game of catch-up, with other employees learning how to do the work of their fired colleagues. Rodríguez also brought in retired workers to compensate for the huge loss.[42] Meanwhile, the disruption had caused grave damage to the Venezuelan economy. Oil production during the disturbances fell from 2.65 million barrels a day to 250,000 barrels.[43] Indeed, it took months before PDVSA could restore production and refining operations. Overall, the lockout caused $14 billion in losses and a quarterly decline of 28 percent in gross domestic product at the beginning of 2003.[44]

Chávez's transformation, and his overcoming of political adversity, has been nothing less than astonishing. Certainly when I was in Venezuela in 1999–2000, I hardly expected the Venezuelan leader to become a figure on the hemispheric, let alone world, stage. Later in 2002, watching the coup unfold from Britain, I figured that Chávez was done for. The combined forces of the United States, the old interests, and the opposition would be too much for him to withstand. I expected Chávez to follow the path of Haitian leader Jean Bertrand Aristide, removed in a coup under similar circumstances. But Chávez and his associate Alí Rodríguez have seemingly overcome their obstacles. After turning back the coup and later the oil lock-out, Chávez has gone on to expand his political agenda throughout the South American region. Alarmingly for George Bush and Washington, Chávez has demonstrated that oil truly can be used as a geopolitical weapon.

After firing recalcitrant staff members, Chávez consolidated his hold over PdVSA. The company, Chávez remarked, "gave us a great opportunity" to move ahead with the government's political and social agenda.[45] Indeed, he moved quickly, shocking political observers who had written him off. Alí Rodríguez promptly discontinued INTESA, the joint venture between American-controlled SAIC and PdVSA.[46] INTESA workers were fired, and the Venezuelan Supreme Court ordered the company to hand over accounting technology to PdVSA.[47] The U.S. Overseas Private Investment Corporation (OPIC), upset by Venezuela's actions, ruled that PdVSA had "expropriated" SAIC's assets and awarded taxpayer compensation to the company. OPIC's decision in turn alarmed the Chávez government. One official remarked, "Accusing Venezuela of expropriating U.S. assets is a serious matter. This may be the beginning of a new type of attack on Chávez."[48]

Having taken care of the company's IT system, Chávez moved on to his main order of business, namely "sowing the petroleum." In 2004, $1.7 billion of the company's $15 billion budget was allocated to fund social programs; this contribution later went up to $4 billion a year.[49] At the Caracas headquarters of PdVSA, a mural shows Chávez and a child superimposed over an oil well. A slogan reads, "Deepening the Bolivarian Revolution in 2005," referring to Simón Bolívar, a Venezuelan leader for independence whom Chávez greatly admires.[50] Alí Rodríguez has remarked that the "new PdVSA" is making a crushing effort to attack "that humiliation of seeing kids in the street, illiterates, people lacking enormous health services."[51] Thus far, the social expenditures seem to have yielded result: the billions of dollars that Chávez spent surely aided him in beating a recall referendum sponsored by the opposition in August 2004.[52]

Although Chávez continues to ship oil to the United States, he has undertaken moves that suggest he may be looking to hedge his bets. For example, he has exerted pressure on foreign oil companies to secure yet more revenue. Since the opening of Venezuela's oil sector under Giusti, the country had earned $25 billion in investments. In 2005, there were 22 foreign petroleum companies operating in Venezuela. Chávez declared a tax hike on oil companies doing business in the Orinoco belt, determined to bring foreign firms into line with the 2001 Hydrocarbons Law.[53] Irate Exxon-Mobil representatives say that the company is paying the new tax rates "under protest." What is more, Chávez has repeatedly stated his determination to reduce his country's dependency on oil sales to the United States. Accordingly, he has begun exploring the sale of parts of CITGO. The PdVSA affiliate owns eight refineries and almost 14,000 gas stations located primarily in the eastern part of the United States. Chávez has complained that CITGO, whose refineries are especially adapted to process heavy crude oil from Venezuela, sells oil to the United States at a discount of two dollars a barrel. "We are subsidizing the U.S. budget," he griped, saying that CITGO contracts were signed before he assumed office in 1999. According to CITGO's 2004 financial reports, the company paid $400 million in dividends to Venezuela but paid almost as much in U.S. taxes. Energy minister Rafael Ramírez, who also serves as PdVSA's president, announced a freeze on plans to expand CITGO in February 2005.[54]

Although it's unclear what exactly this means, it would indeed seem as if Chávez is moving away from the United States. In order to diversify the Venezuelan market for oil, Chávez made plans to begin shipping Venezuelan crude to China, the world's second-largest energy consumer after the United States. "Reaching China is a strategic question," says Ramírez. "It would be a mistake not to have a presence there. They are switching over from coal to more efficient fuels." In Beijing in December 2004, Chávez remarked, "We have reached agreements with China to begin to exploit 15 mature oil fields in eastern Venezuela that have more than one billion barrels in reserves, and a large part of that oil will come to China." Chávez also stated that Venezuela wanted to become a "secure, long-term" petroleum supplier to India, and in March 2005 the two countries concluded an energy cooperation agreement. Transporting oil to Asia, however, could prove logistically difficult. PdVSA has expressed interest in moving oil across Panama to the Pacific Ocean via pipeline. The company is also exploring the idea of building a pipeline across Venezuela's northern border with Colombia, extending to that country's Pacific coast. Shipping oil to Asia carries other logistical and infrastructure problems. For example, China currently has an insufficient deep conversion refining capacity, and transporting petroleum to the Asian giant would be costly due to the long distances involved. Moreover, the Panama pipeline eyed by Chávez already transports 100,000 barrels a day of Ecuadorian crude from the Pacific to the Atlantic. According to analysts, there is no way that the pipeline can be converted to ship Venezuelan oil to China in the opposite direction simultaneously. Finally, China may be interested in Venezuelan oil only in the short run. Beijing is busy exploring for oil and gas closer to its shores in the South China Sea. Would Chávez dare to confront his northern neighbor? Analysts are doubtful. Currently the United States purchases 60 percent of Venezuela's oil exports, and finding new markets could prove daunting to Venezuelan authorities. The fact is, exporting to the U.S. market is convenient due to close proximity and low transportation costs. Additionally, as mentioned, U.S. refineries are adapted to process Venezuela's sulfur-rich crude. Recently there have been some signs that Chávez has backed down from his earlier confrontational posture toward Washington. According to the Venezuelan foreign minister, Chávez has no intention of reducing oil exports to the United States. In fact, the firebrand leader publicly stated in March 2005 that he wants to mend relations with the United States: "We want to continue to send 1.5 million barrels of oil to the United States on a daily basis and to continue doing business." Chávez added, although "we have said things, sometimes, very harsh things, it has been in response to aggressions." Chávez explained, "What I have said is that if it occurs to the United States, or to someone there, to invade us, that they can forget about Venezuelan oil." He clarified that this is just "a theory that we of course do not want, and I hope that the United States does not want it either."

Yet Washington seems to be growing concerned. Any interruption in Venezuelan oil exports to the United States would cause significant disruption to both countries, and Washington is beginning to plan for such a contingency. A potential oil cut-off would represent no small economic loss to the United States, as oil imported from elsewhere would likely be more expensive. The reality is that for the United States, purchasing Venezuelan crude is economically advantageous because the South American nation is geographically close to U.S. ports. In a clear sign of concern, Republican Senator Richard G. Lugar asked the Government Accountability Office (GAO) in late 2004 to study how a sharp decrease in Venezuelan oil imports could affect the U.S. economy. Lugar called on the GAO to review government plans "to make sure that all contingencies are in place to mitigate the effects of a significant shortfall of Venezuelan oil production, as this could have serious consequences for our nation's security and for the consumer at the pump."[55]

CHAPTER THREE

TINA—"THERE IS NO ALTERNATIVE"

In line with his moves to restrict privatization of PdVSA, Hugo Chávez has also frequently opposed the so-called Washington Consensus, a set of U.S.-backed free market policies.[1] The consensus stressed deregulation, privatization of state industries, implementation of austerity plans, and trade liberalization.[2] According to noted economist Joseph Stiglitz, the consensus was largely devised out of the Latin American experience. The broad concepts of the Washington Consensus came to be adopted by powerful institutions, such as the International Monetary Fund, the World Bank, and the U.S. Treasury Department.[3]

In many ways the Washington Consensus paralleled the idea of neoliberalism, that is, free trade in goods and services, free circulation of capital, and freedom of investment. For neoliberals, "the public sector must be brutally downsized because it does not and cannot obey the basic law of competing for profits or for market share." In line with neoliberal ideas, the International Monetary Fund imposed structural adjustment programs, which sought to privatize government industries and services, slash government spending, and promote exports. According to *Multinational Monitor*, a Washington, D.C.-based publication that reports on corporations, the basic idea was "to shrink the size and role of government, rely on market forces to distribute resources and services and integrate poor countries into the global economy." In essence, neoliberalism advocates maximum and efficient exploitation of the world's resources, including labor, raw materials, and markets. Under structural adjustment, countries were obliged to remove obstacles to foreign investment and force governments to orient their economies to produce exports, "typically produced by or sold to multinationals." Neoliberalism then is similar to the idea of globalization, which has stressed a trade-liberalized planet. Many neoliberals have adopted the saying of former British primer minister Margaret Thatcher, who once remarked famously that "there is no alternative" to global capitalism. This slogan is frequently abbreviated as "TINA."[4]

Perhaps no man epitomizes the Washington Consensus more than Robert B. Zoellick. Born in 1953 to a family of German descent, he was raised in Naperville, Illinois. Zoellick, who studied history and economics in college, claims that his first midterms in international trade turned out mediocre. But Zoellick, who was only the second person in his family to attend college, seems to have been something of an overachiever.[5] In 1975, he graduated Phi Beta Kappa from Swarthmore. A product of Harvard Law School, from which he graduated magna cum laude, and the Kennedy School of Government, from which he received a master's in Public Policy,[6] Zoellick later worked as a special assistant at the Treasury Department during President Reagan's second term.[7] During George Herbert Walker Bush's presidency, Zoellick served as under secretary of state for economic and agricultural affairs under Secretary of State James Baker. A high-level operator, he was the leading State Department official presiding over the Uruguay Round, a huge reform of the world trading system which eventually led to the creation of the World Trade Organization (WTO) in 1995. In the waning days of the Bush presidency, Zoellick moved to 1600 Pennsylvania Avenue, where he served as White House deputy chief of staff and assistant to the president. Zoellick used his expertise in trade issues as Bush's personal representative to the G–7 economic summits of 1991 and 1992.[8]

Hardly the stereotypically crude neoconservative, Zoellick admonishes his own country for not placing sufficient emphasis on language study.[9] In meetings, he regales his colleagues with his knowledge of Latin American history and economics.[10] Whiz kid Zoellick became the elder Bush's point man on Latin America, hammering through the North American Free Trade Agreement (NAFTA) accord with Mexico.[11] The agreement, which sought to link the economies of the United States, Canada, and Mexico and create a huge market of 360 million people with an economic output of more than $6 trillion a year, proved incredibly controversial.[12] In the United States, labor unions opposed the measure, fearing it would mean a loss of jobs. Labor groups were joined by a chorus of other environmental and social justice organizations that argued that NAFTA would have a detrimental effect on public health and the environment.[13] At one point, when negotiations hit a tough spot, Zoellick intervened and worked as a special assistant to Bush in his dealings with Mexican president Carlos Salinas de Gortari.[14]

Although Zoellick has played a pivotal role in free trade negotiations, his detractors charge that he is simply a cynic. According to Tom Barry, policy director of the International Relations Center, a liberal policy studies institute based in New Mexico, Zoellick "regards free trade philosophy and free trade agreements as instruments of U.S. national interests." Zoellick, Barry writes, is perfectly capable of morphing into a mercantilist when free trade stands to affect short-term U.S. interests or particular political constituencies.[15] The left leaning British magazine *New Internationalist* calls Zoellick a "trade mercenary."[16] He has been described as an "astute dealmaker" and "an ambitious policy wonk with a towering intellect."[17] With a closely trimmed mustache, carefully combed hair, and spectacles, Zoellick projects seriousness. According to those who have crossed his path, Zoellick displays a blunt and intellectual manner when negotiating.[18]

Although he was no longer in government during the Clinton years, Zoellick must have rejoiced at the expansion of the neoliberal model in the 1990s. Despite the groundswell of opposition, NAFTA was narrowly passed in the U.S. House of Representatives, with a wider margin in the Senate, in January 1994. President Clinton followed up on his successes by inviting hemispheric leaders to Miami[19] to encourage the creation of the Free Trade Area of the Americas (FTAA).[20] The agreement, charged critics, amounted to "NAFTA on steroids."[21] Speaking at the summit meeting in Miami, Bill Clinton proclaimed: "Now we can say that the dream of Simón Bolívar [the great Venezuelan leader of independence against Spanish rule] has come true in all the Americas."[22]Although Clinton's grandiose vision for the future was premature, on the surface at least the president seemed to have considerable support for his ideas. The ebullient Clinton was joined in his calls to form the FTAA by 33 leaders from Canada, South America, Central America, and the Caribbean. As envisioned by Clinton and others, the FTAA sought to consolidate the most extensive free trade area in the world, reaching from Anchorage to Tierra del Fuego and having a combined gross domestic product of almost $13 trillion with 800 million consumers.[23] In seeking to pass the FTAA, the momentum seemed to be with Clinton: in the very same year that world leaders pledged to support the FTAA, the United States, Mexico, and Canada entered into NAFTA.[24] In fact, the FTAA relied on NAFTA rules for guidance in the negotiations.

The association with NAFTA made nongovernmental organizations (NGOs) nervous. NAFTA, they charged, had been a nightmare for the environment and working families. On the U.S. side, the pact had resulted in the loss of hundreds of thousands of jobs, as companies relocated to Mexico in the search for cheaper wages and poorly enforced labor standards. Even worse, Mexico was required to devalue the peso to attract the foreign investment so necessary to a free trade, export-driven economy. The devaluation proved devastating, with 8 million families being pushed from the middle class into poverty. The agreement, they charged, would intensify NAFTA's "race to the bottom" by imposing deregulation and business-friendly privatization throughout the hemisphere.[25] Critics charged that the business community enjoyed unprecedented power over the FTAA negotiating process and no mechanisms were set in place to address labor, human rights, consumer safety, and environmental concerns.[26] According to one damning report, "hundreds of corporate representatives are advising the US negotiators . . . more than 500 corporate representatives have the security clearance to get advance access to FTAA negotiating texts. While citizens are left in the dark, corporations are helping to write the rules for the FTAA." Even worse, some have argued that the neoliberal model, pushed forth through deals like the FTAA, imposes a consumerist, corporately driven American culture on the rest of the world.[27] In a stinging indictment, reporter Greg Palast has written that the FTAA is much more than a simple document relating to trade. "FTAA," he writes, "is an entire new multi-state government in the making, with courts and executives, unelected, with the power to bless or damn any one nation's laws which impede foreign investment, foreign sales or even foreign pollution."[28]

Despite the facade of unanimity at Miami, not everyone agreed with Clinton's trade agenda. Hugo Chávez, for example, was disgusted by Clinton's cheerleading. Chávez believed the U.S. president had perverted and distorted the historical meaning of his hero, Simón Bolívar. Clinton's comments, Chávez remarked, were "a slap in the face of history, and a slap in the face for all of us who know our history and the ideals to which Bolívar devoted his life."[29] As the heads of state toasted each other in Miami, Chávez traveled to communist Cuba.[30] Fidel Castro, the leader of that island nation, had been excluded from the FTAA proceedings for presiding over an authoritarian regime and not promoting free markets. Apparently Castro did not regret the fact that he failed to receive an invitation. The FTAA, he thundered, would "inexorably encourage the annexation of Latin America by the United States."[31] What is more, Castro charged, his exclusion from the FTAA was "a great honor" as the summit was not designed for rebels and "we are rebels." If Cuba had been invited, though, Castro said he would have gone to Miami, "so that they don't think we are afraid of the fascist [Cuban exile] mafia."

As Chávez arrived in Cuba, he saw Fidel waiting for him. "I was surprised," Chávez later remarked. "I hoped to see him, but not in the doorway of the plane." Fidel embraced Chávez, and their relationship and partnership grew over the years. For Chávez, it must have seemed a great honor to meet the revered Fidel. Just two years earlier Chávez had been an officer in the Venezuelan army. Bursting onto the national scene, however, he had launched a military conspiracy against the government of AD president Carlos Andrés Pérez.[32] After the coup failed, Chávez was imprisoned in Yare.[33] During his stay in prison, Chávez became an avid reader. "I read a lot of books about Fidel," he has said. Inspired, he thought, "My God, when I get out of here I am going to have to get to know Fidel!"[34] When Chávez was pardoned and released after serving two years in jail, he formed the MVR, a new political party that included some of his old military colleagues as well as politicians from left-wing civilian parties.[35] Chávez was a relative political neophyte when he traveled to Cuba, however Fidel awarded him honors similar to those extended to heads of state.[36] Over the next ten years, the two men would establish a tight partnership and personal rapport.[37] Perhaps more than anything, the budding friendship was based on antipathy to the Washington Consensus and neoliberalism.

As a young officer in the Venezuelan military, Chávez had firsthand experience with the effects of neoliberal ideas. In the 1980s, as he was moving up in the ranks, Venezuela experienced a painful economic reversal. Faced with rising oil prices during the 1970s, petroleum-importing countries reduced consumption and looked for alternative sources of energy. The increase in prices gave rise to new oil producers, such as those in the North Sea, which in turn led to a loss of market share for OPEC. In 1983, an economic catastrophe hit the country as the Venezuelan currency, or bolívar, tumbled.[38] For Venezuelans, long accustomed to a consumerist lifestyle, it was a rude psychological awakening.[39] It was almost as if Venezuela, having won the lottery, abruptly lost it. The blow must have come especially hard for people such as my landlord in San Bernardino. Formerly a successful international businessman, in 2000 he had to rent out rooms in his condo to foreigners. To me, it looked as if nothing had changed in the apartment since the year 1973. The furniture was of a dated, modernist style, and cheap oil paintings hung on the walls. I was told that San Bernardino was once considered much more affluent. Three blocks from my home was the Hotel Avila, a luxurious hotel built by Nelson Rockefeller. In its day, it was the envy of all Caracas. Today, slums and shantytowns exist side by side with modern skyscrapers. The building where I lived looked as if it had been built sometime during the 1960s or 1970s. A concrete high-rise, the complex had security guards stationed at a front gate. Inside the complex was a drab supermarket that looked as if it had never been renovated. The climate at night in Caracas is quite pleasant and I longed to take long walks. My landlord, however, advised me not to dally: the streets were considered too dangerous. Indeed, San Bernardino was shuttered by 7:30 P.M. At night, lying in bed, I heard gunshots ringing throughout the neighborhood.

For the country once known as the Saudi Arabia of South America, adjusting to the new social reality proved difficult. Venezuela was forced to pay back loans to international creditors taken out during the oil bonanza.[40] Facing declining petroleum revenues, Venezuela had difficulty servicing its $38 billion debt. Luis Herrera Campins, president from 1979 to 1984 from the Social Christian Party (COPEI), attempted to confront the country's economic woes by cutting public spending, thus heralding a shift toward neoliberal deregulation. In 1983, AD candidate Jaime Lusinchi was elected president and attempted to deal with the deepening crisis.[41] His remedy: deepen the process already under way. Lusinchi introduced austerity budgets, cut social services, and renegotiated the debt.[42] The result, however, was discouraging: unemployment and inflation continued to rise.[43] Clearly the nation's leaders were ill equipped to deal with the impending economic collapse. Although chronic poverty had existed even during the oil bonanza of the 1970s, the 1980s and 1990s witnessed social collapse. According to analysts, by the 1990s, poverty afflicted an absolute majority of the Venezuelan population.[44] To this day, the poverty in Caracas is striking. Not surprisingly, electoral participation declined as the public increasingly began to see the two-party system under COPEI and AD as "corrupt, unrepresentative and ineffective in their handling of the economy."[45] As presidential elections neared in 1988, the Venezuelan people hoped that one politician, legendary for nationalizing the petroleum industry, would be able to restore the country's prosperity.[46] His name: Carlos Andrés Pérez, also known as CAP.[47]

CAP, who has spent his whole life in politics, is a survivor. Born in 1922 in the town of Rubio, located in the western state of Táchira, CAP was from a modest background. One of twelve children, his family grew coffee. In 1935, he and his family moved to Caracas where the young CAP pursued law at the Central University.[48] He then became a member of the National Democratic Party, which later became the Democratic Action party, founded by Romulo Betancourt.[49] CAP rose quickly within the party. When a junta overthrew the government of Isaías Medina Angarita in 1945, CAP found work as Betancourt's secretary.[50] After a military coup brought a military government to power, CAP went into exile, returning only when the military regime fell apart in 1958.[51] He later served as deputy and senator in Congress, as well as hard-line Interior Minister in 1963–64 in charge of suppressing left wing guerrilla insurgents, some of them backed by Cuba.[52] There seemed to be no ceiling on CAP's rising fortunes, and in 1973, he was elected president in his own right.[53] By then a middle-aged, balding man with sideburns, CAP regularly derided the United States for its capitalistic greed.[54] He undertook a nationalistic economic policy by nationalizing the oil industry, including Shell and Exxon.[55] CAP rose to power before the economic problems associated with the Campins and Lusinchi administrations. His term coincided with a rise in the country's economic fortunes. The Arab oil embargo led to a windfall in government revenue, which increased by 170 percent.[56] With the government awash in cash, Pérez spent lavishly on grandiose development projects.[57] Unfortunately, the bonanza years also bred corruption and a bureaucratic and inefficient state apparatus.[58] CAP, who served as president until 1979, himself narrowly escaped prosecution for a supposed kickback scandal.[59]

But by 1988, with Venezuelan society hemorrhaging from economic collapse and tired of neoliberal solutions, CAP seemed poised for a political comeback. Following an electoral campaign that evoked the populist symbols of his first government, Pérez was re-elected.[60] On the campaign trail, CAP had denounced International Monetary Fund (IMF) policies as "the bomb that only kills people," leading many to think that, once elected, he would break with the Washington Consensus.[61] So seductive was CAP's rhetoric that left-wing parties threw their support to his campaign.[62] Once swept into power, Pérez surveyed the unenviable economic environment. CAP confronted a fiscal and debt crisis.[63] He surprised his supporters by undergoing an astonishing reversal, selecting a number of figures from IESA, the business school in Caracas, to head his economic team. Having tapped figures from the country's prominent business class to lead his government, CAP then went back on his electoral promises, devising a plan for the neoliberal restructuring of the country in accordance with IMF and World Bank guidelines.[64] Such reforms, which required the elimination of welfare programs, subsidies, and price and wage regulations, posed a dire threat to the Venezuelan poor.[65] But the president's announcements of a 100 percent fuel increase and a 30 percent increase in public transportation prices, provoked popular outrage.[66] Oil was a symbol of national pride, and "cheap oil had sustained a minimal sense of collective involvement in the nation's most lucrative public asset."[67] The people of Venezuela, writes one political observer, "responded to the Pérez government's neoliberal program with a shock treatment of their own."[68] In Caracas, for example, protesters gathered at the key points of the city's public transportation system on the morning of February 27, 1989. At Caracas' main bus terminal, students protested the new transportation fares by occupying the station. From there, the students moved out on to the roadway, where they formed a human barrier blocking entrance to the terminal. Later, they were able to block traffic along one of the main traffic arteries of the city by constructing barricades. Similar protests against fare increases occurred in other major Venezuelan cities.[69]

At the time of the riots, I was in Berkeley studying Latin American history. The events in Venezuela took me by surprise. I had not studied the South American country in much depth and Venezuela did not interest me politically. I was much more centered on the Farabundo Martí National Liberation Front (FMLN) rebels in El Salvador [70]who were actively resisting the U.S. military.[71] A guest lecturer from Venezuela came to our political science class to discuss the riots in Caracas. To me, they seemed to lack any political coherence. I promptly forgot all about the talk and continued to listen to the news coming out of Central America. On November 12, 1989, the *Daily Californian*, the campus newspaper, ran an article entitled "Campus Group Invades General Dynamics' Recruitment Forum." In the piece, a campus reporter noted that a group of 30 protesters, including me, had interrupted a recruitment session led by a leading defense contractor. Protesters had blanketed the recruiting hall with posters decrying U.S. participation in the guerrilla wars in El Salvador.[72] If I, however, or the other student radicals had bothered to pay more attention, we would have put more stock in Venezuelan developments. Indeed, one might even argue that February 27, 1989, sparked the later antiglobalization movement.

The student protests in Caracas on the morning of February 27 soon took on the character of a popular revolt. Once the protesters at the bus station had sufficient strength, they began to block traffic and build street barricades. Next, protesters set fire to a bus and started looting.[73] The riots would come to be known as the *caracazo*, which may be translated as the Caracas "violent blow."[74] As the people sallied forth on to the streets, they scrawled political slogans: "El pueblo tiene hambre" (The people are hungry), "El pueblo está bravo" (The people are angry), and "Basta el engaño" (Enough of the deceit). Some observers claim that the caracazo was misrepresented by the media, which emphasized the looting and riots. According to one account, however, "When people went into shops to take goods, they were often heard singing the national anthem as they did so, many carried the national flag and in many cases people organized the stealing of goods by lining up in an orderly manner." The caracazo therefore "was a semi-organized (though largely non-politicized) expression of working class opposition to neoliberal austerity."[75]

Surveying what increasingly looked to be a popular insurrection, CAP vacillated. On a visit to another province, he initially ignored the disturbances, expecting the violence to peter out.[76] But finally, faced with an unraveling situation, CAP declared martial law on February 28 and sent in the army.[77] Hugo Chávez, then a young officer, was stationed at the Miraflores presidential palace.[78] He watched the developments with growing concern. On the critical day, Chávez was sick and feverish from a bout of measles.[79] The doctor told him to go home.[80] Obeying doctor's orders, Chávez went to Fort Tiuna looking for a friend who could provide him with some gas. As he arrived, the scene piqued his interest. "I see they are taking out the troops," Chávez recalled later, "and I ask a colonel, 'Where are all those soldiers going to?' Because they were taking out logistical units not trained for combat, much less for street fighting. They were recruits scared by the very rifles they carried." The official replied, "'To the street, to the street. That's the order they gave: stop the disturbance as best you can, and so we're going.'"[81] Venezuelans watched in shock as Caracas descended into anarchy. For several days, the capital was in chaos, with criminal gangs roaming the streets. The armed forces responded to the anarchy with a harsh wave of repression and human rights violations.[82] One military officer who witnessed the disturbances later recalled, "It was sometimes very hard when one would go to the hospital . . . there you would see the people standing in line, women with little children . . . hours and hours. It was really a shame to see those things!"[83] In the poor neighborhoods, the repression was especially harsh. On March 1, for example, the army fired on crowds in the slum of Petare, killing more than twenty. By March 4, the disturbances finally ended by March 4. By that time, however, 396 people had died, the vast majority shot by the security forces, and hundreds of stores were destroyed.[84] Although CAP had survived, the Venezuelan masses had demonstrated their hostility to the Washington Consensus and business as usual. The caracazo was a bracing wake-up call for CAP and all of his business-friendly colleagues at IESA. With the two-party system in disarray and neoliberal remedies discredited, how would the elite control further unrest in the streets?

Even more serious were the signs of dissent within the army, which resented having to fire on civilians protesting IMF-imposed austerity measures.[85] After his illness had passed, Chávez took stock of the situation.[86] Reflecting later, he remarked, "That 27th of February of 1989 . . . marked my generation a lot."[87] He had been a longtime critic of the two-party system in Venezuela and had formed a conspiratorial movement, the MBR 200 (Movimiento Bolivariano Revolucionario 200) with three colleagues in 1982 (the MVR, formed in 1994, was the electoral arm of the original MBR 200).[88] According to Steve Ellner, an expert on Venezuelan politics and longtime professor of economic history at the University of Oriente, the MBR 200 was incensed by the rampant corruption prevailing during the oil bonanza and initially wanted merely to bring back clean government. But as a result of social dislocations in the 1980s and the caracazo, the MBR 200 started to analyze socioeconomic problems.[89] In the wake of the caracazo, Chávez now realized "that we had passed the point of no return and we decided that it was time to take up arms. We could not continue to be the custodians of a genocidal regime."[90] The MBR 200, comprised of low-ranking military officers and some left-wing civilians, started to lay the ground work for a coup d'état.[91] CAP finally realized that he would have to backtrack if he wanted to stay in power. Therefore, he softened some of the most controversial aspects of the economic package. Meanwhile, although his shock program reduced inflation and the country's deficit, it also gave rise to unemployment and poverty.[92] For CAP, the economic indicators were not encouraging. In 1989, the poverty rate jumped from 46 to 62 percent. Even more seriously, the percentage of the population facing extreme poverty increased from 14 percent to 30 percent.[93] During the 1991 Gulf War, Venezuela increased its production of crude, thus providing a brief moment of relief for CAP.[94] Yet his popularity was in free fall, and there was no sign that social conflict had abated.[95] Rather, Venezuelan society seemed to be like a pressure cooker. The only missing ingredient was a figure who might articulate the masses' opposition to elite policies of economic restructuring.

On a certain level, an imminent confrontation between Chávez and CAP was unlikely. Both men came from the western part of the country, and both had similar humble origins.[96] As a young, 21-year-old officer, Chávez had received his sword of command from CAP during Perez's first presidential term.[97] Pérez, at least in his earlier incarnation, had mocked the United States and deplored its economic agenda in the Third World. But since his dramatic reversal, CAP had become a symbol for everything that was wrong with the two-party system. On February 4, 1992, Lieutenant Colonel Chávez struck. At midnight, he and 6,000 troops attacked Caracas and three other cities.[98] Years later, Chávez would justify his actions, arguing that the coup was a rebellion against "the dictatorship of the International Monetary Fund, the dictatorship of the Punto Fijo Pact [referring to a 1958 agreement by which leading Venezuelan politicians agreed to share power so as to ensure ongoing stability], and the dictatorship of the Venezuelan oligarchy."[99]

The rebels deployed an impressive array of hardware: columns of tanks and troop carriers drove through the streets. Paratroopers and armored units assembled in key strategic points, including an airbase near to Caracas and La Casona, CAP's official residence.[100] Pérez himself had just fallen asleep when his defense minister called to let him know that a military uprising had occurred in the city of Maracay.[101] According to *Time* magazine's correspondent, at one point a rebel soldier saw he had a clean shot of CAP. The soldier, however, lacked nerve and failed to take his shot.[102] CAP exited the residence through a secret tunnel and soon made his way to Miraflores, the presidential palace in the center of Caracas. But CAP had scarcely arrived when rebel soldiers raked the building with mortar and rifle fire.[103] From his headquarters in the History Museum of La Planicie, Chávez commanded the assault. CAP considered his options. Deciding that his only option was to appeal to the people, he went to the studios of Venevisión TV to make an address.[104] Fortunately for Pérez, the coup plotters failed to inspire a civil insurrection like that which had occurred in 1989.[105] When Chávez failed to take over the presidential palace, he realized that the uprising had been unsuccessful.[106] Twelve hours later, he surrendered but demanded that he also be allowed to speak to the Venezuelan people. Sporting his characteristic paratrooper beret,

Chávez took responsibility for the failed coup.[107] He called for his fellow officers to surrender and declared "for now, we were unable to achieve the goals we had."[108] By the end of the rebellion, 15 soldiers and scores of civilians had perished.[109] Chávez was taken to Fort Tiuna, "a calm, clean, orderly place with clipped lawns and newly painted barracks and stables." Chávez was led into an office on one of the upper floors and sat on a couch.[110] He was later carted off to Yare prison, where he would languish for the next two years.[111]

CAP had once again proven that he was a political survivor who could withstand even the worst scrapes. Although public opinion polls showed that lower-class Venezuelans overwhelmingly rejected his economic reforms, most middle- and upper- class individuals supported the president's policies.[112] Apparently, Pérez had demonstrated that TINA was indeed the only viable political principle. Or had he? As later developments would show, time was not on the side of Pérez or his neoliberal allies in Venezuela. The next blow against the Washington Consensus would come from an unexpected quarter: Mexico.

As I neared my college graduation, I made inquiries among friends about how to live and work in Latin America. I was curious to learn more about political and social conditions south of the border. I learned that Morelia, a quaint colonial Mexican city located in the state of Michoacán, was always looking for English teachers. I flew to San Diego and crossed the border. Ever since the revolution, Mexico had been a one-party state ruled by the Institutional Revolutionary Party (PRI). Traveling by bus through the barren and desolate landscape of Baja, I was struck by the PRI's political slogans literally painted on rocks and boulders.

By the 1990s, many PRI leaders had gone back on their political principles and had endorsed the neoliberal agenda, as CAP had done in Venezuela. Chief among them was President Carlos Salinas de Gortari, who pushed hard for NAFTA. When I was not teaching my classes at the local English school, I would head to the market in Morelia to buy *La Jornada*, Mexico's leading left-wing paper. The newspaper was always full of articles about Salinas's assault on the *ejidos* (common lands). In line with his free market bent, Salinas had moved to privatize the ejidos, which had been protected ever since the revolution under the 1917 constitution.[113] The move had proved controversial in the countryside, where many farmers considered the ejidos sacred and untouchable.

Curious to gauge the local reaction to the PRI's policies, I spoke with some students living with me in my Morelia boardinghouse. Most seemed indifferent to Salinas or cynical about politics. Some did not care for my line of questioning, as their families had been longtime supporters of the PRI. As a result, they could not bring themselves to criticize the party. I could not help noticing that they seemed more interested in listening to American pop music than in discussing politics. I had meanwhile become engrossed in the novels of B. Traven, an enigmatic German exile who had fled political persecution and wound up in Mexico in the 1920s. One of his novels, *Treasure of the Sierra Madre*, about gold miners, had been made into an epic Hollywood film with Humphrey Bogart. I was more interested in Traven's novels set in the southern state of Chiapas. Traven, who had traveled through the rugged Lacandón rain forest, vividly depicted the social conditions of the Mayan Indians and their fight against political oppression. Toward the end of my stay, I traveled to Mexico City where I changed buses for the long trip south to Chiapas. Twelve hours later I saw Indians walking alongside of the road. Amazingly, the women carried loads of firewood by simply placing the strap from the bundle around their foreheads. Unfortunately, although I was later able to travel to a Mayan village and observe a religious ceremony in the local church, my back went out and I had to take it easy. To amuse myself, I visited the Casa Na Balom, an anthropological museum in the town of San Cristóbal de Las Casas. On the last day of my trip I took a bus to visit some lakes near the Guatemalan border. An Indian man got into the vehicle, his face lined with age. I was struck by his gaunt and desolate appearance.

When I later heard of the armed uprising launched by the Zapatista rebels, I thought again of that man. Finally the Mayan Indians had shown the world that they would no longer put up with age-old discrimination and injustice. Shattering the notion of TINA and the supposed unanimity of hemispheric leaders at the Miami summit of the Americas, the Zapatistas, or Zapatista Army of National Liberation, called for autonomy and drastic agrarian and social reform. The government, alarmed that indigenous peoples had challenged neoliberal orthodoxy and NAFTA, sent in the army. Although hundreds died in the ensuing violence, military confrontation led only to stalemate.[114] The Zapatistas, though they had failed to derail NAFTA, attracted international notoriety. Their spokesperson, a mysterious man named Subcomandante Marcos, who wore a black ski mask and smoked a pipe, turned into a symbol of resistance to globalization.[115] Inspiring activists worldwide, Marcos and the Zapatistas held an international conference in Chiapas in 1996 titled "the Intercontinental Encounters for Humanity and against Neoliberalism."[116] Although an uneasy truce reigned in Chiapas, the following year a massacre of 45 peasants brought renewed tensions.[117]

With the pressure building, ex-lieutenant colonel Hugo Chávez, now released from jail and leading his own party, the Movimiento Quinta República, traveled to Mexico City. There he announced his candidacy for the 1998 Venezuelan presidential election. Responding to an invitation by Subcomandante Marcos, Chávez participated in a Zapatista Indian march from Chiapas to Mexico City.[118] In appearing with the Zapatistas, Chávez suggested that he might challenge neoliberalism himself as president. That was certainly a worrying prospect for the Clinton administration. While the Zapatistas had scored an important psychological victory against globalization, they did not seek state power. The possibility, however, of a Chávez victory in Venezuela meant that a major South American country and leading world oil producer might actively campaign against the Washington Consensus.

The idea of further radicalization was not a pleasing notion for Gustavo Cisneros, a prominent member of the Venezuelan elite. He was born in 1945 in Venezuela to a family of Cuban descent.[119] In 2005, *Forbes* magazine estimated Cisneros's worth at $5 billion; he was the 59th richest person in the world.[120] He learned business from his father, Diego, who served as a role model. While other youngsters went on summer vacation, Cisneros observed his father carrying out his routine.[121] In the 1930s, before Gustavo was born, Diego had taken a single truck and turned it into a delivery company. He also owned a concession stand, which he turned into a Pepsi-Cola bottler and distributor.[122] Diego proved to be an enterprising role model for his son. By 1960, he had built up sufficient capital to found Venevisión, which became the country's top broadcaster. Today Venevisión is famous for exporting telenovelas, sultry soap operas, that it supplies to Univisión, a Spanish-language network based in the United States. Currently the network is largely owned by Gustavo.[123] In many ways Gustavo has lived up to his father's aspirations. He went on to study in the United States[124] and took on the family business at age 25. Within 10 years Gustavo was turning the company into an increasingly more international venture, acquiring control over such companies as Spalding, the world's largest sporting goods firm.[125] By the 1980s, the Cisneros family was not only economically powerful but also politically influential. Reportedly Otto Reich, U.S. ambassador in

Venezuela from 1986 to 1989 under Ronald Reagan, established contact with the Cisneros clan during his tenure in Caracas.[126]

In 1995, Gustavo set his sights on even more ambitious projects. In a daring move, he sold off Spalding and amassed a massive war chest of $2 billion. Then he started putting together his massive media empire. In Latin America, Cisneros's media assets are rivaled today only by Rupert Murdoch and the Brazilian conglomerate Globo.[127] Cisneros also helped to bring North American pornography to Latin viewers via an alliance with Playboy Enterprises. Through the venture, Cisneros launched two new adult TV stations, PlayboyTV/América Latina and AdulTVision/América Latina.[128] Described by his admirers as a "visionary," Cisneros has built up an empire. Not only does he have interests in Venezuela; he also established a partnership with AOL Time Warner worth $200 million.[129] In merging with the media and internet giant, Cisneros has sought to bring AOL to the Latin American market.[130] "His business ventures," notes *Latin CEO*, "have risen from successful albeit nationally defined origins to a pan regional conglomerate with operations in virtually every corner of the Ibero American market."[131] Indeed, Cisneros was the first Latin American media magnate to pursue a global vision. According to his biographer, the multibillionaire not only anticipated globalization but astutely took take advantage of it.[132]

Cisneros's $5 billion fortune is not derived solely from his media holdings however. Indeed, just a cursory glimpse at some of his holdings reveals the extent and diversity of his empire: Burger King Venezuela; Cervecería Regional, a beer company; Pizza Hut Venezuela; Miss Venezuela Pageant; Angostura Mining; and the Venevisión International Film Group.[133] The Cisneros Group of companies includes supermarkets and fast food and video franchises. Cisneros sits on the board of Panamerican Beverages, one of the largest Coca-Cola bottling companies.[134]

In his tastes and habits, Cisneros cuts an international figure. Described as "a portrait of gentility," Cisneros dresses in a sweater and tie when speaking with the press and is accompanied by his golden retriever, Arrow. In his apartment on the Upper East Side of Manhattan, he has placed an oil painting of Simón Bolívar, family photos, and a shot of himself with the Pope.[135] An avid art collector, Cisneros and his wife, Patricia Phelps de Cisneros, have funded anthropological exhibits that display the cultures of Venezuela's indigenous peoples.[136] Not surprisingly, Cisneros has been one of the greatest advocates for hemispheric free trade.[137] In 1995, following close on the heels of the Miami Summit of the Americas,

Cisneros went to Denver, Colorado. There he attended a forum designed to foster dialogue between the private and public sector "regarding areas the private sector believes could facilitate progress toward a hemisphere-wide free trade area." Cisneros and other powerful businessmen were happy to offer their input and advice, which was later presented to governments for review. Cisneros served as a commentator on a panel entitled, "Open Access to the Information Marketplace."[138] "Latin America is now fully committed to free trade," he has remarked. "Through those two things," he continues, "globalization and free trade—will improve the per capita income of everybody in Latin America, free from government regulations, interventions, mishandling of the economies, and so forth."[139]

But as the presidential campaign of 1998 neared, Cisneros weighed his options carefully. What would a Chávez victory mean for his financial interests and larger plans for Latin America? The election polarized Venezuela along class lines and led to speculation of increased violence. Amid growing concern, shoppers swarmed supermarkets, stocking up essentials. Bank patrons besieged automatic bank tellers.[140] Prominent investors were concerned, and the affluent elite was already packing and heading to Miami.[141]

CHAPTER FOUR
CHÁVEZ AND HIS FIGHT AGAINST NEOLIBERALISM

Since 1992, Chávez had become a seemingly unstoppable political jugger-naut. Indeed, even as the political fortunes of CAP plummeted, Chávez be-came more and more of a phenomenon. Although he had been a political unknown prior to 1992, it was his TV speech after the coup that ultimately led to his political triumph.[1] Chávez's use of the phrase "for now" and his willingness to assume responsibility for the failed coup made him a hero among the poor and marginalized sectors of the population who had suf-fered under CAP's IMF-influenced policies. Chávez's rising popularity was evident as early as March 1992, when, under martial law, people sponta-neously organized a pot-banging protest (*cacerolazo*). The protesters, who supported the coup, called for CAP's resignation.[2] During the early 1990s, I sensed this growing popularity while traveling in the plains region of west-ern Venezuela where Chávez grew up. Graffiti scrawled on the walls of pub-lic buildings in small towns supported the army colonel.

To make matters worse for CAP, another coup attempt broke out in November 1992, loosely tied to MBR 200. Although the attempt was un-successful, pressure was growing on Pérez to resign.[3] Shortly later, the cacerolazo protesters would see their wishes fulfilled, as the longtime politi-cal survivor faced his professional demise. Convicted of abuse of public funds, he was sentenced to two years and four months in prison. The vet-eran politician, a fixture of the country's politics for five decades, was even thrown out of his party, Acción Democrática.[4] In December 1993, he was suspended from office for misuse of public funds and embezzlement and placed under house arrest. CAP was finally acquitted of embezzlement but convicted on the other charge by the Supreme Court in May 1996.[5] With

CAP's departure, it was abundantly clear that the two-party system was dead.

Rafael Caldera, patriarch of COPEI, organized a group of party dissidents in alliance with the MAS (Movimiento al Socialismo, or Movement Toward Socialism party).[6] In the presidential election of 1993, Caldera's new party, Convergence (Convergencia), was able to triumph by distancing itself from the neoliberal agenda.[7] Even so, Caldera was elected with only a paltry 30 percent of the vote. The elder statesman who had served as president before CAP from 1969 to 1974 astutely campaigned against the earlier privatizations carried out under AD. Caldera was also careful to avoid any criticism of the popular Chávez and the failed coup.[8] Cashing in on the resentment against the two-party system, Caldera pardoned Chávez, who was released from prison in 1994.[9] According to Ellner, the military rebels became politicized in jail. When they were released, they demanded a renegotiation of the foreign debt and tax reform that would lead to a greater distribution of wealth.[10] Chávez went about building his MVR party, traveling to Cuba for his historic meeting with Fidel, and eventually announcing his own presidential candidacy in Mexico.[11]

In the meantime, Caldera proved no more politically consistent than CAP. Confronting a banking crisis and massive capital flight, Caldera went back on his campaign promises, negotiating a $1.4 billion loan from the IMF in 1995 with structural adjustment.[12] In accordance with the institution's recommendations, Caldera announced his plan, the so-called Agenda Venezuela, which promoted deregulation, privatization, and reining in of public spending. The plan was designed to reestablish macroeconomic stability and beat inflation.[13] Cisneros was pleased with Caldera's policies, remarking that the president had restored business confidence in Venezuela and that foreign investors were once again looking at the country as an attractive place in which to invest.[14] With elections approaching again in 1998, who could multibillionaires like Gustavo Cisneros count on to continue the neoliberal opening? In Venezuela Caldera's economic policies proved predictably unpopular and led to strikes, work stoppages, street demonstrations and clashes with police.[15] Although a rise in oil prices in 1997 gave him more leeway, and the president was able to increase public spending while postponing IMF structural adjustment policies, in 1998 the price of petroleum plunged again and forced spending cuts of $6 billion.[16]

Campaigning on an anticorruption, antipoverty platform, Chávez used his charisma and renowned oratory to reach out to the Venezuelan poor and working class.[17]

Irene Sáez, a blond former Miss Universe and mayor of Chacao municipality of Caracas, remained in the election race but was not considered a serious player. The middle and upper classes, fearful of a Chávez victory, threw their support behind Henrique Salas Romer, a businessman who had been educated at Yale. Salas Romer, who as the former governor of Carabobo state had carried out business-friendly policies such as spending cuts, had originally run as an independent. AD and COPEI, once rivals, now joined forces to back Salas Romer and defeat Chávez.[18] But less than two months before the election, Chávez was polling at 39 percent of the vote. In October, 1998, according to the Associated Press, Cisneros met personally with Chávez. The media billionaire declined to comment publicly about the meeting. According to reports, however, Cisneros decided to hedge his bets by organizing positive media coverage of the Chávez electoral campaign. Later, however, Cisneros denied he ever offered the support.[19] In Washington, the Clinton administration grew concerned. It was no secret that Bill Clinton did not wish to see a Chávez government in Miraflores. What is more, the United States denied Chávez a visa to travel to America, claiming that he had staged a coup against a constitutional government.[20] Would a Chávez victory exert a domino-like effect and reverse U.S. moves toward hemispheric free trade? Since the 1994 Summit of the Americas, not much had been done to advance the FTAA. But in April 1998, just months before the election in Venezuela, 34 nations had met in Santiago, Chile. There hemispheric leaders had agreed to set up a Trade Negotiations Committee consisting of vice ministers from every country.[21]

On the campaign trail, Chávez sent conflicting messages about what his economic policies might be. At one point, he threatened to default on Venezuela's foreign debt of $22 billion. Other statements might have given Cisneros pause. Chávez, for instance, promised to increase social spending, in opposition to the usual IMF proscriptions. He also said he would subsidize medicine and basic food and slow down privatization of state industries. Yet, Chávez clearly sought to appease powerful interests in the run-up to the election. The ex-army colonel hired Diego Asencio, a former U.S. ambassador to Colombia and Brazil, to serve as a political consultant. "Chávez," Asencio remarked, "is getting a bum rap as the Antichrist of democracy and free markets."[22] Speaking via satellite to a Miami audience, however, Chávez was careful to avoid discussing the debt question but said that in the event of his electoral triumph he would honor the country's foreign commitments. In defending his previous statements lambasting U.S. free market reforms, he explained that, like Pope John Paul II, he was against "savage" neoliberalism.[23]

In the end, there was no contest: Chávez won the election with 56.2 percent of the vote, the largest margin won by any candidate in the nation's history.[24] In a desperate attempt to revive his flagging political career, CAP, now 76, formed his new Apertura (Opening) political party. In April, 1998, he and his mistress had been charged with depositing money in U.S. bank accounts that exceeded their earnings as public officials. The Public Patrimony Safeguard Court, which was in charge of cases having to do with corruption of high public officials, meanwhile placed CAP under house arrest. Vehemently denying the charges, he claimed that the efforts against him constituted a political vendetta. In seeking a new Senate seat, CAP calculated that he might avoid further prosecution. What is more, he wanted revenge against his arch adversary Chávez. "Have you ever seen a dictator really solve a country's problems?" he asked audiences. CAP, who ran for Senate while serving out his house arrest in Táchira, seemed to head off his legal problems when he won his seat in November, 1998. The Supreme Court set him free from his house arrest. Set free in his home state of Táchira, CAP proclaimed to his supporters, "I am alive!" A scant three months later, the Supreme Court dismissed the charges against CAP as his position as Senator gave him immunity.[25] But his woes were hardly at an end. Under Chávez's new constitution, a new National Constituent Assembly had to be elected. CAP ran again from his native Táchira state, but this time he lost. CAP, who no longer enjoyed his former immunity, moved to the Dominican Republic and spent his time between Santo Domingo, Miami, and New York. In 2001 Venezuelan prosecutors accused CAP of failing to publicly disclose bank accounts; under Venezuelan law politicians must disclose one's assets upon entering and leaving public office. The charges dated back to an earlier 1993 congressional investigation. CAP labeled the charges political persecution "from that man;" apparently a reference to Chávez. Meanwhile the Venezuelan president accused CAP of plotting his assassination; CAP has denied the charges but has remarked, "He [Chávez] must die like a dog, because he deserves it."[26]

Sitting in his new office in Tiuna Fort, Chávez hardly noticed CAP's exhortations. Surrounded by saluting officers in crisp outfits, Chávez conducts the business of state. "Did you know," he remarked to one reporter, "that this is the very room I was brought to as a prisoner on the fourth of February, 1992, after I surrendered? I sat on that very couch over there. Everything is exactly the same." The ex-paratrooper had certainly come a long way from his humble roots in the western state of Barinas.[27] How was he going to challenge the Washington Consensus and reverse his country's economic straits?

In 1998, I was in South Florida, studying Latin America in the history department at the University of Miami. I had already decided to concentrate on Venezuela, and was busy researching the role of the Creole Petroleum Corporation in Lake Maracaibo. Some of my colleagues, however, seemed skeptical about my choice. Very few people studied the country, they warned, and if I wanted a job, I might consider writing my dissertation on a larger country, such as Brazil, Argentina, or Mexico. Having traveled to Venezuela, however, I felt a personal connection to the country and was very intrigued about the pervasive U.S. role in its affairs. But I do not recall feeling very drawn to current Venezuelan politics. I remember watching reports of the Venezuelan election on my beat-up TV in South Miami. Mostly I watched Jorge Ramos, the straightlaced presenter on Gustavo Cisneros's station, Univisión. The coverage was rabidly anti-Chavista and overblown, and I was certainly not sympathetic to the right-wing opposition. Yet, I felt relatively ambivalent about the Chávez experiment. Chávez scored important political victories in his first year through the signing of a new constitution and the creation of a new unicameral legislature.[28] The reforms certainly increased Chávez's power, but I was still skeptical that this new firebrand Venezuelan president would counteract the U.S. driven free trade agenda.

In the fall of 1999, I went to England to continue my studies. I spent my days visiting the library and reading about the oil industry in Venezuela. In the evenings I would work in the college computer room. The news was full of talk about the upcoming meeting of the World Trade Organization (WTO) in Seattle. The WTO, created in 1995 to replace the General Agreement on Tariffs and Trade (GATT), promoted globalization and free trade.[29] WTO treaties, critics charged, favored the interests of multinational corporations and rich countries of the world.[30] Others reported that the United States had disproportionate power over trade negotiations within the WTO.[31] Additionally, some believed that WTO member states adopted WTO treaties in an undemocratic fashion, to the disadvantage of their citizens and the environment.[32] To learn more about what was happening in Seattle, I clicked on to indymedia.org, a new Web site that sought to counter the influence of corporate-controlled media. A large call had been made to protest the WTO meeting on November 30 and to shut down the city with acts of civil disobedience. Participating were not only nongovernmental organizations but labor unions, environmentalists, human rights activists, and anarchists. Although their politics differed, all the groups were united in their opposition to free trade policies sponsored by the WTO.

I read the reports with interest. Early on the morning of the 30, demonstrators began to assemble. By 7:30 A.M. large groups headed to the Seattle Convention Center, where WTO delegates were scheduled to meet. Soon after, seven large-scale disturbances broke out within a radius of two-blocks. The police fired pepper spray at the protesters near the convention center, and at precisely 3:52 P.M. the mayor proclaimed a civil emergency. With the situation on the ground becoming increasingly more chaotic, the governor called in the National Guard and declared a curfew.[33] While the protesters cannot claim that their actions caused the subsequent breakdown in negotiations at the WTO meeting, the Seattle mobilization proved to be popular outside of the United States.[34] Speaking with the *Seattle Weekly*, one Mexican noted, "The attitude among people was that we didn't know you [Americans] had it in you."[35] Significantly, the WTO protests, which spawned the antiglobalization movement, brought the issue of corporate dominance of world trade to the forefront of public consciousness.[36]

After reading the reports on indymedia, I began to get involved in organizing future protests. For years, large financial institutions dominated by the United States had been operating in Latin America, but it seemed that now public consciousness had grown in the United States as well. I fell into e-mail correspondence with other political activists about an upcoming April meeting of the International Monetary Fund in Washington. American activists had put out the call for international solidarity, and I suggested organizing a protest in Britain. The activists' secret weapon at Seattle had been the e-mail list server, and I soon helped to organize a similar list server for the April action. One of my principal contacts was a London anarchist who went by the e-mail pen name "distopia." I went to London and met him, a lean working-class anarchist who sported a beard and a Maoist hat. We agreed to continue our outreach, and I sent out hundreds of e-mails to organizations throughout Britain. The number of individuals on our list server grew exponentially. A meeting at University College London was called. I hopped on the bus, expecting a large turnout. Distopia had rented a classroom for the afternoon. Unfortunately, it was difficult to translate virtual reality into practical action. The turnout for our meeting was disappointing, and our discussion got bogged down in endless suggestions for the April action. Later, at a London pub, distopia attempted to cheer me up. He suggested that we cancel the April plan and instead start to mobilize British activists for an upcoming IMF and World Bank meeting in Prague in September. I returned to Oxford and distributed flyers to student groups and local colleges. In the meantime, distopia, who was involved with a group called Reclaim the Streets, suggested I join him for anticapitalist May Day protests in London, which I did. Spurred on by the successes in Seattle, indymedia reporters were in the streets interviewing the protesters. Reclaim the Streets protesters meanwhile unfurled banners from lampposts. One defaced a statue of Winston Churchill with red paint. Other protesters were more constructive. I was intrigued by some activists who wanted to create greener public space and practiced so-called guerrilla gardening. As the police stood by, the activists put plants in the street. Later, marching to Trafalgar Square, a couple of activists wearing bandannas started to ransack a McDonald's, a poignant symbol of corporate globalization. The vandalism continued for several minutes. Soon not one square inch of the restaurant had not been destroyed or defaced. The police, powerless, stood by idly. Later, however, at Trafalgar Square, the authorities regained control and were able to pen protesters into a small area.

Meanwhile, plans for our September IMF protest were proceeding. Although I knew that I would not be able to attend the fall event, as I would be doing research in the National Archives in Washington, D.C., I nevertheless joined distopia and others for a planning meeting in Prague. The bus trip there was arduous. I sat next to distopia as we headed through the Chunnel and then across Germany. Some of the British activists had never been to continental Europe and seemed genuinely excited to meet their Czech compatriots. In Prague, we made our way on the subway to an outlying suburb. The protesters were to rendezvous at an organic farm, where we would also sleep and take our meals. There I met activists from France, Italy, Spain, Norway, and Germany. One young American woman had helped to organize the IMF protests in Washington in April and had just moved to Prague. The Czechs had organized a loose coalition of environmental, human rights, and anarchist groups in preparation for the September events. The anarchists were young and wanted nothing to do with the old-guard communists. Like the Zapatistas in Mexico, who had no clear leaders (Subcomandante Marcos presents himself only as a spokesperson), our meetings were organized in a "nonhierarchical" fashion designed to prevent any leaders from springing up. At the end of the first day, I joined distopia and others for the convention center where the IMF and World Bank were scheduled to meet. The site was daunting: the center looked as impenetrable as Kafka's castle and stood alone in a huge open space. Any attempt to blockade the site would be challenging.

Although I did not participate in the actual demonstration, I heard about it from my friends. As in Seattle, thousands of protesters clashed with police amid tear gas and more street violence. This time, the IMF allowed representatives from nongovernmental organizations to attend meetings in an effort to fend off criticism about lack of transparency and accountability.[37] Reading about the Prague demonstration on a computer in the Library of Congress in Washington, DC, I realized that the antiglobalization movement was on the ascent. I hooked up with some activists in Washington, and that summer I attended a protest against the Republican convention in Philadelphia. Many of the same protesters who had participated in earlier antiglobalization mobilizations were present. With the date fast approaching for my imminent return to Venezuela, I thought I would try to meet like-minded activists in South America. I had read about some antiglobalization protests in Venezuela on the internet and entered into correspondence with activists in Caracas.

After touching down in Maiquetía airport, I made my way to Caracas. Maiquetía is located on the coast, and to get to the city one must ascend steep mountains ringed with shantytowns. In my hotel the first night in the affluent Altamira section of Caracas, I watched Chávez on TV. He was talking about the history of U.S. oil companies in Venezuela and the struggle to gain control over petroleum revenue. Jetlagged, I drifted off for a while. When I woke up Chávez was still talking. As he spoke, he held up a copy of his new constitution, explaining its political significance to his poor constituents. Watching Chávez, I wondered what connection, if any, existed between him and the Zapatistas and antiglobalization forces in the United States and Europe.

My new acquaintances in Caracas scoffed at the idea that Chávez bore any resemblance to the antiglobalization movement. When I was not in the historical archive in downtown Caracas I spent time with Nelson, a sociologist at the Central University. Like distopia, he also sported a long beard and cap but was a little heavier than my British friend. Although he looked like Karl Marx, Nelson also enjoyed American baseball and took me to see a game in Caracas. He helped to publish *El Libertario*, an anarchist newspaper opposed to right-wing, business-friendly forces and to Chávez and his MVR. To Nelson and his colleagues, Chávez was a vulgar, militaristic demagogue interested in perpetuating his own power. Nelson invited me to a meeting of his circle in a community center in the west of the city. Following Nelson's directions, I took the subway to a poor section of town and got off. The community center doubled as a rudimentary, makeshift radio station. I went to the second floor and met with Nelson's group, comprised of a few student radicals and two older, frail-looking men. Nelson explained that both were anarchists and had fought on the Republican side during the Spanish Civil War during the 1930s. After the Republicans were defeated, they had come to live in Venezuela. When I suggested that the *El Libertario* circle might make common cause with the Chavistas in an effort to keep the United States at bay, one of the older Spaniards looked at me reproachfully. The activists here would have nothing to do with the government. They were determined to promote an anti-authoritarian alternative to Chávez and hoped to open an anarchist bookstore soon in downtown Caracas.

On a certain level I shared my new friends' skepticism: I could not envision Chávez as some kind of prophet of the antiglobalization movement. During his first year in office he seemed to be mostly concerned with smashing what remained of the Pact of Punto Fijo, named after the location Punto Fijo where COPEI and AD agreed to limit the country's political system to competition between the two parties.[38] Even as he consolidated these political gains, Chávez appeased the United States and sought to reassure investors and shore up foreign direct investment.[39] These actions were understandable, given the delicate financial situation during Chávez's first year in office. Venezuela was racked by recession, confronted inflation, capital flight, and low oil prices.[40] Upon traveling to the United States after his election (he was now granted a visa), Chávez threw the first pitch at a Yankees game and then proceeded to the New York Stock Exchange, where he pounded the gavel. John Maisto, Clinton's ambassador in Caracas, supported Chávez. Maisto observed that

Chávez had left U.S. investments intact and sought increased foreign investment. "Watch what Chávez does, not what he says," Maisto advised his superiors.[41]

In seeking to ameliorate poverty, Chávez faced a fundamental contradiction: How can a poor country move ahead within the global context of neoliberalism? In order to reduce unemployment, hasten economic improvement, and reduce indebtedness, Chávez needed capital and investment. However, to achieve these things he would have to negotiate with the IMF, which had exacted a terrible social price in Venezuela during the CAP and Caldera years. The alternative was to somehow delink from the global economy, a path fraught with peril, as demonstrated by the case of Cuba and Chávez's new ally, Fidel Castro.[42] Nevertheless, according to observers, Chávez sought to promote socioeconomic changes during the first year and a half of his rule. In an article entitled "The Radical Potential of Chavismo in Venezuela," Ellner pointed out that Chávez spoke out against neoliberalism and suspended the privatization of the country's health system.[43] Although he paid, "with much sacrifice," Venezuela's foreign debt payments, Chávez proudly announced that "we have not made, nor will we make agreements with the IMF."[44] Echoing the calls of radical anarchists such as distopia, Chávez even proclaimed that the IMF should be "eliminated."[45] The fact is, Chávez now had breathing space. Having pushed for higher oil prices through OPEC, he could afford to avoid a deal.[46]

President Clinton did not seem to view Chávez as much of a threat and pursued a nonconfrontational approach toward Venezuela. But dramatic political developments in the United States would put Chávez on a collision course with the White House. Soon whiz kid and "trade mercenary" Robert Zoellick would be back in power, spelling bad news for Chávez.

Zoellick was out of power in Washington during the Clinton years. However, the small town boy from Illinois did quite well for himself. From 1993 to 1997, he worked as executive vice president at Fannie Mae, the nation's largest mortgage provider.[47] He also served as a member of the advisory board at the infamous Enron corporation[48] and senior international advisor to Goldman Sachs.[49] Indeed, writes one critic, "Zoellick has benefited from direct personal ties with the U.S. financial community and transnational corporations."[50] Meanwhile, however, Zoellick was positioning himself to come back to power in the event of a neoconservative takeover in Washington. In 1998, Zoellick, along with Donald Rumsfeld, Paul Wolfowitz, John Bolton, and William Kristol, signed a letter to Bill Clinton drafted by the Project for a New American Century, a conservative organization focusing on U.S. foreign policy, urging the president to remove Saddam Hussein from power.[51] As the U.S. presidential election of 2000 neared, Zoellick, who had objected to President Clinton's trade policy on the grounds that the administration had promoted social and environmental provisions within free trade organizations, got a job as trade advisor to the George W. Bush campaign.[52] Soon he became close enough to Bush that he got his own personal nickname, "the Adding Machine." Yet, according to the *New Internationalist,* "although the White House values his brain, Zoellick and George W are not good buddies. Instead of hunt'n', fish'n' and gallop'n' across the range his [Zoellick's] hobbies are reading, long-distance running and military history."[53]

During the run-up to the 2000 election, I was in Caracas conducting archival research for my dissertation. Most evenings I sat and watched TV with my landlord, as the streets of San Bernardino were not safe. My landlord spent his days glued to the TV. Chain smoking, he occasionally glanced up from his political talk show to rail against Chávez. On election night I sat on the couch awaiting the electoral returns. To me, Al Gore and George Bush looked relatively indistinguishable on most issues. Certainly, both supported the Free Trade Area of the Americas (FTAA) and sought to continue Clinton's free trade legacy in Latin America.[54] I had gone to the U.S. Embassy in Caracas several weeks earlier to pick up my absentee ballot. I planned to vote for Ralph Nader; unfortunately, the ballot arrived too late on the following day. Like many Americans, I was befuddled by the Florida result. After several hours my landlord went to bed and eventually I was forced to do so as well. Over the next several days I caught up on the electoral news via computer at IESA.

Zoellick played a key role during the Florida recount. In Tallahassee, Zoellick helped former Secretary of State James Baker oversee the Florida recount. According to the *St. Petersburg* (Florida) *Times,* Zoellick proved crucial by helping to map a strategy for Bush and issue Baker's statements to the media. "In that sense," remarked Zoellick, "I got to know Florida very well."[55] After the campaign, Bush rewarded Zoellick's loyalty by naming the Illinois whiz kid U.S. Trade Representative, a cabinet-level position.[56] It now fell to Zoellick to hammer through such crucial agreements as the FTAA. But the next FTAA meeting, to be held in Québec in April 2001, was being targeted by a now-energized antiglobalization movement. Hugo Chávez was also planning a visit.

At the meeting in Québec, George Bush stayed holed up in his hotel. Outside, demonstrators clashed with police amid clouds of tear gas.[57] Bush was joined at the summit by 33 hemispheric leaders intent on building the world's largest free trade zone, "NAFTA on steroids."[58] But how would Bush and his entourage conduct business? Despite the desire of participating countries to avoid a repeat of the violent fiasco of Seattle in 1999, protesters played havoc with the conference's schedules and successfully delayed meetings.[59] Meanwhile meeting attendees had to hide behind a protective cordon of 5,000 Canadian police and a metal fence running around the entire perimeter of the city center. Québec looked like a prison.[60] Frustrated, Bush was obliged to cancel one meeting and postpone others. "If they are protesting because of free trade, I'd say I disagree," he remarked. Bush added, "Trade not only helps spread prosperity, but trade helps spread freedom."[61]

The stakes were high for George Bush, who had been recently inaugurated and had come into office under the pall of the Florida recount fiasco. The FTAA was one of the biggest priorities of his administration. He would have to ram it through to placate corporate interests backing his party. But standing in Bush's and Zoellick's way were congressional Democrats who insisted on labor and environmental protections.[62] To make sure any deal negotiated by Zoellick would not be subject to congressional scrutiny, the president sought to circumvent the democratic process altogether by pushing for so-called fast-track authority (i.e., the ability to submit trade deals to Congress and have legislators simply vote up or down without being able to amend any changes).[63] But Bush's efforts to introduce fast track were not greeted with warmth in Congress and led only to stalemate. As a result, the president's negotiating power was severely weakened as he arrived for the summit in Québec.

For the protesters, too, the stakes were high: they feared—correctly—that the FTAA would lead to unprecedented corporate control over public services. According to the treaty's detractors, the FTAA sought "to introduce 'market competition' into the public sector of local economies throughout the Western Hemisphere. It means, therefore, that all 34 nations involved would have to open up—to private investment—their health care and pension systems, schools, public utilities, and other governmental services."[64] Protesters organized a grassroots "People's Summit," which proposed sustainable economic development and greater social, worker, and environmental protections. Protesters also pushed for recognition of local sovereignty and democratic decision-making. In opposition to Zoellick and Bush's approach of negotiating in secret, the protesters sought greater transparency in the trade negotiating process.[65] Sensing the growing groundswell of opposition, Zoellick, going back on his earlier anti- environmental position, stated that the Bush administration would subject trade deals to environmental review, in accordance with an earlier executive order signed by President Clinton.[66] At the same time, Bush sought to shatter Latin American resistance by calling for bilateral trade pacts with individual Latin American countries.[67]

Adding to Bush's woes was the opposition offered by Brazil and Venezuela. Chávez had in fact raised serious questions regarding the FTAA in a prior meeting with President Cardoso in Brasilia. Both leaders were concerned about efforts to speed up the FTAA to go into effect for 2003 instead of 2005. They did not believe Third World countries displayed the same economic advantages as industrialized countries; therefore they were not yet ready to enter into the FTAA.[68] In Brasilia, Chávez proposed that Latin American regional trade blocs should be strengthened before creating the FTAA, and Cardoso agreed.[69] Cardoso presented a fiery speech during the opening session of the summit, in which he underscored his country's reluctance to adopt *any* free trade deal. "We will insist that free-trade benefits should be equally shared by all participants," he thundered, "that trade opening should be reciprocal and that it should lead to the attenuation rather than the aggravation of the disparities that exist in our region."[70]

The Québec summit seems to have been an epiphany for Chávez. Speaking later at the Fourth Hemispheric Conference Against the FTAA in Havana, Chávez said that the more than 70,000 protesters were subjected to "gas warfare" at the "wall of shame" surrounding the city center. Chávez was particularly repulsed by the bullying attitude of the U.S. diplomats and president. He later recalled the suave hospitality of Jean Chrétien, the Canadian prime minister, who had bragged that the protective wall was "anti-globalizationist-proof" (a claim later dispelled by protesters who ripped down a 50-meter section of the barrier). For Chávez, the Québec summit was like a coming-out celebration. Addressing the conference participants, Chávez paid respects to the radical sociologist and economic historian Andre Gunder Frank, author of the classic work *Capitalism and Underdevelopment in Latin America*.[71] Chávez added that he was disappointed that since the Miami summit of 1994 "we have advanced very little—almost not at all—in the social objectives."[72] In a further shot across Bush's bow, the Venezuelan president declared that the FTAA was "only a possibility, an option, not a written destiny as written on Moses's tablets."[73] Chávez added that it should be the Venezuelan people themselves who would decide about the FTAA and said he would consider submitting the agreement to popular referendum.[74]

Despite this show of independence, Chávez was cordial and respectful toward the United States. On the last day of the summit, he met with Bush and invited him to play baseball. Bush told Chávez he wanted him to be his friend; Chávez replied, in English, "I want to be your friend too."[75] Bush accepted Chávez's invitation to visit Venezuela when he deemed it appropriate.[76] Beneath this display of warm ties, however, lurked mutual suspicion and distrust. At Québec, Chávez had tried, however tenuously, to deviate from TINA. If he were allowed to consolidate his rule he could become a dangerous political example for the hemisphere.

In August 2001, I was finishing up my archival research in Maracaibo. My few months in the oil metropolis had proven profitable, and I had made a lot of progress in the archive, located in a gaily painted Antillean house on the city's main historic street. But the heat had become unbearable, my room had occasional visits from large tropical water bugs, and I was ready to go home to New York. I left Venezuela just as things were beginning to get interesting. Having pushed through significant political reforms in his first two years in office, Chávez now challenged the United States and large financial institutions by instituting measures with significant socio-economic content. These included agrarian reform and a statute affirming state control over all petroleum operations.[77]

Chávez's prestige seemed to be rising just at the time that the antiglobalization movement was sputtering. Speaking with a local newspaper, Jeremy Simer, director of Seattle's Community Alliance for Global Justice, remarked, "In the first year after WTO [in Seattle], people were so energized, but there was a naive idea that we could prevail just by putting 50,000 people on the street." Simer added soberly, "It was a fluke here; the stars aligned in this amazing way based on months of hard work and luck." Since Seattle, activists had to reconcile to the fact that a lot more grassroots organizing had to be done in American communities. "The WTO protests in Seattle," says journalist Geov Parrish, "were a quantum leap forward in terms of public awareness of trade issues. Since then, however, U.S. organizers—unlike their brethren in Latin America—seem to have been stuck trying to take their influence to the next level."[78] The coup de grace came on September 11, 2001. Prior to the attack, I was eagerly anticipating a protest in Washington against the IMF and World Bank set for September 28 to October 4.[79] But the felling of the Twin Towers put a significant damper on protest. The protest, which initially was supposed to focus on large financial institutions, now took on a different, antiwar focus. What is more, turnout was disappointing: I only saw a few thousand people at the rather somber and uninspiring march. Although the antiglobalization movement was able to carry out another protest against the FTAA in Miami in 2003, the event only attracted 20,000 people, achieved little media visibility, and led to a harsh police crackdown. "Miami," says Parrish, "was the first, and perhaps last, test of the possibility for post-9/11 antiglobalization mass protest."[80]

With the antiglobalization movement out of the way, and riding high on a wave of patriotism after the 9/11 attacks, Bush pressed his advantage on trade. Zoellick went on a public relations offensive, arguing that the United States should not be intimidated by terrorism seeking to undermine the U.S. economy. Rather, he argued, the country should counter terrorism with free trade initiatives.[81] Zoellick's longtime efforts were successful in the post-9/11 political climate. In a big blow to labor and environmentalists, the president won his fast-track authority in Congress in a narrow 2002 victory.[82] Zoellick won the respect of the corporate community for gaining bipartisan support for fast track.[83] With the antiglobalization movement on the wane, Bush was at the zenith of his power. Could Chávez become a potent symbol in the fight against globalization? Already there were worrying signs that the Venezuelan leader was no longer such a political maverick on the South American stage. Bolivia had seen antiprivatization protests in 2000, and a scant three months before the Québec summit Ecuador was rocked by violence as Indians protested IMF austerity measures.[84] Quietly, the United States started to initiate dialogue with the Chávez opposition.

By early 2002, U.S.-Venezuelan relations were in tatters as a result of Chávez's tentative moves challenging the neoliberal agenda. His criticism of Washington's war in Afghanistan did not help matters.[85] Meanwhile, Chávez's business supporters had fallen out with the president. "It seems that many had hoped," writes Wilpert, "as had always been Venezuelan tradition, that key big business supporters of the president would be named to important ministerial posts." Chávez, however, let these supporters down by not awarding key ministries to them.[86] The Venezuelan opposition, now with political and economic support from the United States, started to brag that Chávez's days were now numbered.[87] Although Chávez had prevailed against the last champion of market-oriented reforms, CAP, he now faced perhaps a more formidable enemy: Gustavo Cisneros.

The multibillionaire surely did not appreciate Venezuela's growing ties to Cuba or Chávez's challenging of the FTAA. Cisneros's solution? Cultivate high-level support. As early as 1999, he had been able to get an interview with then Texas governor George Bush.[88] As the opposition to Chávez heated up, Cisneros continued to cultivate warm ties to the Bush family. In early 2001, he invited ex-president George Herbert Walker Bush to Venezuela for a fishing trip in the state of Amazonas.[89] Cisneros could now count on other allies in high places, such as his friend Otto Reich.[90] After working as ambassador to Venezuela in the late 1980s, Reich had gone on to become a corporate lobbyist for Bacardi and Lockheed Martin (which sought to provide F–16 fighter planes to Chile). In January 2002, Reich became assistant secretary of state for Western Hemisphere Affairs through a recess appointment.[91] Although Reich and senior government officials have denied there was any U.S. role in the coup or foreknowledge of a plot, the veteran Cuban-American diplomat reportedly met regularly at the White House with alleged coup plotters like Pedro Carmona.[92] Furthermore, Eva Golinger, a pro-Chávez lawyer based in the United States, reportedly uncovered a top-secret document showing that the Central Intelligence Agency had prior knowledge of a coup plot. The document, a Senior Executive Security Brief distributed to the top 200 or so U.S. government officials, was dated April 6, 2002, six days prior to the coup. The brief showed relatively detailed knowledge of the plot.[93]

In the dramatic days leading up to the April coup, Cisneros's Venvisión substituted nonstop vitriolic anti-Chávez propaganda for its regular programming.[94] Cisneros seems to have played a pivotal role in the events that unfolded in the next few days. Indeed, *Newsweek* placed Cisneros "at the vortex of the whole mess."[95] It has been widely reported that Cisneros bankrolled the coup. One day before the coup, April 11, important Venezuelan political and business figures gathered at Cisneros's mansion, where they met with the U.S. ambassador. Later that evening, the alleged coup leaders, including Carmona, met at Venevisión headquarters.[96] "This government was put together at Gustavo Cisneros' office," opposition legislator Pedro Pablo Alcántara later remarked.[97] As the coup plotters were toasting their own success, Chávez was being held captive on the remote Venezuelan island of Orchila. Chávez noticed that a private plane bearing U.S. markings landed on the island. "What was it doing there?" Chávez later asked during a news conference.[98] According to *Newsweek*, the plane belonged to Cisneros.[99] Cisneros has denied the allegations, saying he had played no role in the coup. "That's a fantasy," he said.[100]

In the early hours of April 12, Carmona left directly from Cisneros's office to be sworn in as Venezuela's new president. Later that day, Cisneros and other media executives drove up in their limousines to the presidential palace where they met with Carmona.[101] Carmona appointed Daniel Romero, a lawyer, former private secretary to CAP and a functionary in the Cisneros organization, to be Venezuela's new attorney general.[102] Meanwhile, Venevisión was doing its best to legitimate the new Carmona regime in the public eye. The network did not cover pro-Chávez protests calling for the president's reinstatement. Chávez claimed that TV stations failed to interview his regime's supporters. Instead, Venevisión broadcast a daylong marathon of American films: *Lorenzo's Oil*, *Nell*, and *Pretty Woman*. Station executives claimed that the news blackout was necessary as their reporters had been threatened by violent protesters.[103] Even as Cisneros's network leapt into action, the media magnate was busy talking to Washington officials. On April 13, Otto Reich called Cisneros twice. According to the media magnate, Reich called "as a friend" because Chávez's partisans were protesting at Caracas media outlets.[104]

Significantly, the Carmona regime, helped to power by Cisneros, sought to change course and reestablish Venezuela's links with large financial institutions.[105] Not surprisingly, perhaps, the IMF promptly recognized the new coup government and offered financial assistance. "We are ready to help the new government as far as their immediate needs are concerned," said Thomas Dawson, the institution's director for external relations.[106] With the return of Chávez, however, Cisneros and his neoliberal agenda were dealt a stinging blow. Although the conservative media in Venezuela have suggested that Cisneros might run as a presidential candidate himself in 2006, becoming in the process a kind of Silvio Berlusconi for South America, the outlook does not look so promising for the media magnate.[107]

In fact, the coup seems to have emboldened Chávez to buck the Washington Consensus yet further. In 2005, during his weekly television show *Aló, Presidente*, Chávez proclaimed his support for democratic socialism. Venezuelans, he said, had a clear choice: "Either capitalism, which is the road to hell, or socialism, for those who want to build the kingdom of God here on Earth."[108] Indeed, Chávez's recent moves suggest that he intends to radicalize and deepen the social transformations taking place in his country. At his Ministry for the Popular Economy, officials have already created 6,840 cooperatives employing 210,000 people nationwide.[109] The new cooperatives produce everything from cheese, vegetables and fruits to baked goods, textiles and even shoes.[110] Crucial to Chávez's efforts has been the banking system. Currently regulators demand that private banks set aside 31.5 percent of all loans to agricultural projects, housing construction, tourism, and micro credits (loans to small, start-up businesses).[111] Chávez also recently sent in the Venezuelan military to seize a Heinz plant that makes ketchup. Company representatives blasted the move as "a violation of property rights and free trade as well as due process."[112] The government declared that the plant had been bought illegally, had been closed for many years, and that 80 percent of the firm already belonged to workers. Respected Venezuela analyst Greg Wilpert reports that Chávez is investigating the cases of 700 other closed enterprises. Later the government will evaluate whether they are suitable for worker takeovers via expropriation.[113] Under article 115 of Chávez's new constitution, private property must serve the public good and general interest. If a company does not live up to this principle, the government may expropriate but with just compensation.[114] Such moves have made Chávez unbelievably popular, with an approval rating of 70 percent.[115] The government's actions have radicalized workers, who "have begun taking matters in their own hands" by occupying factories and businesses.[116]

Ellner, a veteran observer of Venezuelan affairs, is skeptical about Chávez's radical pretensions. "Venezuela," he has said, "is far from having developed a new economic system that would allow Chávez to package and export a model to the rest of Latin America." So far, he continues, Chávez has not established "anything close to socialism." If Chávez has indeed come up with a new model, it is based on state prioritization of public needs and the encouragement of worker cooperatives and small producers in the countryside and city. Chávez, explains Ellner, has rejected alliances with large capitalist groups but has sought a kind of rapprochement with them. Nevertheless, Chávez's six and a half years in power have demonstrated that Third World governments can defend national sovereignty from the likes of the United States. Simultaneously, Chávez has promoted a "nationalist, progressive agenda that . . . confronts capital."[117]

In Washington, the alarm bells were going off. Zoellick, who became deputy secretary of state in February 2005, said Latin American countries should ally together to protect democracy against "creeping authoritarianism" in the region. He singled out Chávez in particular, accusing the president of carrying out "terrible things" and being a new "Pied Piper of Populism."[118] It was difficult to see, however, how Zoellick's comments would encourage any kind of bloc that would stand against Chávez. Indeed, in pushing his ideas, Chávez was much more in sync with developments in wider South America than Zoellick was.

In the Argentine capital of Buenos Aires, Angel Carrizo has become a baker. His improvised oven is made out of old washing machines cut in half with an opening for wood fuel. Carrizo bakes bread every day and sells it for 1.20 pesos a kilo, as opposed to 1.80 in the bakeries. With the money, Carrizo and his crew can buy flour from a wholesaler and feed 160 poor children from the area. Carrizo used to run errands for a mechanic. But he lacks the spare parts for his car, which has not run for years. Carrizo's wife operates two donated sewing machines and has created a clothing bank. She recycles donated clothing and provides it for next to nothing to the needy.

Carrizo and his wife are *piqueteros*, poor residents who go out on the highways, stop traffic, and burn tires. Many are homeless and have worn-out shoes. On the highway, they might be shot or killed by the police.[119] During a typical roadblock, the piqueteros might demand release of their colleagues from jail, police withdrawal, food parcels, state- funded employment, repudiation of the country's foreign debt, a living wage, unemployment benefits, and government investment in electricity, health, and paved roads. With traffic snarled, trucks get backed up, factories cannot receive their supplies, and agribusiness cannot ship grain. "Like a debilitating strike," remarks James Petras, a former sociology professor at Binghamton University and adviser to the jobless in Argentina, "it hampers the elite from accumulating profits."[120] If they survive to protest another day, the piqueteros return to houses with tin rooves and mud walls. They run community kitchens, libraries, gardens, and even clinics. Most piqueteros lack political experience and get involved in protest because they are starving.[121] Although many work in the informal economy as vendors, day workers, or household laborers, others formerly had well-paying jobs.[122] Like the Zapatistas in Chiapas, many piquetero organizations are structured in an egalitarian fashion.[123] According to Petras, the piqueteros practice grassroots democracy by reaching collective decisions at the neighborhood and municipal level.[124]

The piqueteros were in the vanguard of a new movement that sought to overturn Argentina's free market policies. In the midst of a bleak depression in 2001, the unpopular Fernando de la Rúa government had followed the dictates of multilateral lending agencies dominated by the U.S. Treasury Department.[125] In an effort to pay off the country's foreign debt, de la Rúa sought assistance from the IMF and instituted austerity measures.[126] But trade liberalization, privatization, and drastic cuts in social spending led to a popular backlash in December of that year. When organized looting of supermarkets and violent clashes erupted, de la Rúa proclaimed a 30-day state of siege. Tens of thousands of Buenos Aires residents disobeyed the order and took to the streets in a spontaneous *cacerolazo*, or pot and pan banging demonstrations. De la Rúa was forced to resign, and the country was thrust into a period of political uncertainty.[127] Néstor Kirchner, who had denounced the neoliberal policies of the past, came to power in May 2003. Kirchner immediately negotiated an agreement with the IMF to reschedule $84 billion in debt payments over three years. According to the Council On Hemispheric Affairs, "by repaying the IMF, Argentina gains economic autonomy from an overarching authority which has chronically undermined Latin America's economic prosperity."[128]

The arrival of Kirchner, accompanied by the election of Luiz Inácio Lula da Silva of the Workers' Party (Partido dos Trabalhadores [PT]) in Brazil in October 2002 and the rise of the center-left government of Tabaré Vázquez in Uruguay in 2004 constituted a major shift in South American politics. Such sweeping political developments were not lost on Hugo Chávez, who was ideally positioned to become a hemispheric leader challenging the tenets of globalization.

Having survived the coup attempt, Chávez grew more confrontational by the day. The FTAA, he charged, did not "attend to social problems, education, housing, the retired, children facing hunger."[129] Never one for subtlety, Chávez charged that the FTAA was the "path to hell."[130] Chávez was surely not out of sync with the popular mood. Indeed, during his tenure as U.S. Trade Representative, Zoellick failed to secure a Free Trade of the Americas agreement.[131] Although he had been successful in hammering through Bush's fast track, Zoellick faced an obstacle in Brazil, which was wary of intellectual property rules among other things. With a number of countries missing their FTAA deadlines for submitting negotiating offers, Zoellick pared down his goals and started to hammer through two-track free trade deals with Central America. In a recognition of the changing political reality, Zoellick conceded that the mood was quite different from the heady days of 1994 in Miami. "Now you have to narrow it down to what you think you can reasonably accomplish," he remarked. "The times change. In the 90s there was a different sense of economic progress in the region. Obviously, you've got different governments."[132]

Zoellick might have been referring to Venezuela, which proclaimed its own trade agreement in December 2004. What South America most needed, Chávez explained, was "integration for life—not colonialism, but the happiness of our peoples."[133] Venezuela has charged that the FTAA's negotiating process is undemocratic, that the agreement undermines sovereignty and democracy by bolstering the power of corporations, and that privatization spells death for poor people across the hemisphere.[134] Chávez has proposed instead the "Bolivarian Alternative for the Americas,"[135] known by its Spanish acronym, ALBA.[136] The agreement, which differs from the FTAA in that it "advocates a socially-oriented trade block rather than one strictly based on the logic of deregulated profit maximization," provides for fluid exchange of goods and services in a way that circumvents international banking systems and corporate interests.[137] Already Cuba and Venezuela have signed many documents pertaining to ALBA, and initiatives involving other countries are under way. Venezuela currently ships oil to Cuba in exchange for the services of nearly 20,000 Cuban doctors and teachers. An ALBA agreement is also being hammered out with Kirchner's Argentina, under which Venezuela is to provide oil in exchange for cattle.[138] One of the more interesting provisions of ALBA has to do with the creation of a "Compensatory Fund for Structural Convergence," which would supervise and distribute financial assistance to economically vulnerable countries.[139]

Located 230 miles south of Buenos Aires, Mar del Plata is normally a peaceful Argentine beach resort. But during the Fourth Summit of the Americas in November 2005,[140] the city was turned into a riot zone as activists protested the presence of President George Bush.[141] The protesters included piqueteros, anarchists, and community and labor groups. At one point, demonstrators hurled a Molotov cocktail and set a bank on fire. In an effort to get the situation under control, police fired tear gas.[142] By the time the rioting started, the streets of Mar del Plata were largely deserted.[143]

But this summit was noteworthy not so much for the protests outside the conference but for the fiery address delivered by Hugo Chávez. Speaking before a crowd of 25,000 at the World Cup Stadium, Chávez baptized the site as "the gravesite of the FTAA." Basking in his newfound fame as a hemispheric leader, Chávez took advantage of the occasion to promote his own plan, the ALBA.[144] Joining Chávez in the stadium was Argentine soccer star Diego Maradona, Bolivian presidential candidate Evo Morales, and Cuban singer Silvio Rodríguez. The three had ridden aboard the so-called ALBA Express, a train from Buenos Aires to Mar del Plata.[145] By all indications, the event was a public relations coup for Chávez, whose rising popularity seemed to contrast starkly with the ever-plummeting fortunes of Bush. To make matters worse for the beleaguered U.S. president, the summit itself ended in a fiasco. Owing to resistance not only from Venezuela but also from the Mercosur nations of Brazil, Argentina, Uruguay, and Paraguay, which argued that the FTAA would damage their economies, the conference failed to reach any agreement on a trade deal. Twenty-nine of the thirty-four countries represented agreed to continue FTAA talks in 2006, while the five dissenters insisted on waiting for the result of a WTO meeting in Hong Kong.[146]

Mar del Plata seemed to highlight Venezuela's growing political importance in the region. For Chávez, ALBA is only one of many hemispheric initiatives designed to weaken the thrust of U.S.-sponsored neoliberalism. For example, the Venezuelan leader has proposed the creation of a Bank of the South as a means of "consolidating a multipolar world" and combating the IMF.[147] Chávez, who recently withdrew Venezuela's foreign currency reserves from the United States and placed them in European banks, has suggested that he would like to place them in a newly created South American bank. "By god, don't tell me that's impossible," he remarked.[148] Venezuela has said that it would help to create such a bank with a $5 billion initial deposit.[149] Chávez recently bought $950 million in Argentine bonds in an effort to foster creation of the new bank.[150] If that was not confrontational enough, Chávez has spoken out against the immorality of Latin America's foreign debt. In an inflammatory move, he suggested that the issue of the external debt be submitted to a regional referendum and that the peoples of Latin America be asked whether they support paying the debt or investing the money in health and education.[151] Such a move was probably unrealistic, but Chávez has been somewhat successful at chipping away at the Washington Consensus. In 2005, he got Kirchner of Argentina and Lula of Brazil to join Venezuela in agreeing to negotiate their foreign debt not on an individual basis but as a collective bloc.[152] Chávez also urged that 10 percent of the Latin American foreign debt go toward an International Humanitarian Fund that would help to fund social programs without any of the usual neoliberal conditions. He garnered support for his plan at the Iberian American presidential summit, which met in 2003.

It is clear that Chávez has come a long way since Québec. As Ellner writes, "Chávez's success places in doubt the view that effective resistance by Latin American and Caribbean countries to the free-market neoliberal order is no longer possible."[153]

CHAPTER FIVE
CHÁVEZ'S CIVIL—MILITARY ALLIANCE

General John Craddock was furious. Venezuela, he exclaimed, constituted a threat which represented "a danger for the hemisphere." In 2005, the officer, recently appointed to head the U.S. Southern Command overseeing all U.S. military and intelligence operations in Latin America, voiced his concern that democracy was being eroded in Venezuela. In an interview with the Miami daily *El Nuevo Herald,* Craddock remarked, "I believe that there is a danger for Venezuela's neighbors if this process [Chávez's consolidation of power] is exported." With the exception of Cuba and Venezuela, Craddock complained, the United States maintained good relations with its Latin American counterparts. The general's comments underscored the significant deterioration in military ties between the two nations.[1]

To Craddock and others in the U.S. military establishment, Venezuela's moves to cultivate military ties to Cuba were worrying. What is more, since coming to power Chávez had used the Venezuelan army to deepen the process of social transformation in the country by carrying out public works projects. Even worse, Chávez ordered the army to carry out expropriations of large landholdings. The president's moves to appoint military officers to the board of PdVSA and deploy troops to occupy oil installations came as further proof that he was intent on "militarizing" the oil company. On top of all this, Chávez also secured weapons and arms sales, which sent up warning signals in Washington.

For the Venezuelan armed forces, Chávez's military policies constituted a profound transformation. Historically, the United States had enjoyed warm ties to the Venezuelan military.[2] As early as the Juan Vicente Gómez period (1908–1935),[3] the United States backed the repressive military state. With burgeoning oil operations in the Maracaibo Lake region, the United

States viewed Gómez as a stabilizing force.[4] But the Venezuelan military was a plague on the country, rounding up dissidents and throwing them in appalling dungeons. In the prisons, inmates had to "submit to whipping, hunger and thirst and infamous tortures . . . such as being hung up by their sexual organs, beaten with a thousand stripes . . . kept in cells with practically all light and air excluded, poisoned in some cases and slowly starved to death in others."[5] Marcos Pérez Jiménez, another military dictator who ruled from 1948 to 1958, was similarly brutal. But Pérez was a staunch anticommunist and the United States maintained close military ties. When Venezuela returned to civilian rule, Washington continued to cultivate those ties to the South American nation. With this support, the military could put down young student radicals such as Alí Rodríguez, who had taken to the mountains. Yet as Venezuela reeled from social and political chaos in the 1980s and 1990s, many officers began to turn away from the United States in disgust. One such man is the current minister of defense, Jorge Luis García Carneiro. Surely the bane of the U.S. Southern Command and General Craddock, Carneiro is a charismatic middle-age man. Like Chávez and many other officers in the Venezuelan military, he is of mixed race. Tall and lean, Carneiro wears a crisp uniform and sports a mustache. In response to Craddock's recent broadside, Carneiro was scathing and dismissive. Venezuela, he said, no longer paid any attention to this type of remark because "this has been the policy of the Bush Administration."[6]

How did the Venezuelan military undergo such a dramatic reversal, and what does it portend for the United States? To answer these questions, it is instructive to examine Carneiro's career. Born in the parish of El Valle, Caracas, in 1953, Carneiro is almost Chávez's exact contemporary. The future general grew up in a poor family. His house was located right next to Tiuna Fort, where Chávez was held during the 1992 coup and where he later took up his duties as president. At 14, Carneiro witnessed a terrible earthquake that hit Caracas and as a boy was impressed by the military, who rescued people. Inspired by the example of the soldiers, Carneiro went into the military academy.[7] During the 1970s, the Venezuelan military academy was brought up to university standing. Students began to learn political science and to read about Venezuelan reality. They began to exchange experiences with other university students and to broaden their intellectual horizons.[8] Going into the military was hardly an unusual career path for a young and ambitious man. As Carneiro has explained, there was no discrimination within the Venezuelan military, and those of humble means could ascend through the ranks. "There is no military caste as exists in other countries," Carneiro has said. "We are not part of a caste like in other countries where the commanders of the armed forces are upper class with impressive last names. No, normally the armed forces here are very linked to the people."[9] Indeed, in Venezuela most of the senior officers come from poor urban and rural backgrounds.[10]

As Carneiro came up through the ranks, the soldiers who had saved civilians from natural disaster were his role models. Yet he was also aware of problems within the armed forces. In 1971–72, when Carneiro was still a cadet, the military still had a very counterinsurgency outlook. Cuban-inspired guerrillas still were at large in the country, and Carneiro was startled by the brutality of some of his peers. It was then, as a cadet, that Carneiro met Chávez. The two men struck up a close friendship. "I have a special affinity for his [Chávez's] personality," Carneiro has remarked, "I cannot deny it." They spent four years together in the military academy; later Chávez went to a separate unit and Carneiro was transferred to the state of Apure.[11]

It is no wonder that Carneiro started to develop a social consciousness about the country's problems. As a soldier in Apure, he would have had to been blind not to observe the tough conditions. Apure, which lies in the llano, is a vast region occupying 8.34 percent of Venezuelan territory, about 600,000 square miles. The llano boasts abundant wildlife including freshwater dolphin, manatees, armadillos, anteaters, capybaras, and capuchin monkeys. Unfortunately for the local inhabitants, the llano is also home to other more dangerous animals: caimans, pumas, jaguars, and boa constrictors. The area is characterized by a punishing tropical climate. During the dry season, lasting from November to April, large areas of swamp disappear and the water levels drop along the state's 68 important courses of water, making navigation tough.[12] In the wet season the landscape changes dramatically, with trees and pastures becoming green. Meanwhile, "the heavy rains, usually accompanied by thunder and lightning, occur almost without exception during the hottest part of the day; the temperature may drop as much as 8 or 10 degrees in a quarter of an hour . . . When the sun comes up, it rapidly heats the air and burns off any fog, and afternoon temperatures are about 90 degrees."[13]

During a trip to Venezuela in the mid-1990s, I traveled to the state of Barinas, home of Hugo Chávez, to the north of Apure. A friend of an acquaintance of mine, who owned a ranch on the llano, offered to put me up.

The ranch hands' day began at 5:30 in the morning, and I rose with the men. One cannot help but rise at that hour, as the cacophony of bird sounds is deafening. I remember how the hands headed for the covered corral to milk the cows. Rounding up the cows was a rough business. At one point I watched as four horsemen forced cows across a muddy bog. It was a bloody mess, as some cows fell and were almost trampled. Many of the ranch hands and their wives were from neighboring Colombia. Later at breakfast we ate oily arepas, rice, and eggs. One woman explained to me that her father had abandoned her and her mother was dead. Some of the ranch hands had kids in school, and they complained bitterly about the Venezuelan educational system, which they said was terrible. The living conditions were also quite rudimentary: some of the men merely strung up their hammocks in a glorified stable. The men wanted to grow a watermelon patch on the ranch, but this was against the owner's rules. So they compensated by going fishing in the local stream, where they collected small, mostly bony fish such as piranha. In general, the woman explained, there was never enough money to get by once they had bought their food.

For the young Carneiro, it must have been a jarring experience. Having grown up amid poverty in the capital, he was then shipped off to Apure to witness harsh rural conditions. "It was a painful situation," he remarked, "a scene of poverty in the country."[14] Like Chávez, Carneiro came up through the ranks when counterinsurgency operations were winding down and only a few guerrilla nuclei stayed active. "When soldiers patrolled peasant zones in the frontier," writes Marta Harnecker, "what they found was not a guerilla force but poverty." Carneiro and others could see with their own eyes that the view pushed by Latin American elites, "that the poor are poor because they drink, because they have no initiative or will to work, because they are not very intelligent," was wrong.[15] Nevertheless, Carneiro had not reached the point of wanting to overturn democracy and did not join Chávez's conspiratorial MBR 200.[16] As the social crisis deepened in the 1980s, however, many officers began to question their political allegiances. The caracazo was like a cold shower. According to Harnecker, some troops felt a sense of indignation when called to repress civilians.[17] One military official who had to travel to El Valle, Carneiro's old neighborhood, was ashamed to take care of cadavers and the wounded.[18] When Chávez recuperated from his illness and returned to his duties at Miraflores after the caracazo, presidential guards approached him and he decided to join the MBR 200.[19]

Even as many officers were turning away from the traditional parties and their North American patrons, the United States continued to exert influence over the Venezuelan armed forces. Although beginning with Carneiro's generation, most officers were trained not in the U.S. School of the Americas but at the Venezuelan military academy, some soldiers still found their way to the infamous Fort Benning, Georgia, military base. One was Efraín Vásquez.[20]

The town of Columbus, Georgia, has had long standing ties to the military. As far back as the Civil War, in fact, Columbus had an arsenal and was active in arms manufacture. Located just to the south of Columbus is Fort Benning, one of the largest infantry bases in the world.[21] In 1984, the base began to host the School of the Americas, a training facility formerly located in Panama.[22] The base was the Defense Department's main Spanish-language training facility for Latin American military staff.[23] The town of Columbus promptly became the center of national controversy. The School of the Americas was accused of training Latin American military officers working for regimes that carried out human rights violations.[24] Graduates of the school have included such infamous figures as Manuel Noriega, Efraín Ríos Montt and Roberto D'Aubuisson.[25] The school's detractors refer to the institution as the "School of Assassins."[26] Every year, protesters descend on the town of Columbus and gather just outside Fort Benning.[27] Efraín Vásquez, a Venezuelan lieutenant colonel, spent a full year there in 1988, taking a course titled "Command and General Staff Officer Training."[28]

Though Vásquez had nothing to do with army abuses in Central America, some of his School of Americas peers were implicated in serious human rights abuses. About a year after Vásquez graduated, I was sitting in my student cooperative in Berkeley reading the *New York Times*. The front page had a gory story about another massacre in El Salvador: six Jesuit priests, their housekeeper, and her teenage daughter were killed at the University of Central America. A United Nations Commission determined that 19 of the officers involved in the massacre were School of the Americas graduates. As a result of these scandals, pressure on Congress increased to stop funding the school. In 2000, a motion to shut the School of the Americas in the House of Representatives was narrowly defeated. Feeling the mounting pressure, the Pentagon gave the school a new name, the Western Hemisphere for Security Cooperation (WHINSEC). However, the school continued to offer the same courses as before. Critics of the school viewed the change of name as cosmetic and a cynical maneuver to avoid public criticism. Officially, WHINSEC continued to receive financial support from the U.S. government.[29]

In 1992, Chávez's coup revealed the deep fissures within the Venezuelan armed forces. While the MBR 200 abhorred the political elites who put down civilian unrest with the assistance of U.S. military training, a sizable number of officers remained tied to the two-party system. When Chávez launched his infamous coup d'état against CAP, Carneiro was serving as a local commander carrying out border missions in rough terrain within Apure state. It was not unusual, he remarks, to spend up to four months away from his family at a time. On February 4, Carneiro was shocked to see Chávez on national television. "That's my friend!" he said to himself. "What did he do? Did he rise up against the government?" Carneiro says his reaction to the coup was not all that positive: he had grown up during Venezuela's return to democracy and could not condone a violent overthrow of the system. Nevertheless, the country was plagued by corruption, poverty, and negligence, and Carneiro asked himself whether Chávez could be right.[30]

Although Chávez was able to build positive public opinion around himself during his famous surrender speech, in which he proclaimed that the rebels would cease their struggle "for the time being!" the aborted coup revealed a great chasm between the military and society at large.[31] The MBR 200 was not a strictly military movement; it also contained civilians, but Chávez was reportedly wary of their participation. During the coup, the military did not supply promised weapons to civilians.[32] Once on the presidential campaign trail, however, Chávez argued that civil-military relations needed to be reformed. The armed forces, he argued, had been unjustly excluded from the process of national development.[33]

But what role did Chávez envision for the army? Even if he hoped to change the role of the military in society, I was wary of his intentions. For me, the Venezuelan army was an institution to be shunned, not encouraged. During my trip to Venezuela in the mid-1990s, I noted how callously the local armed forces in the llano treated detainees. On the ranch where I had stayed, Colombians sometimes fell afoul of the local authorities. At one point, one ranch hand was picked up for not having his papers in order. I accompanied some of the hands to visit the man in jail. We traveled by truck to where he was being held, interestingly enough in a rundown town called Libertad. The jailers did not strike me as terribly enlightened. The local commander was not in Libertad, and this meant the ranch hand's case could not be settled promptly. And when would the colonel be back? we asked. "In a while," said one of his subordinates. We were allowed, however, to bring our man some food. We walked down the hall to the detention cell, a big concrete room. There were no beds, and a couple of men were stretched out on the floor. Our man grabbed the plate of fish prepared by one of the women at the ranch, sheepishly not meeting our gaze. As we were walking out, I asked one ranch hand why we had to bring food to the jail. The prisoners, he explained, were dependent on what the soldiers gave them. Sometimes, he added, the authorities didn't feed them.

While I was in Caracas in 1999–2000, shortly after Chávez's electoral victory, I was often struck by my bus driver's attire. Every day I would take the metro from the presidential archive at Miraflores to the Bellas Artes stop. There, I would get off and take a bus up the hill to San Bernardino. The driver was always dressed in military khakis and judging from the badges on his shirtsleeve, he was an officer. If he was at all resentful of having to forsake his normal army duties to drive a city bus, he gave no sign. Day after day he would put up with the honking, pollution, and congestion. Although I still carried the memory of the military and their indifference to detainees in the llano, I admired this officer for his stoical public service.

As it happens, the case of my military driver was hardly atypical. During my stay in Venezuela, Chávez undertook a profound reform of military policy. In keeping with his suspicion of civilian politicians, he sought to expand the role of the armed forces in social and economic development. Under the Social Emergency and Internal Defense and Development Plan, popularly known as the Plan Bolivar 2000, the government funneled large sums of social welfare funds to military units working at the state level.[34] According to Chávez, 40,000 troops were involved in the effort.[35] The army became a visible presence on the streets, perhaps surprising many ordinary Venezuelans accustomed to thinking that soldiers would stay in the barracks. The armed forces became involved in infrastructure projects and public transportation. Additionally, troops distributed consumer goods to the poor and even provided medical services.[36] Chávez, who had been horrified by the caracazo, was intent on restoring public trust. In a symbolic move, he initiated Plan Bolivar on February 27, 1999, ten years to the day after the

caracazo. "Ten years ago we came out to massacre the people," Chávez remarked. "Now we are going to fill them with love." In addition to the army,
the air force, national guard, and navy also sought to assist the civilian population. Many Venezuelans woke up to find the navy helping to organize
local fishermen into cooperatives and repairing boat engines at the local
wharf. The air force meanwhile carried poor passengers with their chickens
in helicopters and planes in areas lacking highway infrastructure.

At isolated border posts, the National Guard assisted indigenous peoples by shuttling them in boats from one village to the next. The guard also
brought in medicine and doctors, and built houses to the natives' specifica-
tions. For Chávez, the idea of helping indigenous peoples carried personal
resonance. As a young man, he had brought sheet metal and poles to the Indians in the remote village of Barranco Yopal in Apure state. The Indians
would make winter huts out of the materials. Most of the babies there died
of malaria, tuberculosis, or other diseases. Many women were raped or
forced to prostitute themselves. "They were ghosts," Chávez related,
"scorned by most of the population. They sometimes stole in order to eat."
Determined to reverse social inequalities and historic discrimination,
Chávez sent military agricultural engineers to work under the supervision of
local chiefs, who sported Plan Bolivar caps. Later, Chávez boasted, "those
natives were happy, their faces changed." The Indians took Chávez to see
their crops. On just nine acres of land, they had been able to produce sugar-
cane, watermelons, bananas, corn, and papayas. They were eating better and
had received small outboard motor boats to go fishing.[37]

When Chávez was elected, Carneiro was working as the director of the
Military Academy. In February 1999, he was given command over the 21st
brigade in the university town of Mérida. When Chávez launched the Plan
Bolívar, Carneiro established a rapport with the student body. "I was able to
make some amazing friendships," he remarked, "to the point that . . . they
named me vice president of the University of the Andes." Carneiro was the
first soldier awarded such a position. Carneiro, himself from a humble background, claims that he knew how to attract working-class students. "I
wanted to satisfy their basic necessities," he says. "Student residencies didn't
have electricity, there was total darkness, scarcity of water, sanitary problems." He got to know the situation and eliminated the problems. The commander from El Valle also faced deplorable conditions in schools. At one
point, he relates, students blocked the principal avenue in Merida demanding improved conditions for their local school. Carneiro went to take a look

at the school, where he was shocked to find that the building was part of an old police installation. First-, second-, and third-graders were studying in compounds that had served as the old jail; boys and girls had to share one bathroom. Carneiro was struck by the contrast between the school and a nearby air-conditioned bullfighting and cock ring. Local officials, he noted caustically, viewed the ring as more important than the schools. Carneiro was able to improve the school and supply it with all its services. Before, during the caracazo, civilians feared the army, but now they had "a certain respect and admiration for us, because for them we represent something."[38] Clearly, Plan Bolívar had a radicalizing effect on Carneiro. And to the chagrin of the Chávista opposition, Carneiro was not alone. Many officers, particularly the more junior ones, "became more socially aware and engaged" as a result of civic action programs.[39]

Inspired by developments in Mérida, Carneiro got his old friend Chávez's attention and proposed the so-called Wasp Plan, an ambitious construction initiative. Under the plan, local inhabitants built their own houses with assistance from the military. Soldiers provided machines to construct building blocks and offered courses along with civilian technicians and masons. Wasp Plan led to increased employment in local communities.[40] For example, in the western town of San Cristóbal, the capital of Táchira—CAP's home state—Carneiro met with some success. Carneiro constructed Wasp housing units with the support of the locals. I had been to the town in the mid-1990s, riding in a huge Buick cab. The shacks ringing the town contrasted dramatically with the large gas-guzzling car and the Marlboro billboards on the highway.[41] The military had seemingly succeeded in reversing much of its negative public image. But in tapping the military to carry out ambitious projects, Chávez aroused considerable political controversy.

The military, now assigned to important roles in public policy, had become a political actor in its own right. Indeed, not only had the military assumed an active role in helping the civilian population, but many officers themselves campaigned and were elected to political office.[42] Not all sectors of the population were pleased about the new prevalence of the military in civilian affairs. On his left, Chávez had to worry about Patria Para Todos, Alí Rodríguez's party, which withdrew from Chávez's coalition in protest over his moves to appoint military figures to senior cabinet positions.[43] On his right, Chávez had to be concerned about the opposition media.[44] Just after Plan Bolívar was launched, "millions of dollars were reported as paid to phantom companies or companies that had not provided any service."[45] The media used the incident as ammunition against the president.[46]

While Chávez admits that some officers took advantage and skimmed money during Plan Bolívar, he has defended his overall policy. During his first year in power, Chávez faced a very unfavorable political outlook. Most Venezuelan governorships and mayoral districts were in the hands of his opponents, as was Congress and the Supreme Court.[47] Chávez had campaigned promising poverty relief, but in the first year of his presidency, he was distracted with political battles and reforming the constitution.[48] To make matters worse, the new budget was already decided on, the price of oil stood at $7 a barrel, and economic recession meant that few resources were available for poverty alleviation.[49] People were clamoring for fundamental change and, Chávez says, there was "an immense level of expectations generated by our triumph." Thousands of people had gathered around his palace with their sick children, demanding jobs. They slept on the pavement and would not let his car pass.[50] To solve his problems, Chávez turned to the institution most likely to carry out his plans at the national level: the military.[51]

There is no denying that Plan Bolívar achieved tangible results. The government repaired thousands of schools, hospitals, clinics, households, churches, and parks. Additionally, a whopping 2 million Venezuelans received medical assistance; almost 1,000 inexpensive markets were established; more than 2 million children were vaccinated; and thousands of tons of garbage were collected. Plan Bolívar, which lasted from 1999 to 2001, led to greater civilian-military cooperation, a remarkable feat in a country where people no longer had much faith in government.[52] Ordinary Venezuelans, reeling from political and economic collapse, did not withdraw their support for Chávez despite corruption charges stemming from Plan Bolívar. Chávez's moves surely got the attention of conservative policymakers in Washington. What were his real intentions? Nothing could be more frightening to the neoconservatives than the prospect of a radical civil-military alliance.

Chávez did not assuage U.S. fears when he sought to cultivate military ties to Cuba. In November 1999, in the midst of Plan Bolívar, Chávez and a Venezuelan military mission traveled to the island nation to carry out an "exchange of experiences." High-level diplomatic talks continued, to the consternation of Washington. *El Universal*, a Caracas daily, reported in late 2001 that Sergio Cardona, a Cuban navy captain and military attaché in Caracas, toured Venezuela with his Venezuelan counterparts. Cardona remarked that the military relationship between the two countries was very tight.[53]

In an incendiary move, Chávez also began to appoint military figures to PdVSA. To Washington, nothing could be worse than the Venezuelan oil sector becoming militarized by a leader with close ties to communist Cuba. In October 2000, Chávez appointed General Guaicaipuro Lameda Montero, a colleague from the Military Academy, as director of the state oil company.[54] The appointment of Lameda, who had no previous experience in the oil sector, underscored Chávez's growing desire to bring PdVSA under firmer government control. The Lameda announcement came shortly after the appointment of General Cipriano Martínez Morales as PdVSA's vice president.[55] Later Chávez fired the president of CITGO, PdVSA's subsidiary in the United States, and replaced him with another general.[56]

Even as Chávez stacked PdVSA with officers whom he felt would support him, the president moved against the old guard. In a provocative move, he assumed control over military promotions and assignments.[57] Furthermore, he merged the army, navy, and air force into a sole, unified command.[58] In a blow to the entrenched officer corps, he shunted aside, retired, or placed on extended leave some generals and admirals who had not supported his 1992 coup.[59] Opposition was not long in coming. In March 2000, a group of retired, supposedly apolitical officers formed the Institutional Military Front, which accused Chávez of politicizing the military. The president, officers argued, was using the armed forces as his own personal instrument. Chávez moreover was using the military to perform public works projects, which should be left in the hands of civilians. Reportedly, some military figures were more comfortable in their traditional role of defense. Even worse, a group of civilians and military figures formed a new group, the Patriotic Military Junta, who called for Chávez's resignation. The group's spokesman, Captain Luis Eduardo García Morales of the National Guard, had been part of a military unit that stayed loyal to CAP during Chávez's coup.[60] In a taped speech, García stated, "We want to return to the barracks. We are tired of being used in that archaic Plan Bolívar which underutilizes us, which has served to defraud the nation."[61] Later García referred to the Patriotic Junta as a "movement of Venezuelans tired of traditional parties" and "deceived by the leaders of the 4F" [referring to Chávez's failed coup].[62] Reportedly, Chávez personally summoned García, and the two spoke for six hours. While it is unclear what they discussed, Chávez's entreaties did not dissuade the young officer, who would continue his opposition in later months.[63]

Meanwhile, Chávez even had to be worried about former collaborators. One such man was Francisco Arias Cárdenas, one of Chávez's military coup conspirators in 1992, who was elected to the governorship of the important oil state of Zulia in 1995.[64] Under Chávez's new constitution, new elections were called in 2000, and Arias ran for president against his erstwhile comrade in arms. "Like the president," remarked the Associated Press, "he [Arias] says he wants to govern for the poor. But unlike populist President Hugo Chávez, Arias talks more about good management than revolution, courts private investors and gets along with the Catholic Church."[65] What is more, Arias spoke fondly of the United States and was critical of Chávez's ties to Fidel Castro. Chávez depicted Arias as a "traitor," bought and paid for by a "rancid oligarchy." In the end, Arias was no match for the folksy and charismatic Chávez: Chávez received 59.7 percent of the votes cast, compared with just 37.5 percent for Arias.[66]

Arias's defeat must have come as a relief for Chávez. The president might have hoped that after 2001, opposition from conservative officers would wither and die. By that time, Plan Bolívar had entered a new phase. As Chávez remarked, "There are no longer hundreds of soldiers in the streets." Having consolidated more political control over the country, now Chávez could rely on governors and mayors to help carry out social programs. The military simply had to act as project coordinators at the local and regional level.[67]

But by late 2001, there were yet more points of friction that would lead to irrevocable political conflict. One such problem area were the Bolivarian Circles. Formed in December 2001, the Circles grouped some 700,000 Venezuelans into neighborhood associations.[68] These civic action groups, Chávez said, would empower the people by allowing them to lobby the government for funding more effectively.[69] Without popular mobilization, Chávez understood, his Bolivarian Revolution would surely lose potency. The president accordingly called on supporters to form groups of 7 to 11 people who would educate their neighbors concerning the new constitution. Bolivarian Circles also should form cooperatives, attend to the needs of their neighborhoods, or obtain bank loans.[70] Chávez and the National Assembly meanwhile allocated credit lines for small businesses, particularly those owned by the poor, women, and indigenous peoples.[71] It was surely a shrewd move: through the Bolivarian Circles, Chávez could circumvent the old government bureaucracy and consolidate his base.[72] Members of the Circles worked together to feed the hungry; provide after-school care for poor children; secure resources for small businesses; assist in literacy, education, and vaccination programs; and perform other public services.[73]

The aims sounded benign, but soon inflammatory charges started to surface surrounding the Circles. The Institutional Military Front charged that Chávez and government officials distributed army-issued weapons to the Circles in an effort to turn them into a fearsome force that could even rival the army. Even worse, charged the Front, the Bolivarian Circles obtained military training from communist Cuba. Cuban doctors, officers argued, had infiltrated Venezuela to train Circles members.[74] Meanwhile, over at PdVSA, General Lameda, Chávez's own pick to head the oil company, viewed the Bolivarian Circles as "shock troops."[75] The regime defended itself against the charges, dismissing the idea of armed Bolivarian Circles as absurd.[76] Venezuela analyst Greg Wilpert adds, "The vast majority of these [Bolivarian Circles] are unarmed community groups, as numerous international reporters have already discovered. It is pure opposition propaganda to present these as some kind of paramilitary group."[77]

Captain García, however, was not persuaded. In June 2001, he called for "pacific civil disobedience" to stop "Hugo." In an escalating war of words, García attacked the Chávez regime for its ties to Cuba and accused it of having links to the Colombian guerrillas and drug smugglers. "What an embarrassment you are," García remarked, adding that "the people put you there and they can also remove you, we're tired already." García suggested a number of people who could comprise an honest cabinet. In a clear sign that conservative elements in the military were unhappy about Chávez's oil policy, García recommended that ex-PdVSA president Luis Giusti be included in his new cabinet.[78] Clearly, by late 2001, the Chávez opposition was gathering steam. Although the president was surely aware of the growing political discontent, he did not suspect that one of his own commanders, Efraín Vásquez, might be among the conspirators.

After completing his course at the School of the Americas at Fort Benning, Vásquez returned to Venezuela. He rose to the rank of general, and became commander of the military garrison at Maracaibo in the state of Zulia.[79] There, Vásquez had to confront critical local issues, such as the kidnapping of Venezuelan ranchers by Colombians and poppy production in the border zone.[80] After Chávez came to power, Vásquez helped to carry out Plan Bolívar in his district, pledging to place mobile clinics at the service of poor residents in Zulia. Six hundred civilian and military personnel would be put to work as part of Chávez's initiatives.[81] Later, Vásquez reported to Chávez personally at Miraflores Palace on the military's progress.[82] In 2002, now army commander in chief, Vásquez denied that there was any discontent within the ranks. "I am very on top of all military units so as to sense up close the attitude of officials under my command," he remarked. "The military doesn't depart from the doctrines and dogmas that are dictated under our Constitution," he added. In any case, Vásquez said he did not get involved in political questions.[83]

Despite this apparent show of unity, Vásquez reportedly began to meet with Otto Reich of the U.S. State Department, a man who had been named to WHINSEC Board of Visitors, a body which was to review and advise "on areas such as curriculum, academic instruction, and fiscal affairs of the institute."[84] But if Vásquez thought that overthrowing Chávez would be a straightforward affair, he underestimated the determination of General Carneiro, one of Chávez's senior commanders who had been radicalized by Plan Bolívar.

CHAPTER SIX

THE TEST OF CHÁVEZ'S CIVIL-MILITARY ALLIANCE

At the Puente Llaguno, a bridge located one block from the presidential palace of Miraflores in Caracas, pro-Chávez supporters readied themselves for confrontation.[1] It was here, on the streets of the capital, that the ultimate fate of Hugo Chávez would be decided. It was April 11, 2002, and the situation looked as if it would become ugly when between 100,000 to 200,000 anti-Chávez protesters redirected their march from the PdVSA offices to Miraflores. The new protest route would put the anti-Chávez demonstrators on a direct collision course with a pro-Chávez demonstration.[2] Then, quite dramatically, a raging gun battle broke out on the Llaguno Bridge.[3] Most of those killed in the subsequent shootout were Chávez supporters.[4] But who was responsible for the violence? In seeking to discredit the Chavistas, the private media broadcast a video of the Chávez supporters, some of whom were members of the Bolivarian Circles, firing off the bridge.[5] A voiceover to the video intoned, "Look at that Chávez supporter . . . see how he unloads his gun at the peaceful opposition march below."[6]

Irish filmmakers, however, later released footage showing that there were no protesters under the bridge. In fact, the footage shows that Chávez gunmen were cowering under fire in between taking shots of their own.[7] "What the video didn't show viewers," remarks Venezuela analyst Eva Golinger, "was how it manipulated the setting and failed to include the wider angle of the scene." Golinger says the street below was empty and metropolitan policemen allied to the Chávez opposition shot at Chavistas from behind vehicles and buildings.[8] In subsequent court testimony, police officers admitted that they had been ordered to fire on the crowd on the bridge, which prompted the Chavistas to fire back.[9]

It was time for Efraín Vásquez to leap on to the national stage.

On April 11, Vásquez was the only high military official to call for Chávez's resignation. In a startling rebuke to the president, Vásquez refused to implement Chávez's Eagle Plan.[10] Under the plan, which allowed for the deployment of troops to keep public order, Chávez could muster troops around Miraflores. At the critical moment, Vásquez halted deployment of troops from Tiuna Fort to the presidential palace, arguing that Chávez's order was unconstitutional.[11] In a nationally televised address, he declared: "Mr. President, I was loyal to the end, but today's deaths cannot be tolerated."[12] Flanked by his officers, Vásquez ordered his troops to stay confined to their base.[13] The general has justified his actions by saying that he could not stomach using heavy military equipment against unarmed civilians, which would have resulted in more deaths. He has always maintained that he was not a coup plotter. It was the killing of "defenseless" Venezuelans, he maintained, who were participating in a "peaceful" demonstration that had motivated him to act against the government.[14]

Very soon, however, the veteran School of the Americas graduate would have to contend with his counterpart, General Carneiro. Chávez ordered Carneiro to activate the Eagle Plan and send troops to Miraflores. However, Carneiro quickly realized he was unable to help his friend: not one battalion obeyed his order.[15] Meanwhile, Carneiro's associates warned him to stand down so as to avoid "a bloodbath amongst brothers."[16] At Tiuna Fort, Carneiro had the unmistakable impression that he was being detained by fellow officials, although they did not explicitly state this to be the case.[17]

Inside Miraflores, a bewildered Chávez tried to assess the situation. In a later interview, the president admitted that he distrusted some senior military officers and that he was not surprised that some participated in the coup. But Vásquez's defection came as a surprise.[18] After Vásquez delivered his speech, senior generals in the National Guard—a force charged with internal security—as well as navy admirals issued their own TV and radio statements condemning Chávez's directives as illegal.[19]

In the midst of the media frenzy demonizing the Chávez gunmen at Llaguno Bridge, dissident military officers intervened, arguing that the president had ordered his supporters to fire on the anti-Chávez protest marchers.[20] Joining Vásquez and other officers in the coup against Chávez was none other than Captain García of the Venezuelan Patriotic Junta.[21] Chávez also faced an obstacle in General Lameda at PdVSA. Despite Chávez's hopes, Lameda had implemented a pro-business agenda at the oil company. Facing a total reversal of his plans, Chávez had had to backtrack and removed Lameda, his own pick, from oil company management two months before the coup took place. However, the general had not gone quietly. In March, he publicly denounced Chávez's economic policies and was increasingly touted by the media as a possible political rival to the president.[22] The Chávez government later charged that Lameda was involved in the April coup.[23]

Vásquez went to the presidential palace to negotiate Chávez's ouster early on April 12.[24] A group of nine high military officials read a communiqué in which they rejected the president's governing authority. "The Constitution," they said, "obliges us to avoid more spilling of blood and that obligation leads to the peaceful departure of the president."[25] Chávez has claimed that the officers revolted for diverse reasons. Some, he explained, were frustrated at not being promoted fast enough. Still others were influenced by the anti-Chávista ideological campaign and feared that the president would weaken the military by strengthening civilian militias. Although some officers actively planned for the coup, he has said, others were confused and did not understand what was happening politically.[26]

Chávez was arrested by National Guard forces and flown to a small Caribbean island and military base, La Orchila.[27] Meanwhile the Bolivarian Circles had grown restive. About 3,000 pro-Chávez protesters gathered at Miraflores on the night of April 11. The streets looked like a battleground, with rocks and bottles strewn across the entire area.[28] As violence and confusion reigned, Carneiro, at Fort Tiuna, wondered what to do. Feeling ill at ease, he mingled with Carmona and other military officials celebrating and drinking after their victory. Apparently, Carneiro's peers did not fear him. They openly admitted that they had been planning a coup for years. However, during the confusion the coup plotters fought over new positions in government. Carneiro was able to slip back to his house in the predawn hours of April 12.[29]

As Carneiro and loyal Chávista officers sought to regroup, Vásquez was reportedly in close touch with the Pentagon. On the night of April 12, continuing to midday on April 13, the general coordinated with his U.S. patrons.[30] Meanwhile, the U.S. military attaché attended a news conference given by Vásquez. (This was not the first time that U.S. military personnel had been among the conspirators. Reportedly, the U.S. military attaché was at Fort Tiuna "during the preparation for and up until the coup."[31]) For a supposed reluctant participant in the April developments, Vásquez certainly carried out the desires of the new Carmona regime with gusto. According to a report on Fox News, he quickly worked to "identify, disarm and dismantle" the Bolivarian Circles.[32]

But Vásquez underestimated the civil-military alliance at his own risk. He was only one of two senior commanding officers within the new Carmona regime. Although several retired generals supported the coup, just 200 out of 8,000 officers joined the effort.[33] Chávez was supported by the majority of the troops, the noncommissioned officers, and young officers.[34] In addition, the rebels controlled almost no combat troops. Although plans for the coup had been in the works since the summer of 2001, their efforts were largely improvised. In Maracay, home to the nation's armored, airborne, and air forces, troops refused to accept the new regime. Even in Caracas, Carmona's control "was spotty at best."[35]

At 6 A.M. on the morning of April 12, Carneiro returned to Tiuna Fort, where the coup plotters informed him that he was to be relieved of his command. Carneiro left the building in disgust. Outside, crowds had gathered and wanted to enter the fort. What had happened to their president? they wanted to know. Already there had been rumors that Chávez had not resigned and had, in fact, been kidnapped. Carneiro grabbed a megaphone and declared that the army did not agree with Carmona violating the constitution. Amid cheers and applause, Carneiro demanded Carmona's resignation. Meanwhile, Carneiro put on music to entertain and calm the crowds—Alí Primera, a Venezuelan protest singer from the 1960s who championed the plight of the poor.[36]

Meanwhile Carneiro communicated with colleagues, including General Baduel,[37] paratrooper commander of the 42 Airborne Brigade[38] based in Maracay and founding member of the MBR 200.[39] Carneiro informed his colleague that many garrisons did not agree with the coup and wanted to restore constitutional order.[40] Baduel came out against the Carmona regime, which inspired pro-Chávez protesters to take to the streets and set up barricades in Maracay. In Caracas, some soldiers serving in the palace regiment considered launching a commando-style operation to kidnap the coup conspirators, but they decided to bide their time and wait.[41]

With Carneiro turning up the heat out in the streets and popular disgust growing with Carmona's cancellation of the 1999 constitution (approved in a popular referendum by almost 80 percent of voters), civil unrest escalated.[42] In El Valle, Carneiro's old neighborhood, cacerolazos and protests broke out on the streets in the early evening. Protesters even blocked the highway leading from Caracas to the coastal city of La Guaira. Across the country, the Bolivarian Circles met and prepared for a popular response against Carmona.[43] Meanwhile pro-Chávez crowds gathered at army barracks, singing the national anthem. The protesters yelled to the soldiers, "¡Soldado, consciente, busca a tu presidente! ["Soldier, with conscience, go and find your president!"] and "¡Soldado, amigo, el pueblo está contigo! ["Soldier, friend, the people are with you!"].[44] Within a very short period of time, an impressive web of communication developed, linking pro-Chávez elements in the military and the Bolivarian Circles.[45]

The coup plotters responded to the unrest by sending out the metropolitan police.[46] In light of developments, it is ironic, to say the least, that Vásquez would justify Chávez's ouster based on the idea of respect for human rights and preservation of the constitution. In fact, according to available information, at least 40 deaths occurred in the course of the coup, only 16 of them, by best estimates, on April 11. The newly restored Chávez regime later said that up to 68 people were killed. According to Associated Press reporter Andrew Selsky, who cited two local human rights organizations, many of the later deaths occurred when police shot on pro-Chávez demonstrators in poor neighborhoods.[47] The apparent evidence of non-Chávez forces repression exposed the political bankruptcy of the coup government. Soon, Vásquez and his associates would be overcome by the Chávista civic-military alliance.

The end was swift. In a critical miscalculation, Carmona had neglected to replace the security troops at Miraflores.[48] At 10 A.M. on the morning of April 13, the palace regiment, which had been in touch with Carneiro, stormed Miraflores.[49] Carmona took refuge at a nearby military base. Junior and midranking officers commanding combat units notified their superiors that they would only support a return to constitutional rule.[50] Now the only challenge was to get the word out that the coup regime was in disarray. Once again the Bolivarian Circles took charge, staging a protest at the offices of state-owned Channel 8 television. Officers and protesters forced the police to let them into the station, where they broadcast a video repudiating the Carmona regime. Meanwhile, hundreds of thousands of people were on the streets. According to one observer, "The atmosphere was defiant, slogans echoed throughout: 'Pueblo, escucha, únete a la lucha' [People, listen, unite in the struggle]; 'Chávez, amigo, el pueblo está contigo' [Chávez, friend, the people are with you]."[51]

On April 13, with the coup fast unraveling, Vásquez was the first dissident officer to demand the revocation of the Carmona decree, which dissolved parliament and fired the country's governors and mayors. What could have caused this change of heart? *The Economist* suggested, rather implausibly, that the dissolution of the National Assembly and suspension of the constitution was too much for the old School of the Americas graduate.[52] It is more likely that Vásquez simply sensed the popular mood had turned against the coup. Reportedly, he withdrew his support from Carmona after consulting with the U.S. government.[53] Meanwhile General Baduel helped to organize Chávez's rescue from prison on the island of Orchila.[54] Chávez returned early on April 14 with the coup regime toppling in less than 48 hours.[55] It had been one of the shortest-lived governments in Latin American history.[56]

I read about developments in Venezuela while in Britain. Writing my dissertation on a tight deadline, I did not have much time to think about Hugo Chávez. But perhaps I had been wrong about the military in Venezuela. Surely the events of April 2002 demonstrated that the armed forces could in fact be a force for positive social change. What particularly struck me was that not only had the military actually fought to oppose the United States, but it had won. As a student of Latin American history, I knew that it was not very often that the White House failed to achieve its objectives in the region. I also found compelling the role of the Bolivarian Circles. Without a doubt, there was something of a personality cult around Chávez. On the other hand, the coup had demonstrated that civilians had become a potent political force in their own right. Once I returned to New York after my dissertation defense in the fall of 2002, I began to follow events much more closely.

Chávez did not disappoint. Taking advantage of the changing political landscape he removed 400 mostly senior officers, replacing them with more radical soldiers.[57] General Baduel was rewarded for his loyalty: he was promoted to army chief of staff.[58] And what of Vásquez? Although Chávez fired the senior general, who was detained at Fort Tiuna, the Supreme Court later ruled that he did not rebel but intervened to fill a "power vacuum." The verdict caused an uproar among the president's supporters, who claimed that the court answered to the opposition. In 2005, however, the court annulled the earlier decision, allowing the attorney general to charge Vásquez and other officers with military rebellion.[59] Recently the Colombian government denied Vásquez and others political asylum.[60] Captain García meanwhile went into exile in South Florida. Reportedly, he has provided military training to a Cuban-Venezuelan paramilitary group called the F–4 Commandos. The group conducted exercises in a shooting range near the Everglades. García was quoted as saying "We are preparing for war." Nonetheless, he claims his movement opposes military coups.[61]

Perhaps García's unsubtle metaphor was not altogether misplaced. In the wake of the coup, Chávez helped to spread the Bolivarian Circles and consolidate power. By late 2002, there were 70,000 Circles in the country compared to 8,000 at the time of the coup. Most were based in poor Caracas barrios, where 60 percent of the city's population resided. The expansion of the Circles alarmed the opposition yet further, which demanded that Chávez disband them.[62] As the country became increasingly polarized, some original founders of the Bolivarian Circles said they felt disillusioned. Ernesto Alvarenga, a member of the opposition Solidarity Faction in parliament, claimed that the Circles had become more and more militant and no longer resembled the community groups that he had foreseen.[63] But Chávez harbored few illusions about the opposition and its tenacious determination to unseat him. Without the Bolivarian Circles, he might not have survived the coup attempt. In late 2002, he had the opportunity to call on them again for support.

In an effort to get rid of the unflappable Chávez once and for all, the opposition launched its oil lockout in late 2002. Petroleum exports were crippled as PdVSA was virtually shut down. "A protracted battle involving the country's oil supply," remarked the *Christian Science Monitor*, "could be the difference in whether Chávez stays or goes."[64] With Chávez seemingly engaged in endless trench warfare with his foes, the president looked for strategic allies. Once again, the Bolivarian Circles provided crucial assistance. They provided volunteer labor, defended oil installations, and contacted former oil workers and technicians.[65] What is more, many oil workers were themselves members of the Circles. Once the oil lockout hit, these workers created an important support network that resulted in oil production recovery "in record time."[66]

Again, as in April, the civilian base was joined by the military at a critical moment. In a sign of fiery determination, Chávez took to the airwaves and remarked that Venezuelan law allowed him to use the army to guarantee the operation of oil-related public services like refineries, gas stations, and distribution.[67] Meanwhile, the Minister of Defense and high-ranking military officials met with the Minister of Energy and Mines and oil industry officials.[68] As tensions escalated, the National Guard even commandeered delivery trucks to make sure that gas stations remained open. Predictably, the opposition decried Chávez for militarizing the country.[69] However, the opposition's protests were to no avail, as Chávez survived the oil lockout with his regime intact.

But now Chávez took no chances: he pressed even harder for a broad military role in society. The first order of business was to secure PdVSA: the oil company, according to military officials, could be subject to future industrial sabotage.[70] Carneiro announced that the armed forces would now closely monitor the oil industry so as to deter alleged CIA infiltration.[71] In a dramatic move called "Operation Black Gold," Carneiro dispatched 1,000 soldiers to western Venezuela. Chávez said he was carrying out the move to catch those responsible for a recent decline in oil production.[72] In Maracaibo, military officials denied that PdVSA was being militarized; to the contrary, said one officer, "the armed forces are socializing and getting close to the people. Oil workers will constitute themselves as cooperatives and will form part of reserves and strategic units."[73] The military even announced that PdVSA workers would be taught how to operate anti-aircraft defense systems and artillery.[74]

Surveying the political landscape in Venezuela, Washington policymakers were not pleased. Having suffered two severe rebuffs in Venezuela through the failed coup and the oil lockout, the neoconservatives sought to further isolate Chávez by appointing a well-connected insider to the U.S. Southern Command in Miami: John Craddock. A senior military assistant to Secretary of Defense Donald Rumsfeld,[75] Craddock had been deployed to both Operation Desert Shield and Desert Storm.[76] As head of the Southern Command, Craddock was responsible for Central America, South America, and Guantánamo base in Cuba.[77] As such, he has been responsible for the handling of detainees at the prison facility at Guantánamo, Camp X-ray. Since its inception in 2002, the camp has been subjected to harsh criticism by Amnesty International, which charged that the U.S. military has subjected detainees to illegal practices. Prisoner testimony and photographs strongly suggest that al Qaeda detainees may have been subject to torture techniques similar to those documented at the infamous Abu Ghraib prison in Iraq.[78] Craddock, who it should be said arrived at his post in 2004 after the allegations of detainee abuse first surfaced, has shot back at Amnesty International, calling the group "shrill" and "uninformed."[79] What did Craddock's appointment portend for U.S.-Venezuelan relations? Clearly, by appointing such a hard-liner, Rumsfeld was being provocative. With the arrival of Craddock, U.S.-Venezuelan military ties, already in tatters, took a turn for the worse.

Prior to my studies in England, I studied Latin American history at University of Miami. There, I became aware of the activities of the U.S. Southern Command. I had become particularly incensed about its role in Colombia, a country that I was familiar with from my travels. A technologically advanced center, the U.S. Southern Command is located in a nondescript building at 3511 NW 91 Avenue. In the late 1990s, when I was in Miami, the center had an annual budget of more than $500 million. Craddock's predecessor, Charles Wilhelm, was intent on rolling back left-wing guerrillas in Colombia. In order to do that, however, he had to establish tight connections to the Colombian military brass, some of whom allegedly had connections to right-wing paramilitary death squads and who had studied at the School of the Americas. Yet there was no grassroots movement against Southern Command.[80] Carrying on from my earlier activism, I publicized Wilhelm's links to prominent Colombian military officers on my own Web site and conducted talks at Florida International University and University of Miami about U.S.-Colombian military ties.

More recently, in an effort to assure ongoing funding, Southern Command has sought to declare a war on terrorism in Latin America by "erroneously labeling drug trafficking and 'radical' populist movements as al Qaeda threats."[81] Craddock has kept with historic precedent and promised that he will continue military to military contact with Latin American militaries with corrupt and brutal pasts.[82] He also continued links with the Western Hemisphere Institute for Security Cooperation (WHISC) (formerly the School of the Americas), by presiding over the graduation of Latin American officers. Craddock also went on the diplomatic offensive. In an interview with the Miami daily *El Nuevo Herald,* the general warned of the ominous threat of "radical populism." Craddock singled out Venezuela, which in his view represented a "danger for the hemisphere."[83]

The Venezuelans were hardly intimidated by Craddock. In an inflammatory move, Chávez severed ties to the WHISC. The center, Chávez charged, had "deformed the minds of many Latin American soldiers."[84] Chávez's vice president, José Vicente Rangel, went even further, proclaiming that the WHISC was a training school for dictators, torturers, and terrorists.[85] In condemning WHISC, the Chávez government was responding to the pleas of Father Ray Bourgeois, a longtime opponent of WHISC. In an effort to shut down the military facility, Bourgeois went on Venezuelan national television and personally met with Chávez. Venezuela's withdrawal was a big blow to the school. Over the years, more than 4,000 Venezuelan soldiers have graduated from the center. According to organizers working to close WHISC, Chávez's move has energized their movement.[86]

In a further blow to the rapidly deteriorating relationship with the United States, Chávez also announced that Venezuela would indefinitely terminate bilateral military exchanges. For decades, the two countries had enjoyed reciprocal military relations. While U.S. officials were posted to Fort Tiuna as well as other Venezuelan air bases in Maracay, 90 Venezuelan officers were enrolled in U.S. military academies.[87] But the April coup led to a deterioration in relations between the two nations. "The failure of the rebellion," noted a U.S. military report, "means that the officers remaining in the armed forces after 11 April are those who have had less contact with and sympathy for the United States."[88]

Speaking on his weekly television program *Aló, Presidente* in April 2005, Chávez lashed out at the White House, declaring that U.S. military instructors based in Venezuela had abused the country by making disparaging remarks about his government. "Some of the [U.S. officers] were waging a campaign in the Venezuelan military," Chávez remarked, "making comments, talking to Venezuelan soldiers, criticizing the president of Venezuela." He added that "all exchanges with U.S. officers are suspended until who knows when. There will be no more combined operations, nothing like that." Chávez justified his decision by remarking that the U.S. military office in Fort Tiuna was nothing less than an "organ of the CIA . . . conspiring against the government." He declared that a U.S. navy officer was apprehended taking photos of an army base in the country's interior. All in all, Chávez charged, the Venezuelan authorities were wary of an American invasion and the behavior of U.S. officers had hardly helped to ameliorate these concerns. Reacting to Chávez's address, the U.S. Embassy in Venezuela released a statement saying that the United States regretted the president's decision. William Brownfield, the U.S. ambassador, said that since Venezuela had terminated the program, it was now up to Chávez to reestablish military relations.[89]

But such a proposition hardly seemed likely by 2004–05, as Chávez moved to further ties with Fidel Castro. Although Venezuelan-Cuban diplomatic and economic ties had been warm for some time, Chávez now expressed increasing interest in furthering military relations. Such a development was hardly surprising, given a vicious row with the United States over U.S.-made F–16 fighter jets. Venezuelan officials have complained bitterly that the United States has refused to provide spare parts or service their fleet of 22 U.S. F–16s purchased in 1982.[90] The United States, Chávez charged, was reneging on its commitments to provide Venezuela with the parts.[91] In a harsh rebuke to U.S. President Bush, Chávez said he would consider shipping the F–16 jets to Cuba and China. "When someone does not comply with a contract then the other party is authorized to no longer recognize the contract," Chávez announced.[92]

With Venezuelan-U.S. military ties at a new low, Chávez turned to new defense partners by 2005. As a sign of the warming relations, Chávez sent his older brother Adán to Cuba to serve as the new Venezuelan ambassador.[93] A former left-wing university professor in Mérida, Adán had been elected to the constituent assembly in 1999 and was an enthusiastic political supporter of his brother.[94] In an alarming development for Washington, a Venezuelan military delegation traveled to Cuba. There, the Venezuelans participated in joint maneuvers and observed a MIG–29 fighter jet demonstration.[95] Chávez has also purchased 100,000 AK–47 Kalashnikov semiautomatic rifles and 40 helicopters from Russia, as well as transport planes and patrol boats from Spain.[96]

Asked about the Venezuelan arms purchases, Defense Secretary Rumsfeld remarked, "If you have a country that ends up buying 100,000 AK 47s you have to ask the question: What are they going to do with them all? One has to worry about the proliferation of these weapons."[97] Meanwhile, Colombia, a key U.S. ally in the region, has accused Chávez of supporting the Revolutionary Armed Forces of Colombia (known by their Spanish acronym, FARC) guerrillas in that country.[98] But who is a threat to whom? Even as Rumsfeld was turning up the rhetoric, the United States was arming Colombia. The Chávez government has argued—plausibly—that it must patrol and guard its 1,400-mile border with Colombia. A violent area, the border is subject to incursions by drug traffickers, left-wing guerrillas, and right-wing paramilitaries. In 2004, six Venezuelan soldiers and one oil engineer were killed in Apure along the Colombian border. Their assailants have not been identified. In that same year, more than 100 Colombian paramilitaries were apprehended at a ranch near Caracas; apparently they were planning to destabilize the Chávez regime. As a result of these types of incidents, Venezuelan officials say, the country needs the rifles and helicopters.[99] The Venezuelan small arms arsenal, Chávez argues, is over 50 years old, and the country does not have enough boats and vehicles to patrol the coast and the Colombian border.[100]

Nothing infuriates Venezuelan diplomats more than Washington's hypocrisy when it comes to the Andean region. Recently I attended a political fundraising event in midtown Manhattan, where Venezuelan and Cuban diplomats criticized the United States. I was surprised to see an old acquaintance of mine, the head archivist at the Historical Archive of Miraflores in Caracas. Since my time in Venezuela, he had become a diplomat and was now representing his country at the United Nations. In Caracas he had seemed rather self-effacing, but now he was transformed. Colombia, he remarked with conviction, was a brother nation to Venezuela. It was Washington, he declared, that was dividing the two countries. The United States, not Venezuela, was destabilizing the region. The Chávez government, my old friend declared, would defend its sovereignty and independence. The crowd applauded raucously.

August 28, 2004: Along Caracas's parade route of Los Próceres, the people kept coming. Wave upon wave of Chávez supporters, some wearing overalls and carrying picks and shovels, others pushing wheelbarrows, presented an impressive spectacle. The people were part of the "Vuelvan Caras" or "Turning Lives Around" program that sought to carry out community infrastructure projects. The wheelbarrows were meant to highlight new labor and employment opportunities under Chávez's social programs or missions that have improved health, education, housing, and employment conditions. In a sign of growing civil-military ties, the president's supporters were joined by members of the armed forces along Los Próceres. "The new Venezuela is born," Chávez announced proudly during the parade.[101]

To the Bush White House, the growing radicalization of the military and its role in carrying out important programs must have come as yet another disagreeable development. Chávez, for example, has used the military to help carry out land reform and business expropriations. A radical army captain, Eliecer Otaiza, was put in charge of Venezuela's National Land Institute, which oversees implementation and management of land reform. "Chávez apparently felt that it was necessary to put Otaiza in charge," writes

Wilpert, "because of the 2 million hectares slated to be redistributed in 2005, 1.5 million were to come from estates that are privately owned."[102] Land reform, Chávez declared, should be carried out through negotiation with landowners, but if no agreement was reached then the army could be called in.[103] Recently, the pro-Chávez governor of Monagas state called in the Venezuelan army, which seized a Heinz ketchup plant. Although the operation had been closed for nearly a decade, company officials protested that the seizure violated property rights. The dramatic move came amid ambitious moves by the government. Officers were in the process of evaluating over 700 closed enterprises that might be suitable for worker takeovers via expropriation. Meanwhile, reports Wilpert, "Workers at many other factories and businesses have begun taking matters in their own hands, not waiting for the government to act in the expropriation of idle factories."[104]

Meanwhile, the Venezuelans seemed to be developing an appreciation for the Cuban civil-military model. During a visit to Cuba, in fact, a Venezuelan general remarked that he was particularly interested in the island nation's promotion of popular participation in the nation's defense program. "We are convinced," the official added, "that security is not the exclusive prerogative of the army, but a duty of all civilians."[105] In line with this spirit, Chávez recently announced that he would increase the size of the military reserves from 100,000 to 1.5 million Venezuelans so as to "defend, with the people, the sovereignty and greatness of this land." The reserve force will be the largest in Venezuelan history. Personally, Chávez remarked, he abhorred war. But Venezuela needed to be prepared. "If anyone were to come here and to try to seize the fatherland from us, we would make them bite the dust," Chávez proclaimed in 2005 in a typical rhetorical flourish.[106] Earlier in 2005, 20,000 reservists sporting olive green fatigues marched before Chávez at a Caracas military academy. The reserve force will answer directly to the head of state.[107] General Carneiro has declared that the force will facilitate further civil-military links. Reserve troops, he remarked, will be deployed to help in national development and to back up Chávez's mission programs.[108]

Monitoring developments from the United States, Donald Rumsfeld and his protégé John Craddock must have wondered how Venezuela had managed to slip out of their control. The Venezuelan military had certainly come a long way since the coup of 1992, notable for a lack of civilian participation. For U.S. military planners, Chávez's encouragement of civilian-military ties could not have come as a welcome development.

CHAPTER SEVEN
CHÁVEZ'S SOUTH AMERICAN OIL DIPLOMACY

Without a doubt, Chávez has proven that he is an adept political survivor. Even as President Bush's popularity plummets, Chávez's stature has grown throughout Latin America. "Mr. Bush, I'm going to make another bet with you. I've bet you a dollar to see who lasts longer—you in the White House or me here in Miraflores [palace]," the cocky Chávez recently remarked.[1] If current trends continue, Chávez may well be the winner. The Venezuelan president has hardly been idle since surviving the April 2002 coup. In an effort to succeed politically and to avoid the fate of Fidel Castro, whose regime was isolated by the United States, Chávez has sought key allies. The prospect of South America uniting behind Chávez was hardly a pleasing prospect for Washington policymakers, but there was little the Bush White House could do.

Astutely, the Venezuelan president has used oil as a means of forging alliances. In 1999, fresh from electoral victory, Chávez remarked that PdVSA and Petróleo Brasileiro (Petrobrás), Brazil's state-run oil and gas giant, were reviewing plans to form a larger joint oil company.[2] The Venezuelans were intent on creating Petrosur, a company encompassing the southern cone of Argentina, Brazil, and Uruguay. Petrosur would supply oil to countries under preferential financial terms and encourage large-scale infrastructure, such as pipelines and refineries.[3] It also would coordinate oil distribution, exploration, and processing. Oil wealth would be channeled into social programs for education, healthcare, and job creation.[4]

Eventually, Chávez hoped, Petrosur and other regional oil agreements would lead to the creation of Petroamérica, which would cover all of Latin America.[5] What have been the implications for U.S. business? In recent years, there was a gigantic consolidation in the oil industry, with Exxon merging with Mobil, British Petroleum with Amoco, and Chevron with Texaco.[6] Chávez's plan to involve state-run oil companies in formidable hemispheric alliances[7] stands to sideline these large behemoths.[8]

Chávez has said that an energy partnership with Brazil "could become the axis for the process of integration that is under way." In São Paulo, Chávez met with business leaders and stated that coordination among Latin American oil producers "will allow us to be the energy epicenter of the region and the world."[9] This is hardly an understatement. Petrobrás, which recently ranked as the fifteenth largest oil company in the world, produces more than 2 million barrels of crude oil a day.[10] If Petroamérica were to become a reality, the new behemoth would control 11.5 percent of the world's oil reserves and could help to raise the material conditions of over 530 million people.[11] For Washington, Chávez's moves were surely suspect. The Venezuelan leader was clearly attempting to diversify his country's export market. Currently, the United States purchases up to 80 percent of Venezuelan petroleum exports.[12] If Petroamérica ever came to fruition, it would threaten the untrammeled access of U.S. oil companies to Latin America's subsoil riches.[13]

At a dinner in honor of Chávez, former Brazilian president Cardoso stated that Petroamérica could lead to "projects of great impact, that generate jobs and revenue."[14] Chávez, however, seemed to look further. "This integration," he remarked, "must go beyond the economic [sphere]. There must also be a cultural, social and political integration that one day could lead to the creation of a federation of Latin American and Caribbean nations."[15] This federation, Chávez added, would help "combat the perverse effects of globalization that only takes into account economic matters and ignores education, culture, health, poverty and misery."[16]

For Chávez, oil and energy integration was merely the first stepping-stone that would unite South America against U.S. objectives in the hemisphere. Chávez has remarked that he wanted to create "a Petro-América, a great multinational enterprise. We have petroleum, gas, everything we need to build a powerful and large bloc, all we need is the will to do it."[17]

In July 2002, Chávez traveled to Guayaquil, Ecuador, for a summit of Latin American leaders. There, in a remark that surely must have rattled Washington, Chávez stated, "I propose that we form Petroamérica, a kind of South American OPEC."[18] Even worse from the White House's perspective, yet another left-wing politician soon looked to succeed Cardoso. What would the imminent election of Luiz Inácio Lula da Silva mean for Chávez's

Petroamérica? The emergence of a Brazilian-Venezuelan axis and furthering of energy ties was hardly an encouraging prospect for the Bush White
House.

The Brazilian Northeast is a rugged region known for its brutal semi desert
climate. Rain is scarce and many rural inhabitants are dependent on subsistence agriculture.[19] The Northeast is home to the state of Pernambuco, an
area covered in scrubby trees and bush called *caatinga*.[20] This drought resist-
ant vegetation has adapted to the extreme climate of the *sertão* (backlands).
Because rainfall is so erratic, drought plagues the sertão, and leads to
hunger.[21] During the region's long dry spells, local inhabitants have been
forced to eat lizards, rodents, centipedes, and even cacti.[22] In addition, the
Northeast has historically been plagued by a highly unequal system of land
ownership, illiteracy, and a high rate of child mortality in relation to the rest
of the country.[23] Child prostitution is also particularly pronounced in this
poverty-ravaged region.[24]

It was into this harsh and brutal environment that Luiz Inácio Lula da
Silva was born in 1945. He lived with his family in the city of Garanhuns in
Pernambuco. His father was frequently absent and his illiterate mother
raised Lula and the other seven children largely by herself.[25] When Lula's
parents separated in 1956, his mother and siblings moved to the city of São
Paulo.[26] As a child he worked as a shoe shine boy and peanut seller, learning
to read later at the age of 10.[27]

Lula's early childhood, while certainly filled with hardship, was hardly
unique. Historically, millions of northeasterners have sought to escape the
appalling standard of living in their home region and have migrated to
Brazil's large cities.[28] São Paulo can seem daunting to newcomers. The city
of 17 million is plagued by crime, kidnappings, and robbery. High rise
apartment buildings equipped with sophisticated security systems are common. "Those with enough money," remarks the *New York Times*, "sought
haven from the threat of carjackings and other crimes by equipping their
automobiles with armor plating, hiring bodyguards or even acquiring helicopters."[29] Poverty-stricken newcomers are frequently obliged to take shel-
ter in *favelas* (shantytowns made up of shacks)[30]

Lula, however, opted to stay in São Paulo, where he acquired work at
Villares Industries, a metallurgical plant.[31] In the 1960s, he lost a finger during an industrial accident.[32] But by this time the young man was involved in
activities that could have cost him his life. In 1964, the Brazilian military

took over in a U.S.-backed coup d'état and held power for next twenty-one years.[33] Lula courageously defied the repressive political climate and became active in the labor movement. In 1975, he became the president of the São Paulo local of the 100,000 strong Metallurgists's Trade Union.[34] Lula, who sported a scruffy beard, T-shirt, and baseball cap,[35] led a bitter strike in the São Paulo automotive industry in 1980. According to the Associated Press, it was one of the few brazen challenges to the authorities of that era, and Lula spent several weeks in jail.[36] That same year, undeterred by the authorities, Lula helped to found the left-wing Partido dos Trabalhadores (PT), or Workers Party.[37]

Lula also took a keen personal interest in the fate of Petrobrás. During the 1990s, the Cardoso regime pursued market economic policies pleasing to Washington.[38] Like Chávez's predecessors in Venezuela, Cardoso was careful to appoint business leaders and bankers to management positions at the state oil company.[39] In May 1995, oil workers went on strike to demand wage increases and a halt to privatization schemes.[40] As the prolonged strike continued, Lula traded accusations with Cardoso. At one point the firebrand labor leader even faxed Cardoso to say that the continuation of the conflict was "essentially the result of the intransigence of a government that should have the capacity to negotiate." In a terse rebuke, Cardoso remarked: "It is unfortunate that Lula is using a strike that is causing the people so much hardship just to make political points. To confuse respect for the law with intransigence shows a lack of understanding of the exercise of democracy."[41] Meanwhile Petrobrás management punished workers tied to the anti-privatization strike by sending chastising notes and handing out 29-day suspensions.[42] Cardoso furthermore called out the military to run the oil refineries. The workers, who received scant support from the public which was suffering from fuel shortages, went back to work once the strike was declared illegal.[43] Although Petrobrás had not been completely privatized, Cardoso had achieved an important public relations victory.[44] The Brazilian Senate, feeling the public backlash against the strikers, approved the Cardoso administration's constitutional amendment allowing greater private investment of any origin in the oil sector.[45] Cardoso signed the Petroleum Investment Law in 1997, which opened up the Brazilian petroleum industry to foreign investment.[46] In 2000, the government went so far as to sell 28.5 percent of its shares in Petrobrás. More than half of the shares were sold to foreign investors.[47]

Lula ran for president on the PT ticket in the October election of 2002. As the election neared, Washington policymakers looked on in alarm. What if Lula should win? As scholar Immanuel Wallerstein has put it, "Brazil is a major country in the world-system. Its large size, its large population, its role as a leader of Latin America . . . all mean that what happens in Brazil is of great consequence in terms of both the geopolitical arena and the structure of the world-economy."[48] The last thing the Bush administration wanted was a radical labor firebrand running Brazil, the world's ninth largest economy and certainly the largest in Latin America.[49] Even worse, what if Lula should help to further a Venezuela-Brazil bloc that was hostile to U.S. interests?

As Chávez had done, Lula criticized global trade policies that left Third World countries at a disadvantage.[50] Would Lula, in line with earlier militancy on the Petrobrás issue, join in an energy alliance with Chávez? The significance of the Brazilian election was not lost on Chávez, who publicly congratulated his new counterpart. "Viva Lula!" he exclaimed. Having barely survived a coup attempt, the Venezuelan president hoped to end his diplomatic isolation. Surveying events from Venezuela, Chávez hoped that Lula would join him in challenging the Washington Consensus. Brazil, he remarked, was advancing and would show the rest of Latin America how to defy "savage" neoliberalism.[51] In a token of his goodwill, Chávez sent Lula a special gift: a replica of Simón Bolívar's sword. The sword arrived on the day of the Brazilian election, which also happened to be Lula's birthday.[52]

Although Lula categorically dismissed the idea of forming a bloc of anti-American countries, much of the Brazilian public looked to him to change course on the Washington Consensus.[53] Cardoso's market-friendly economic policies made the country attractive to foreign investment and helped to stave off inflation, but they also left the country vulnerable to financial shocks on the world market.[54] When financial crisis hit Asia and Russia in the late 1990s, stocks plunged in Brazil and investors began to pull their money out of the country.[55] Billions poured out of Brazil in capital flight and the government devalued the Brazilian currency, the real.[56] Even with an International Monetary Fund bail-out, the influx of foreign capital dried up and the country's public debt mushroomed. In the wake of international financial crises, the government was obliged to freeze wages and cut jobs in the state sector.[57] Given the tremendous economic hardship, Lula's electoral performance (the former shoeshine boy was elected with 61 percent of the vote) was hardly surprising.[58]

In a jab at Washington, Lula promptly made a point of halting privatization of the energy sector.[59] Following Lula's election, he halted price hikes on fuel and appointed a new energy minister Dilma Rousseff.[60] Rousseff, a member of the PT, was a former guerrilla fighter against the military dictatorship.[61] She was infamous for her role in taking part in a daring 1969 "expropriation" of $2.5 million from a former governor. Like her counterpart Alí Rodríguez in Venezuela, Rousseff was a left-wing radical, had fought against military regimes between 1964 and 1985, had languished in jail for three years, and had been tortured.[62] In an encouraging nod to Rousseff, Lula sought to provide his new energy minister with the last say in deciding which foreign companies may operate in Brazil.[63] In another sign that Lula would not broach a return to the Cardoso years, he appointed José Eduardo Dutra, a PT senator from a poor northeastern state, to head Petrobrás.[64] Dutra, a geologist by training, had formerly worked at Petrobrás, where, as a union organizer, he had opposed moves to privatize the company.[65] Dutra promptly packed upper management with PT members.[66] Just as PdVSA had increased social spending under Alí Rodríguez so as to reduce poverty, Dutra pledged to have Petrobrás contribute $100 million to government anti-poverty programs.[67]

To the White House's relief, however, Lula was not nearly as combative as Chávez toward the United States. Gone by now was Lula's scruffy image, replaced by tailored suits. The Brazilian even had his teeth repaired.[68] Unlike Chávez, who sought to radicalize the military, Lula assuaged conservative elements in the armed forces. Prior to the election, he gave a speech in which he praised former military authorities—who had jailed him for prior labor activities—for promoting internal development.[69] In a move designed to ingratiate himself further with Washington, in June 2004, Lula sent the largest military contingent to Haiti to protect the newly installed regime there after the ousting of democratically elected president Jean Bertrand Aristide. Observers say Aristide was kidnapped at gunpoint with the connivance of Washington. Following developments in Haiti, U.S. Secretary of State Colin Powell suggested that Brazil might be worthy of a seat on the UN Security Council.[70] Chávez by contrast snubbed the Bush administration by refusing to recognize the new government in Port-au-Prince.[71] In a jibe at Lula, he decried the participation of Latin American troops in the United Nations peacekeeping mission sent to Haiti and even offered refuge in Venezuela to exiled President Aristide.[72]

Apparently, Lula had no plan to conclude any kind of radical civic-military alliance à lá Chávez. Indeed, according to political observer Tariq Ali, during Lula's first year in office, the MST (Movimento dos Sem-Terra, or Movement of the Landless), which had been a historic pillar of the PT, was subjected to much more repression than under Cardoso.[73] James Petras, an adviser to the landless and jobless in Brazil and Argentina, had harsh words for the Pernambuco native son. "The biggest loser in the debacle of Lula's regime," he said, "has been the Landless Workers Movement . . . scores of peasant activists have been killed, tens of thousands of land squatters have been forcibly evicted." Lula, he says, "has continually reneged on every promise of agrarian reform."[74]

In his economic orientation, too, Lula has disappointed some of his more ardent supporters. One year after assuming the presidency, the liberal *Nation* magazine gushed, "The bearded political leader they call Lula is the new phenomenon of globalization, a man with audacious ambitions to alter the balance of power among nations."[75] Lula pushed for better terms of trade for poor countries and sought to improve political and economic ties amongst Mercosur nations.[76] The new Brazilian leader was tough in World Trade Organization negotiations, refusing to yield to the usual U.S. pressure tactics and thus ensuring the wrath of Robert Zoellick.[77] Yet, Lula faithfully pays Brazil's external debt, maintains a primary budget surplus beyond the amount demanded by the International Monetary Fund, and pushes through regressive pension reform.[78] Reportedly, Chávez's relationship with Lula was strained in November 2004, when the Venezuelan leader criticized regional governments' moves to place macroeconomic policies over social needs. "The 250 or 300 million poor in Latin America plead for justice," Chávez said. The remarks apparently irritated Lula, who had aspirations to become a prominent hemispheric leader.[79]

Public disaffection with Lula was placed into bold relief during the 2005 meeting of the World Social Forum in the Brazilian city of Porto Alegre.[80] When Hugo Chávez arrived at the meeting, he was welcomed with cries of "Here Comes the Boss!"[81] Speaking at the Gigantinho stadium, Chávez had the crowd on its feet as he denounced U.S. hegemony and proclaimed his aim of consolidating socialism in Venezuela. "Only with socialism can we transcend capitalism," he thundered.[82] But, the Venezuelan leader added, it was time to jettison the old model of state socialism, creating a more humanist model.[83] The crowd responded with cries of "Chávez Sí, Lula No." Chávez motioned for them to stop, calling for a broad "anti-imperialist front."[84] He defended Lula, remarking that at the beginning of his own administration, many criticized him for not proceeding faster with radical political change. But, Chávez said, "each process has several phases and different rhythms that not only have to do with internal situations in each country, but with the international situation at the time."[85]

What kind of common ground could exist between the feisty ex-paratrooper and provocateur and the now moderate and economically conservative Lula? Despite their differences, Chávez quickly moved ahead with his oil diplomacy.

From the very outset, oil was key in solidifying the Chávez-Lula alliance and easing the political differences between the two South American leaders. Word of the PT victory could not have come at a better time for Chávez. In December 2002, the Venezuelan president was facing the devastating oil lockout, designed to put further pressure on the regime.[86] As a result, Venezuela was forced to import gasoline for internal use.[87] In a clear sign that Brazil would not kowtow to Washington in its effort to isolate Venezuela, Petrobrás shipped 520,000 barrels of oil to its Andean neighbor.[88] President Cardoso, serving out the last days of his presidency before Lula's arrival, approved the oil shipment.[89] However, according to the *New York Times*, "there are indications that his successor-elect, Luiz Inácio Lula da Silva . . . was also involved in the decision."[90] In moving to help Chávez, Lula reportedly had his own pragmatic concerns. If Chávez was overthrown, he remarked privately, "tomorrow" it would be his turn, and this could give rise to a domino effect throughout the region.[91]

In January 2003, during a breakfast meeting in Brasilia on Lula's first day in office, Chávez asked Lula if Brazil might send technical experts from Petrobrás to replace many of the 30,000 PdVSA workers who had joined the oil lockout. Lula said that he would consider Chávez's request. Chávez also pressed Lula about plans to launch Petroamérica.[92] Lula's actions further inflamed the Venezuelan opposition, which condemned Brazilian interference.[93] In another move which surely angered the opposition yet further, Chávez was personally on hand to oversee the unloading of fuel from the Brazilian tanker *Amazonian Explorer*, which docked at the Venezuelan port of Puerto La Cruz.[94] But would Lula follow through and provide technical assistance to PdVSA during the strike? Antonio Carrara, the coordinator of the main oil workers' union at Petrobrás, remarked that "We are against sending Petrobrás workers to Venezuela mainly because of security issues." Carrara added, "That would put our workers at risk . . . at this point we can't even see a resolution for what is happening in Venezuela."[95] Dutra, however, remarked that Petrobrás was interested in helping Venezuela resume oil production.[96] Then, in a clear sign that he would not be intimidated by Washington, Lula offered Petrobrás specialists to help operate several Venezuelan refineries.[97] By April 2003, production had been almost restored.[98]

Why would Lula stake so much on helping his Venezuelan counterpart? A degree of self-interest might have been involved. In the late 1990s, Brazil only produced about two-thirds of its own oil consumption needs and was not a petroleum exporter.[99] In fact, though Brazil hopes to be oil self-sufficient in a few years, it has relied on Venezuela for oil imports.[100] The idea of regional energy self-sufficiency was appealing to Brazil. During the oil crisis of the 1970s, the country had been hit hard. Its debt burden had increased, obliging leaders to subject Brazil to harsh macroeconomic policies.[101]

Given Brazil's difficulties, it is not surprising that Lula sought to cultivate energy ties with Chávez. In April 2003, following the oil lockout in Venezuela, Chávez and Lula agreed to invest $2.5 billion in the construction of a new refinery in Pernambuco to be jointly owned by Venezuela and Brazil.[102] For Lula, building the new refinery was a social and economic imperative. The Northeast was a huge, poverty-stricken area with a population of 40 million,[103] almost a quarter of the Brazilian population of 170 million, and nearly double Venezuela's population of 24 million.[104] During the four years of the refinery's construction, 230,000 people would be employed.[105] The refinery was set to produce 200,000 barrels a day of heavy crude.[106] In addition, Chávez and Lula planned to improve energy infrastructure between the two countries by building a gas pipeline.[107] Chávez also concluded an agreement that allowed for Brazilian participation in the production of natural gas off the Venezuelan coast. In yet another project, Brazil and Venezuela agreed to produce 150,000 extra barrels of heavy crude in the Orinoco Oil Belt.[108] Capping it all off, Chávez established PdVSA do Brasil, thus binding the countries even closer together.[109]

Clearly, Lula is no Chávez. But the Venezuelan leader has moved his Brazilian counterpart into his corner through skillful oil diplomacy. In the wake of the Venezuelan oil lockout, Lula seemed to be veering closer and closer toward joining Petroamérica. He sent Petrobrás president Dutra to meet with Alí Rodríguez to discuss plans to further energy integration.[110]

According to the BBC, energy deals signed by Lula suggested that "the Brazilians have moved in President Chávez's direction."[111] Speaking at Miraflores, where the two leaders concluded joint energy agreements, Lula commented that the "two countries are establishing a true strategic alliance."[112]

By all indications, Chávez has been successful wielding oil as his trump card. With energy ties growing between Brazil and Venezuela, the United States will find it increasingly more difficult to prod Lula into isolating Chávez diplomatically. For his part, Chávez must surely hope that energy agreements with Brazil will encourage Lula to support his other ambitious hemispheric objectives. Having solidified ties with Brazil, Chávez focused on Argentina, where he hoped to pull off another coup through oil diplomacy.

Speaking to the crowd during the recent Summit of the Americas in Mar del Plata, Argentina, Chávez completely upstaged President Bush, who was forced to flee from piqueteros and protesters upset at his free trade policies. In a sense, it is hardly surprising that Mar del Plata should be such a focal point of discontent. A medium-size coastal city of some 600,000 people, Mar del Plata's traditional industries have been fishing and textiles. Historically the city had also been a favored tourist destination for the Argentine elite. I learned of the city through Martín, a colleague of mine at Oxford University. He and I both arrived in England at the same time in 1999, and we shared a common academic supervisor at the Latin American Centre. A scholar of Argentine political history during the early twentieth century, Martín accompanied me on my research trips to the Public Records Office, a historical archive located in Kew Gardens, London. During our long rides, Martín filled me in on life in Argentina and his native Mar del Plata.

Martín explained that at the end of the 1930s and especially after the era of *Peronismo* in the 1950s, Mar del Plata became a vacation spot for the middle and working classes, the latter of whom had been favored by social policies of the Peronist regime. Soon hotels had sprung up all over the city. In particular, Martín told me, during the 1970s, Mar del Plata experienced a construction boom and massive tourism. But by the 1990s, the city had fallen on difficult economic straits. Its industries, particularly textiles, had been adversely affected by neoliberal policies pursued by the central government.

In 2002, I graduated and lost contact with Martín. But later, as I read the headlines about Chávez in Mar del Plata, I e-mailed my old colleague.

He replied that as a result of neoliberal policies of the 1990s and the economic collapse in 2001, unemployment rose in his city, affecting approximately 20 percent of the economically productive population. Even worse, the city was devastated by a collapse of the tourist industry in 2001–02. Ominously, shantytowns started to emerge on the outskirts of the city. Thousands of young men and women left, particularly for Spain, thus "repeating in an inverse sense the migratory movement of their grandparents and great-grandparents."

Not surprisingly, Martín added, in December 2001, "Mar del Plata was one of the urban centers which experienced marches and demonstrations during the economic and political collapse." Mar del Plata's middle class were a part of these marches; they had been adversely affected by a government freeze on bank withdrawals. Protesters holding savings accounts even burned down the façade of banks or carried out street theater at the municipal palace. The piqueteros also began to organize in Mar del Plata, blocking streets and main roads.[113]

It is no wonder that Chávez would receive such a warm welcome by activists in Mar del Plata. But would he be able to advance his hemispheric agenda with the new president, Néstor Kirchner? On the surface at least, there seemed to be some convergence of views. Kirchner, having taken power in 2003, distanced himself from the Washington Consensus and denounced the neoliberal policies that had generated social dislocation.[114] But some observers see Kirchner as a cynical figure. They argue that he has dampened social protest and the piquetero movement by carefully co-opting, isolating, and imprisoning militant leaders.[115] In fact, argues James Petras, "Whatever the occasional difference between the U.S. and Kirchner, it is clear that he has accomplished one of the primary conditions for U.S. domination—he has demobilized the movements and taken the country out of the 'danger zone' of a popular upheaval against the neo-liberal system constructed during the 1990's."[116]

Kirchner, Petras adds, has respected all privatizations carried out by his predecessors and championed the agroindustrial sector over the rural poor. Moreover, he supports the Free Trade Area of the Americas as long as Argentina can secure concessions for its agrobusiness interests. Eager to please Washington, he has sent troops to Haiti to defend the government there; in this sense his foreign policy is similar to that of Brazilian president Lula. Fortunately for Kirchner, Argentina has seen strong growth, for the most part a result of a commodities boom resulting from double-digit industrial growth in China. The Argentine president has been left with sufficient re-sources to increase social spending and provide some pension and minimum wage increases.[117]

Faced with disparities in their outlook, what might Chávez have in common with Kirchner and the new government in Argentina? Again, Chávez sought to build bridges with oil. Argentina in fact is the fourth largest hydrocarbon producer in South America after Mexico, Venezuela, and Brazil and had the fifth largest reserves behind Mexico, Venezuela, Ecuador, and Brazil.[118] The country is also a major producer of natural gas and has the third largest gas reserves in Latin America.[119]

During the 1980s and 1990s, Argentina, like Brazil and Venezuela, had sought to privatize its state-run oil company, Yacimientos Petrolíferos Fis-cales (YPF).[120] Like PdVSA in Venezuela, YPF had been an institution in Argentina. The company had even built whole towns and cities.[121] It was the third largest state-run oil company in South America, after PdVSA and Petrobrás.[122] In 1992, the state-run gas company, Gas del Estado, was priva-tized.[123] In 1993, YPF was sold outright.[124] By 1994, U.S. direct investment in the Argentine petroleum industry had reached $773 million.[125] In 1999, the Spanish Repsol bought YPF for $13.5 billion, resulting in one of the largest oil and gas corporations in the world.[126]

Unfortunately, according to analysts Kirchner maintains "strategic al-liances with Spanish oil company Repsol to preserve the sector's privatiza-tion."[127] The president's unwillingness to renationalize YPF, which recently accounted for approximately 39 percent of the country's oil production, is surely a blow to creating a Petrosur with real teeth.[128] Yet Kirchner did in-troduce a bill into Congress allowing for the creation of a largely state-owned company, Enarsa (Energía Argentina Sociedad Anónima). The company would explore, exploit, produce, generate, transport, distribute, and market oil and gas and sell energy on the domestic and international market. In addition, Enarsa would hold permits to explore and exploit all offshore concessions that were not already awarded.[129]

Surely, economic circumstances had forced Kirchner to act decisively. Although the Argentine economy had been in a state of collapse, by early 2003, the economy showed signs of recovery.[130] Along with recovery, how-ever, demand for natural gas began to rise. By early 2004, the country was experiencing shortages.[131] Much as Chávez had led an assault on PdVSA, Kirchner now led a forceful attack on the gas companies, accusing them of not ensuring supply to the local market and failing to expand areas covered by the local grid.[132]

Under the National Law on Hydrocarbons, the companies were obliged to comply with Kirchner's demands. Additionally, in a heartening endorsement of Kirchner's call, the Argentine Congress approved the creation of Enarsa. Within the new company, the state held 53 percent of the shares, the provinces owned 12 percent, and private investors held 35 percent. Under the law, Enarsa had the ability "to intervene in the market in order to prevent situations of abuse arising from the monopoly or oligopoly position" of companies.[133]

Clearly, Kirchner's energy policy was beginning to converge with Chávez's. To help it cope with energy shortages, in 2004, Venezuela supplied Argentina with emergency fuel oil.[134] It was the first time that Argentina, an energy exporter, had imported fuel from Venezuela.[135] In return for Venezuelan oil supplies worth more than $300 million, Argentina traded cattle, agricultural products, and medical equipment.[136] Kirchner also agreed to supply farm machinery in exchange for more fuel oil and to repair and build PdVSA's oil tankers in Argentine shipyards.[137]

As in the case of the Brazilian refinery, the shipbuilding deal stands to ameliorate social dislocation. Reportedly the agreement will generate at least 1,500 jobs. The Argentines are to build four tankers worth $200 million. The first tanker will be baptized *Eva Peron*, named after the former Argentine president's wife. In his usual personal touch, Chávez visited one of the shipbuilding plants where the tankers are to be constructed.[138]

Chávez was ecstatic that his plans for energy integration seemed to be gaining widespread acceptance, establishing a worrying precedent for Washington. As Ellner has pointed out, the U.S. economy is bolstered by use of the dollar as the world's preeminent currency for international exchange. But under Chávez, Venezuela has moved toward nonmonetary barter deals for its oil with other South American countries, thus bypassing the dollar.[139]

These novel deals were followed up with even closer collaboration: Kirchner soon signed a joint venture agreement between PdVSA and Enarsa that included production, refining, and distribution of natural gas and petroleum by-products.[140] According to the *New York Times*, Chávez's trade deal proved wildly popular among Argentines. In Buenos Aires, Chávez was mobbed by crowds when he inaugurated Venezuela's first state-owned gas station forming part of the food-for-oil program.[141] Kirchner planned to set up a full 600 joint Enarsa-PdVSA gas stations throughout Argentina by the end of 2005.[142] Furthermore, Chávez entered into a joint agreement with Argentina to purchase an existing refinery called La Rhasa. The Argentine plant processes 8,000 barrels of crude per day, and PdVSA hopes to increase capacity. La Rhasa, according to PdVSA officials, would service its new gas stations planned for Argentina and Uruguay.[143]

The consolidation of a new energy alliance was certainly a positive development for Chávez. In 2005, the last domino on the Atlantic coast of South America elected a left-of-center government. Uruguay, a tiny beef- and wool-producing country wedged between Brazil and Argentina, had turned against U.S.-backed military dictatorship and the Washington Consensus.[144] With Uruguay in the fold, Chávez stood to make yet further political inroads.

CHAPTER EIGHT

CHÁVEZ AND THE INFORMATION WAR AGAINST THE BUSH ADMINISTRATION

Born in 1934, José Mujica grew up in a modest house on the outskirts of the Uruguayan capital of Montevideo. He was politically active from an early age and worked as a left-wing student activist as an adolescent.[1] Mujica came of age in a troubled time in his nation's history. Starting in the mid-1950s, Uruguay was gripped with economic stagnation, inflation, and political corruption.[2] As labor unrest mounted, Uruguayan society saw the rise of an urban Marxist guerrilla movement known as the Tupamaros, named after the Indian rebel Túpac Amaru. The Tupamaros started out in the early 1960s carrying out kidnappings and staging spectacular jailbreaks of fellow imprisoned rebels.[3] Seeing themselves as modern-day Robin Hoods, the Tupamaros robbed banks and distributed the money to the poor.[4] In the mid-1960s, Mujica joined up with the Tupamaros, becoming part of the organization just as the war was heating up. Mujica took part in daring guerrilla operations and went underground.[5]

The United States and the Nixon administration responded by training the Uruguayan police in interrogation and torture techniques.[6] Dan Mitrione, a former policeman from Richmond, Indiana, and then a member of the FBI, was sent to Uruguay in 1969 as an advisor for the U.S. Agency for International Development.[7] Mitrione had had previous experience training the Brazilian police in the early and mid-1960s. During this time the police widely tortured dissidents and killed undesirables through use of death squads.[8] In Uruguay, Mitrione was affiliated with the Uruguayan police's Office of Public Safety and instructed his students in how to torture using electrical implements.[9] Mitrione is reported to have said, "The precise pain, in the precise place, in the precise amount, for the desired effect."[10]

As tensions in Uruguay escalated, the Tupamaros kidnapped Mitrione.[11] They then tried to use him as a bargaining chip, demanding the release of a large number of prisoners for Mitrione's life. The Uruguayan government refused and Mitrione was murdered. Later, Frank Sinatra and Jerry Lewis put on a benefit show in Mitrione's memory.[12] White House spokesperson Ron Ziegler described Mitrione as someone who "devoted service to the cause of peaceful progress in an orderly world . . . [Mitrione] will remain as an example for free men everywhere."[13]

Meanwhile, the military was able to defeat the Tupamaros and took power in a 1973 coup. The country soon had the dubious distinction of having the world's highest percentage of political prisoners to the general population.[14] I first became aware of the Tupamaros in Berkeley when I saw the famous film by Costa-Gavras, *State of Siege.* Based loosely on the Tupamaro insurgency, it grippingly portrays the clandestine lives of the rebels as they flee from the police. The French actor Yves Montand plays Philip Michael Santore, modeled after Dan Mitrione. In the film, Santore is unrepentant about training the police in Uruguay.

Today, Mujica does not like to talk about his past. However, it is known that at one point, he suffered six bullet wounds, he was imprisoned on four occasions, and amazingly he managed to escape from prison twice. In total, Mujica spent fifteen years in prison.[15] In 1985, jailed Tupamaros received amnesty and Mujica finally got out of jail.[16] Uruguay was just returning to democratic rule, and Mujica became a leader of the Movement of Popular Participation (known by its Spanish acronym MPP), a political party formed by former Tupamaros.[17] Mujica's party became a member organization of the ruling Broad Front (Frente Amplio), a coalition of political parties formed in 1971 including socialists, Communists and other left leaning politicians.[18]

But Uruguay, having survived the dark years of U.S.-backed military rule, was now pummeled by Argentina's debt default and later currency devaluation.[19] Unemployment skyrocketed and wages plummeted.[20] By 2004, an unprecedented 32 percent of Uruguayans had fallen below the poverty line.[21] In an eerie echo of Argentina, there was a wave of panicky bank withdrawals prompting the government to suspend all banking operations.[22] Like Brazil and Argentina, the country became burdened by billions of dollars in debt as the economy contracted and the International Monetary Fund provided emergency aid.[23]

For ordinary Uruguayans, the changes were difficult to accept psychologically. Historically the country was known as a strongly middle class nation characterized by upward social mobility. Uruguay had long enjoyed a system of costly social welfare programs, an extensive social security system, old-age pensions, a superior educational system, and high literacy rates.[24] Despite the financial assistance offered by the International Monetary Fund, the public showed it had no stomach for free market solutions. In a 2003 plebiscite, it voted by more than 60 percent against partial privatization of the country's oil company, known as ANCAP (Administración Nacional de Combustibles, Alcohol y Portland).[25]

Developments in Uruguay looked to be increasingly in Hugo Chávez's favor.

José Mujica wept as he was sworn in to chair the Senate in February 2005. Since his release from jail, the former guerrilla fighter had gone on to become a senator. Now he was about to become Uruguay's new minister of agriculture.[26] The voters had just elected Tabaré Vázquez, a socialist and member of the Broad Front, as their new president.[27] Vázquez was born and grew up in La Teja, a working-class Montevideo neighborhood; his father, a trade union leader, worked in an ANCAP refinery.[28] Vázquez became a cancer specialist and worked as the president of a soccer team.[29] In 1989 he was elected mayor of Montevideo under the Broad Front.[30] In the 2004 presidential election, Vázquez garnered 51 percent of the vote, thus eliminating the need for a second runoff.[31]

As the new government was sworn in, thousands of Uruguayans filled the streets of Montevideo. Chanting "Ur-u-guay!" and waving flags, the people celebrated the election of the 65-year-old socialist leader. Confetti flew and fireworks thundered overhead. While on the campaign trail, Vázquez had pledged to help the poverty-stricken and that message resonated well among Uruguayans wary of Washington's free market proscriptions.[32] As one of his first initiatives in office, Vázquez signed a $100 million antipoverty program.[33] But carrying out social initiatives will prove difficult. When Vázquez was inaugurated, his country faced a massive $13.2 billion debt. The new president pledged to keep up payments and to adhere to monetary goals established by the International Monetary Fund.[34]

In a sign that the new government was not prepared to tangle with Washington, Vázquez's Broad Front promised to preserve the country's regressive tax system. The regime also pledged to keep paying the foreign debt and to stockpile an enormous government surplus so as to prevent any default. While the moves surely must have come as a disappointment to Vazquez's more left-wing supporters, the transition in government went smoothly, "explained in part by the weakness of social resistance owing to unemployment, emigration, and the aging of the population." What is more, though the era of the Tupamaros was certainly violent, Uruguay has no historic tradition of popular insurrection.[35]

Might Venezuela radicalize politics within Uruguay? With no proven hydrocarbon resources, Uruguay is completely dependent on oil and gas imports. With Argentina fearing that its energy crisis might continue into 2005 owing to soaring gas demand, Vázquez turned to Chávez.[36] The Venezuelan leader, keen to consolidate his alliance with the newly emerging regimes along the Atlantic coast, was magnanimous. Proffering up yet another replica of Simón Bolívar's sword, he offered the gift to Vázquez upon the latter's assumption of power.[37] In Montevideo, Chávez announced that he would supply 40,000 barrels of oil per day to Uruguay.[38] Under the agreement, Venezuela will supply oil to Uruguay for 25 years under preferential terms. Uruguay will receive two-thirds of the petroleum by bartering its meat and milk with Venezuela. Low-interest loans will pay for the rest of the oil.[39]

In a further sign of the improving ties, PdVSA stated it would open a commercial office in Montevideo, and Chávez personally toured the La Teja refinery.[40] Chávez said Venezuela would help to bring the plant to full production capacity so as to process Venezuelan crude. Eventually the Venezuelan president hopes to eventually double La Teja's capacity in order to refine extra-heavy Venezuelan crude from the Orinoco Oil Belt.[41] "Venezuela will provide very big support to such a small country as this, where the energy problem is of crucial importance," Vázquez noted.[42]

Most important of all, Vázquez agreed to his country's joining Petrosur. As he entered into the agreement, the Uruguayan president remarked on TV that "the empire [apparently Vázquez meant the United States] exists and there was and have been attempts to achieve total hegemony and we are opposed to that."[43] Chávez's energy minister, Rafael Ramírez, signed an agreement with the Brazilian minister of energy and mines and 1960s radical Dilma Rousseff, as well as with the Argentinean minister of public works, Julio De Vido, to create Petrosur.[44]

The new company will collaborate on future projects in the Venezuelan Orinoco "heavy oil belt," the Brazilian Abreu de Lima refinery, and new oil and gas exploration as well as production in Argentina.[45] With Uruguay aligning itself with the oil bloc, Chávez seems to have enhanced his stature. He even entered into negotiations with Petropar, the Paraguayan state-owned energy company.[46] Chávez agreed to ship 8,600 barrels of petroleum products a day to Paraguay with a 25 percent discount and no interest.[47] In return, Paraguay will provide Venezuela with food products, such as meat and soybeans.[48]

Even worse from the perspective of Washington, Chávez has extended his oil diplomacy throughout the Andean region. Chávez has pushed for his own plan, PetroAndina, which would sell discounted oil to Bolivia, Ecuador, Peru, and Colombia.[49] PetroAndina, as Chávez envisions it, would allow for the mutual provision of energy resources and joint investment in projects.[50] "We have petroleum, gas, everything we need to build a powerful and large bloc," the president has said. "All we need is the will to do it. A great agreement among Venezuela—an oil-producing country, Colombia—an oil-producing country—and Ecuador, Peru, and Bolivia, which have large quantities of natural gas, a great multinational energy enterprise."[51] Although the political equation in the Andes is very murky and unclear already Chávez has met with some success in using oil as a geopolitical weapon against the United States. In fact, he has stated that one of the crucial reasons why U.S.-Venezuelan relations have deteriorated so noticeably is his insistence on carrying out oil accords throughout South America.[52]

In a first step toward building up Petroamérica, Venezuela has already sold natural gas to Ecuador.[53] Chávez also recently suggested that Ecuador might refine its oil in Venezuela and has agreed to help the state-run oil company PetroEcuador to modernize its technical and operational infrastructure.[54] Chávez may hope that such moves may ingratiate Venezuela with the new Ecuadorian president, Alfredo Palacio, who has moved to sign a free trade agreement with the United States and supports the U.S.-sponsored drug war. Chávez is clearly hoping that his energy diplomacy may move Palacio away from the U.S. orbit. In a novel gesture, he has even offered to buy up Ecuadoran debt.[55] (The policy was reminiscent of Venezuelan diplomacy in Argentina, where Chávez followed up his oil deals by buying $500 million in Argentine bonds[56]). To the south of Ecuador, in Peru, a retired army colonel named Ollanta Humala is surging in the polls in advance of the April 2006 presidential election.[57] Humala, who compares

himself to Chávez and is an outspoken critic of the United States, has proclaimed his intention to nationalize Peru's "strategic enterprises."[58]

In Colombia, right-wing president Álvaro Uribe has implemented pro-
U.S. market policies as well as the America-funded drug war. But even here
Chávez has met with some success, recently concluding a $200 million deal
to build a joint gas pipeline that will form part of a regional energy network.[59] According to *Oil and Gas Journal*, Colombia had 1.54 billion barrels
of proven crude oil reserves in 2005, the fifth-largest in South America.
Colombia exports approximately half of its oil production, with the greatest
share of those exports shipped to the United States.[60] The growing energy
ties between Venezuela and Colombia make it harder for the United States
to isolate Chávez. In fact, one political observer remarks that if Colombia is
"not exactly with Chávez [it is] not prepared to be Washington's ram against
him."[61] With Colombia having the potential to join Petroamérica, the
prospect of a possible further leftist upset in the Colombian election in 2006
surely reinforces the seriousness of the situation for the White House.[62]
Chávez has also set his sights on Mexico, the country from which he
launched his presidential ambitions in 1998 while participating in a Zapatista march. If Mexico should elect Andrés Manuel López Obrador of the
PRD (Party of the Democratic Revolution) in 2006, this "could precipitate a
tectonic shift for the Bush administration's ill-reputed Latin America team,
leading them from a grudging acceptance of South America's left-of center
governments to the use of Cold War–style tactics against them." According
to political analyst DeLong, "The nightmare scenario for the Bush team
would . . . be Chávez inviting Mexico's state-owned oil company, Pemex,
into a cooperative arrangement with the Venezuelan leader's oil trading
bloc, 'Petrosur.'" Mexico and Venezuela are leading suppliers of U.S. oil. In
fact, a combined Obrador-Chávez bloc would account for upward of a quarter of all U.S. oil imports.[63]

Clearly, Chávez has been able to use oil as a geopolitical weapon. If political trends continue to shift leftward, the Venezuelan leader will become
even more entrenched. Chávez, however, hopes oil diplomacy will be
merely the first stepping-stone toward deeper political and social integration. One encouraging result of his oil diplomacy has been the creation of a
hemispheric TV station that has the White House on edge.

A short, stocky, middle-age man with a gray ponytail, Aram Aharonian
hardly cuts the figure of someone who would represent a threat to the Bush

White House.[64] And yet, as the new director general of Telesur,[65] Aharonian is a man to be reckoned with. Chávez's 24-hour Spanish-language satellite TV channel broadcasts across Latin America, and Aharonian hopes that one day it will rival the likes of CNN en Español, BBC, and Fox News.[66] "This is a dream, a dream of a lot of people," says Aharonian. The U.S. media, he says, provides a superficial view of Latin America and concentrates only on disasters. "Why do we have to continue seeing ourselves through the eyes of others?" he asks.[67] "Telesur's reason for being," says Aharonian, "is the need to see Latin America with Latin American eyes." It is time, he believes, to wage "an ideological fight." In his public comments, Aharonian leaves no doubt as to where he stands vis-à-vis the United States: "Commercial TV tells us today that there is a liberating coalition in Iraq saving the Iraqis when we know it is a genocidal invasion." Television, he says, cannot be left in the hands of "the enemy."

Personally, I had become much less skeptical about Chávez as a result of my research into his social programs. But on a gut level, the idea of state-funded TV was a bit suspect to me. To get a better idea of Aharonian's ideas, I went back to read some of his earlier pieces. In a recent article in the Caracas monthly newspaper *Questión* entitled "RR: Rhetoric or Reality?" Aharonian sketched out his views concerning social and political changes in Venezuela. Although he is complimentary of Chávez's accomplishments in the fields of health and education, he writes that the regime must do more to encourage participatory democracy in order to give more power to the poor.

In another recent article, published in the wake of Chávez's victory in regional elections, Aharonian writes that the president must give up his confrontational politics and start to govern. "The reality," he writes, "is that the climate of confrontation that Venezuela experienced for years encouraged a situation in which many governors and mayors elected under the Chávez banner are really not suitable for governance, they don't have experience in politics or public administration." The article made me think that Aharonian is not a mere mouthpiece of the Chávez regime. Indeed, when pressed, Aharonian insists that Telesur will be completely independent. He asks why more people do not voice similar concerns about the independence of private TV media.[68]

Aharonian is the symbol of Chávez's new South American internationalism. A veteran Uruguayan journalist, he witnessed the counterinsurgency war against the Tupamaros and his country's descent into chaos. Aharonian, who worked for Uruguayan newspapers such as *La Verdad*, found the political climate increasingly difficult.[69] In accordance with "national security," media outlets were closed down, particularly those of the opposition. Journalists could stay in the country and be imprisoned, or go into exile. Aharonian chose the latter and headed for Buenos Aires; he later moved to Venezuela in 1985.[70] After the horrible climate of fear in Uruguay, Venezuela came as a relief for Aharonian. The journalist thrived in his new home, working for United Press International and Prensa Latina, the official Cuban news agency; he also directed *Questión*, the Spanish-language version of the Parisian newspaper *Le Monde Diplomatique*. Before joining Telesur, Aharonian worked as president of the Foreign Press Association of Venezuela from 1999 to 2003.[71]

With Aharonian, a man so intensely opposed to U.S. influence in Latin America, at the helm of Telesur, I was curious to see what the programming of the new station was like. I called my old acquaintance at the Venezuelan Mission to the United Nations, who said that I would need Deep Dish TV, a grassroots satellite network, to watch Telesur.[72] In my Brooklyn apartment I only had corporately owned Time Warner cable. A month later I got another e-mail, instructing me to go to the new Telesur link. It turned out that one could now watch the station online. Eager to finally catch a glimpse of "TeleChávez," as Chávez's detractors have referred to the new Telesur network, I clicked on to the Web site.

Telesur, which operates as an affiliate of state-sponsored Venezolana de Televisión, showcases documentaries, movies, and some entertainment programming. The network places strong emphasis on informative content, which accounts for 40 percent of all programming, and has correspondents throughout South America.[73] Telesur's programming differs widely to the usual fare served up on the American media. The new South American network broadcasts serious documentaries on an array of subjects, such as the indigenous movement in Bolivia and the destruction of the Amazonian rain forest. Culturally, the station caters more to Latin than North American tastes, with programming on tango, for example. A novel-sounding program, "Nojolivud" (whose name comes from the phonetic Spanish spelling of "No Hollywood"), broadcasts films made outside "the Hollywood system."[74] In line with its programming bent, Telesur has notable left-wing figures on its advisory board, including

African American actor Danny Glover and Uruguayan writer Eduardo Galeano.[75]

According to Aharonian, the governing board of the company is comprised of "journalists, communicators and people from the Latin American audiovisual world." It includes Aharonian himself; Ana de Escalom, of Channel 7 Buenos Aires; Beto Almeida, of Brazil's journalist guild; Ovidio Cabrera, ex-vice President of Cuba's Radio TV; Jorge Enrique Botero, Telesur's director of information in Colombia, and Andrés Izarra, Telesur's president, a professional journalist who formerly reported for CNN.[76] He is also Chávez's Minister of Communications and Information.[77] Izarra's father, William Izarra, is a former air force officer and currently serves as Chávez's deputy foreign minister. In a recent fiery speech William declared, "The media are more important than [military] divisions."[78] Perhaps sensitive to charges of bias, Aharonian declared that none of the individuals on the governing board, except for Andrés Izarra, officially represented the government's point of view.[79] Recently Izarra resigned his post as information minister, declaring that he wanted to reassure the public that Telesur would not suffer from conflicts of interest.[80]

Flush with oil revenue, Chávez set aside an initial $2.5 million for the network. "For the first time in the history of Venezuela," comments Aharonian, "the earnings of petroleum are reaching the people and the surpluses have given the opportunity to promote this Latin American project of communicational integration." Organizers have sought out sponsors, but in sharp contrast to Cisneros's Univisión, Telesur will offer no commercial advertising. Although, "there will be advertisements from private and public institutions, with such sponsors having nothing to do with the editorial line," says Aharonian. Currently Telesur represents a multistate project, with Venezuela putting up 51 percent of the funding, followed by Argentina with 20 percent, Cuba with 19 percent and Uruguay with 10 percent.[81] Additionally, Telesur has concluded an agreement to share material with TV Brasil, a state-run company.[82]

According to Izarra, Telesur is the first example of a continent-wide station owned jointly by a number of governments. In a worrying sign for Bush, Telesur managers announced their intention to form a cooperation agreement with Al Jazeera, an Arabic-language news channel. Under the agreement, Al Jazeera would open a central office in Caracas. According to Izarra, however, the deal was never concluded.[83] Telesur's satellite signal is available in South America, Central America, North America, Western Europe, and northwest Africa.[84] The station has correspondents in Argentina, Brazil, Colombia, Cuba, Peru, Mexico, and the United States.[85] Watching Telesur over the Internet, I could not help thinking about the proposed arrangement with Al Jazeera. I recalled reading a recent news report alleging that President Bush suggested bombing the Al Jazeera offices in Qatar while in a meeting with British prime minister Tony Blair. The Middle Eastern network had reportedly irked Bush for its damaging coverage of the U.S. war in Iraq.[86] Perhaps, I thought, correspondents for the newly formed Telesur should take care.

I had some difficulty hearing Telesur broadcasts over the Internet, no matter how high I turned the volume up on my computer. Apparently, I was not the only one who experienced technical difficulties. During one news report, a correspondent in Montevideo strained to hear the voice of the anchorwoman in Caracas. Despite the technical difficulties, I was somewhat impressed with Telesur. For a new network, it had certainly come far. I was intrigued by a long, in-depth news segment about the South American trading bloc Mercosur, which Venezuela had recently joined. A correspondent in Uruguay interviewed average people on the street to ask them what they thought about closer Venezuelan-Uruguayan integration. One young man responded that it was important that Chávez was launching initiatives that could combat U.S. influence.

There was a short commercial break—an ad funded by PdVSA with a voice intoning "energy for integration,"—then it was back to the news: some short reports from Peru showing protesting Indians and students blocking highways in Bolivia. In an apparent effort to provide lighter fare, the reports were followed by a short piece about Tai Shan, a baby panda in the Washington, D.C., zoo. The news show also carries professional sports reports. Although Telesur is nowhere near as glitzy and sensationalistic as Fox News, for example, I wondered whether the network was making a conscious effort to imitate the appearances of other TV anchors. The woman news presenter on Telesur was pretty, nicely dressed, and wore makeup and earrings. I could not help feeling a bit disappointed: I had read that, in stark contrast to Univisión celebrity anchor Jorge Ramos, who wears a jacket and tie, Telesur had hired Ati Kiwa as anchor, an indigenous Colombian woman who wears traditional dress.[87] Where was she?

Before I could give this more thought, the news show ended and we were in the midst of a documentary about anarchism in Argentina at the turn of the twentieth century. The producers interviewed learned historians and journalists about the politics of the era, while I strained to hear their voices. What, I wondered, would ordinary Venezuelans make of this programming? Will millions of Venezuelans, weaned on telenovelas and Gustavo Cisneros's sensationalistic fare, tune in? What about Latin Americans in other countries?

Venezuelans historically have had long-standing cultural ties to the United States. For example, the country is famous for its American-style beauty pageants. During a trip to Venezuela in the mid-1990s, I found myself stuck in Maracaibo on my way to Mérida. Standing in a yuppie bar in the historic downtown area, I was struck by a peculiar sight: ten adolescent girls posing for a camera. A man was filming them as they leaned over the grille of the balcony in suggestive poses.

I asked the patrons what was happening. They said that the girls were studying to be models. The girls blew kisses at the camera, looking like little Lolitas. I fell into a conversation with the cameraman, who explained that he was from Caracas and shot videos. I was surprised to learn that these girls were not working class, but middle class. Obviously they were not studying to be models out of economic necessity; rather, being a beauty queen was considered a great honor.

Chávez clearly hopes that Venezuelans, and other South Americans will undergo a kind of psychological and spiritual transformation and start to take pride in their own culture. But it is far from clear that Telesur will be a successful vehicle for cultural change. According to Greg Wilpert, Venezuelans are tired of the shrill anti-Chávez media but are also skeptical of public media. "If Telesur offers the original quality programming that its promoters claim it will, then it will be able to cast away its widely-acknowledged reputation for being a vehicle for Chávez-funded propaganda," Wilpert believes.[88]

Commercially, the South American–based Telesur represents a challenge to U.S.- based media conglomerates. Less than a third of TV programming in the region originates in Latin America. A full 70 percent of the programming is imported, with 62 percent coming from the United States.[89] In a sign of the growing information war between the United States and Venezuela, U.S. House Representative Connie Mack, Republican of Florida, gave a feisty speech on the floor of the House shortly before Telesur premiered. "In Hugo Chávez's Venezuela," he thundered, "there is no free press—just state-controlled anti-American propaganda."[90] Telesur, Mack charged, was "patterned after Al Jazeera," and threatened to spread anti-American ideas across Latin America.[91]

Reacting with alarm to developments in South America, Mack successfully pushed through a congressional amendment to the Foreign Relations Reauthorization Bill "to initiate radio and television broadcasts that will provide a consistently accurate, objective, and comprehensive source of news to Venezuela."[92] Under the amendment, the Broadcasting Board of Governors (BBG), a quasi-independent company in charge of spreading Washington's "public diplomacy" broadcasting programs worldwide,[93] will allow the Voice of America and Radio/TV Martí to beam anti-Chávez messages to Venezuela.[94]

According to the Council on Hemispheric Affairs, "Mack's move on behalf of his Miami-Dade county constituents reflects the expanding political clout and fiercely anti- Chávez sentiment of the area's rapidly growing Venezuelan exile community."[95] Curtis Reed, president of the Tampa-based Free Venezuela organization, said that Telesur was going to promote "the revolutions of Chávez and Castro, instigating anti-Americanism."[96] The Mack proposal was not included in the Senate's version of the foreign relations bill, and it is not clear whether the fate of the amendment might be decided in conference committee. If the legislation makes its way past that hurdle, President Bush would have to decide whether to sign off on the measure.[97] The White House did not comment on Mack's proposal.[98]

The Venezuelan Congress reacted to the escalating electronic war by passing a resolution condemning the U.S. House decision. In a typical riposte, Chávez hailed the Mack amendment "a preposterous imperialist idea" and pledged to jam the signal of U.S. broadcasts.[99] "Just like Fidel Castro has been able to neutralize Radio Martí's signal," Chávez said, "we too shall neutralize any signal."[100]

With all of Chávez's initiatives in full swing, the question is: Where is hemispheric integration headed? "The possibility of South American unity," notes political analyst DeLong, "is more imminent today than at any time since Simón Bolívar's original vision of continental solidarity."[101] Michel Alaby, president of the Brazilian Association of Market Integration, a São Paulo lobbying firm, adds: "Energy integration is crucial. The tendency is for South America to become totally integrated within a generation or two."[102] But what kind of integration is South America headed towards? According to DeLong, the region's presidents are striving toward a European Union–type model with all its attendant institutions. Such a model would certainly be more sensitive to the social impact of market policies than the proposed Free Trade Area of the Americas.[103]

In another parallel to the European Union, Chávez has pushed for a new South American currency modeled after the euro, surely an unwelcome development for Washington.[104] In an interview, Chávez remarked, "We can establish 2012 as the target date for Latin America, or at least the Andean Community, to have a common currency." Chávez would like to name the new currency the sucre, "in honour of that great man who was murdered by the oligarchs who betrayed Bolívar."[105] Chávez was referring to Antonio José de Sucre, a superior Venezuelan military commander who enlisted in the wars of independence against Spain in 1811. Sucre fought in decisive campaigns in Ecuador, Peru, and Colombia. With the help of Bolívar, he became the first elected president of Bolivia. He was assassinated while seeking to preserve the unity of Gran Colombia, comprised of Ecuador, Colombia, and Venezuela.[106]

The drive toward regional integration was on display at Puerto Ordaz, Venezuela, in March 2005, where Chávez gathered with other hemispheric leaders. Chávez declared to the world that heads of state need to "accelerate the South American integration project as a geopolitical component because it is the only path that we have: the Latin American Union."[107] He and other leaders reaffirmed their commitment to create the so-called South American Community of Nations, which would merge the two main trading blocs, the Andean Community of Nations and Mercosur.

The two blocs are enormously important, with a combined population of 360 million, a $1.3 trillion gross domestic product and an export market of $181 billion. (Recently, Chávez reaped real benefits from his oil diplomacy when Kirchner supported Venezuela's admission to Mercosur. Kirchner remarked, "For Argentina, it is not only an honor, it is above all a necessity to have Venezuela with us [in Mercosur], so as to deepen the changes that we want to bring about.")[108] In order to facilitate greater trade integration, regional governments have pledged to construct major infrastructure projects—pipelines, highways, railways, and airports. "If these projects are completed," DeLong writes, "they will represent an unprecedented step forward towards the goal of South American unity and economic self-sufficiency."[109]

Certainly the recent moves are hugely significant in an economic sense. But Chávez surely must be pleased about the political overtones as well.

The South American Community of Nations, Chávez believes, must be fundamentally driven by politics and social needs. With the recent political shift in Brazil, Argentina, and Uruguay, governments see greater hemispheric unity as a means to counteract Washington's plans for the region. Simply put, DeLong adds, "The region's center-left governments typically view the FTAA as a possible threat to their fragile economies, environments and workers' rights."[110]

The only risk for Chávez is that even as he forges ahead with his oil deals, he could lose popularity at home. Alfredo Keller, an independent pollster in Caracas, says that Chávez is losing ground. According to national polls carried out in the summer of 2005, 75 percent of Venezuelans disapproved of the favors Chávez showered on other nations. "Venezuelans don't like their resources going to foreigners," Keller says, adding: "At home problems such as cost of living, housing, unemployment, remain unchanged . . . and people are wondering: Whose leader is he?"[111] Chávez, however, is undaunted. "Only united can we be free, that is the great challenge," he has remarked.[112]

CHAPTER NINE
IN THE ANDES, TURNING THE TIDE AGAINST THE UNITED STATES

On my first night in Caracas in 1999, I watched Chávez speak on national television on a small black-and-white television in my hotel room. He was sitting in front of a tall oil painting of Simón Bolívar and constantly referred to the Great Liberator. Chávez's incessant harping on Bolívar struck me as a bit ludicrous. What could be the relevance of Simón Bolívar now in the twenty-first century? U.S. politicians did not seek to identify themselves as "Washingtonians," so why the strong identification with the independence era in Venezuela? Chávez did not stop with his speeches; he went so far as to rename Venezuela the Bolivarian Republic of Venezuela. When I was applying for my Venezuelan visa in New York in 1999, a woman at the consulate confided to me that when Chávez changed the name of her country, it had cost the authorities financially: they had to redo all of the official stationery.

Although Chávez's strong personal affinity with Bolívar might seem anachronistic, it is understandable in light of the country's history. During the Bolivarian era, Venezuela exerted great leverage on the international stage. In 1819, Venezuela achieved independence from Spain and joined with its neighbors Colombia, Ecuador, and Panama to form the new Gran Colombia federation. The architect largely responsible for this accomplishment, Simón Bolívar, saw regional unification as a way of countering the emerging power of the United States.[1] Bolívar was also responsible for liberating the Andean nations of Peru and Bolivia from the Spanish yoke.[2] Unfortunately for the Great Liberator, Gran Colombia proved ephemeral, and the new country was dissolved in 1830 following the secession of Venezuela and Ecuador.[3] Since the passing of Bolívar, no Venezuelan leader, military or civilian, has lived up to his cult status.

Today, Hugo Chávez seeks to revive the Bolívarian dream by cultivating solidarity within the Andean region, a troubled area prone to political instability, violence, and ethnic tensions. In an interview, he remarked: "What we propose is to recapture the original idea, under which our republic was founded—Simón Bolívar's idea of a multipolar international system . . . Bolívar proposed Great Colombia, the integration of what is presently Venezuela, Colombia, Ecuador, Peru, Bolivia and Panama into one great republic. Bolívar had a multipolar vision of the world. We do not want a unipolar or bipolar world."[4]

For Bolívar, one of the most vexing problems was how to liberate indigenous peoples from centuries of economic and social oppression. Two hundred years later, Indians still are the poorest members of society and continue to suffer racism and exclusion at the hands of affluent whites. The United States has exacerbated these long- standing problems by pushing for its own agenda within the region, an agenda that includes fighting the drug war, which has led to a growing militarization in the Andes, and pressing for neoliberal orthodoxy. These policies have hit indigenous peoples especially hard. Now, however, Indians have risen up, demanding political and social equality. Indigenous peoples have grown increasingly restive, mobilizing against the Washington Consensus and the U.S.-fueled drug war.

For the White House, the political stakes were high. According to indigenous activists, Washington has sought to portray Indians as a destabilizing force. In the post- 9/11 world, the United States has equated indigenous movements with terrorism. In a December 2004, report issued by the U.S. National Intelligence Council entitled "Global Trends 2020—Mapping the Global Future," the government depicts both indigenous activism and Islamic radicalism as threats to U.S. national security. The National Intelligence Council works with the CIA and other government agencies. Its report, charge indigenous leaders, is "a veritable x-ray" of potential "counterinsurgency scenarios" from now until the year 2020.

Indeed, Washington views the Andean region as the "hottest" area in Latin America, because of emerging indigenous movements in Bolivia and Ecuador. "It's true that indigenous peoples are a threat, from the point of view of the political and economic powers-that-be," said Ricardo Díaz, an indigenous Bolivian legislator, "but we aren't, because our struggle is open, legal and legitimate." The National Intelligence Council report, adds anthropologist Pedro Ciciliano of the National Autonomous University of Mexico, is "exaggerated and fraught with errors typical of U.S. intelligence based on biased information." Ciciliano adds, "Indigenous people can be considered a threat, because they are poor and are pressing for their rights, but they don't represent a terrorist threat."[5]

These claims notwithstanding, the United States seems intent on turning back the course of indigenous movements in the Andean region. In Venezuela, Chávez is acutely aware of the potency of indigenous struggle and has done much to cultivate ties with the Indians. With unrest heating up across the region, Chávez's moves will certainly draw attention from Washington policymakers in future.

It is hardly surprising that Chávez would take up the cause of the region's indigenous peoples. He himself was born in the Venezuelan llano, and has a provincial accent. The area has had a history of racial conflict going back centuries. During the Spanish colonial period, some rebellious black slaves who managed to escape from plantations and haciendas fled to the llano and became a problem for the authorities. Slaves started to live in *cumbes* (escaped communities where collective forms of work were practiced). The blacks mixed with the Indian population and carried out daring raids on cattle ranches.[6] Interracial mixing alarmed the white elite in Venezuela: escaped slaves, they feared, might have a radicalizing effect on the Indian population. Accordingly, in 1785, the authorities drafted laws prohibiting blacks from living with Indians "because they only corrupt them with the bad customs which they generally acquire in their breeding and they sow discord among the same Indians."[7]

Physically, Hugo Chávez is a *pardo*, a term used in the colonial period to denote someone of mixed racial roots.[8] "Chávez's features," writes a magazine columnist, "are a dark-copper color and as thick as clay; he has protruding, sensuous lips and deep-set eyes under a heavy brow. His hair is black and kinky. He is a burly man of medium height, with a long, hatchet-shaped nose and a massive chin and jaw."[9] In an interview, Chávez remarked that when he first applied to the military academy, he had an afro. From an ethnoracial standpoint, Chávez is similar to many of his fellow Venezuelans. Indeed, today 67 percent of the population is mestizo, 10 percent are black, and 23 percent are white.

Chávez has not sought to distance himself from his ethnic heritage. "My Indian roots are from my father's side," he remarked. "He [my father] is mixed Indian and black, which makes me very proud." Chávez also has boasted of his grandmother, whom he says was a Pumé Indian. While on duty with the military, he toured the country and became aware of economic exploitation and racial discrimination. In 1998, while campaigning for president, Chávez made a commitment to champion the rights of Venezuela's half-million indigenous peoples. After he was elected, he squarely addressed the issue of indigenous rights by addressing it on his weekly call-in program, *Aló, Presidente.*[10]

Chávez came to power just as Venezuela's indigenous peoples were clamoring for their rights. The country has a small but diverse indigenous population, concentrated far from Caracas on Venezuela's borders with Guyana, Brazil, and Colombia. Indians number just 1.5 percent of the country's 23 million people and are divided into 28 different ethnic groups. The most substantial group is the Wayúu; 200,000 reside in Zulia on the Colombian border. I occasionally saw some of the dirt poor Indians selling their wares on the streets of Maracaibo. Like Chávez himself, Venezuelan Indians were radicalized by the 1989 caracazo riots against the International Monetary Fund neoliberal programs and founded their own organization, the Venezuelan National Indian Council.[11] Once Chávez became president, three longtime indigenous activists were elected to the Venezuelan National Assembly, and prominent native leaders currently hold positions in government.

Chávez made good on his promises by working to codify Indian rights in the new 1999 constitution. Article 9 proclaims that while Spanish is the official language of Venezuela, "Indigenous languages are also for official use for Indigenous peoples and must be respected throughout the Republic's territory for being part of the nation's and humanity's patrimonial culture." In chapter eight of the constitution, the state recognizes social, political, and economic organization within indigenous communities, in addition to their cultures, languages, rights, and lands. In a critical provision, the government also recognizes land rights as collective, inalienable, and nontransferable. Later articles declare the government's pledge not to engage in extraction of natural resources without prior consultation with indigenous groups. In a novel move, Chávez has had the constitution translated into all of Venezuela's languages.[12]

Chávez's critics claim that the Venezuelan president is trying to radicalize the country's indigenous peoples by feeding them Cuban propaganda—

hardly welcome news for Washington. In the remote state of Amazonas, Chávez has pushed his so-called Mission Robinson program, which teaches indigenous peoples how to read and write in Spanish. The program is named after Simón Rodríguez, Simón Bolívar's tutor, who traveled under the pseudonym Samuel Robinson while living in exile. Until Chávez came to power, Puinave Indians inhabiting the island of Pedro Camejo on the Orinoco River had difficulty communicating with the outside world. In Puerto Ayacucho, the nearest city which is a two-hour drive or three-day walk beyond the Indians' canoe landing, natives found it difficult to ask for assistance or healthcare.[13]

But now, a literacy instructor fires up a generator that powers a TV, videocassette recorder, and videotapes provided by communist Cuba. The Spanish-language cassettes begin with a slogan from José Martí, Cuba's liberation hero: "To be cultured is to be free."[14] Cuba's educational assistance forms part of a larger program that provides 12,000 volunteer teachers, doctors, and trainers (who instruct "facilitators" on how to provide literacy instruction) to Venezuela, in part to compensate Chávez for discounted oil sales. Mission Robinson is modeled loosely after Cuba's literacy brigades, which swept through the island nation in 1961 after Castro came to power. Chávez's critics say he is playing politics and trying to win over Venezuela's indigenous peoples, who traditionally were not involved in national politics. Officials involved in Mission Robinson deny that the Cuban-made presentations are designed to win over Venezuelans to the virtues of a workers' state.[15]

What does Chávez's promotion of indigenous rights mean for the United States? The Venezuelan leader's domestic moves seem to form part of a larger regional strategy. Chávez hopes that he can become a spokesman for indigenous peoples across South America, who are in open revolt against U.S. policies. In neighboring Colombia, the conflict between the nation's Indians and the U.S.-supported government has been particularly acute. The 90 indigenous groups in Colombia make up just a tiny fraction of the population: 2 percent of 44 million people.[16] However, they have suffered disproportionately. Victimized at the hands of the military as well as local landowners, they have protested growing U.S. involvement in their country and escalating militarization. Surveying the troubled landscape in Colombia, Chávez sensed political possibility.

In the mid-1990s, I was in the Colombian capital of Bogotá teaching English and doing translation work. I had done some reporting for a local radio station in New York about issues affecting the Latino community and wanted to write some stories about social conditions in Colombia. I was renting an apartment in La Candelaria, a colonial neighborhood in downtown Bogotá where Bolívar himself had once resided. Although I rather fancied the bohemian area, some Bogotanos I met were shocked that I dared to live in the neighborhood. They advised me to exercise caution.

I was careful not to stay out too late at night, but at one point I found myself in a dodgy situation. As I got off a bus early on New Year's Day, an adolescent boy approached me on a deserted street. His hair was matted and he had a dirty gray blanket slung over his shoulders. I quickly recognized him as one of the neighborhood's *gamines* (homeless street urchins). The boys routinely stopped pedestrians asking for change. I had always been a bit wary of the gamines and tended to avoid them. Victimized and abandoned by society, the boys often turned to *bazuco*, the highly addictive residue left from the production of cocaine.[17]

Before I could react, the boy darted in front of me, demanding money. I emptied my pockets and handed him the coins, but he would not believe that I had given him all my spare cash. He produced a knife and started coming at me. Just when I thought my luck had run out, a group of revelers exited a nearby building. Seeing what was going on, they cried out at the boy to stop. The boy ran off.

Few people in La Candelaria had much sympathy for the gamines, viewing the boys instead as a public menace. After my narrow escape, I had to agree. I did not, however, condone the campaign of "social cleansing" aimed at eliminating the gamines from the city streets. Although you seldom read about it in Colombia's conservative daily newspapers, the campaign against street children was escalating. I spoke about the situation with Tom Quinn, the *Time* correspondent in Bogotá and editor of the *Colombian Post*, an English-language newspaper. A dashing American with a long gray mustache, Tom was a long time expatriate. He explained that prominent business owners in the downtown business district disliked the gamines and hired policemen to go out and "eliminate"—meaning kill—them. The phenomenon was referred to as "social cleansing," the "serial killing of members of a social group in order to 'clean out' or 'impose order' on a criminal or unsightly populace."[18]

Through my own readings and conversations with Colombians I had met, I learned that social cleansing against the gamines was only one part of a larger violent picture. The country was in the midst of an intractable war with the Marxist Fuerzas Armadas Revolucionarias de Colombia (FARC) guerrillas, but the government used the conflict as a justification to go after anyone who disturbed the social order. The country was a human rights nightmare, with the armed forces carrying out extrajudicial killings and assassinations. The elite was intent on pursuing Washington's neoliberal program, so in vogue during the 1990s. Many of the poor and disadvantaged turned to drug cultivation. The United States, under the Clinton administration, provided millions of dollars in military aid to fight drug trafficking. The army and its right-wing paramilitary allies targeted the FARC, labor leaders, human rights activists, and indigenous activists.

Tom was critical of the U.S. drug war and foreign journalists in Colombia who sought to justify U.S. foreign policy. Something of a swashbuckling adventurer, he had bought a farm in the rural state of Cauca, where he had lived for many years. He spoke to me of the plight of the Nasa Indians, who were in a bitter struggle with a multinational timber corporation, Cartón de Colombia. Through Tom, I was able to make contact with an agronomist based in Cali who seemed interested in having me write an article about the Nasa. Perhaps somewhat foolheartedly, I agreed and took the long bus ride down from the mountains to Cauca.

Cauca is a highly strategic corridor located in southwestern Colombia. The Pan- American Highway passes through the department, facilitating vital commerce and transfer of goods. In Cauca's northern section, which is mountainous and neglected by the authorities, the FARC have set up a stronghold. In the valleys and cities, powerful movers and shakers—sugar barons, drug lords, and ranchers—wield economic power. These groups forge alliances with multinational capital with the hope of setting up megaprojects to exploit the area's natural resources.[19] Meanwhile, as the group Amazon Watch explains, during the 1990s "intensive competition for land turned resentful eyes towards the indigenous communal land base."[20]

There are 32 departments or states in Colombia, each one electing its own governor.[21] The department of Cauca has one of the highest concentrations of Indians in Colombia, comprised of Nasa, Yanagona, Coconuco, and Guambiano peoples.[22] The Nasa number some 200,000 people and as such, they are one of the largest of the country's 90 indigenous groups.[23] There, the Indians have had to live in a constant state of fear and unease. Landowners often fund paramilitary terror campaigns to forcibly displace them.[24] According to the Cauca Regional Indian Council, the 270,000 local

Indians occupy only 18 percent of the department's 7.5 million acres. The Indians claim large landowners kicked them off the best land long ago and they have been left with the poorest-quality farms.[25] And as mentioned, indigenous peoples have had to put up with long-standing racism. The capital of Cauca, the quaint colonial town of Popayán, has long been a bastion of reactionary sentiment. According to Bill Weinberg, a long-time journalist who has written on Colombia, for many years Indians were prevented from even crossing a colonial-era bridge leading to the town center. The name of the structure: the Bridge of Humility.[26]

The Cali agronomist drove me into the hills beyond the city. We then said goodbye and he left me in the mountains. In the Indian village of La Paila, I met Luis Labio, a Nasa Indian and a local member of the municipal council. La Paila was full of rudimentary houses without electricity. The community was locked in a protracted struggle with Cartón de Colombia, which had resettled a group of subcontracted peasants on lands claimed by the Indians. The farmers, a mixture of mestizos but also additional Nasa Indians, were planting reforested pine for the company. As I later learned, many of the workers had formerly cultivated coca. Working for the company, the subcontracted workers would at least now be able to avoid any conflict with the law. The Nasa who were not working for Cartón in the new pine company meanwhile claimed legal right to the lands. "You have to understand," Labio told me, "that we were the first ones here." He explained the violence-prone history of the area to me as we hiked up and down steep mountain slopes. Although Labio was older than I, I could not keep up the pace and frequently had to stop to catch my breath.

Labio had personally known great hardship and loss. His uncle Luciano had been in the vanguard of the Nasa land struggles, helping to occupy the timber company's lands. In the early 1980s, the FARC appeared in the area and tried to recruit the Nasa to fight against Cartón de Colombia. When the Nasa refused to join, tensions began to mount. One day a group of men in uniforms—Labio believes it was the FARC—arrived in La Paila and murdered Luciano and his wife. The trouble did not end there. On another occasion Labio's cousin Miguel was driving in his truck when armed men stopped him, according to witnesses at a military checkpoint. Miguel's body was later found dumped nearby. Because the body was dressed in military fatigues, the army claimed Miguel was a guerrilla who was killed in combat. Labio told me that he also feared for his life. "I've been threatened constantly," he told me.[27] It is a wonder that I did not come to harm at La Paila.

Young and naïve, I might have been targeted by either the army or the guerrillas. Fortunately, I was able to make my way back to Cali; the agronomist admitted that he never slept overnight at La Paila.

I always wondered what happened to Luis Labio. After my article was published, I lost track of the Indians' struggle and eventually returned to New York. I was interested to learn later that the Nasa were in the forefront of social struggle in Colombia, staging numerous occupations of property belonging to large landholders, claiming the lands formed part of their ancestral homelands. However, the Nasa paid a high price for their militancy; top leaders were murdered by both the FARC and the Colombian army.[28] The Nasa were fast gaining international recognition and becoming a potent force. But where could they turn for inspiration? Within the Andean region, Hugo Chávez was fast garnering a reputation as a defender of indigenous rights; he had become a potent psychological symbol for the Nasa and others.

Barranco Yopal is a remote village located some 300 miles south of Caracas in the state of Apure.[29] For Chávez, Barranco Yopal carries personal meaning. He used to visit the town in his youth. In an interview with Marta Harnecker, he explained:

> I used to go to Barranco Yopal and bring cans and sticks to the Indians, because they made houses with those materials to spend the winter season there, but in the summer they used to go away. They were nomads: hunters and gatherers, as they were 500 years ago. I saw Indian women giving birth there . . . The majority of those babies died of malaria, tuberculosis, of any type of illness. They [the Indians] used to spend the time drunk in town. The Indian women used to prostitute themselves, many times they were raped. They were ghosts, disrespected by the majority of the population. They used to steal to eat. They didn't have any conception of private property: for them it wasn't robbery to go into an area and grab a pig to eat it if they were hungry.[30]

Chávez returned to Barranco Yopal in October 2005, where he handed over indigenous land titles, boat motors, and vehicles.[31] In all, Chávez distributed 1.65 million acres to indigenous communities in the states of Apure, Anzoátegui, Delta Amacuro, and Sucre. The move forms part of the so-called Mission Guaicaipuro, which will provide land titles to all of Venezuela's 28 indigenous peoples. By the end of 2006, Chávez's Mission Guaicaipuro plans to award land titles to 15 more indigenous groups. In

Barranco Yopal, Chávez granted titles recognizing collective ownership of ancestral lands to the Cuiba, Yuraruro, Warao, and Kariña tribes. It was in fact the second such land transfer, the first having been decreed in August 2005, when Chávez awarded communal lands during the sixteenth World Festival of Students and Youth in Caracas. At the ceremony, he handed out 313,824 acres to six Kariña indigenous communities living in the states of Monagas and Anzoátegui.[32]

Some Indians at Barranco Yopal felt that the government still needed to provide more assistance. "We want the government to help us with hunger, with credit," remarked Pedro Méndez, a Yuraruro Indian. He said that his community had requested an electrical generator and loans to help plant more crops. Others, such as Librado Moraleda, were more positive. A 52-year-old Warao Indian from a remote village in the Orinoco River delta, Moraleda was present for Chávez's ceremony in Barranco Yopal. "Previously," he declared, "the indigenous people of Venezuela were removed from our lands. This is historic. It is a joyful day." Moraleda received a land title and a government pledge of $27,000 to construct homes as well as plant cassava and plantains.[33]

Chávez was rapidly becoming a dangerous symbol for indigenous rights in the region. His approach to land disputes certainly provided a stark contrast to Colombia. In Bogotá, Colombia's new leader and close U.S. ally Álvaro Uribe watched developments warily.

I learned of Álvaro Uribe while studying in Oxford. Just as I arrived at the university, the Colombian politician was leaving. He had been lecturing at St. Antony's College, where I was also affiliated.[34] From my colleagues at the Latin American Centre, I heard that Uribe had been a controversial figure on campus. Apparently, some activists had come up from London to protest Uribe's alleged ties to right-wing paramilitaries. Unfortunately, they had shown up on the wrong day and Uribe was not in class. I regret not having had the opportunity to study with the man. I would have liked to ask him about his alleged relationship with Pablo Escobar, the head of the Medellín cartel.

In terms of his personal background, Álvaro Uribe provides a stark contrast to his Venezuelan counterpart Hugo Chávez. One of five children, Uribe, who is white, was born in 1952.[35] Unlike the colorful Chávez, Uribe has been described as bookish and lacking a sense of humor.[36] His father, a wealthy cattle rancher, was an important figure in the town of Salgar, in the southwestern part of Antioquia department. Antioquia is the richest, most religious, and most conservative province in the country.[37] Medellín, located 145 miles northwest of Bogotá, is the capital of Antioquia department. It was there that Uribe would later make his political career.[38] In the 1970s, Uribe studied political science at Medellín's University of Antioquia.[39] A large city of around 3 million, Medellín nevertheless preserves a kind of rural feel.[40] I was there for two days and was struck by the verdant vegetation that surrounded the metropolitan center. Unlike Bogotá, Medellín seems much more modern, efficient, and clean. Despite the city's dangerous reputation, I found it to be very pleasant. On the other hand, it is certainly true that by the 1980s Medellín had become unbelievably brutal. The city became home to a violent drug cartel, and the murder rate was one of the world's highest.[41]

Uribe started to embark on his political career just as the drug trade was peaking. In 1976, he became the head of the Real Estate Office of the Public Works Department of Medellín.[42] He then became Director of Civil Aviation, where he was accused of granting licenses to pilots accused of shipping cocaine. Uribe, who was later cleared of the charges, has vehemently denied any wrongdoing.[43] From there, he became mayor of Medellín and was elected in 1982.[44] In his capacity as mayor, however, Uribe allegedly accepted money from Pablo Escobar, a notorious drug kingpin, for two urban regeneration schemes.[45] At about the same time, Uribe experienced personal tragedy; his father was gunned down by FARC guerrillas on the Uribe ranch.[46] According to a declassified report written by the U.S. Defense Intelligence Agency, Uribe's father was killed because of his ties to the drug business.[47]

The death of his father did not slow Uribe down, and the ambitious young man doggedly moved ahead with his political career, serving two terms as a senator, from 1986 to 1994.[48] Allegations about ties to drug trafficking would continue to dog Uribe, however. According to the same report by the Defense Intelligence Agency, Uribe was "dedicated to collaboration with the Medellín cartel at high government levels." The report, written in 1991, goes on to say that Uribe was a "close personal friend" of Pablo Escobar. When the report, which was obtained under the Freedom of Information Act, was made public in 2004, Uribe's spokesman dismissed the findings and top U.S. officials warned that the report might be inaccurate.[49]

Despite persistent allegations about his ties to drug traffickers, Uribe was successful at building his political career. In the early 1990s he went to

Harvard and got a degree in business administration.[50] In 1995, he became governor of Antioquia, where he pushed the controversial CONVIVIR (which can roughly be translated, ironically, as "getting along") program, a network of rural security cooperatives. According to the BBC correspondent in Colombia, some of the cooperatives became fronts for paramilitaries.[51] In 1998, Uribe was awarded a Simón Bolívar Fellowship to teach at Oxford University. In 2002 he returned to his troubled country hoping to become the next president. Uribe, "a diminutive bespectacled technocrat, who looks more at home behind a lectern than as a commander in chief," nevertheless was elected.[52] According to Justin Podur, a writer who has authored many articles on Colombia, the Antioquia native was successful "because a hard core of 5.8 million voters in a population of about 44 million believed his promise that he would eradicate the guerillas by escalating the civil war in the country."[53]

What would the presidential victory of one of Colombia's white elite landholders mean for the Nasa and their struggle for justice in Cauca? The signs did not look promising for the Indians. Showing his contempt for the Nasa, Uribe disbanded the Agrarian Reform Institute,[54] replacing it with an institute for rural development with miniscule budget. The minister of Agriculture, who was himself a businessman, remarked, "no more priming the pump of agrarian reform."[55] During an indigenous march and protest in 2004, Uribe traveled personally to Popayán to meet with Indian leaders. There he tried to dissuade the Indians from mobilizing. "We cannot impede protests," he said, "but we can preserve the rights of all citizens." Uribe said he would use public force to break up any blockades. In a move that surely had a chilling effect on the Indians, Uribe warned protesters that armed groups may have infiltrated the march.[56]

Yet the Indians were not intimidated. In fact, the Nasa became more politicized and began to take on issues of larger hemispheric importance. Indigenous leaders in Cauca were particularly concerned about the rush to privatize natural resources. For example, in 1999, the Colombian state privatized a local dam. The Nasa feared that under the Free Trade Area of the Americas (FTAA), water would be diverted from indigenous lands to service powerful agribusiness interests in the valley below. One Nasa leader commented, "The development of savage capitalism, in which the ends justify the means—this we don't want. We don't want destructive development, as in the U.S. We want development that comes from the base and represents our own traditions. We don't hold the land in a capitalist sense. We hold it in the spirit that we are a part of it."[57] For years, the Nasa have sought to implement their own alternative indigenous-based development proposal, based on communal land ownership, bilingual education, and healthcare rooted in traditional medicine.[58]

Such moves were putting the Nasa more squarely in Chávez's corner, to the detriment of the United States. As early as October 2002, facing an imminent oil lockout, Chávez recognized the political importance of the indigenous question and organized the First International Meeting of Resistance and Solidarity with Indigenous Peoples and Campesinos. The changes taking place in Venezuela, Chávez proclaimed, were the first sign that the peoples of Latin America were uniting against the neoliberal order.[59] The following year in Caracas, Chávez followed up his indigenous bridge building with his so-called Congreso Bolivariano de los Pueblos (Bolivarian Congress of Peoples). The meeting was held at Chávez's newly-founded Bolivarian University in Caracas.[60] According to the organization's Web site, the congress was born out of a desire to represent "popular, democratic and patriotic forces" in Latin America so as to foster integration and unity. The congress called on not only indigenous peoples, but campesinos, workers, women's groups, and others to participate.

I was struck by the tone of the Web site. "We must unify or drown," reads one passage. "No country," it continues, "can save itself on its own." Lack of unity, reads one manifesto, has "brought us to misery, backwardness, and dependency." What kind of unity does the congress have in mind? "We are an organization of peoples," reads the site. Fundamentally, organizers do not seek a unity based on economists, academics, or legislators. In a warning sign to George Bush, the organizers state, with a rhetorical flourish, "Who will stop the offensive of the FTAA if not the peoples of Latin America? Who will defend our natural resources from the rapacious foreigner if not our own organized peoples?" The FTAA, which seeks to "annex" Latin America, is to be replaced by an alternative proposal: integration with sovereignty and development like that pushed for by Chávez under the ALBA. To that end, the congress will seek to build consciousness in Latin America about the FTAA and its long-term implications for the region and to foster cooperation against "common enemies." Fundamentally, Latin American countries needed to unite so as to stop paying "extortionist" external debt.

The congress also seeks to practice "participatory" democracy, as demonstrated in Venezuela, and every April 13 the organization calls for a

celebration throughout Latin America of the "Day of Participatory and Pro-
tagonist Participatory Democracy," in honor of the civilian-military alliance
that topped the Carmona regime in 2002. The congress, however, does not
seek to become a political party; rather, the idea is to form "a tool of struggle" that shall foster a new identity based on historical roots, culture, and "an
authentic Bolivarian doctrine of liberation."[61] Is the congress some kind of
cynical instrument used by Chávez to advance his profile internationally and
to gain control over hemispheric politics? According to the congress's Web
site, the initial headquarters of the organization will be located in Caracas.[62]
Political analyst Alberto Garrido says the congress cannot be reduced to the
influence of any one person. Although Chávez has played an important role,
the congress is comprised of different groups that have vastly distinct histo-
ries and trajectories.[63] Although the congress is ideologically inchoate, what
seems to unite it is participants' hostility to the Washington Consensus.

Significantly, at the second Bolivarian Congress in 2004, attended by
indigenous leaders from Colombia, organizers agreed to struggle not only
against the FTAA but also against the "militaristic and interventionist policies of the Bush administration" and the U.S. military presence in Colombia.[64] Such rhetoric surely must have rung alarms in Washington. One of
the linchpins of U.S. policy in the Andean region has been the war on drugs,
fought with massive amounts of American military aid. Would Chávez's efforts at indigenous diplomacy threaten that effort? For many indigenous
groups in Colombia, the prospect was encouraging.

At the heart of the U.S. drug effort in the Andes is the so-called Plan
Colombia. Indigenous peoples in Cauca have come out forcefully against
the plan, a $1.3 billion U.S. aid package principally aimed at training and
equipping the Colombian army.[65] In 1999, some 13 million U.S. drug users
spent about $67 billion on illicit drugs.[66] According to a Washington group
specializing in drug policy, Colombia is responsible for almost 90 percent of
the world's cocaine.[67] Throughout the 1990s, the United States put a heavy
emphasis on interdiction as a key component in the overall war on drugs.[68]
According to Amazon Watch, although Colombian authorities "originally
pitched Plan Colombia as an effort to strengthen the peace process and
boost economic development, with U.S. aid, the Plan became a predomi-
nantly military initiative to eradicate drug trafficking."[69]

A shortsighted policy? Critics say yes. In recent years coffee prices have
plummeted, obliging farmers to plant coca in rural areas hit hard by unem-

ployment.[70] The United States has not acted to stamp out this social crisis in the Colombian countryside. Under the 1999 Alianza Act, the U.S. Senate provided a three-year, $1.6 billion emergency aid package for Colombia. But, 90 percent of the money went to the military and police. Social programs and economic development received less than 10 percent of the funds. According to the Center for Defense Information, converting Colombia's coca and poppy fields to other cash crops would cost $4 billion. Only $50 million was provided for crop substitution over three years under the act.[71]

According to reports, Plan Colombia has had a dire social effect on the country. Since its implementation, paramilitary groups allegedly tied to the state have committed an increasing number of massacres of the civilian population, including indigenous activists. Additionally, under Plan Colombia the authorities initiated a controversial program of aerial fumigation of illegal coca and poppy crops. Herbicide spraying has damaged the ecology, destroyed food crops, and forced farmers to flee the land.[72]

Colombia's escalating drug war has fallen disproportionately on the nation's indigenous peoples.[73] For thousands of years indigenous peoples throughout the Andean region have cultivated the sacred plant of coca for ritual and medicinal purposes. In fact, mass production of coca and drug abuse run against traditional indigenous beliefs. However, economic hardship has pushed many Indians into cultivating coca leaf for commercial purposes.[74] In the department of Putumayo, home to the Nasa as well as other Indian groups, an observer reported that spraying had devastated subsistence farms and gardens and polluted rivers.[75]

The U.S. drug strategy has even fallen under harsh criticism by politicians in Washington. According to Democratic senator Patrick Leahy, fumigation in Colombia has not led to any fall in U.S. demand.[76] Undeterred, George Bush has persevered. During a visit to the coastal Colombian city of Cartagena, Bush said he would press lawmakers to continue military aid to Colombia in the future, remarking "My nation will continue to help Colombia prevail in this vital struggle."[77]

What logical reason can there be for the ongoing drug war in Colombia? Indigenous leaders suggest an insidious rationale. About one-quarter of Colombian territory is legally recognized as belonging to Indians. Some of the nation's most important natural resources lie on indigenous territory, including significant quantities of oil. Under the Colombian constitution, the Indians have the right to control these natural resources. "Indigenous land rights and decision-making authority regarding natural resources threaten access to resources, which is fundamental to multinational mining and energy corporations," explains Al Gedicks, professor of sociology at the University of Wisconsin-La Crosse and author of the book *Resource Rebels: Native Challenges to Mining and Oil Corporations.*[78] U.S. oil companies, like the Los Angeles-based Occidental, have supported Plan Colombia and lobbied President Bush to protect oil installations. According to Amazon Watch, in a gross misstatement, an Occidental representative testified that the Colombian military was "vastly under-armed."[79]

Occidental relies heavily on the Colombian armed forces for protection. In 2001, soldiers occupied lands belonging to the U'wa Indians, who were struggling against the encroachment of the oil giant in northeastern Colombia. A violent police crackdown left three Indian children dead. Meanwhile, paramilitaries began to surround U'wa lands and dislodged 400 indigenous people from the Caño Limón pipeline region of Norte de Santander.[80] Word of the U'wa struggle attracted support from Hollywood celebrities, including Martin Sheen, Susan Sarandon, and Pierce Brosnan.[81] On the other side of the fence has been President Bush, who recently requested $98 million to protect the pipeline. One report has noted, "The growing strategic importance of Colombian oil for the Bush administration is likely to place indigenous peoples living on oil-rich lands in further danger of abuses and displacement."[82] Critics have noted that Plan Colombia has been executed unevenly inside of Colombia. Much effort has been invested in stamping out coca production in Putumayo, a FARC stronghold. Needless to say, the guerrillas have steadfastly opposed neoliberal reforms promoted by the likes of Uribe. Although the FARC tax the coca farmers, the guerrillas call for development plans that would allow peasants to cultivate alternative crops.[83] Moreover, the FARC has carried out agrarian reform programs in Putumayo.[84] Could the U.S.-fueled drug war be an effort to eliminate FARC strongholds populated by native populations? "Much of the $1.8 billion worth of U.S. military aid since 2000," notes one report, "has provided for the training, weapons and attack helicopters for the army's anti-drug battalions operating in this Amazon jungle area on the frontier with Ecuador."[85]

Even as the U.S. and Colombian army target Putumayo, they ignore other key drug-producing areas of the country. In northern Colombia, right-wing paramilitary leaders such as Carlos Castaño have held sway. Castaño announced on national TV that the drug trade provided 70 percent of the funding for the United Self Defense Forces of Colombia, a loose coalition of paramilitary factions. The glaring inconsistency between the government's handling of Putumayo, on one hand, and northern Colombia, on the other, is not lost on indigenous leaders. From their perspective, "the hidden agenda behind the drug war is the elimination of obstacles to massive U.S. and international investment in mega-projects including mines, dams, roads and canals that will allow the efficient exploitation of Colombia's rich natural resources as envisioned in the Free Trade Area of the Americas."[86] Recently, the Bush administration seemed to drop the pretense that Plan Colombia was designed to fight drug trafficking. In a post-9/11 $28.9 billion supplemental antiterrorism package, the United States allowed military aid to be used against the State Department's list of terrorist organizations, including the FARC and right-wing paramilitaries. The only problem was that Uribe was not fighting the paramilitaries at all; instead he has sought to negotiate with them while rebuffing talks with the guerrillas. Even worse, claim human rights advocates, the military has collaborated with the paramilitaries. The Colombian government denies the charges.[87]

What is the connection between the U.S.-funded drug war in the Andes and Hugo Chávez? Washington is concerned about keeping Venezuela in its corner on the fight on drugs. Although Venezuela is not a big drug producer, according to one report up to 30 percent of Colombian cocaine gets transshipped through the country.[88] In recent years, Chávez has taken measures that challenge Washington's efforts in the region. In the process, he has increased his visibility among indigenous peoples. Chávez has criticized Plan Colombia for promoting a growing militarization of the region that threatens to spill over the Venezuelan border.[89] He also rails against Washington's aerial fumigations of coca in Colombia.[90] Venezuelan vice president José Vicente Rangel said that Plan Colombia would create more displaced persons inside Colombia that could destabilize the 1,379 mile-long border.[91] In a further inflammatory move designed to irk Washington, Chávez prohibited U.S. overflights of Venezuelan airspace to combat the drug war.[92] Chávez also ordered government officials to cease cooperation with the U.S. Drug Enforcement Agency, accusing it of drug running and espionage.[93]

Stung, President Bush took Venezuela off his list of allies in the war on drugs, claiming that Chávez had not done enough to cooperate with joint narcotics efforts. John Walters, the U.S. drug czar, remarked that in the past

Venezuela had cooperated with American efforts, but that Chávez "no longer wants a productive relationship." To make matters worse, the White House said Venezuela "failed demonstrably" to halt the flow through Venezuela of 150 tons of cocaine and increasing amounts of heroin, largely coming from neighboring Colombia and headed for American streets. The United States also accused Venezuela of not eliminating coca and poppy fields along the Colombian border and supporting the FARC by allowing the guerrillas sanctuary and providing weapons.[94]

Washington also charged that Chávez failed to address corruption within the military ranks and law enforcement. In a rapidly deteriorating diplomatic spat between the two countries, Venezuelan officials said the Chávez government was doing its utmost to stem the flow of drugs. During the first eight months of 2005, the regime claims to have seized a record of 18.7 tons of cocaine, compared to 19.6 tons total in 2004. By attacking the Chávez government over the drug issue, Venezuelan officials argued, Washington was simply acting for political motives.[95]

If political developments in Colombia start to shift, Chávez could emerge as a very powerful leader within the Andean region. Given his well-known position on the Free Trade Area of the Americas and his moves to thwart the U.S.-led drug war, he is well placed to become an important role model for Colombia's indigenous peoples. But how likely is political change to occur in Colombia? Again, once more it is indigenous peoples, and specifically the Nasa, who have been in the vanguard of the struggle against President Uribe. For the past four years, the Indians have stood out as a peaceful beacon in an otherwise horrifying political environment.

With their stern-faced, unarmed Indigenous Guards—a force of 7,000 men and women—the Nasa have driven out rebels and soldiers alike from their homelands in Cauca. According to the *New York Times*, the Nasa courageously confront all outside armed forces with ceremonial three-foot batons decorated with green and red tassels, the colors of the Nasa flag. The Nasa have gained attention within Colombia, but their struggle has earned them acclaim in the United Nations.[96] "We are not a threat to the world, or to the United States," said one indigenous activist from Cauca. "On the contrary, we hold out a hope, an alternative for humanity."[97]

Recently 2,000 Nasa invaded 19 farms in Cauca with a combined area of 10,000 acres. The Indians say the land, owned by absentee landlords, was promised to them by the government decades ago. Initially the police tried to expel the Nasa with batons and tear gas. The Indians fought back with sticks, stones, and slingshots, surprising many Colombians who were more accustomed to seeing the Nasa as passive victims. Eventually, the police gave up trying to dislodge the militants. "We'll resist as long as necessary," one of the Indians remarked. "Our objective is the land, and until we get it, we're not moving from here, even if it costs us our lives."[98]

In a trend that alarms Washington, indigenous peoples have been successful at building bridges with other social actors in Colombia. In 2005, they carried out a protest march in regional capitals in opposition to Uribe's plans to carry out a free trade treaty with the United States, Peru, and Ecuador. The Indians were joined by labor unions, students, and others in a massive 24-hour general strike.[99] According to investigative journalist Garry Leech, Uribe has willingly worked with the International Monetary Fund to establish economic policy, and Colombia has become "the latest poster child for neoliberalism."[100] The mobilization succeeded in shutting down the capital of Bogotá. "Uribe, paramilitary, the people are pissed off," chanted the protesters.[101]

Will popular forces be able to translate growing mobilization on the ground into concrete political gains? "Until recently," writes David Coddon of the Center for International Policy, "few even bothered to ask this question."[102] With opinion polls showing Uribe maintaining a 70 percent approval rating, the Nasa's prospects looked dim indeed.[103] However, the Indigenous Regional Council of Cauca has its own political party, the Indigenous Social Alliance, which holds seats in the Colombian Congress.[104] Also, the Independent Democratic Pole, a new left-wing party, received the backing of indigenous representatives. The Democratic Pole supports a negotiated settlement with the FARC, social justice, and respect for human rights.

The party has enjoyed some recent successes, most notably the election of Luis Eduardo Garzón, a former communist and labor leader, as Bogotá mayor.[105] Garzón, a staunch critic of U.S. policy who has advocated drug legalization and suspension of coca fumigation, has been an enthusiastic Chávez supporter. In 2003, he even participated in a pro-Chávez demonstration along the Colombian–Venezuelan border.[106] Antonio Navarro Wolf, the Democratic Pole's candidate against Uribe in the May 2006 election, is a senator and cofounder with Garzón of the Pole. He has demonstrated a long-term commitment to economic justice, human rights, and peace negotiations with the guerrillas. Although Navarro Wolf has been growing in popularity, his chances may be slim and Uribe will certainly be a formidable opponent.[107] According to polls, Uribe probably will avoid a runoff election and win more than 50 percent of the vote in May 2006.[108]

According to experts, however, Uribe may be politically vulnerable, as he has not been able to militarily defeat the FARC. In fact, the guerrillas seem to be growing more active.[109] A political upset for the Democratic Pole in 2006 would send shock waves throughout the region. An electoral triumph for Navarro Wolf, writes Leech, "would bring Colombia in line with other South American nations that have taken a turn to the left in recent years. It would also likely lead to a shift in relations between Colombia and both the United States and Venezuela."[110]

CHAPTER TEN

THE CHÁVEZ-MORALES AXIS

If the prospects for an indigenous upset in Colombia seem remote, in neighboring Ecuador, the political outlook looks more promising. Unlike Colombia, where indigenous peoples make up a tiny fraction of the population, Ecuador's Indian movement has the power to shake the government.[1] In this small Andean nation, Indians account for approximately 40 percent of the total population of 13 million.[2] Indigenous peoples are particularly noticeable in the mountainous Sierra, where I observed them in the summer of 1990 as a college student. I had been working at the Strand Bookstore in New York City and was thrilled to be free of the city. It was my first trip to South America, and Ecuador made a big impression on me.

Touring the country north of Quito, I was particularly struck by the indigenous women who wore gold necklaces twined around their necks in rings almost to the chin. In the marketplace in the town of Otavalo, men sported long pigtails and pleated white trousers. The local Indians are expert weavers and display beautiful shirts, vests, and hats. I also noted how they had their produce stacked symmetrically in the food stalls. I had already gotten sick earlier in my trip from unwashed produce but broke down and ate a cherimoya. The fruit, which is common in Ecuador, has a green skin but is white on the inside.

Later I walked to the nearby San Pablo Lake. In my diary, I noted: "It was truly one of the most stunning scenes I've seen. The lake is placid, and up above is a towering volcano." Halfway around the lake, I came to an isolated Indian village. From all sides I heard the sound of violins. I thought I saw some Indians dancing behind a building and tried to see what was happening. But, feeling intrusive in the village, I decided not to do any further spying. Later in my trip I developed a keen interest in Andean music. On the streets of Quito, bands of Indians play traditional music. I was moved by the sound of the gigantic flutes and the *charango*, a small guitar-like instrument. I was so taken by the charango that I later managed to acquire one and even took lessons from an Ecuadoran musician. I also made a brief attempt to learn some expressions in Quechua, for me a beautiful-sounding language.

Although picturesque, Ecuador is a country with long-standing racial tensions. For centuries, Ecuador's indigenous peoples have been excluded from power and have suffered systematic discrimination at the hands of whites. Like the Nasa in Colombia, Ecuador's Indians fear that their traditional lands are being exploited to serve a rapacious United States bent on corporate expansion. Fueling resentment has been the role of U.S. missionaries in the country, who, indigenous activists charge, hasten the penetration of U.S. corporations.

For example, according to indigenous leaders from the Huaorani tribe of the Ecuadoran Amazon, missionaries "worked in conjunction with the petroleum industry"[3] which led to environmental and social problems in their homeland. According to one journal specializing in indigenous affairs, "Beginning in 1967 with Texaco's discovery of the Oriente oil field, oil companies have constantly used missionaries as a method of quelling indigenous animosity and relocating the indigenous peoples from possible drilling sites."[4]

John Perkins, the author of the recently released book *Confessions of an Economic Hit Man*, writes about an evangelical group called the Summer Institute of Linguistics that worked with the Huaorani Indians of the Amazon basin during the early years of oil exploration.[5] Perkins, who says he was originally recruited by the super secretive U.S. National Security Agency, later worked for private corporations. His job, as he described it in a radio interview, was to get poor countries like Ecuador into debt.[6] According to Perkins, whenever seismologists reported to corporate headquarters that a particular region might contain oil, the Summer Institute of Linguistics went in and encouraged the indigenous people to move off their land and relocate to missionary reservations.[7] The evangelical group has categorically denied that it ever had any involvement with the oil industry.[8] The sensational allegations eventually led the Confederation of Ecuadorian Indigenous Nationalities (CONAIE) to request the expulsion of the group. The missionaries, charged CONAIE, were linked to the U.S. CIA.[9]

For many Ecuadorans, the idea of U.S. missionaries acting without much oversight in far-flung regions of the country stirs up nationalist sentiment and wounded pride. Hugo Chávez, seeking to reinforce his standing with the CONAIE and Andean indigenous peoples, has reaped maximum political advantage by exploiting the issue.

It was vintage Chávez. In an inflammatory speech given in October 2005, the Venezuelan president proclaimed that the American missionary group New Tribes Mission constituted a "true imperialist invasion" and was working with the CIA. Remarking that he did not "give a damn" about the international consequences of his decision, Chávez said the missionary group would soon have to abandon its jungle bases in his country.[10] New Tribes had over 160 missionaries operating within Venezuela at the time of the expulsion. The missionaries worked with 12 indigenous groups in Amazonas and several other states. According to Venezuelan officials, the missionaries had 29 landing strips within the country.

Retired general Alberto Müller Rojas, a military adviser to the Chávez government and former governor of Amazonas state, was not surprised by the increased pressure on New Tribes. Within the missionary organization, he commented, "There are distinct [religious] denominations, principally those Protestant groups of the Baptist tendency which Pat Robertson belongs to." According to Müller, television evangelist Pat Robertson, who recently caused international controversy by calling for Chávez's assassination on his TV show, was "tightly linked" to New Tribes. New Tribes and Robertson, he continued, were part of the same Protestant movement that so strongly supported President George Bush.

Although Chávez's move was certainly dramatic, it is not as if the issue of New Tribes was a novel one in Venezuela. For years, accusations had swirled that the evangelical outfit was involved in espionage and committed ethnocide while carrying out its missionary work among indigenous peoples.[11] Perhaps due to New Tribes' far-flung infrastructure, by the 1970s, the missionaries had come under widespread public fire. The first salvo came from Pablo Anduza, the former governor of Amazonas, who remarked in 1973 that missionary education was alien to Indian traditions and " . . . missionary teachings encourage the creation of an artificial society which separates children from parents."[12]

The second blow came from Julio Jiménez, a Guajibo Indian. In 1976, Jiménez publicly disclosed that, in 1958, he was sent by New Tribes to the United States to take specialized courses with the Summer Institute of Linguistics. Jiménez said that he believed missionary work had a pernicious effect on the indigenous lifestyle: "New Tribes has done more harm than good, and they should be expelled."[13] On the main campus at the Central University of Caracas, the public mood was turning against the New Tribes Mission. At a seminar held at the School of Sociology and Anthropology, various indigenous leaders called for its expulsion. But the public relations nightmare for New Tribes was just beginning. In late 1976, Carlos Azpurua released a new 18-minute film, *I Speak to Caracas*. The film featured the historian and shaman of the Yecuana people, Barne Yavari, who tells the camera: "They [the missionaries] prohibit all our customs . . . our drinks, our mythology, music and our form of life. I don't mean that no North American has helped me spiritually. We don't need spiritual help because we have our religion." Yavari goes on to tell the people of Caracas that his people have their own God, Wanadi. "It's not known how he began nor who made him," says Yavari. "Wanadi has been my beginning."

I Speak to Caracas was a sensation, hitting Venezuela like a bombshell. The film earned various prizes at home and abroad. Suddenly, the role of New Tribes Mission and the plight of Venezuelan Indians hit the international stage. The film was shown at hundreds of forums in universities, film clubs, unions, parishes, public libraries, legislative assemblies, and even border posts. Everyone from indigenous leaders to public law firms participated in the forums accompanying the film's screenings. The organizers eventually published a document entitled "Let Us Stop Ethnocide," in which they called for an end to the war that "these missionaries carry out against culture and the lives of our Indians."[14]

The missionaries also faced opposition from the military. Particularly critical was the report filed by Antonio Mariño, who headed the Amazonas military command in 1978. The report alleged that the evangelical group had not remained in its own demarcated jurisdiction, nor had it complied with Venezuelan aeronautical regulations. Rather, allegedly it had conducted scientific espionage on behalf of transnational companies, had tried to impersonate Venezuelan military officers by appearing in their uniforms when meeting with the Indians, and had even attempted to bribe military authorities.[15]

Despite growing public opposition, the missionaries were able to count on high-level support from the corrupt two-party system, the Venezuelan Evangelical Council, and the U.S. Embassy in Caracas. Although the Venezuelan congress and the military launched separate investigations, high-level action was never taken. In August 1981, José Vicente Rangel, then a deputy in Congress, requested that the investigation into New Tribes be reopened. Rangel, a longtime fixture of Venezuelan politics, had run un-successfully for president twice on the MAS (Movement Towards Socialism) ticket, in 1973 and 1978. An aggressive opponent of U.S.-backed military regimes in Venezuela, Rangel was particularly incensed by the case of New Tribes. Although the Ministry of Justice and Interior Relations ultimately heeded Rangel's calls and carried out another investigation, the results were never made public. Despite the investigations and media attention, no mis-sionary was ever put in jail.[16]

The political mood, however, would eventually shift against the mission-aries. In 1999, after Hugo Chávez was elected president, he named Rangel minister of external relations. The veteran politician went on to serve as minister of defense under Chávez and later as his vice president. Increas-ingly, New Tribes Mission was becoming more vulnerable and isolated in Venezuela. Formerly, the missionaries could count on the support of many members of the traditional two-party system. But those parties, by the time of Chávez's rise to prominence, had fallen into disgrace. What is more, while New Tribes had earlier lobbied the U.S. Embassy in Caracas to protect its interests, American diplomats now had little influence over Chávez.

As he proclaimed New Tribes' expulsion in October 2005, Chávez as-tutely played on wounded national pride. "We don't want the New Tribes here. Enough colonialism! 500 years is enough!" the Venezuelan president thundered.[17] Chávez said he had become aware of New Tribes' alleged espi-onage through his own military intelligence, although, as mentioned, no proof has been made public. While addressing Indians in Barranco Yopal, Chávez confided that he had seen an "incredible" report and video concern-ing the matter.[18]

In the wake of Chávez's announcement, Venezuelan military officials remarked that they were studying how to remove New Tribes' missionary bases. However, according to New Tribes, the Venezuelan military has al-ready acted, occupying some of its facilities in areas inhabited by the Pumé tribe. The governor of Amazonas state, Liborio Guarulla, has sought to comply with the expulsion order. Guarulla will request the withdrawal of missionaries operating in the Upper Orinoco, home to Yekuana and Yanomami Indians. Guarulla added that he will comply with the law without resorting to force.[19]

For its own part, New Tribes remarked, "We hope that President Chávez will reconsider his decision and allow us an opportunity to clarify misunderstandings and misinformation that exists regarding the work of New Tribes Mission in Venezuela. New Tribes Mission is not and has never been connected in any way with any government agencies. Our goal is to serve indigenous people."[20] According to the Venezuelan newspaper *El Universal*, U.S. ambassador William Brownfield noted that he would seek to facilitate negotiations between New Tribes and the Venezuelan government. He categorically denied any link between the CIA and New Tribes.[21] The U.S. State Department is apparently following the matter with concern, and holds out hope that the missionaries may yet be allowed to stay as the Venezuelan government has not given any official expulsion order.[22]

But why did Chávez wait six years after gaining power before expelling the missionaries? It is not as if the charges against New Tribes are anything new. On a certain level, it would seem that Chávez had simply been opportunistic. Pat Robertson's inflammatory comments made the president look like a persecuted martyr. In fact, Chávez may have calculated that he had nothing to lose and everything to gain by expelling the missionaries. Speaking with the press, Rangel remarked that the government's decision was designed to restore national sovereignty.[23] Playing to Venezuelans' sense of wounded pride, Chávez said that New Tribes had set up a state within a state, made unauthorized flights, and set up luxurious settlements in the midst of poverty. "These violations of our national sovereignty have to stop," he declared.[24]

Chávez's announcement at Barranco Yopal of New Tribes' expulsion was timed perfectly to coincide with Columbus Day, which Chávez has renamed Indigenous Resistance Day. Alexander Luzardo, a sociologist and longtime New Tribes critic, remarked that Chávez's decision "complies with what is stipulated in the constitution of 1999, which establishes indigenous peoples' right to self-determination and to respect for their beliefs, values and customs."[25]

Chávez's nationalist moves to protect indigenous peoples from the clutches of North American missionaries seem designed to appeal to the likes of Luis Macas. The president of Ecuador's CONAIE, Macas personally cosigned a letter denouncing missionaries for allegedly collaborating with oil companies in an effort to uproot Indians in the Ecuadoran Amazon.[26] If Chávez seeks to win over indigenous sentiment and become a truly

"Bolivarian" figure within the Andean region, he will have to build lasting ties to politically influential figures such as Macas.

A Quechua Indian, Macas was born in the Saraguro region in the Andean highlands[27] in 1950.[28] Macas's father was also an indigenous leader. In his youth, the younger Macas used to pass out food and *chicha*[29] (a fermented drink common in the Andes),[30] during *mingas*[31] (communal work projects)[32] organized by his father. At the age of 20, Macas became the secretary of the local *cabildo* (council) in Saraguro. Since there were no schools in his community, Macas was obliged to leave to pursue his education, but continued to maintain contact with indigenous leaders in his hometown.[33] Macas later received a doctorate in law at Ecuador's Central University,[34] went on to become a lawyer,[35] and received a scholarship to study anthropology in Quito. He came of age during a repressive period of political dictatorship in Ecuador. In 1978, authorities frustrated his attempts to organize a meeting among Amazonian, Sierra, and coastal Indians.[36]

Macas, who dresses in a distinctively dark poncho and sombrero from his home town of Saraguro,[37] had to confront not only political repression but ingrained racism. In Ecuador, anything associated with "Indian" was considered insulting and equated with ignorance. In many editions of the Royal Academy of the Spanish Language Dictionary, the terms "Indian shit," "Indian porter," "to play the Indian" (act stupid) can be found. One leader of the CONAIE recalled, "I used to cry when I was called 'Indian,' as I wasn't raised as an indigenous person. As an adult I had to struggle to recover my own language and cultural heritage."[38]

However, dramatic developments on the political stage would soon make Macas's work easier. In August 1979, after 10 years of military dictatorship, Ecuador returned to democratic rule, and Jaime Roldós was sworn in as president. In a historic move, Roldós made his first speech to Congress in Quichua, the main indigenous language in Ecuador. According to the *New Internationalist* magazine, "Politicians and landowners never forgave him, despite the use of indigenous icons—such as Ruminahui, who led the fiercest resistance against the Spanish conquest—for patriotic purposes."[39] With the return of democratic rule in 1979, Macas was finally able to carry out his historic conference[40] and in 1980 helped to found the CONAIE.[41]

As indigenous peoples enjoyed the more open political climate in Ecuador, Roldós boldly accused the Summer Institute of Linguistics of collaborating with the oil companies and ordered the missionaries' expulsion.[42]

The move hardly ingratiated him with Washington, nor did his vocal support of the Sandinista regime in Nicaragua win him any accolades with the newly elected Reagan administration.[43] In May 1981, Roldós died in a suspicious air crash.[44] According to Perkins, Roldós's death was not an accident. The Ecuadoran president, he believes, was assassinated because he "opposed that fraternity of corporate, government, and banking heads whose goal is global empire. We Economic Hit Men failed to bring Roldós . . . around, and the other type of hit men, the CIA-sanctioned jackals who were always right behind us, stepped in."[45] Roldós's presidential successor reinstated the Summer Institute of Linguistics.[46]

Although U.S. officials might have been relieved that Roldós was no longer running Ecuador, the indigenous movement now went on the offensive. Eventually the CONAIE would take up important issues that were on Chávez's agenda. The Indians not only called for the expulsion of North American missionaries but demanded land reform, an end to U.S. militarization in the region, and an end to the Washington Consensus. In an alarming warning sign for George Bush, there seemed to be growing ideological affinity between social movements in the Andes and the firebrand Venezuelan leader. To make matters worse for Washington policymakers, Luis Macas was becoming a figure on the national stage and a key power broker.

Established white society was, in the words of the *New Internationalist*, "shocked out of its complacency"[47] when, under the guidance of Luis Macas,[48] who became CONAIE president in 1990,[49] Ecuador's Indians began to assert growing militancy. Responding to Macas's call, more than a million Indians stopped working in a massive general strike in May of that year. In a display of growing force and militancy, Indians blocked highways and cut off food supplies to Quito.[50]

In a confrontational move, 160 CONAIE activists even occupied the Santo Domingo Cathedral in Quito, demanding immediate resolution of land disputes within highland communities. The very next day, indigenous peoples from the Amazon and elsewhere marched to Quito and demanded respect for the nation's agrarian reform law, funding for bilingual education, and a constitutional amendment declaring Ecuador a multinational state. A significant characteristic of the 1990 indigenous uprising was support from non-Indian sectors of society, such as students and labor. The Indians ultimately abandoned the cathedral. Although the government did not accede to all the demands, president Rodrigo Borja, who was more conciliatory than some of his predecessors and who had recognized the legitimacy of CONAIE, restored bilingual education.

In the following years, Macas found himself in the midst of a growing maelstrom of political activity. When the government signed an agrarian reform law, designed to create a free market for farm produce, strengthen individual land titles, and abolish the land reform agency, Macas organized massive protests by the CONAIE. Macas argued that the "breakup of communal lands will mean the dissolution of indigenous communities by destroying their geographical and political integrity."[51] In response to mounting pressure, the government agreed to reform the law.[52]

In an ominous development for American policymakers, Indians protested the Washington Consensus by opposing privatization of Ecuador's social security system.[53] They also protested austerity measures, which included price increases for electricity, telephone services, and public transport.[54] The CONAIE also has staged protests against the signing of a free trade agreement with the United States. Macas charged that the agreement would result in the ruination of local agriculture and the privatization of water resources.[55] CONAIE has demanded a popular referendum on the free trade agreement to let the public decide.[56] When the CONAIE offices in Quito were ransacked in a suspicious break-in in November 2005, Macas claimed that the attack was linked to his organization's opposition to the free trade agreement. The intruders made off with CONAIE's documents, folders, and computer disks.[57]

To make matters worse for Washington, Indians also opposed growing U.S. involvement in Ecuador. In 1990, the same year I made my trip to Ecuador, the Summer Institute of Linguistics was expelled—again—in response to CONAIE protests.[58] Indigenous peoples were also concerned about the violence and drug cultivation that was spilling over the border from the north. In southeastern Colombia, the Cofán Indians were decimated by the government's crop fumigation practices. As paramilitaries threatened their communities, the Cofanes became refugees and fled over the border into Ecuador. Unfortunately for the Indians, paramilitaries followed them there and in 2002 forced both the Cofanes and Quichuas to abandon their farms, crops, and animals under threat of death.[59]

As the violence spread into Ecuador, the U.S. has increased its military presence in the Andean nation. The U.S. military air base in Manta is vitally important in carrying out antinarcotics operations in neighboring Colombia.

The base has proven quite controversial in Ecuador. In 2000, over 1,000 activists attended the First Worldwide Anti-Imperialist Encounter at Manta, and protesters marched through the streets decrying the U.S. military presence.[60] CONAIE and Luis Macas rejected Plan Colombia and demanded the withdrawal of U.S. forces from the Manta base.[61]

What is obviously most worrying for Washington is that this indigenous movement might link up with Hugo Chávez in Venezuela. Already there have been disturbing signs: CONAIE officials attended the Second Congress of Bolivarian Peoples.[62] There Ecuadoran Indians struck a confrontational note, declaring that coca leaf was "a symbol of Latin American dignity." It was important, noted the participants, to condemn all "North American imperialism against coca-producing countries."[63] Humberto Cholango, president of the Kichwa Confederation of Ecuador, has declared that "no one can stop this [Bolivarian] Revolution in Venezuela, we will keep on defeating the Creole oligarchies and the Yankees . . . the time has come for South America to rise up to defeat the empire . . . Long live the triumph of the Venezuelan people."[64] In 2004, CONAIE condemned the "fascist" opposition in Venezuela and warned the United States not to interfere in the recall referendum organized against Chávez.[65] In addition, Pachakutik, the political wing of CONAIE, has warmly embraced Chávez, hailing the triumph of the Venezuelan MVR in recent elections for the Venezuelan National Assembly.[66]

Given the sheer numbers and militancy of the indigenous movement in Ecuador over the past 15 years, it should be able to steer the country away from U.S.-backed policies. Unfortunately, the Indians have not been able to achieve far-reaching change. "The Ecuadorean case," writes one observer, "provides many insights into both the possibilities and the pitfalls of social movements when involved in government."[67] The case of Luis Macas is fairly illustrative of this frustration.

Macas's meteoric rise seemed to suggest that the indigenous movement might be able to translate its grassroots organizing into concrete electoral gains. In 1996, Macas became the first indigenous person elected to the National Congress. He served as a legislator for the Pachakutik Movement. Macas seemed to be on the cusp of a political revolution. By 1998, there were eight indigenous representatives in congress.[68] In 2000, Macas scored an important victory. Amid Indian protests in Quito against the government's economic policies and plans to scrap the national currency in favor of the U.S. dollar, President Jamil Mahuad was forced to resign.[69]

As protesters took over the national parliament, an army unit looked on and even joined the people. The demonstrators declared Lucio Gutiérrez, an army colonel, as the next president. Later, Gutiérrez reportedly took part in a march from parliament to the presidential palace, which had been vacated by Mahuad. Like Chávez, Gutiérrez was of mixed racial background and a mestizo.[70] As the Mahuad government crumbled, Gutiérrez helped to form a short-lived junta government.[71] In another striking parallel to Chávez, Gutiérrez was imprisoned by the military for his disobedience, and he languished in jail for six months. When Gutiérrez got out of jail, he ran for president in 2002 promising to overturn corruption and poverty.[72]

With the help of the indigenous movement, which delivered a large portion of the rural vote, Gutiérrez won the presidency with 54 percent of the vote.[73] With Gutiérrez's assumption of power, Macas sensed that the country had entered a historic juncture and that the indigenous movement had come of age. Before the election, Gutiérrez had won Macas over by promising that he would help indigenous communities. Now the veteran CONAIE organizer accepted a job as Gutiérrez's minister of agriculture.[74] The ministry historically had catered to the interests of Andean landowners.[75] At his new job, Macas sought to shape policy on land reform.[76]

But Gutiérrez, unlike Chávez, reneged on his promises. Specifically, the former colonel embraced conservative economic policies.[77] In fact, the indigenous movement's honeymoon lasted just seven months.[78] "The rupture occurred precisely in August 2003," Macas remarked. "The worst thing he [Gutiérrez] did was to begin negotiations" with the International Monetary Fund.[79] Feeling disillusioned, the indigenous leader resigned his post.[80] Clearly, Gutiérrez had submitted to pressure from foreign lenders, obliging him to cut social programs so as to pare down the debt. Adding to the public's dislike of their new president, Gutiérrez backed Plan Colombia and the escalating drug war.[81] The coup de grâce came when Gutiérrez tried to stack the Supreme Court with his supporters, sparking massive protests in Quito once again. In response, Gutiérrez declared a state of emergency. He was forced to abandon the presidential palace when the armed forces withdrew their support and congress voted to sack him. As Gutiérrez fled the country for Brazil, Alfredo Palacio, the vice president, was sworn in as Ecuador's new leader.[82]

From Macas's point of view, the damage had been done. Gutiérrez had followed a systematic policy designed to destroy the indigenous movement by a policy of divide and rule. Gutiérrez diffused the Indians' power by disbursing funds and awarding key positions to indigenous leaders.[83] Today, in the wake of the Gutiérrez debacle, some indigenous leaders have suggested that their movement must get back to the grassroots and begin a process of self-critique.[84] Macas meanwhile has gone back to CONAIE, winning a second term as the organization's president. He will face a difficult challenge unifying the nation's indigenous groups and building bridges with other popular forces, such as labor.[85] He has also organized protests against the new Palacio government, which has sought to sign a free trade agreement with the United States and continue government support for Plan Colombia.[86]

Although the political outlook in Colombia and Ecuador may be murky, Chávez can count on a key ally in Bolivia, Evo Morales. Unlike Nasa leaders in Cauca and Luis Macas in Ecuador, Morales has actually managed to take power. An indigenous Aymara Indian and former coca leaf farmer, Morales says he represents the United States' "worst nightmare."[87] Morales is a former leader of coca-growing unions who led farmers in often violent challenges to U.S.-directed coca eradication programs. During that time, the United States treated Morales as persona non grata.[88] According to Morales, Plan Colombia represents the "extermination of indigenous peoples."[89] Elected as the first wholly indigenous president in Latin America in December 2005, Morales is the embodiment of a new indigenous awakening that could inspire social movements across the region.[90] Such a prospect further emboldens Chávez and concerns the White House.

Events stand to fortify Chávez's hand. The Venezuelan leader has always had a certain following in Bolivia among indigenous peoples. As early as 2000, Chávez traveled to Bolivia, whose population is two-thirds indigenous and is the poorest country in South America. There, he was greeted by an outpouring of support. During his official state visit, a popular demonstration in favor of the Bolivarian process took place.[91] The *Miami Herald* published a piece alleging that Chávez had financed a road blockade in Bolivia organized by the Aymara Indian leader Felipe Quispe. Chávez denied the accusations, saying that the reports constituted a "ferocious international campaign" to isolate Venezuela.[92] The U.S. State Department said it was concerned that the Venezuelan leader was supposedly offering support to violent indigenous movements.[93]

In the presidential elections of 2002, charges of Chávez's supposed interference in Bolivia's internal affairs resurfaced. This time it was the turn of *La Prensa*, a Bolivian daily, which claimed that Chávez had offered $300,000 to Evo Morales to finance the indigenous leader's presidential campaign. Again, Chávez denied the reports.[94] Whether he actively supported Morales's campaign is unclear, but the Venezuelan leader certainly did not attempt to hide his warming diplomatic ties with the coca grower. When Sánchez de Lozada won the election, Chávez returned to Bolivia to attend the inauguration. While staying in his hotel in the capital of La Paz, Chávez was received by Morales, who had come in second in the election. Later, both men declared the need for strengthening the indigenous movement within the *altiplano*, a broad upland plateau located in southwest Bolivia. In a sign of the friendly ties, Chávez personally invited members of Morales's party, the Movement Towards Socialism (known by its Spanish acronym of MAS) to Venezuela to observe the deepening of the Bolivarian process.[95] Morales returned the favor by helping to organize a street march in Caracas to support Chávez, then in the midst of the oil lockout of 2002–03.[96]

Once Chávez had survived the disruptions caused by the Venezuelan opposition, he met personally with Morales, who was then a Bolivian congressman, in April 2003. According to one journalist who was present, the meeting was jovial and went smoothly. Chávez received Morales at Miraflores at about one in the morning, along with Blanca Chancoso, an indigenous leader from Ecuador, and Rafael Alegria, a peasant farmer activist from Honduras. "From an unlit garden, Chávez emerged from the shadows wearing jeans, a t-shirt and blue sneakers," and the three greeted him excitedly. The activists sat down at a table with Chávez and the Venezuelan president announced, "I don't drink but let me offer you some wine." Someone called, "We know how to drink, and to make a toast. To Bolivarian unity!"

As they sat and talked, Chávez and the activists discussed the issue of security of leaders and activists opposed to U.S. policies. As the time came to say good-bye, the men shook hands, embraced, and took a group photo as a souvenir. "The hurricane of revolution has begun," Chávez remarked, "and it will never again be calmed."

"We'll keep the flame burning, *comandante*," Alegría added.

"We will return, and there will be millions of us," said Chancoso.

"Thank you, President Chávez," said Morales. "I leave here full of ideas for the struggle ahead."[97]

A scant two and a half years later, Morales's opportunity finally arrived. Wearing a short-sleeved shirt and jeans, he sat down with local inhabitants[98] in the tropical lowland province of Chapare[99] before going to vote in the presidential election. As he enjoyed a breakfast of fish and boiled yucca, a campesino sporting a cowboy hat rode a buffalo through the village, brandishing a checkered, rainbow-colored Aymara flag called a *wiphala*. The Indians say the flag should become the new emblem of a reborn Bolivia.[100] During Morales's campaign for president, the wiphala flew from every one of his campaign vehicles.[101]

Scenes like this one horrify Bolivia's European and mixed-race elites. For centuries, they have ruled over the impoverished Indian majority who have had to endure entrenched racism. A recently released study by the World Bank suggests that not much has changed for the Aymara. According to the study, 74 percent of Bolivia's Indians live in poverty. What is more, Bolivia's indigenous population has 3.7 fewer years of schooling than the non-Indian population. Additionally, the incidence of child labor is four times higher among Indians than nonindigenous children.[102]

Nevertheless, in recent years the Aymara, Bolivia's largest ethnic group, have achieved significant political gains. From 1993 to 1997, an Aymara Indian served as the country's vice president, and indigenous mobilization has only increased under Morales.[103] According to the London *Independent*, Morales cultivates indigenous support and "litters his conversation with Aymara references and reminders that Europeans have been exploiting the indigenous people for 500 years."[104] Indigenous gains have alarmed the non-Indian population. Racism now seems to be moving out into the open, with cases of light-skinned youths harassing indigenous protesters and yelling racial epithets. The protesters in turn pull the neckties from people and call them "white men."[105]

After casting his vote in Chapare, Morales gave a press conference. Flanked by men and women *cocaleros* (coca farmers) Morales declared that he would not change a previous policy that allowed each Chapare farming family to cultivate coca leaf on 0.4 acres of land.[106] Morales, who has a broad Indian face, is a quiet-spoken man with a calm but charismatic style.[107] As he spoke, the cocaleros casually chewed coca leaf.[108] Morales is in favor of the legalization of coca growing but opposes production of cocaine.[109]

Coca is a key ingredient used to make cocaine but, in Bolivia, is also highly valued by Indians for traditional medicinal purposes.[110] Morales supports the cultivation of coca leaf for religious ceremonies and native products, such as herbal tea sold in local markets.[111] "Long live coca, no to the Yankees," he cried to his supporters.[112] That kind of talk endears Morales with his supporters. Coca, whose leaves were used for medicinal and religious ends by the ancient Inca, forms an integral part of indigenous culture. The leaf supplies energy and allows the Indians to stave off hunger. Indeed, coca enabled indigenous peoples to endure harsh conditions in the tin and silver mines, where they toiled as slaves for the Spanish. Many still labor in the mines today.[113]

Perhaps it is no coincidence that Morales would wind up his campaign in Chapare, a region that he cares about deeply. Chapare has been a haven for illegal cultivation of coca.[114] In fact, Chapare produces 90 percent of Bolivia's coca crop.[115] Up until recently, it was illegal to cultivate coca in Chapare and the U.S. Drug Enforcement Agency had special operations teams in the area. Chapare became the scene of heated clashes between cocaleros and the authorities.[116] In an interview, Morales remarked, "In the Chapare there have been confrontations . . . between U.S. soldiers and Quechua and Aymara indigenous people who resist. From our point of view this is unconstitutional and illegal."[117]

Morales laments the lack of economic opportunities for local inhabitants in Chapare.[118] Although the United States has worked to provide cocaleros with alternative crops, such as bananas and coffee, there is little monetary incentive for the farmers to plant these crops. Depressed markets mean that farmers earn as little as one-tenth of what they might with coca, which yields three to four harvests per year.[119] "We have never seen alternative development," remarks Morales perfunctorily.[120]

Morales, whose mother was Quechua and whose father was Aymara, was born in 1959.[121] His family hailed originally from a tin mining town in the high Andes, where Morales grew up poor in the cold highlands.[122] Four of his six siblings died before their second birthday.[123] Morales's father herded llama,[124] an animal common to the Andes used by the Indians for transport of goods. Though they are generally gentle creatures, if they become irritated they may spit or hiss.[125] Evo, who left school after the third grade, helped his family survive by herding llama and helping with farming and cattle raising.[126] To distract himself from the tough conditions he experienced growing up, he worked as a trumpet player in a band.[127]

When the mining industry fell on hard times in the late 1970s, Evo and his family were forced to migrate to the coca-growing heartland in Chapare to look for a better life. His family was joined by thousands of others who had also migrated to the tropical lowlands.[128] Morales became active in the cocaleros' union and, in that role, was at the forefront of protests against the government's coca eradication policies.[129] In 1988, he became the executive secretary of a coca growers' federation of unions, and in 1997, he was elected to Congress.[130]

Morales's resistance to the U.S. coca eradication program is what has made him such a unifying figure of popular protest in Bolivia.[131] Bolivia is the third largest cocaine producer, after Colombia and Peru; the State Department has announced that if Bolivia does not eliminate coca, U.S. foreign aid to the poverty-stricken nation might be jeopardized.[132] That kind of heavy-handedness causes resentment amongst Bolivians. For many indigenous people, the United States has placed too much blame on the cocaleros and not enough on the addictive appetites of Americans.[133]

In a further move that rankled coca farmers, in 2001, the United States created a special Bolivian army unit to carry out eradication. María Luz Gomez, a cocalera in Morales's home state of Cochabamba, told *Time* magazine, "The army soldiers come to my house and shout, 'You b_____ Indian coca sellers!'" Gómez indignantly added, "Without the coca, we can't have a life here." Even worse, the special narcotics unit has been accused of numerous killings of cocalero leaders in Cochabamba. According to witnesses, one leader, Casimiro Huanca, was shot in the back by soldiers during a protest.[134]

When questioned about the U.S. role in Bolivia, Morales bristles. "If they want to talk about the war on drugs, fine," he says. "But the discussion should start with demand and not supply." Morales adds that he is willing to sign an agreement to combat drug smuggling. "If they cut demand we'll work to cut supply," he says. "But at the moment it's not the traffickers that are in jail it's the farmers."[135] For Morales, the drug war is "just a pretext. For the U.S. government, drugs are just an excuse for the U.S. to increase their power and control over other countries."[136] Morales has pledged to depenalize coca leaf production, which would surely damage the United States drug strategy in the region.[137] As the Bolivian presidential election neared in late 2005, the United States looked on warily.[138] A victory for Morales could, in the words of *Time* magazine, signify a "washout" for Washington's drug eradication program.[139]

Some question whether Morales would really dare to decriminalize coca leaf. If he did press for such a measure, he would become a hero to indigenous peoples in Ecuador and Colombia. Already, similar moves are under way in neighboring Peru, where the regional government of Cuzco acted to legalize coca.[140] Andean nations acting in concert to decriminalize coca would be a huge setback for the United States and a coup for Chávez. Speaking during his show *Aló, Presidente*, Chávez seemed to sympathize with the plight of Bolivia's indigenous peoples and their right to cultivate coca. He said that Bolivian farmers "used to survive from coca, but they can't produce it now; the campesinos are not guilty of the fact that chemicals have been made to convert coca into cocaine."[141]

If Morales ever withdrew from the coca eradication program, the United States would surely vote against Bolivian requests for loans from the World Bank, International Monetary Fund, and the Inter-American Development Bank. All these institutions are vital if Morales ever hopes to pay back Bolivia's debt and fuel its economy.[142] Morales had better think carefully about intimidating capital. As one recent report has noted, "Unlike Venezuela under Chávez, Bolivia is much more dependent on foreign aid and lacks the economic strength to go it alone."[143] Recent moves by Morales suggest that he may be drifting away from Washington's orbit and seeking to cultivate Chávez as a key ally. In early 2006, Morales traveled to Caracas where the Venezuelan president offered $30 million in assistance for social programs and pledged to supply Bolivia with 150,000 barrels of diesel fuel per month in exchange for agricultural products.[144]

Going against the logic of the international financial system certainly presents challenges for Morales, but his radical Aymara supporters seem determined to defy the United States.[145] During a campaign rally for Morales, a volunteer handed out coca leaf from a plastic bag to miners still wearing their helmets. There were no police in sight. Meanwhile, the crowd chanted, ""Now, Now, Now, Evo Presidente!" A singer grabbed a microphone and yelled, "The place to eradicate coca is in the noses of those gringo sons of bitches!"[146]

In the central city of Cochabamba, capital of the larger department of the same name, Evo Morales shouted to his supporters, "Beginning tomorrow Bolivia's new history really begins, a history where we will seek equality, justice, equity, peace and social justice."[147] The United States' "worst nightmare" had occurred in December 2005. Morales had won the election handily with 51 percent of the vote compared to 32 percent for the right-wing candidate Jorge Quiroga.[148] Quiroga, described as "conspicuously European-looking," typically sported a red polo shirt.[149] Morales was the first elected indigenous president in Bolivia's history. For native leaders throughout the region, his election came as a sign of hope. In Ecuador, Luis Macas remarked that Morales's triumph was a historical landmark unlike anything witnessed "since the time of Spanish colonialism."[150]

Macas was not the only one exulting. Chávez sent Morales a note of congratulation. The Bolivian election, Chávez declared, had been a "battle for dignity and sovereignty." Chávez was ecstatic that, in his view, the patriotism of Bolívar and Sucre, one of the Liberator's generals sent to rule over Bolivia, had finally triumphed.[151] As he had before with Lula, Chávez offered a replica of Bolívar's sword to the new Bolivian president.[152] For Chávez, Morales's election came as a true geopolitical triumph. In an earlier interview, Morales had declared, "If I was president of Bolivia, I would like to accompany the people of Cuba and Venezuela, and two men, Fidel Castro and Hugo Chávez, who are liberating forces in America."[153]

Such declarations alarmed the U.S. State Department, which in June 2005 warned of growing links between Chávez and Morales at the Organization of American States.[154] General James Hill, commander of the U.S. Southern Command in Miami prior to General Craddock's arrival, went even further. He stated that Morales received direct financial support from Chávez. For his part, Morales denies receiving any financial support from Chávez.[155] The coca leader, who identifies himself as a "Bolivarian,"[156] said that he had never requested external assistance. "Those accusations always occur," he declared. "Evo Morales is accused of everything, in Bolivia I am responsible for everything, if I am outside of the country I am a problem for the government, if I was in the cemetery surely I would continue to be a problem."[157] Nevertheless, Morales makes no effort to hide his sympathies. He has remarked that he shares Chávez's desire to liberate Latin American countries from the yoke of the United States.[158]

The prospect of a Chávez-Morales axis is cause for worry for the Bush administration. Not only does Morales oppose the drug war, but he has taken a hard line on Bolivia's energy policy. A key plank of the Morales campaign was the nationalization of the hydrocarbon industry.[159] Bolivia contains significant oil reserves and the second largest gas reserves in

South America, after Venezuela.[160] Currently six multinational companies control the gas industry in Bolivia, the so-called transnacionales (Bolivians, according to one correspondent, practically spit out the word), including Exxon.[161] Many of Morales's supporters speculate that he will expropriate oil and gas facilities within a couple of months after assuming the presidency. Morales himself talks tough, saying "we cannot give away what was given to us by Pachamama."[162]

Morales has been able to exploit the politically explosive issue to his advantage. In the 1990s, Bolivia was in the vanguard of the Washington Consensus, privatizing its oil and gas industry.[163] The International Monetary Fund, which recommended the move, promised increased income from foreign investment. It never happened. As a matter of fact, government revenue plummeted. Life was rosy, however, for the multinationals, which took in unprecedented profits.[164] Neoliberal economics did little to aid Bolivia's people: today more than 65 percent of the country is still living under the poverty line. "The privatization schemes," writes *The Nation* magazine, "rather than bringing prosperity as promised, have provoked a wave of anger against international financial institutions and the United States." Popular anger over the mishandling of hydrocarbon wealth led Bolivia to the brink of disintegration, with two presidents forced out of office in less than two years by popular protest. The demonstrations helped to catapult Morales onto the national stage.[165]

Not surprisingly, Morales's heated rhetoric bashes neoliberal economics. "The worst enemy of humanity is capitalism," he has said.[166] Speaking in Caracas after his election, Morales added that Bolivia will join "the anti-neoliberal and anti-imperialist fight."[167] In his rhetoric, Morales owes much to Hugo Chávez. Indeed, the Bolivian indigenous leader has complimented the Venezuelan president, who in Morales's eyes formed part of Latin America's antiglobalization movement. According to Morales, his party MAS also sought to form part of the international network combating globalization.[168]

In line with his anti-neoliberal bias, Morales also criticizes the Free Trade Area of the Americas. "From the point of view of the indigenous people here," Morales says, "the FTAA is an agreement to legalize the colonization of the Americas."[169] In his hostility to the FTAA, Morales shares ideological affinity with Chávez. In 2004, Morales attended the Congress of Bolivarian Peoples in Caracas, which attacked the U.S.-imposed trade agreement.[170]

On energy policy, Morales would like to resist the neoliberal trend. According to Carlos Villegas, Morales's economic adviser, contracts with transnational companies are illegal and need to be renegotiated. In 2005, MAS drove through a new law in Congress that raised taxes on the gas companies to 50 percent. "So far," says Villegas, "the government has failed to enforce this law. We are going to enforce it and we're going to extend it."[171]

While Morales could "extend" the pressure by expropriating the companies, such action would likely land him in lengthy court battles, and foreign investment could dry up.[172] Any moves toward nationalization could prompt the companies to sue in private closed-door arbitration, away from the scrutiny of a public judge in an international court. The companies could claim rights over the $3.5 billion they already invested in Bolivia and also seek to reclaim expected profits totaling tens of billions more. Writes *The Nation*, "For a country like Bolivia, whose annual revenues are only a little more than $2 billion a year, that's no small threat."[173]

A hopeless situation? If the companies are unwilling to renegotiate their contracts, other countries could step into the breach. Could Chávez get the gas industry up and running in Bolivia? It is a prospect that surely provokes concern in the oil-dominated Bush-Cheney White House. Recently, Chávez pledged to support Morales if Bolivia nationalizes its gas industry.[174] Some experts have pointed out that Venezuela lacks the necessary expertise in gas extraction. A second question is whether Venezuela could afford to bankroll such a daunting enterprise, given Chávez's lavish spending on social programs at home.[175]

Nevertheless, recent developments suggest that energy integration is at least on the agenda. Ex-guerrilla fighter Alí Rodríguez has been busy meeting with his Argentine counterparts. The Venezuelans and Argentines have both agreed that YPFB (Yacimientos Petrolíferos Fiscales Bolivianos), a Bolivian state company, should help to form Petrosur.[176] In 2003, Morales went on Chávez's TV show, *Aló, Presidente*, where the indigenous leader remarked that resources like oil could form the basis of Latin American unity.[177] The following year, while attending the Congress of Bolivarian Peoples, Morales gave his fervent support to Petroamérica and expressed hope that Bolivia might one day be able to join the company. Petroamérica, Morales asserted, could block the encroaching "North American empire."[178]

EXTENDING OIL DIPLOMACY TO THE UNITED STATES

Far away from the stormy politics of South America, Hugo Chávez has recruited key allies in Washington, including Congress member José Serrano. One of three Puerto Rican representatives in the U.S. Congress, Serrano has devoted his life to the service of his political constituents in the South Bronx.[1] Serrano's district, which includes great landmarks such as Yankee Stadium, is 63% percent Latino, the highest percentage of any New York congressional district. Historically, the area has been heavily Puerto Rican, however in recent years the district has seen the arrival of other groups from Latin America.[2]

Serrano was born in Mayagüez, a major port and city in Western Puerto Rico, in 1943. Growing up on the island, Serrano strongly identified with the local culture. As a child, his parents, José and Hipolita, took him to celebrate the *fiestas patronales* (the patron saint feasts). "The powerful combination of the spirituality and music at these festivals," remarked the *Puerto Rico Herald*, "filled young José with a pride in Puerto Rico that he retained when, at seven years old, he moved with his family to New York." Like many other Puerto Ricans in the Bronx, Serrano faced trying social conditions. He grew up in the projects, and his family was poor. He and his younger brother attended the public schools, and later Serrano took classes at Lehman College, which forms part of the City University of New York.[3]

Serrano is one of the most liberal members of Congress and once remarked, "I embrace that label. To me, liberal reflects my concern for people like those in my community who don't always share in the economic prosperity of the country and my concern for the vitality of public institutions, including schools and hospitals."[4] An ardent defender of bilingual education, he also has led efforts to improve police training and ties between the local police force and the community so as to combat police brutality. To fight asthma and other pulmonary illnesses common among his constituents, Serrano has expressed interest in environmental questions, pressing for development of cleaner fuels. He also has taken a keen interest in the fate of his native island. For example, he has opposed the training by the U.S. Navy in the Puerto Rican island of Vieques.[5]

Serrano additionally has been a leading critic of President Bush's foreign policy. For example, he advocates ending the embargo on Cuba, and in 1995, he helped to bring Fidel Castro to visit the Bronx.[6] Serrano was also one of only three House members to vote for immediate withdrawal of U.S. troops from Iraq.[7] As the ranking Democrat on the House subcommittee that funds the State Department and the National Endowment for Democracy, Serrano has raised concerns about the role of the Bush administration in the April 2002 coup against Chávez. "It is not our place to be working to undermine his [Chávez's] government," Serrano has said.[8]

In September 2005, Serrano's Bronx constituents were greeted to an unusual sight. Dressed in dark pants and his trademark red shirt, Hugo Chávez kissed, hugged, and mixed with local residents. He then "mixed it up with gusto with a Dominican band, almost as if he were courting voters." Chávez played a güira, a cylindrical aluminum percussion instrument. He then grabbed two maracas and began swaying to the music. The band sang, "¡Ooh, ah, Chávez no se va!" (Chávez is not leaving). The Venezuelan leader had come to the Point Community Development Corp. on Garrison Avenue. Earlier, Chávez had been at the United Nations, where he had blasted the Bush administration. Now, moving from table to table, Chávez was surrounded by aides, reporters, bodyguards, and beaming Bronx residents eagerly taking pictures. According to Serrano, who helped set up the event, Chávez himself asked to meet local people.[9]

In a move that surely pleased Serrano, who has campaigned to clean up the local environment, Chávez had instructed CITGO CEO Félix Rodríguez to undertake a study of the Bronx River and ways to clean the waterway.[10] But Chávez had an even more radical offer for Bronx residents; he offered to provide cheap fuel oil to the poor. Since Venezuela already owns CITGO gas stations in the United States, Chávez had a ready-made distribution system. Serrano was all too pleased to help broker the deal. "My constituents are facing some of the highest energy bills in recent history," he said, "even as oil companies are reporting the largest profits in recent memory."[11]

Concerned that notoriously greedy New York City landlords would pocket the savings, Serrano involved local nonprofit housing corporations in the discount fuel program. Under the Chávez-Serrano plan for the South Bronx, each resident will be awarded vouchers for rent reductions and for "infrastructure and quality-of-life improvements" in buildings.[12] "The idea is to make sure the financial help goes directly to the poor, not the middle-man," Serrano remarked.[13] Apparently Chávez's public relations bid in the South Bronx was very successful. Serrano said, "Chávez went to the poorest congressional district in the nation's richest city, and people on the street there just went crazy. A lot of people told me they were really mesmerized by him. He made quite an impression."[14]

Chávez's offering formed part of a larger plan designed to help poor communities across the United States. In Boston, CITGO will sell oil at $1.35 a gallon, far below the market price of about $2.25 a gallon, resulting in huge savings for Massachusetts homeowners who could save about $180 for each 200-gallon shipment, enough fuel to last approximately three weeks.[15] Venezuela will also provide fuel oil to poor Mexican Americans in Chicago. Chávez has even offered to ship low-cost gasoline to Native American tribal communities in the United States. "There is a lot of poverty in the U.S. and I don't believe that everything reflects the American Way of Life. Many people die of cold in the winter. Many die of heat in the summer," Chávez remarked during his weekly TV show in August 2005. "We could have an impact on seven to eight million persons," he added.[16]

What is more, in the wake of Hurricane Katrina, Chávez provided relief assistance to the poverty-stricken and largely African American victims of the disaster. The head of CITGO set up disaster relief centers in Louisiana and Texas in the wake of the hurricane and provided humanitarian aid to thousands of victims. Volunteers based at CITGO refineries in Lake Charles, Louisiana, and Corpus Christi, Texas, provided medical care, food, and water to approximately 5,000 people. In Houston, volunteers from CITGO headquarters provided similar assistance to 40,000 victims. Additionally, Venezuela provided hundreds of thousands of barrels of oil in energy assistance to the United States.

Chávez's moves are sure to play well in the inner city. In light of the high price of oil in 2005—it has reached $70 a barrel—the price of heating oil is expected to skyrocket and become unaffordable to many poor people of color. By providing cheap oil to marginalized communities fed up with price gouging, Chávez shrewdly overshadows George Bush. The U.S.

president, along with the Republican party, has long ignored the social needs of America's inner cities, as evidenced by the botched hurricane relief operation in New Orleans. Unlike the U.S. government, which was hobbled by Hurricane Katrina and which had to redirect much of the winter's energy assistance program to hurricane victims, Chávez is ideally positioned to help poor communities of color. Venezuela owns 14,000 gas stations and eight refineries in the United States through CITGO, and none of its oil infrastructure was damaged by Hurricane Katrina.

If Chávez's recent moves are any indication, the Venezuelan leader is determined to use oil for political advantage, embracing any allies that he can muster in the battle of wills with President George Bush. Julia Buxton, a scholar at Bradford University who has written extensively on Venezuela, recently remarked, "He [Chávez] clearly needed to build constructive alliances with more liberal sections of American society and open a way to insulate himself against his Washington enemies."[17] In an effort to create his visibility in the United States, Chávez launched an ad campaign in America's top newspapers, including the *New York Times, Washington Post, USA Today*, and the *Houston Chronicle*. The full-page ads read, "How Venezuela is keeping the home fires burning in Massachusetts," and discussed CITGO's moves to supply poor state residents with fuel.[18]

Chávez's diplomacy seems to form part of a larger, long-term strategy of forging ties with racial minorities. In January 2004, TransAfrica Forum sent a delegation of influential artists, actors, activists, and scholars to Caracas to meet with government officials. The group included screen actor Danny Glover (*Lethal Weapon, The Color Purple*), who expressed his excitement at the social changes taking place in Venezuela. Glover, who has called President George Bush a racist, remarked that the U.S. media's portrayal of Venezuela "has nothing to do with reality" and stated that his presence in Venezuela was "to listen and learn, not only from government and opposition politicians, but to share with the people, those who are promoting the changes in this country and we want to be in contact with those who benefit from those changes."[19]

Glover and others later presided over the inauguration of a new "Martin Luther King Jr." school in the coastal town of Naiguatá. The area is home to large numbers of Afro-Venezuelans. The school inauguration was the first official Venezuelan recognition of the importance of the slain civil rights leader. The government also launched a photo exposition to honor Dr. King. Speaking at the event, the Venezuelan ambassador to the United

States, Bernardo Álvarez, declared that "the visit by members of the TransAfrica Forum represents a struggle that goes beyond the figure of Martin Luther King, his struggle, his ideas and the African-American social movements inspired by him. This is a struggle aimed at defending people's rights, not only in the United States, but in the hemisphere and the world."[20] Glover, clearly touched by the occasion, commented, "This isn't Danny Glover the artist. I'm here as a citizen, not only of the U.S., but a citizen of the world. We understand fully the importance of this historical moment."[21] Chávez later honored the late Dr. King during his radio and TV show *Aló, Presidente;* Glover and others were invited on air to participate.[22]

Chávez has been keen to cultivate his budding friendships with prominent African Americans. In July 2005, Danny Glover and singer Harry Belafonte were invited to the ceremonial launching of Chávez's new TV station Telesur. Glover was impressed with the new media initiative, but criticized the station for not having any people of African or indigenous descent on its advisory board. Chávez himself remarked to Glover, in English, "Danny, I am with you." Meanwhile, Chávez has also cultivated ties with civil rights leader Jesse Jackson. During a visit to Caracas, the veteran African American activist condemned Pat Robertson's call for Chávez's assassination. Coinciding with Jackson's stay in the country, the Venezuelan National Assembly declared a special session to commemorate Dr. King's "I Have a Dream" speech.

National Assembly member Nohelí Pocaterra, an indigenous woman of Wayuú descent, addressed parliament in her native language and later in Spanish. Pocaterra compared Chávez's struggle for equality in Venezuela with Dr. King's civil rights work. Speaking later at the National Assembly, Jackson discussed the role of King during the civil rights struggle. Jackson praised Venezuela for outlawing slavery before the United States did. "You in Venezuela ended the system of slavery in 1854," he remarked.[23] At the end of his speech, Jackson received thunderous applause from Venezuelan lawmakers.

Washington is unlikely to receive Chávez's warming ties to liberal African Americans, and his oil diplomacy in the South Bronx, with gratitude. "Cutting oil prices must seem like the worst sort of radicalism to the Big Oil companies and their buddies at the Bush-Cheney White House," writes Juan González of the New York *Daily News.* Indeed, just as Bush's popularity is flagging over the war in Iraq and botched relief efforts at home, Chávez has emerged as the most charismatic South American leader in recent times. "Advanced by individuals such as President Chávez," remarks Bill Fletcher of TransAfrica, "the recognition of the on-going reality of racism, and the struggles against it by the African descendant and Indigenous populations, could have a momentous impact on the politics and future of Latin America, let alone the entire Western Hemisphere."[24]

NOTES

INTRODUCTION

1. "Robertson: U.S. Should assassinate Venezuela's Chávez, State Department Says Comment 'Inappropriate,'" CNN Web site, August 23, 2005, http://www.cnn.com/2005/US/08/23/robertson.Chávez.1534/ (accessed March 2, 2006); "Venezuela Vice President Slams Robertson," Associated Press, August 24, 2005, posted on ABC News Web site, http://abcnews.go.com/GMA/wireStory?id=1063308 (accessed March 2, 2006); Jackie Frank, "U.S. Evangelist Calls for Assassination of Chávez," Reuters, August 23, 2005, posted on *Boston Globe* Web site, http://www.boston.com/news/nation/washington/articles/2005/08/23/us_evangelist_calls_for_assassination_of_Chávez/ (accessed March 2, 2006); Anne Gearan, "Newsview: White House Distances Robertson," Associated Press August 24, 2005, posted on ABC News Web site, http://abcnews.go.com/Politics/wireStory?id=1065568&CMP=OTC-RSS-Feeds0312 (accessed March 2, 2006).
2. "Canciller duda de posición de EEUU sobre declaraciones de Robertson," *El Universal*, August 26, 2005, http://www.eud.com/2005/08/26/pol_ava_26A604731.shtml (accessed March 2, 2006); Transcript: Hugo Chávez Interview, *ABC Nightline*, September 16, 2005, http://abcnews.go.com/Nightline/International/story?id=1134098&page=1 (accessed March 2, 2006); Jefferson Morley, "Venezuela's 'Anti-Bush' Fears," *Washington Post*, March 17, 2005, http://www.washingtonpost.com/wp-dyn/articles/A41572–2005Mar16.html (accessed March 2, 2006).
3. Nikolas Kozloff, "*Fox News* Venezuela Coverage: 'Fair and Balanced' or Quasi-Official U.S. Government Propaganda?," Council on Hemispheric Affairs, Memorandum to the Press 05.48, 29, April 2005, http://www.coha.org/NEW_PRESS_RELEASES/New_Press_Releases_2005/05.48_Fox_%20News_the_one.htm (accessed March 2, 2006); Transcript: Hugo Chávez Interview, *ABC Nightline*, Marta Harnecker, *Hugo Chávez Frías, un hombre, un pueblo* (Havana: Editorial de Ciencias Sociales, 2002), 179; Greg Wilpert, "Poll: Chávez Enjoys 71.8% Approval Rating in Venezuela," *Venezuela Analysis*, July 27, 2005, http://venezuelanalysis.com/news.php?newsno=1702 (accessed March 2, 20006); "Death Threat May Bolster Chávez's Popularity Before Election," August 24 2005, Bloomberg.com Web site, http://www.bloomberg.com/apps/news?pid=71000001&refer=latin_

america&sid=aW0HtBbsP0qU (accessed March 2, 2006); Ian James, "Venezuelan Oil Deals Become Issue in Country's Presidential Race," Associated Press, February 1, 2006, posted on *Boston Globe* Web site, http://www.boston.com/news/local/rhode_island/articles/2006/02/01/venezuelan_oil_deals_become_issue_in_countrys_presidential_race/?rss_id=Boston.com+%2F+News+%2F+Local (accessed March 2, 2006).

4. Jonah Gindin, "A Brief Recent History of Venezuela's Labor Movement, Re-Organizing Venezuelan Labor," Venezuela Analysis, October 18, 2004, http://venezuelanalysis.com/articles.php?artno=1296 (accessed March 2, 2006); Daina Green and Barry Lipton, "Report on Venezuela's Trade Union Situation," Venezuela Analysis May 26, 2004, http://www.venezuelanalysis.com/articles.php?artno=1183 (accessed March 2, 2006); Jon Quaccia, "National Endowment for Death Squads? The AFL-CIO and the NED," Venezuela Analysis, December 21, 2004, reprinted from *Against the Current*, http://www.venezuelanalysis.com/articles.php?artno=1340 (accessed March 2, 2006).

CHAPTER 1

1. Nikolas Kozloff, "Venezuela's Chávez: Oil is a Geopolitical Weapon," Council on Hemispheric Affairs, Memorandum to the Press 05.35, March 28, 2005, Council on Hemispheric Affairs Web site, http://www.coha.org/NEW_PRESS_RELEASES/New_Press_Releases_2005/05.35%20Venezuela%20Oil%20the%20one.htm (accessed March 2, 2006); Daniel Fisher, "A Friend in Need?" *Forbes*, January 6, 2003, http://www.forbes.com/archive/forbes/2003/0106/096_2.html?token=NCBNYXIgMjAwNiAwNDozO-To1MSArMDAwMA%3D%3D (accessed March 2, 2006).

2. Kozloff, "Oil is a Geopolitical Weapon," Energy Information Administration (EIA), Venezuela Country Analysis Brief, June 2004, EIA Web site, http://www.eia.doe.gov/emeu/cabs/venez.pdf#search='Venezuela%20Country%20Analysis%20Brief, %20June%202004' (accessed March 2, 2006); Fisher, "A Friend in Need?"; "Oil Tops $70 a Barrel," *Sun Sentinel*, (Fort Lauderdale, Florida), August 29, 2005, http://www.sun-sentinel.com/news/weather/weblog/hurricane/archives/2005/08/oil_tops_70_a_b.html (accessed March 2, 2006); Gillian Wong, "Oil Prices Hover Around $59 a Barrel," Associated Press, February 17, 2005.

3. Geri Smith, "Is Venezuela's Chávez Killing the Golden Goose?" *Business Week*, March 14, 2005, http://www.businessweek.com/magazine/content/05_11/b3924086_mz058.htm (accessed March 2, 2006).

4. Center for Strategic and International Studies (CSIS), Web page on Luis Giusti, "Expert Profile: Luis Giusti, Senior Adviser," http://www.csis.org/component/option,com_csis_experts/task,view/type,34/id,152/ (accessed March 2, 2006); "Manager: Luis Giusti," *Business Week* (International Edition), October 26, 1998, http://www.businessweek.com/1998/43/b3601030.html (accessed March 2, 2006).

5. Yensi Rivero, "Environment-Venezuela: Freshwater Weed Strangling Lake Maracaibo," Inter Press Service (IPS), June 5, 2004, http://ipsnews.net/send-news.asp?idnews=24054 (accessed March 2, 2006); Aurelio de Vivanco y Villegas, *Venezuela al día* (Caracas: Imprenta Bolívar, 1928), 575.

6. EIA, "Venezuela Country Analysis Brief."

7. CSIS Web page, "Expert Profile: Luis Giusti, Senior Adviser," *South America, Central America and the Caribbean 2005* (London: Europa Publications, 2005), 867; "Petróleos de Venezuela S.A," Hoover's Company in Depth Profiles, January 4, 2006; Alfredo Carquez, "Giusti garantiza aporte fiscal de Bs. 3,8 billones, PdVSA dejará de percibir Bs 1,7 millardos en ganancias netas del 98," *El Nacional,* July 7, 1998.

8. "Manager: Luis Giusti"; Pablo Bachelet, "Oil, Politics and Venezuela," *Petroleum World,* June 27, 2005; Rafael Ramírez, "A National, Popular, and Revolutionary Oil Policy for Venezuela," Venezuela Analysis, June 9, 2005, http://www.venezuelanalysis.com/articles.php?artno=1474 (accessed March 2, 2006).

9. Tim Padgett, "The Latin Oil Czar, Can a Former Guerrilla Lead Venezuela's Oil Monopoly to do Well by Doing Good?" *Time,* July 18, 2004, http://www.time.com/time/globalbusiness/article/0,9171,1101040726–665069,00.html (accessed March 3, 2006); Bernard Mommer, "Petróleo Subversivo," in Steve Ellner, Daniel Hellinger (eds), *La politica venezolana en la época de Chávez: clases, polarizacíon y conflicto* (Caracas: Editorial Nueva Sociedad, 2003), 168–69.

10. Bernard Mommer, "Changing Venezuelan Oil Policy," *Oxford Energy Comment,* April 1999, http://www.oxfordenergy.org/comment.php?9904 (accessed March 3, 2006).

11. Fisher, "A Friend in Need?"

12. "Venezuela Plans Major Petrochemicals Expansion," Reuters, May 9, 1996, Factiva Database.

13. "Hydrocarbons Law Tightens Grip on Venezuela's Oil Industry," Alexander's Gas and Oil Connections, November 28, 2001, http://www.gasandoil.com/goc/news/ntl15170.htmL (accessed March 18, 2006).

14. "PdVSA Chief Speaks Out," Alexander's Gas and Oil Connections, March 4, 1998."

15. "Venezuela Sees 1995 Production, Reserves Rising," Reuters, December 26, 1994, Factiva Database.

16. "Venezuela's Chávez Squeezes Oil Companies," Bloomberg.com Web site, August 24, 2005, http://quote.bloomberg.com/apps/news?pid=nifea&&sid=a3z63_HrIvtc (accessed March 3, 2006).

17. Dick Parker, "Defending Chávez's 'Bolivarian Revolution,'" *Red Pepper,* July 2003, http://www.redpepper.org.uk/July2003/x-July2003-venezuela.html (accessed March 3, 2006); "Manager: Luis Giusti."

18. "Appointment of Army General to Venezuela Oil Company Could Mean More Politics, Less Oil," CNN Web site, October 16, 2000, http://archives.cnn.com/2000/WORLD/americas/10/16/venezuela.oil.reut/ (accessed March 3, 2006); Ernesto Villegas Poljak, "Presidente de PdVSA gana

148 millones de bolívares al año," *El Universal*, October 10, 1996, http://www.el-universal.com/1996/10/10/pol_art_M10LU.shtml (accessed March 3, 2006); "Energy—PdVSA Dispute Rumbles on—The Government Sacked Three Senior Executives," *Latin American Economic and Business Report, Latin American Newsletters*, April 11, 2002 (Factiva Database).

19. Adam Easton, "Oil Industry Locks Horns with Chávez," BBC Web site, March 17, 2002, http://news.bbc.co.uk/2/hi/americas/1877770.stm (accessed March 3, 2006).

20. Julia Buxton, "Economy," in *South America, Central America and the Caribbean 2005* (London: Europa Publications, 2005), 870.

21. Padgett, "The Latin Oil Czar."

22. Martín Sánchez, "Venezuela Rejects U.S. Ruling on Alleged PdVSA Expropriation of Assets from CIA-linked Firm," Venezuela Analysis, July 15, 2004, http://www.venezuelanalysis.com/news.php?newsno=1310 (accessed March 3, 2006).

23. "About SAIC, Company Overview," SAIC Web site, http://www.saic.com/about/overview.html (accessed March 3, 2006); Anitha Reddy, "SAIC's New Chief Has Big Plans, Dahlberg Seeks to Consolidate Contractor's Far-Flung Units," *Washington Post*, February 6, 2004, http://www.washingtonpost.com/ac2/wp-dyn/A17539-2004Feb5?language=printer (accessed March 3, 2006).

24. Paula Shaki Trimble, "SAIC Enhances Defense Services," April 3, 2001, *Federal Computer Week*, http://www.fcw.com:8443/fcw/articles/2001/0402/web-saic-04-03-01.asp (accessed March 3, 2006).

25. William D. Hartung and Michelle Ciarrocca, "Arms Trade Resource Center, the Ties that Bind: Arms Industry Influence in the Bush Administration and Beyond," A World Policy Institute Special Report, World Policy Institute, October 2004, http://www.worldpolicy.org/projects/arms/reports/TiesThat Bind.html (accessed March 3, 2006).

26. "SAIC Wins Global IT Outsourcing Contract from Marathon," PR Newswire, July 21, 2004, http://www.prnewswire.com/cgi-bin/stories.pl?ACCT=104&STORY=/www/story/07-21-2004/0002214800&EDATE= (accessed March 3, 2006).

27. Sánchez, "Venezuela Rejects U.S. Ruling."

28. Bruce Bigelow, "SAIC to Recoup Some Losses in Venezuela Deal," *San Diego Union-Tribune*, July 20, 2004, http://www.signonsandiego.com/news/business/20040720-9999-1b20saic.html (accessed March 3, 2006).

29. Walter Martínez, "In This Largest Energy Reservoir of the World, Great Interests Placed Their Sights Here," Interview with Energy and Mines Minister Rafael Ramírez, Part 2, Venezuela Analysis, January 27, 2004, http://www.venezuelanalysis.com/articles.php?artno=1096 (accessed March 3, 2006).

30. "Windfalls of War, Science Applications International Corporation," Center for Public Integrity, Web site, http://www.publicintegrity.org/wow/bio.aspx?act=pro&ddlC=51 (accessed March 3, 2006); Bruce Bigelow, "'Heart' of SAIC Reveals Plans to Step Down," *San Diego Union Tribune*, April 9, 2003,

http://www.signonsandiego.com/news/business/20030409-9999_1b9beyster. html (accessed March 3, 2006); Mark Lewellen-Biddle, "Voting Machines Gone Wild!" *In These Times*, December 11, 2003, http://www.inthesitimes. com/site/main/article/660 (accessed March 3, 2006).

31. "Manager: Luis Giusti."

32. Kozloff, "Oil is a Geopolitical Weapon."

33. Alma Guillermoprieto, "The Gambler," *New York Review of Books*, October 20, 2005, Vol. 52, No. 16, http://www.nybooks.com/articles/18355 (accessed March 3, 2006).

34. Kurt Abraham, "Situation at Venezuela's PdVSA Deteriorates," *World Oil*, October 1999, http://www.worldoil.com/magazine/MAGAZINE_DETAIL. asp?ART_ID=247&MONTH_YEAR=Oct-1999 (accessed March 3, 2006); Stuart Wilkinson, "New Venezuelan Hydrocarbons Law Struggles Forward," *World Oil*, October 2001, Vol. 222, No. 10, http://www.worldoil.com/maga-zine/MAGAZINE_DETAIL.asp?ART_ID=1577&MONTH_YEAR=Oct-2 001 (accessed March 3, 2006).

35. Neil Mackay, "Official: U.S. Oil at the Heart of Iraq Crisis," *Sunday Herald*, October 6, 2002, http://www.sundayherald.com/28285 (accessed March 3, 2006); "Strategic Energy Policy, Challenges for the Twenty First Century," Independent Task Force on Strategic Energy Policy, April 2001, Baker Insti-tute Web site, http://bakerinstitute.org/Pubs/study_15.pdf (accessed March 21, 2006); Edward S. Morse and Amy Myers Jaffe, *Strategic Energy Policy, Challenges for the 21st Century* (New York: Council on Foreign Relations, 2001), 46.

36. CSIS Web site, Experts Web page.

37. CSIS Web site, Expert Profile, Luis Giusti, Senior Adviser, "Luis E. Giusti, Member of the Board," Centre for Global Energy Studies, http://www. cges.co.uk/?cdn=governingboard&pt=Governing+Board&nav=governing-board&lnav=associates (accessed March 3, 2006).

38. Canadian Broadcasting Corporation Web site, "The Fifth Estate, Conspiracy Theories, the Saudi Connection," originally broadcast on October 29, 2003, http://www.cbc.ca/fifth/conspiracytheories/saudi.html (accessed March 3, 2006); Oliver Burkeman and Julian Borger, "The Ex-presidents' Club," *The Guardian*, October 31, 2001, http://www.guardian.co.uk/Archive/Article/ 0,4273,4288516,00.html (accessed March 3, 2006).

39. Fisher, "A Friend in Need?"

40. "Castro cree que 'nada ni nadie detiene a Chávez,'" *El Universal*, July 30, 2000, http://www.eluniversal.com/2000/07/30/pol_art_30112AA.shtml (ac-cessed March 3, 2006); "Giusti Denies Castro Charges," *The Oil Daily*, Au-gust 1, 2000 (Factiva Database); "Ex-Venezuelan Oil Chief Denies Castro's Charges," Reuters, July 30, 2000 (Factiva Database); Gilles Trequesser, "Cuba Raises 'Reward' in Alleged Venezuela Spy Claim," Reuters, July 29, 2000 (Factiva Database).

41. *Apuntes estadísticos del estado Zulia, tomados de orden del ilustre Americano, Gen-eral Guzmán Blanco, Presidente de la República* (Caracas: Imprenta de la

Opinión Nacional, 1875), 20; Samuel C. Snedaker, "Mangroves: Their Value and Perpetuation," in *Nature and Resources* 14, No. 3, July-September 1978, 7.

42. Shell Archive [London], *Eighth Annual Report: The Caribbean Petroleum Company 1921*, 102; Ralph Arnold, George Macready, and Thomas Barrington, *The First Big Oil Hunt: Venezuela 1911–1916* (New York: Vantage Press, 1960), 289.

43. Stephen Rabe, "Anglo-American Rivalry for Venezuelan Oil 1919–1929," *Mid-America* 58, No. 2, April-July 1976, 99.

44. Ibid., 102.

45. George Philip, *Oil and Politics in Latin America: Nationalist Movements and State Companies* (New York: Cambridge University Press, 1982), 45; Jonathan Brown, "British Petroleum Pioneers in Mexico and South America" (Austin: Institute of Latin American Studies, University of Texas at Austin, 1989), 38.

46. Rabe, "Anglo-American Rivalry for Venezuelan Oil 1919–1929," 99. Public Records Office [PRO] [London], Foreign Office (FO) 371/5723, A 9248, Howard, first name illegible, to Marquess of Kedleston, Madrid, December 1, 1921.

47. PRO, FO 371/5723, A 9248. The basis for these claims was made by Dr. Cardenas, Venezuelan minister in Holland, who, it should be pointed out, was said to be a personal enemy of Borges.

48. [National Archives (NA)] 831.00/982, intercepted telegram, signed Davis, originally Winslow to Hurley, London, March 3, 1921, forwarded to Secretary of State Charles Evans Hughes.

49. PRO, FO 371/17619, A 1496, Annual Report 1933, Mr. E. A. Kelling to Sir John Simon, Petroleum Department to Under Secretary of State, March 2, 1921, 4. NA, 831.00/982, intercepted telegram.

50. PRO, FO 371/17619, A 1496, Annual Report 1933.

51. PRO, FO 371/5723, A 9248; Howard, first name illegible, to Marquess of Kedleston.

52. Sandra Flores, "The Gómez Administration and the Oil Workers," (Venezuela, 1908–1935), master's thesis, University of Texas at Austin, 2001, 22.

53. Flores, "The Gómez Administration and the Oil Workers," 14. According to Lieuwen, a 5-bolívar daily wage in 1925 was worth $1 U.S. See Lieuwen, *Petroleum in Venezuela*, 50.

54. NA, 831.504/9, Sloan to Secretary of State.

55. "Snuffing Out a Half-Million Dollar Blaze," *The Lamp*, August 1925, 26.

56. Aníbal R. Martínez, *Chronology of Venezuelan Oil* (London: George Allen and Unwin Ltd. 1969), 50.

57. Henri Pittier, *Trabajos Escogidos* (Buenos Aires: Ministerio Agricultura y Cría, Imprenta López, n.d.), 86–87.

58. "Lake Exploration Extends Seven Miles from Shore," *Oil and Gas Journal*, December 25, 1941, 152.

59. Lourdes Bello, Judith Díaz, Luisa Pernalete, et al., *El fin de los pueblos de agua y el petróleo* (Caracas: Biblioteca de Trabajo Venezolana, Colección Raíces Mi Pueblo, Vol. 7, Cooperativa Laboratorio Educativo, 1980), interview with Sra. Antonia Rall, 7, 8, 12.

60. Brian McBeth, *Juan Vicente Gómez and the Oil Companies in Venezuela, 1908–1935* (New York: Cambridge University Press, 1983), 154.

61. Acervo Histórico del Estado Zulia [Maracaibo] (AHZ) 4, 1928, Calamidades Públicas, Incendio de Lagunillas, Pedro Pinto S. to Secretario General de Gobierno, Santa Rita, June 18, 1928.

62. NA, RG 84/848, Archer Woodford to John Bernhard, Maracaibo, December 23, 1939, Archivo Histórico de Miraflores [Caracas] (AHM), 1–1–3, Informe Sobre Situación i Necesidades de Ciudad Ojeda, Junta Pro Mejoras de Ciudad Ojeda, Alberto Nuñez, Eugenia Zamarripa, Carlos R. Prieto, to Medina, Ciudad Ojeda November 16, 1942.

63. Luis Vallenilla, *Oil: The Making of a New Economic Order: Venezuelan Oil and OPEC* (New York: McGraw-Hill, 1975) 46.

64. Charles Bergquist, *Labor in Latin America, Comparative Essays on Chile, Argentina, Venezuela, and Colombia* (Stanford, CA: Stanford University Press, 1986), 239, 240, 242; Wayne C. Taylor and John Lindeman, *The Creole Corporation in Venezuela* (Washington, D.C.: National Planning Association, 1955), 87; Morris, *Nelson Rockefeller*, 119–120; George Ives, "Creole's Venezuela Indoctrination School," *World Oil*, September 1, 1947.

65. Freedom of Information and Privacy Acts, Subject: Creole Petroleum Corporation, File Number: 64-HQ–28947, Federal Bureau of Investigation, A. Lewis Russell to J. Edgar Hoover, Caracas, October 23, 1961, 64–28947.

66. Freedom of Information and Privacy Acts, Subject: Creole Petroleum Corporation, File Number: 64-HQ–28947, Federal Bureau of Investigation, United States Department of Justice, Federal Bureau of Investigation, Re: Possible Hijacking of Tanker Esso Caripito, Norfolk, Virginia, March 20, 1963.

67. "World Economic Forum 2002—Profiles: Alí Rodríguez," *Financial Times*, January 29, 2002, http://specials.ft.com/wef2002/FT3BYRXU1XC.html (accessed March 3, 2006); "El Secretario General de la OPEP, Nuevo Presidente de Petróleos de Venezuela," EFE, April 21, 2002.

68. Rodríguez was born in 1937, so he is seven years older than Giusti. "World Economic Forum 2002, Profiles Alí Rodríguez," *Financial Times* Web site.

69. Padgett, "Latin Oil Czar."

70. Esperanza Márquez, "Alí Rodríguez araque, el personaje y su receta," *El Mundo*, August 10, 2002, http://www.elmundo.com.ve/ediciones/2002/08/10/p1-14s1.htm (accessed March 3, 2006).

71. "World Economic Forum 2002—Profiles: Alí Rodríguez."

72. Padgett, "The Latin Oil Czar."

73. "World Economic Forum 2002—Profiles: Alí Rodríguez"; Edgar Elías Osuna, "Las dos versiones del Comandante Fausto," *El Universal*, March 4, 2003, http://buscador.eluniversal.com/2003/03/04/opi_art_04290DD.shtml (accessed March 22, 2006).

74. "El Secretario General de la OPEP," EFE; Márquez, "Alí Rodríguez Araque, el personaje y su receta."

75. Padgett, "The Latin Oil Czar—Alí Rodríguez Named Venezuela's Foreign Minister," EFE, November 21, 2004, reprinted at *Latin Petroleum* Web site, http://www.latinpetroleum.com/cgi-bin/artman/exec/view.cgi?archive=17& num=3817 (accessed March 3, 2006).

76. Padgett, "The Latin Oil Czar."

77. Fisher, "A Friend in Need?"

78. Michael McCaughan, *The Battle of Venezuela* (London: Latin America Bureau, 2003), 31.

79. Michel Chossudovsky, *La miseria en Venezuela* (Valencia, Venezuela: Vadell Hermanos, 1979) 16, 19.

80. Judith Ewell, *Venezuela: A Century of Change* (Stanford, CA: Stanford University Press 1984), 182.

81. Carlos Aznárez, *Los sueños de Bolívar en la Venezuela de hoy* (Editorial Txalaparta, 2000), 63; Marco Vinicio Salas M., *Los recios pueblos de Barinas* (Mérida: Ediciones Merap, 1998), 145.

82. Jon Lee Anderson, "The Revolutionary," *New Yorker,* September 10, 2001, http://www.newyorker.com/printables/archive/020422fr_archive03 (accessed March 3, 2006).

83. Vinicio Salas, *Los recios pueblos de Barinas,* 11.

84. "Transcript: Hugo Chávez Interview," ABC News Web Site, Sept 16, 2005, http://abcnews.go.com/Nightline/International/story?id=1134098&page=1 (accessed March 3, 2006).

85. Guevara, *Chávez, Un hombre que anda por ahí,* 74.

86. "Transcript: Hugo Chávez Interview."

87. Guevara, *Chávez, Un hombre que anda por ahí,* 77.

88. Dieterich, *La cuarta vía al poder,* 34.

89. Guevara, *Chávez, Un hombre que anda por ahí,* 77.

90. Dieterich, *La cuarta vía al poder,* 34.

91. Guevara, *Chávez, Un hombre que anda por ahí,* 77, 79.

92. Ibid., 78, 79.

93. Ibid., 80.

94. David Blank, *Politics in Venezuela* (Boston: Little Brown and Co., 1973), 36, 28.

95. Ibid., 29.

96. Ibid., 89.

97. Blank, *Politics in Venezuela,* 28; Amalio Belmonte Guzmán, Dimitri Briceño Reyes, et al., *Ensayo sobre Historia Política de Venezuela,* 1917–1968 (Caracas: Academia Nacional de La Historia, 1981), 119.

98. Blank, *Politics in Venezuela,* 89.

99. Judith Ewell, *Venezuela: A Century of Change* (Stanford: Stanford University Press, 1984), 142.

100. Chossudovsky, *La miseria en Venezuela,* 70.

101. Ibid., 75.

102. Guevara, *Chávez, un hombre que anda por ahí,* 77; Anderson, "The Revolutionary."

103. "Transcript: Hugo Chávez Interview."

104. Guevara, *Chávez, un hombre que anda por ahí*, 81; Dieterich, *La cuarta via al poder*, 34.

105. Ricardo de Sola, "La vivienda y la construcción en Venezuela," in Corporación Venezolana de Fomento, *Contribución al estudio de la vivienda* (Caracas: Ediciones C.V.F., 1959), 19.

106. Amalio Belmonte Guzmán, Dimitri Briceño Reyes, et al., *Ensayo sobre historia política de Venezuela, 1917–1968* (Caracas: Academia Nacional de La Historia, 1981), 119.

107. Ibid., 120.

108. Ewell, *Venezuela: A Century of Change*, 139.

109. Blank, *Politics in Venezuela*, 65.

110. Ibid., 45.

111. Ibid., 44.

112. Belmonte Guzmán, Briceño Reyes, et al., *Ensayo sobre historia política de Venezuela*, 120.

113. Blank, *Politics in Venezuela*, 45.

114. John Powell, *Political Mobilization of the Venezuelan Peasant* (Cambridge, MA: Harvard University Press, 1971), 110.

115. Ewell, *Venezuela: A Century of Change*, 140.

116. Blank, *Politics in Venezuela*, 46.

117. Ewell, *Venezuela: A Century of Change*, 123.

118. Blank, *Politics in Venezuela*, 45; Ewell, *Venezuela: A Century of Change*, 139.

CHAPTER 2

1. "Mérida," Encyclopedia Britannica Online, http://www.britannica.com/eb/article–9052129 (accessed March 3, 2006).

2. Greg Wilpert, "The Main Obstacle is the Administrative Structure of the Venezuelan State," Venezuela Analysis, July 24, 2004, http://www.venezuelanalysis.com/articles.php?artno=1224 (accessed March 3, 2006); Bernard Mommer, "Changing Venezuelan Oil Policy," *Oxford Energy Comment*, April 1999, http://www.oxfordenergy.org/comment.php?9904 (accessed March 3, 2006); Abraham, "Situation at Venezuela's PDVSA Deteriorates"; Mommer, "Changing Venezuelan Oil Policy"; José Zambrano, "Oil: New PdVSA President—OPEC's Loss is Venezuela's Gain," Inter Press Service, April 22, 2002 (Factiva Database).

3. *South America, Central America and the Caribbean 2005*, 867; Luis Lander and Margarita López Maya, "Oil and Venezuela's Failed Coup," *Foreign Policy in Focus*, April 26, 2002; "Venezuela's Chávez Basking in Spotlight as OPEC Summit Begins," Associated Press, September 26, 2000, posted at CNN Web site, http://edition.cnn.com/2000/WORLD/americas/09/26/venezuela.opec.ap/ (accessed March 3, 2006); Padgett, "The Latin Oil Czar"; Fisher, "A Friend in Need?"; "U.S. Energy Secretary in Venezuela Seeking Cheaper Oil," Reuters, October 21, 2000, posted at CNN Web site, http://archives.

cnn.com/2000/WORLD/americas/10/21/venezuela.richardson.reut/index.ht
ml (accessed March 3, 2006).

4. "Venezuela's Chávez Courts OPEC Chief for the Top Job at PdVSA," AP-
    Business, April 18, 2002; "Venezuela's Chávez Basking in Spotlight as OPEC
    Summit Begins"; Marc Frank, "Cuba Gets First Venezuela Oil in 5 Months,"
    Reuters, September 15, 2002 (Factiva Database).

5. EIA Web site, "International Energy Annual 2000, Oil and Gas Market
    Chronology: 2000," http://www.eia.doe.gov/iea/chron2000.html (accessed
    March 2, 2006); Wilpert, "The Main Obstacle is the Administrative Structure
    of the Venezuelan State"; "Analysis: OPEC's Income in Danger as Multina-
    tionals Return"; "Venezuelan Becomes OPEC President," Alexander's Gas and
    Oil Connections, December 5, 2000, http://www.gasandoil.com/goc/news/
    ntl01969.htm (accessed March 3, 2006); "World Economic Forum 2002—Pro-
    files: Alí Rodríguez"; Zambrano, "OPEC's Loss is Venezuela's Gain." Greg
    Wilpert, "Venezuela's New Constitution," Venezuela Analysis, August 27,
    2003, http://www.venezuelanalysis.com/articles.php?artno=1003 (accessed
    March 3, 2006), Joachim Bamrud, "Another Fujimori," Latin Business Chroni-
    cle, November 26, 2001, http://www.latinbusinesschronicle.com/reports/com-
    mentary/chavez.htm (accessed March 3, 2006), South America, Central
    America and The Caribbean 2005. 867. Lander and López Maya, "Oil and
    Venezuela's Failed Coup," Wilpert, "The Main Obstacle Is The Administrative
    Structure of The Venezuelan State," Padgett, "The Latin Oil Czar, "Abraham,
    "Situation at Venezuela's PDVSA Deteriorates."

6. "U.S. Energy Secretary in Venezuela Seeking Cheaper Oil"; Greg Palast,
    "OPEC Chief Warned Chávez About Coup," The Guardian, May 13, 2002,
    http://www.guardian.co.uk/oil/story/0,11319,714504,00.html (accessed March
    3, 2006); Lander and López Maya, "Oil and Venezuela's Failed Coup."

7. "Venez. Prez Foes To Pass The Hat," Associated Press, January 4, 2002,
    reprinted at CBS Web site, http://www.cbsnews.com/stories/2003/01/05/
    world/main535304.shtml (accessed March 3, 2006), Matthew Robinson,
    "Venezuelan oil to keep flowing during Dec 10 strike," Reuters, December 5,
    2001 (Factiva Database)

8. Alexandra Olson, "Ex-President of Venezuelan State Oil Company Accuses
    Government of Eroding Morale," Associated Press, March 4, 2002 (Factiva
    Database); Fred Pals, "Former PdVSA Head Lameda Warns Venezuelan
    President of Turmoil," Dow Jones International News, March 5, 2002 (Fac-
    tiva Database).

9. "Country Analysis: Venezuela," Alexander's Gas and Oil Connections, Janu-
    ary 24, 2003, http://www.gasandoil.com/goc/news/ntl30454.htm (accessed
    March 3, 2006); CBC Web site, CBC News Online, in Depth: Venezuela,
    August 16, 2004, http://www.cbc.ca/news/background/venezuela/oil.html
    (accessed March 3, 2006); Easton, "Oil Industry Locks Horns with Chávez,";
    Margarita López Maya, Luis Lander, and Edgardo Lander, "The Military
    Coup in Venezuela," Foreign Policy in Focus, April 15, 2002; Jonah Gindin, "A
    Brief Recent History of Venezuela's Labor Movement, Re-Organizing

Venezuelan Labor," Venezuela Analysis, October 18, 2004, http://www. venezuelanalysis.com/articles.php?artno=1296 (accessed March 3, 2006).

10. Eva Golinger, "NED Back on the Offensive in Venezuela," Vheadline, November 28, 2004, http://www.vheadline.com/readnews.asp?id=23482 (accessed March 3, 2006).

11. Palast, "OPEC Chief Warned Chávez About Coup."

12. C. R. Chávez, "Luis Giusti: 'No estamos violando la Constitución Nacional,'" *El Universal* (Caracas), November 5, 1996, http://buscador.eluniversal.com/1996/11/05/pet_art_S05LUI.shtml (accessed March 3, 2006); "Carmona, de líder empresarial a efímero presidente," *El Pais*, April 14, 2002, http://elpais-cAlí.terra.com.co/paisonline/notas/Abril142002/carmona.html (accessed March 3, 2006); "Pedro Carmona, presidente por un día," BBC Mundo, April 14, 2002, http://news.bbc.co.uk/hi/spanish/news/newsid_ 1925000/1925832.stm (accessed March 3, 2006); Pedro Carmona, "Un compás de espera," *El Universal*, December 19, 1998, http://www.el-universal. com/1998/12/19/opi_art_007.shtml (accessed March 3, 2006); Pedro Carmona, "Petróleos de Venezuela," *El Universal*, March 30, 2002, http:// buscador.eluniversal.com/2002/03/30/opi_art_OPI4.shtml (accessed March 3, 2006); "Profile: Pedro Carmona," May 27, 2002, BBC News Web site, http://news.bbc.co.uk/2/hi/americas/1927678.stm (accessed March 3, 2006). Carmona was elected president of Fedecámaras in 2001. See "Carmona, de líder empresarial a efímero presidente."

13. "Pedro Carmona, presidente por un día"; Rocío Caza and Gilberto Rivero, "Sucesos, Decomisan arsenal en quinta de Pérez Recao," *El Mundo*, April 25, 2002, http://www.elmundo.com.ve/ediciones/2002/04/25/p1–20s1.htm (accessed March 3, 2006); "'No participé en reuniones en las que se hablase de golpe,'" *El Universal*, May 16, 2002, http://buscador.eluniversal.com/2002/ 05/16/pol_art_16110AA.shtml (accessed March 8, 2006); Juan Tamayo, "Venezuelans Linked to Coup Attempt Said to Be in Miami," *Miami Herald*, April 26, 2002; Sebastián de la Nuez, "Héroes y villanos," *Tal Cual* (Venezuela), May 3, 2002, http://www.talcualdigital.com/ediciones/2002/05/ 03/f-p8s1.htm (accessed March 3, 2006).

14. Greg Wilpert, "Coup in Venezuela: An Eyewitness Report," Common Dreams, April 12, 2002, http://www.commondreams.org/views02/0412–08.htm (accessed March 3, 2006); Luis Lander and Margarita López Maya, "Oil and Venezuela's Failed Coup," *Foreign Policy in Focus*, April 26, 2002; Kim Bartley and Donnacha O'Briain, "Who's Right? The Filmmakers Respond," *Columbia Journalism Review*, June 2004, http://www.cjr.org/issues/2004/3/bartley-docu. asp (accessed March 3, 2006); *South America, Central America and the Caribbean 2005*, 868; "Altos oficiales desconocen autoridad del presidente Chávez," *El Universal*, April 12, 2002, http://buscador.eluniversal.com/2002/04/12/pol_ art_12112BB.shtml (accessed March 3, 2006); "Timeline: Venezuela, a Chronology of Key Events," BBC Web site, December 6, 2005, http:// news.bbc.co.uk/2/hi/americas/country_profiles/1229348.stm (accessed March 3, 2006).

15. Tamayo, "Venezuelans Linked to Coup Attempt Said to Be in Miami"; Lander and López Maya, "Oil and Venezuela's Failed Coup"; Parker, "Defending Chávez's 'Bolivarian Revolution'"; "'No participé en reuniones en las que se hablase de golpe,'" *El Universal*.
16. Greg Palast, "OPEC Chief Warned Chávez about Coup."
17. "BBC Profile: Pedro Carmona"; "The Great Escape," Inter Press Service, June 19, 2002, posted on latinamericapress.org.; Tamayo, "Venezuelans Linked to Coup Attempt Said to Be in Miami"; Caza and Rivera, "Sucesos, Decomisan arsenal en quinta de Pérez Recao".
18. "'No participé en reuniones en las que se hablase de golpe,'" *El Universal*.
19. Frank, "Cuba Gets First Venezuela Oil in 5 Months"; Kozloff, "Oil is a Geopolitical Weapon," "Al-Jazeera: The New Power on the Small Screen," *The Independent* (Online Edition), October 26, 2005, http://news.independent.co.uk/media/article322273.ece (accessed March 3, 2006).
20. *South America, Central America and the Caribbean 2005*, 868.
21. "Rodríguez' Decision to Leave OPEC Not Easy," Alexander's Gas and Oil Connections, May 16, 2002, http://www.gasandoil.com/goc/news/ntl22063.htm (accessed March 3, 2006).
22. Zambrano, "OPEC's Loss is Venezuela's Gain."
23. "Rodríguez' Decision to Leave OPEC Not Easy," Alexander's Gas and Oil Connections.
24. Zambrano, "OPEC's Loss is Venezuela's Gain."
25. Hugo Chávez, *El golpe fascista contra Venezuela, "aquí está en juego la vida de la patria" discursos e intervenciones, diciembre de 2002-enero de 2003* (Havana: Ediciones Plaza, 2003), 295.
26. Bridget Broderick, "Venezuela: Another Bosses' Strike," *International Socialist Review* Issue 27, January–February 2003, http://isreview.org/issues/27/venezuela.shtml (accessed March 3, 2006).
27. Andy Webb-Vidal, "Oil Power to the People is Priority for Rodríguez," *Financial Times*, December 30, 2002; *South America, Central America and the Caribbean*.
28. Chávez, *El golpe fascista contra Venezuela*, 295.
29. Ibid., 295.
30. Greg Wilpert, "Collision in Venezuela," *New Left Review* 21, May–June 2003.
31. Chávez, *El golpe fascista contra Venezuela*, 296.
32. John C. K. Daly, "UPI Energy Watch," July 16, 2004, posted at *Washington Times* Web site, http://www.washtimes.com/upi-breaking/20040716–024248–5903r.htm (accessed March 3, 2006); Sanchez, "Venezuela Rejects U.S. Ruling."
33. Fabiola Sánchez, "Expropriation Claim by U.S. Firm Will Not Curb FDI," Associated Press, July 16, 2004, reprinted at *Latin Petroleum* Web site, http://www.latinpetroleum.com/cgi-bin/artman/exec/view.cgi?archive=17&num=3484&printer=1 (accessed March 3, 2006).
34. Webb-Vidal, "Oil Power to the People is Priority for Rodríguez."
35. Easton, "Oil Industry Locks Horns with Chávez".
36. Webb-Vidal, "Oil Power to the People is Priority for Rodríguez".

37. "Venezuela Importing Gas to Ease Oil Strike," CNN Web site, December 29, 2002, http://edition.cnn.com/2002/WORLD/americas/12/29/venezuela. strike/ (accessed March 3, 2006).

38. Webb-Vidal, "Oil Power to the People is Priority for Rodríguez."

39. "Continúan despidos de gerentes de PdVSA," El Universal, December 24, 2002, http://buscador.eluniversal.com/2002/12/24/eco_art_24111EE.shtml (accessed March 3, 2006); South America, Central America and the Caribbean 2005.

40. Sánchez, "Venezuela Rejects U.S. Ruling."

41. South America, Central America and the Caribbean 2005.

42. Greg Wilpert, interview with Alí Rodríguez, "The Main Obstacle is the Administrative Structure of the Venezuelan State," Venezuela Analysis, July 24, 2004, http://www.venezuelanalysis.com/articles.php?artno=1224 (accessed March 3, 2006).

43. South America, Central America and the Caribbean 2005, 868.

44. Sánchez, "Venezuela Rejects U.S. Ruling."

45. Chávez, El golpe fascista contra Venezuela, 142.

46. Sánchez, "Venezuela Rejects U.S. Ruling."

47. Sánchez, "Expropriation Claim by U.S. Firm Will not Curb FDI."

48. Sánchez, "Venezuela Rejects U.S. Ruling."

49. EIA report, Country Report on Venezuela, June 2004.

50. Smith, "Is Venezuela's Chávez Killing the Golden Goose?"

51. Paula Chahín, "Alí Rodríguez, presidente de PdVSA: "Todo recurso natural pertenece a los pueblos"; Punto Final, No. 579, October 29, 2004, http://www.puntofinal.cl/579/Alí.htm (accessed March 3, 2006).

52. "Venezuela Pérez Wins Recall Vote," Associated Press, August 16, 2004, reprinted at CBS News Web site, http://www.cbsnews.com/stories/2004/03/03/world/main603747.shtml (accessed March 3, 2006).

53. Smith, "Is Venezuela's Chávez Killing the Golden Goose?"; Pascal Fletcher, "Venezuela Slaps Higher Taxes on Orinoco Oil Deals," Reuters, October 11, 2004, reprinted at Latin Petroleum Web site, http://www.latinpetroleum.com/cgi-bin/artman/exec/view.cgi?archive=17&num=3718&printer=1 (accessed March 3, 2006).

54. Kozloff, "Oil is a Geopolitical Weapon"; Marianna Párraga, "Hidrocarburos/Afinan venta de Ruhr Oel en una oferta mixta de firma rusa, Paralizada expansión de Citgo," El Universal, February 6, 2005, http://www.el-universal.com/2005/02/06/imp_eco_art_06124A.shtml (accessed March 3, 2006).

55. Kozloff, "Oil is a Geopolitical Weapon"; Sarah Wagner, "Chávez and Foreign Minister Say U.S.-Venezuela Relations Can Improve," Venezuela Analysis, March 18, 2005, http://www.venezuelanalysis.com/news.php?newsno=1554 (accessed March 3, 2006); "U.S. Reviews Oil Supply Relationship with Venezuela," Alexander's Gas and Oil Connections, Vol. 10, Issue 2, January 27, 2005, http://www.gasandoil.com/goc/news/ntl50403.htm (accessed March 3, 2006); "U.S. Senator Worried About Cutoff of Venezuelan Oil," Reuters, January 13, 2005, reprinted at Boston Globe Web site, http://www.boston.com/news/nation/washington/articles/2005/01/

13/senator_worried_about_cutoff_of_venezuelan_oil?mode=PF (accessed March 3, 2006).

CHAPTER 3

1. Pablo Bachelet, "Reaching New Policy Deal for Latin America, the Washington Consensus Has Become an Ugly Term, Invoked as the Cause of Latin America's Woes," *Miami Herald*, January 2, 2006, http://www.miami.com/mld/miami-herald/business/special_packages/business_monday/13527922.htm?source=rss &channel=miamiherald_business_monday (accessed March 3, 2006).
2. Marcela Sánchez, "A Plea for a Broader Consensus for Latin America," *Washington Post*, July 14, 2005, http://www.washingtonpost.com/wp-dyn/content/article/2005/07/14/AR2005071401343.html?nav=rss_opinion/columns (accessed March 3, 2006).
3. "Unraveling the Washington Consensus, an Interview with Joseph Stiglitz," *Multinational Monitor*, April 2000, Vol. 21, No. 4, http://multinationalmoni-tor.org/mm2000/00april/interview.html (accessed March 4, 2006). George Bush Presidential Library Web site, Appointment of Robert B. Zoellick as Deputy Chief of Staff to the President, August 24, 1992, http://bushlibrary.tamu.edu/research/papers/1992/92082406.html (accessed March 4, 2006), White House Web site, "United States Trade Representative, Ambassador Robert B. Zoellick," http://www.whitehouse.gov/government/zoellick-bio.html (accessed March 4, 2006)
4. Susan George, "A Short History of Neoliberalism," Conference on Eco-nomic Sovereignty in a Globalising World, March 24 26, 1999, posted on Global Policy Forum, http://www.globalpolicy.org/globaliz/econ/histneol.htm (accessed March 4, 2006); Tom McFeat, "In Depth: Summit of the Americas, What is Globalization?" CBC News Online, January 7, 2004, http://www.cbc.ca/news/background/summitofamericas/globalization.html (accessed March 4, 2006); "20 Questions on the IMF," *Multinational Monitor*, April 2000, Vol. 21 No. 4, http://multinationalmonitor.org/mm2000/00april/economics.html (accessed March 4, 2006).
5. Robert B. Zoellick, "Africa and Trade: How to Increase Hope and Opportu-nity," Transcript of Ambassador Robert Zoellick speaking at the University of Pretoria, Pretoria, South Africa, February 18, 2002, U.S. Embassy in South Africa Web site, http://usembassy.state.gov/posts/sf1/wwwhv1z.html (ac-cessed March 4, 2006). George Bush Presidential Library Web site, Appoint-ment of Robert B. Zoellick as Deputy Chief of Staff to the President, August 24, 1992, http://bushlibrary.tamu.edu/research/papers/1992/92082406.html (accessed March 4, 2006), White House Web site, "United States Trade Rep-resentative, Ambassador Robert B. Zoellick," http://www.whitehouse.gov/government/zoellick-bio.html (accessed March 4, 2006)
6. White House Web site, "United States Trade Representative, Ambassador Robert B. Zoellick".

7. Tom Barry, "Profile, Robert Zoellick," International Relations Center, June 28, 2005, International Relations Center Web site, http://rightweb.irc-online.org/profile/1397 (accessed March 27, 2006).

8. White House Web site, "United States Trade Representative, Ambassador Robert B. Zoellick"; "Understanding the WTO: Basics, the Uruguay Round"; World Trade Organization Web site, http://www.wto.org/english/thewto_e/whatis_e/tif_e/fact5_e.htm (accessed March 4, 2006).

9. Zoellick, "Africa and Trade".

10. "Worldbeaters," *New Internationalist*, March 2005.

11. Barry, "Profile, Robert Zoellick."

12. Michael G. Wilson, "The North American Free Trade Agreement: Ronald Reagan's Vision Realized," Executive Memorandum #371, November 23, 1993, Heritage Foundation, http://www.heritage.org/Research/Tradeand-ForeignAid/EM371.cfm (accessed March 4, 2006); Office of NAFTA and Inter-American Affairs, "The North American Free Trade Agreement, Seven Years of Success," *Export America*, September 2001, 12, http://www.trade.gov/exportamerica/NewsFromCommerce/nfc_NAFTA.pdf (accessed March 4, 2006).

13. David Brooks and Jonathan Fox, "IRC Americas Program Special Report, NAFTA: Ten Years of Cross-Border Dialogues," March 2004, International Relations Center Web site, http://americas.irc-online.org/reports/2004/0403nafta.html (accessed March 4, 2006).

14. Barry, "Profile, Robert Zoellick."

15. White House Web site, "United States Trade Representative, Ambassador Robert B. Zoellick," International Relations Center Web site; "IRC Strategies and Principles," http://www.irc-online.org/strategies.php (accessed March 4, 2006); "IRC Staff," http://www.irc-online.org/staff/index.php (accessed March 4, 2006); Barry, "Profile, Robert Zoellick".

16. "Worldbeaters."

17. Barry, "Profile, Robert Zoellick"; "Worldbeaters."

18. "Worldbeaters."

19. Michael Keefer, "Hugo Chávez Frías and the Sense of History," Centre for Research on Globalisation, May 6, 2005, http://www.globalresearch.ca/index.php?context=viewArticle&code=MIC20050506&articleId=167 (accessed March 27, 2006). Final Vote Results For Roll Call 575, HR 3450, North American Free Trade Agreement Implementation, 17 November 1993, U.S. House of Representatives Web site, http://clerk.house.gov/evs/1993/roll575.xml (accessed March 4, 2006), U.S. Senate Roll Call Votes 103rd Congress - 1st Session, "On Passage of the Bill (H.R. 3450), November 20, 1993, U.S. Senate Web site, http://www.senate.gov/legislative/LIS/roll_call_lists/roll_call_vote_cfm.cfm?congress=103&session=1&vote=00395 (accessed March 4, 2006)

20. International Forum on Globalization Web site, "The Free Trade Area of the Americas and the Threat to Water," http://www.ifg.org/programs/ftaawater.htm (accessed March 4, 2006).

21. "FTAA, Frequently Asked Questions," Global Exchange report, last updated September 13, 2005, http://www.globalexchange.org/campaigns/ftaa/faq. html (accessed February 26, 2006).

22. Keefer, "Hugo Chávez Frias and the Sense of History."

23. International Forum on Globalization Web site, "The Free Trade Area of the Americas and the Threat to Water"; Scott Miller, "Western Hemisphere Trade Meeting Opens in Miami, Trade Ministers Aiming for Ambitious, Balanced Agreement," *Washington File* (a product of the Bureau of International Information Programs, U.S. Department of State), November 20, 2003.

24. International Forum on Globalization Web site, "The Free Trade Area of the Americas."

25. "FTAA, Frequently Asked Questions," Global Exchange.

26. International Forum on Globalization Web site, "The Free Trade Area of the Americas."

27. Mike Hanlon, "Globalization Allows Societies to Express Cultural Strengths," *Seattle Post Intelligencer*, November 28, 2003, http://seattlepi. nwsource.com/opinion/150070_hanlon28.html (accessed March 4, 2006).

28. Greg Palast, "Chávez Versus the Free Trade Zombies of the Americas," GregPalast.com, November 30, 2003, http://www.gregpalast.com/detail. cfm?artid=295&row=1 (accessed March 4, 2006).

29. Keefer, "Hugo Chávez Frias and the Sense of History."

30. Hampden McBeth, "The Not So Odd Couple: Venezuela's Hugo Chávez and Cuba's Fidel Castro," Council on Hemispheric Affairs, June 21, 2005, http://www.coha.org/NEW_PRESS_RELEASES/New_Press_Releases_ 2005/05.62_The_Not_So_Odd_Couple_Venezulas_Hugo_Chávez_and_ Cubas_Fidel_Castro.htm (accessed February 24, 2006).

31. "Castro ataca al ALCA y pide plebiscito," BBC, May 2, 2001, http://news. bbc.co.uk/hi/spanish/news/newsid_1307000/1307771.stm (accessed February 26, 2006).

32. "Profile: Hugo Chávez," BBC News Web site, December 5, 2002, http:// news.bbc.co.uk/2/hi/americas/1925236.stm (accessed February 24, 2006). Carlos Batista, "Fidel Castro, el gran ausente de la cumbre de las Américas," Agence France Presse, January 12, 2004 (Factiva Database). Guevara, *Chávez un hombre que anda por ahí* (Melbourne: Ocean Press 2005, 97)

33. Alberto Garrido, "Proceso cubano y la izquierda venezolana, El eje revolucionario Chávez-Castro," *El Universal* (Caracas, Venezuela), June 27, 2004.

34. Guevara, *Chávez un hombre que anda por ahí*, 97.

35. "Profile: Hugo Chávez," BBC News Web site; Jon Lee Anderson, "The Revolutionary," *New Yorker*, September 10, 2001.

36. David Coleman, "Venezuelan President Hugo Chávez Frías Postpones 24-hour Visit to Havana," Vheadline, December 12, 2004, http://www.vheadline.com/readnews.asp?id=23941, (accessed February 24, 2006); Dalia Acosta, "Cuba: Castro Strengthens Vital Ties with Colombia, Venezuela," Inter Press Service, January 18, 1999 (Factiva Database).

37. McBeth, "The Not So Odd Couple."

38. Eduardo Ortíz, *Análisis socioeconómico de Venezuela* (Caracas: Fundación Centro Gumilla, 1997), 9.

39. Ibid., 13.

40. *South America, Central America and the Caribbean 2005* (London: Europa Publications, 2005), 865; Ortíz, *Análisis Socioeconómico de Venezuela*, 9.

41. Julia Buxton, "Economy," in *South America, Central America and The Caribbean 2005*, 876. "Herrera Campíns, Luis," *Encyclopædia Britannica*, Encyclopædia Britannica Website, http://www.britannica.com/eb/article–9000878 (accessed February 24, 2006), Robert D. Crassweller, "The Western Hemisphere," book review of *Copei: Ideología y Liderazgo* by Ricardo Combellas, *Foreign Affairs*, Summer 1986, http://www.foreignaffairs.org/19860601fabook10949/ricardo-combellas/copei-ideologia-y-liderazgo.html?mode=print (accessed February 24, 2006), Jorge Jorquera, "Neoliberalism, the Erosion of Consensus and the Rise of a New Popular Movement," Vheadline (Web site dedicated to news from Venezuela), July 10, 2003, http://www.vheadline.com/readnews.asp?id=9399 (accessed February 24, 2006). "Venezuela," Latin American Andean Group Report, July 30, 1987 (Factiva Database)

42. Carrie Figdor, "President Lusinchi Announces Austerity Economic Package," Associated Press, July 17, 1986 (Factiva Database). "Herrera Campíns, Luis," Encyclopædia Britannica, Encyclopædia Britannica Website, http://www.britannica.com/eb/article–9000878 (accessed February 24, 2006)

43. "Herrera Campíns, Luis," *Encyclopedia Britannica*.

44. Kenneth Roberts, "Polarización social y resurgimiento del populismo en Venezuela," in Steve Ellner and Daniel Hellinger (eds.); *La política venezolana en la época de Chávez* (Caracas: Editorial Nueva Sociedad, 2003), 80, 81.

45. *South America, Central America and the Caribbean 2005*, 865.

46. Ibid.

47. "Press Digest—Venezuela—July 26," Reuters, July 26, 2004. (Factiva database)

48. "Pérez's Corruption Case Ends in Conviction," Reuters, May 30, 1996; "Ex-President Pérez to Be Freed, Prepares New Political Party," Agence France-Presse, September 18, 1996; "Pérez, Carlos Andrés," *Diccionario de historia de Venezuela* Vol. 2 (Caracas: Fundación Polar, 1997), 550.

49. "Pérez's Corruption Case Ends in Conviction"; "Success Turns Sour for Carlos Andrés Pérez," November 30, 1992, Latin American Business News Wire Notimex/Federal News Service (Factiva Database).

50. Ewell, *Venezuela a Century of Change* (Stanford: Stanford University Press, 1984), 94–5; "Pérez's Corruption Case Ends in Conviction."

51. John C. Fredriksen, "Pérez, Carlos Andrés," *Biographical Dictionary of Modern World Leaders: 1992 to the Present* (New York: Facts on File, Inc., 2003), Facts on File, Inc., *World History Online*, www.factsonfile.com (accessed March 27, 2006).

52. "Success Turns Sour for Carlos Andrés Pérez," Latin American Business News Wire Notimex/Federal News Service, November 30, 1992 (Factiva Database); "Pérez's Corruption Case Ends in Conviction".

53. *South America, Central America and the Caribbean 2005*, 865.

54. Padgett, "Democrat or Demagogue?"
55. *South America, Central America and the Caribbean 2005*; "Petróleos de Venezuela, S.A."; Hoover's Company in Depth Profiles, January 4, 2006 (Factiva Database); Alan Petzet, "Venezuela (Petróleo de Venezuela, S.A., Company Profile) (The Role of State Oil Companies)," *Oil and Gas Journal*, August 16, 1993 (Factiva Database).
56. *South America, Central America and the Caribbean 2005*, 865.
57. Padgett, "Democrat or Demagogue?"
58. *South America, Central America and the Caribbean 2005*, 865.
59. Ex-Venezuelan Pres. Calls Corruption Allegations 'A Farce,'" Dow Jones International News, December 19, 2001 (Factiva Database); Padgett, "Democrat or Demagogue?"
60. Roberts, "Polarización social y resurgimiento del populismo en Venezuela," 84, *South America, Central America and the Caribbean 2005*, 865.
61. Michael McCaughan, *The Battle of Venezuela* (London: Latin America Bureau, 2003), 32.
62. Ibid.
63. "Pérez, Carlos Andrés," Fundación Polar, 555.
64. "Pérez Conducts a Tame Reshuffle," *Latin American Weekly Report*, August 9, 1990 (Factiva Database); "Pérez, Carlos Andrés," Fundación Polar, 556.
65. McCaughan, *The Battle of Venezuela*, 32.
66. Margarita López Maya, "The Venezuelan Caracazo of 1989: Popular Protest and Institutional Weakness," *Journal of Latin American Studies*, 117, Vol. 35; Issue 1, February 1, 2003 (Factiva Database).
67. McCaughan, *The Battle of Venezuela*, 32, 33.
68. Jorquera, "Neoliberalism, the Erosion of Consensus and the Rise of a New Popular Movement." Vheadline, July 10, 2003, http://www.headline.com/prinks_news.asp?id=9399.
69. López Maya, "The Venezuelan Caracazo of 1989".
70. "World has Underestimated Venezuela's Chávez, Colombian Ex-minister Warns," BBC Monitoring Americas, October 5, 2005 (Factiva Database).
71. "Chronology of 11-Year Civil War in El Salvador," Reuters, September 26, 1991 (Factiva Database)
72. Jennifer Packer, "Campus Group Invades General Dynamics' Recruitment Forum," *The Daily Californian* (Berkeley), November 15, 1989, 5.
73. López Maya, "The Venezuelan Caracazo of 1989."
74. Kartherine Ellison, "Venezuela Steers a New Course: As Oil Profits Fund a Socialist Revolution, President Hugo Chávez Picks a Fight with His Country's Biggest Customer—the United States," *Smithsonian*, January 1, 2006 (Factiva Database).
75. McCaughan, *The Battle of Venezuela*, 33.
76. Ibid.
77. McCaughan, *The Battle of Venezuela*, 33 López Maya, "The Venezuelan Caracazo of 1989."

78. Heinz Dieterich, *La cuarta vía al poder, Venezuela, Ecuador, Colombia* (Bogotá: Grijalbo 2001), 182.

79. Gabriel García Márquez, "The Enigma of Chávez, Deliberate Ambiguity Breeding Doubts and Hopes," *Le Monde Diplomatique*, October 4, 2000, reprinted at ZNet, http://www.zmag.org/content/LatinAmerica/marquez_Chávez-enigma.cfm (accessed February 24, 2006).

80. Dieterich, *La cuarta vía al poder, Venezuela, Ecuador, Colombia*, 182.

81. Márquez, "The Enigma of Chávez."

82. López Maya, "The Venezuelan Caracazo of 1989."

83. Marta Harnecker, *Militares junto al pueblo* (Caracas: Vadell Hermanos, 2003), 131.

84. López Maya, "The Venezuelan Caracazo of 1989."

85. Harnecker, *Hugo Chávez Frías, un hombre, un pueblo*, 18.

86. Dieterich, *La cuarta vía al poder, Venezuela, Ecuador, Colombia*.

87. Harnecker, *Hugo Chávez Frías, un hombre, un pueblo*.

88. Harnecker, *Hugo Chávez Frías, un hombre, un pueblo*, 19; *South America, Central America and the Caribbean 2005* 565; "Political Forces," Country Briefings Venezuela, *The Economist* Web site, from the Economist Intelligence Unit, Source: Country ViewsWire, July 26, 2005, http://www.economist.com/countries/Venezuela/profile.cfm?folder=Profile-Political+Forces (accessed February 25, 2006).

89. Steve Ellner, "President Hugo Chávez of Venezuela," *Z Magazine*, December 1999 http://www.zmag.org/zmag/articles/Chávez.htm (accessed February 25, 2006); Steve Ellner, "The Radical Potential of Chavismo in Venezuela: The First Year and a Half in Power," *Latin American Perspectives*, Issue 120, vol 28, No 5, September 2001, 8, 9

90. Harnecker, *Hugo Chávez Frías, un hombre, un pueblo*.

91. Martín Sánchez, "Venezuela's Chávez and Supporters Celebrated Anniversary of the Feb. 4th Rebellion," Venezuela Analysis, February 5, 2004; Marquez, "The Enigma of Chávez."

92. "Venezuela coup fails, but nation ill at ease," St. Petersburg Times, November 28, 1992 (Factiva Database), McCaughan, The Battle of Venezuela, 32, Edgardo Lander, "The Impact of Neoliberal Adjustment in Venezuela, 1989–1993," Latin American Perspectives, Issue 90, Vol. 23, No. 3, Summer 1996, 53, 55, Fundacíon Polar, Diccionário de historia de venezuela, volume 3, "Pérez, Carlos Andres" (Caracas: Fundacíon Polar, 1997), 551, 558–9

93. McCaughan, *The Battle of Venezuela*, 32.

94. "Petróleos de Venezuela, S.A.," Hoover's Company in Depth Records, January 4, 2006 (Factiva Database).

95. Vivian Sequera, "Profile of Embattled Venezuela President Carlos Andrés Pérez," Associated Press, May 20, 1993.

96. Jon Lee Anderson, "The Revolutionary," *New Yorker*, September 10, 2001, http://www.newyorker.com/archive/content/?020422fr_archive03 (accessed March 18, 2006); "Pérez, Carlos Andrés," *Encyclopedia Britannica* Web site,

http://www.britannica.com/eb/article–9059222?tocId=9059222&query=vene
zuala, (accessed February 26, 2005); "Pérez, Carlos Andrés," *Diccionario de
historia de Venezuela*, Vol. 2 (Caracas: Fundación Polar, 1997), 550.

97.   McCaughan, *The Battle of Venezuela*, 30.

98.   Padgett, "Democrat or Demagogue?"; Harnecker, *Hugo Chávez Frías, un
      hombre, un pueblo*, 23.

99.   Sánchez, "Venezuela's Chávez and Supporters Celebrated Anniversary of the
      Feb. 4th Rebellion."

100. Bruce Nelan, "Venezuela: No Time for Colonels, A Coup Fails When Civil-
      ians Prove Unwilling to Trade Their Government, However Flawed, for a
      Military Dictatorship," *Time*, February 17, 1992.

101. Márquez, "The Enigma of Chávez."

102. Padgett, "Democrat or Demagogue?"

103. Nelan, "Venezuela: No Time for Colonels"; Márquez, "The Enigma of
      Chávez"; Padgett, "Democrat or Demagogue?"

104. Márquez, "The Enigma of Chávez."

105. Daniel Hellinger, "Visión política general: la caída del puntofijismo y el
      surgimiento del chavismo"; Ellner and Hellinger (eds.), *La política venezolana
      en la época de Chávez*, 49.

106. Sánchez, "Venezuela's Chávez and Supporters Celebrated Anniversary of the
      Feb. 4th Rebellion."

107. Márquez, "The Enigma of Chávez."

108. Sánchez, "Venezuela's Chávez and Supporters Celebrated Anniversary of the
      Feb. 4th Rebellion."

109. Padgett, "Democrat or Demagogue?"

110. Anderson, "The Revolutionary."

111. Márquez, "The Enigma of Chávez"; Richard Gott, *In the Shadow of the Liber-
      ator* (London: Verso, 2000), 127.

112. Roberts, "Polarización social y resurgimiento del populismo," 85.

113. Wesley R. Smith, "Research, Trade and Foreign Aid, Salinas Prepares Mexi-
      can Agriculture for Free Trade," Backgrounder #914, October 1, 1992, Her-
      itage Foundation Web site, http://www.heritage.org/Research/Tradeand
      ForeignAid/BG914.cfm (accessed February 25, 2006).

114. Garance Burke, "Mexico: A Deadly Standoff: How a Hot Rebellion Turned
      into an Ongoing Low-Intensity Conflict, Timeline," *Frontline*, August 2003,
      PBS Web site, http://www.pbs.org/frontlineworld/fellows/mexico0803/time-
      line.html (accessed February 25, 2006); "Mexicans Vote in Rebel-sponsored
      Indian Rights Referendum," CNN Web site, March 21, 1999, *http://www.
      cnn.com/WORLD/americas/9903/21/mexico.rebels/* (accessed February 25, 2006).

115. "Profile: The Zapatistas' Mysterious Leader," BBC News Web site, March
      11, 2001, http://news.bbc.co.uk/2/hi/americas/1214676.stm (accessed Febru-
      ary 25, 2006); Rachel Neumann, "On the Road With the Zapatistas, Part 1:
      Mexico City or Bust, the Zapatistas Hit the Road on a March for Indigenous
      Rights," *Village Voice* Web site, February 28, 2001, http://www.villagevoice.
      com/news/0109,zap1,22660,1.html (accessed February 25, 2006).

116. "Second Declaration of La Realidad, Words of the Zapatista Army of National Liberation in the Closing Act of the First Intercontinental Encounter for Humanity and Against Neoliberalism (read by Subcomandante Insurgente Marcos)," EZLN Web site, August 3, 1996, http://www.ezln.org/documentos/1996/19960803.en.htm (accessed February 25, 2006).

117. "Zapatistas Blame Mexican President for Massacre," BBC News Online: World: Americas," BBC Web site, December 27, 1997, http://news.bbc.co.uk/2/low/americas/42109.stm (accessed February 25, 2006); Susan Ferriss, "Zapatista Autonomy Now a Fact of Life," *The Atlanta Journal-Constitution* Web site, December 28, 2003, http://www.ajc.com/news/content/news/1203/28mexico.html (accessed February 25, 2006).

118. "Chávez desafía a gobierno venezolano," *El Universal*, September 13, 1997, http://buscador.eluniversal.com/1997/09/13/pol_art_13116DD.shtml (accessed March 4, 2006).

119. Christina Hoag, "Venezuelan Billionaire Shares His Entrepreneurial Vision in New Book," *Miami Herald*, April 5, 2004 (Factiva Database).

120. "World's Richest People, 2005," *Forbes* Web site, undated, http://www.forbes.com/static/bill2005/rank_76.html?passListId=10&passYear=2005&passListType=Person&searchParameter1=unset&searchParameter2=unset&resultsHowMany=25&resultsSortProperties=%252Bnumberfield1%252C%252Bstringfield2&resultsSortCategoryName=Rank&fromColumnClick=&bktDisplayField=&bktDisplayFieldLength=&category1=category&category2=category&passKeyword=&resultsStart=76 (accessed February 25, 2006).

121. Anna Carugati, "Cisneros Group of Companies' Gustavo Cisneros," *World Screen* Web site, January 2005, http://www.worldscreen.com/interviewscurrent.php?filename=0105cisneros.htm (accessed February 25, 2006).

122. J. P. Faber and Reese Ewing, "Cisneros Goes Online," *Latin CEO: Executive Strategies for the Americas*, December 1999, reprinted at FindArticles.com, http://www.findarticles.com/p/articles/mi_m0OQC/is_1_1/ai_100439900 (accessed February 26, 2006).

123. Carugati, "Cisneros Group of Companies' Gustavo Cisneros"; "Historia," Venevisión Web site, http://www.Venevisión.net/canal/index.asp (accessed February 26, 2006).

124. "Gustavo A. Cisneros," Arthur M. Blank Center For Entrepreneurship at Babson College Web site, undated, http://www3.babson.edu/ESHIP/outreach-events/Gustavo-A-Cisneros.cfm (accessed May 15, 2006)

125. Faber and Ewing, "Cisneros Goes Online."

126. Carlos Fazio, "Otto Reich, experto en operaciones encubiertas, según el Congreso de EU," *La Jornada* (Mexico City), April 29, 2003, http://www.jornada.unam.mx/2003/04/29/029n1mun.php?origen=mundo.php&fly=1 (accessed March 4, 2006).

127. Faber and Ewing, "Cisneros Goes Online."

128. "Nuevos canales para adultos Playboy anunció alianzacon el Grupo Cisneros," *El Universal*, October 9, 1996, http://www.eud.com/1996/10/09/eco_art_C09PLA.shtml (accessed March 4, 2006).

129. "Miami: the Cross road for Hemispheric Growth; Gustavo Cisneros Discusses with Latin CEO the Competitive Advantages of Miami to Headquarter the Free Trade Area of the Americas," *Latin CEO: Executive Strategies for the Americas,* August-September 2002. "AOL firma pacto con Cisneros," *El Universal,* December 16, 1998, http://www.el-universal.com/1998/12/16/eco_art_16210BB.shtml (accessed March 4, 2006).

130. "AOL firma pacto con Cisneros," *El Universal,* December 16, 1998, http://www.el-universal.com/1998/12/16/eco_art_16210BB.shtml (accessed March 4, 2006).

131. "Miami: The Crossroad for Hemispheric Growth."

132. "Presentaron en Madrid biografía de Gustavo Cisneros," *El Universal,* February 24, 2004, http://buscador.eluniversal.com/2004/02/24/cul_art_24205C.shtml (accessed March 4, 2006).

133. "World's Richest People, 2005," *Forbes* Web site, Faber and Ewing, "Cisneros Goes Online."

134. Global Information Infrastructure Commission Web site, Gustavo A. Cisneros.

135. Faber and Ewing, "Cisneros Goes Online."

136. "De un vistazo," *El Universal,* February 25, 2001, http://buscador.eluniversal.com/2001/02/25/apo_art_25380BB.shtml (accessed March 4, 2006); "Presentaron en Madrid biografía de Gustavo Cisneros"; Yasmín Monsalve, "La Orinoquia venezolana baña tierras alemanas," *El Universal,* July 29, 1999, http://buscador.eluniversal.com/1999/07/29/cul_art_29313AA.shtml (accessed March 4, 2006).

137. "Americas Society to Honor Gustavo Cisneros at 23rd Annual Spring Party Gustavo Cisneros to Receive Gold Medal," Americas Society Distinguished Service Award, June 2, 2003, Council of the Americas Web site, http://www.americas-society.org/coa/publications/PR-June-2-03-SpringParty.html (accessed February 26, 2006).

138. Market Access and Compliance Web site, Western Hemisphere Trade and Commerce Forum, Panel 2: "Open Access to the Information Marketplace," Denver, July 1-2, 1995, http://www.mac.doc.gov/ftaa2005/FORUM/APPEND2.TXT (accessed May 12, 2006).

139. Faber and Ewing, "Cisneros Goes Online."

140. "Venezuela Tense as Voters Prepare to Pick President; Populist Chávez Seen as Front-Runner in Sunday Ballot," CNN Web site, December 5, 1998, http://www.cnn.com/WORLD/americas/9812/05/venezuela.elex/ (accessed February 26, 2006).

141. Jane Bussey, "Venezuelan Candidate Has Image Problem Abroad," *Miami Herald,* September 19, 1998.

CHAPTER 4

1. Márquez, "The Enigma of Chávez."

2. Sánchez, "Venezuela's Chávez and Supporters Celebrated Anniversary of the Feb. 4th Rebellion".

3. *South America, Central America and the Caribbean 2005*, 866.
4. Tim Padgett, "Democrat or Demagogue? In 1992 Hugo Chávez Tried to Take Power in Venezuela by Force. Now He May Win a Democratic Presidential Election," *Time* International, November 23, 1998 (Factiva Database).
5. "Pérez Rodríguez, Carlos Andrés," *The Columbia Encyclopedia*, Encyclopedia.com Web site, http://www.encyclopedia.com/html/P/Pérez-C1a.asp (accessed February 26, 2006); "Ousted Venezuelan Leader Sentenced," Associated Press, May 30, 1996, reprinted at *Houston Chronicle* Web site, http://www.chron.com/content/chronicle/world/96/05/31/venezuela.html (accessed February 26, 2006); "Venezuela Ex-Chief Ordered Detained," AP Online, December 20, 2001 (Factiva Database).
6. Jorquera, "Neoliberalism, the Erosion of Consensus and the Rise of a New Popular Movement."
7. "Venezuela: Caldera's Win Is Rejection of Neo-Liberalism," Inter Press Service Global Information Network, December 6, 1993 (Factiva Database)
8. "Publications, Venezuela: Human Rights Developments," Human Rights Watch Web site, http://www.hrw.org/reports/1995/WR95/AMERICAS–11.htm (accessed February 26, 2006); "Global Integrity: Venezuela: Corruption Timeline," Center for Public Integrity, Web site, http://www.publicintegrity.org/ga/country.aspx?cc=ve&act=timeline (accessed February 26, 2006); Jorquera, "Neoliberalism, the Erosion of Consensus and the Rise of a New Popular Movement."
9. Sánchez, "Venezuela's Chávez and Supporters Celebrated Anniversary of the Feb. 4th Rebellion."
10. Ellner, "The Radical Potential of Chavismo in Venezuela."
11. Sánchez, "Venezuela's Chávez and Supporters Celebrated Anniversary of the Feb. 4th Rebellion"; "Chávez desafía a gobierno venezolano," *El Universal*; Coleman, "Venezuelan President Hugo Chávez Frías Postpones 24-hour Visit to Havana," Vheadline.
12. C. P. Pandya and Justin Podur, "The Chávez Government's Economic Policies," Venezuela Analysis, reprinted from *ZNet*, January 22, 2004, http://www.venezuelanalysis.com/articles.php?artno=1092 (accessed February 25, 2006).
13. Robert Díez, "Venezuela," *LatinFinance*, September 1, 1998 (Factiva Database); Robert Taylor, "Agenda Slips on Oil Price," *The Banker* 74 (Vol. 148, No. 869), July 1, 1998 (Factiva Database); "Venezuela: President Rafael Caldera Faces Mounting Protests against Economic Measures," NotiSur-Latin American Political Affairs, April 5, 1996 (Factiva Database).
14. Luisa Amelia Maracara, "Inauguraron otra planta con una inversión de $150 millones, Duplicarán producción de Regional," *El Universal*, 6, 1997, http://www.eud.com/1997/12/06/eco_art_06221AA.shtml (accessed March 4, 2006).
15. "Venezuela: President Rafael Caldera Faces Mounting Protests."
16. *South America, Central America and the Caribbean 2005*, 866.
17. Greg Wilpert, "Mission Impossible? Venezuela's Mission to Fight Poverty," Venezuela Analysis, November 11, 2003, http://www.venezuelanalysis.com/articles.php?artno=1051 (accessed February 26, 2006).

18. "Venezuela Tense as Voters Prepare to Pick President; Populist Chavez Seen as Front—Runner in Sunday Ballot," CNN Web site, December 5, 1998, http://www.cnn.com/WORLD/americas/9812/05/venezuela.elex/ (accessed February 26, 2006)

19. "Two Tied For Lead in Venezuelan Presidential Race," Reuters, October 22, 1998 (Factiva Database), Bart Jones, "Ex-soldier softens tone, but Venezuela polarized over candidacy," Associated Press, October 25, 1998 (Factiva Database), David Adams and Phil Gunson, "Media accused in failed coup," *St. Petersburg Times* (Florida), April 18, 2002 (Factiva Database), "Mail Call: A Continuing Concern," Letters, *Newsweek International* (Atlantic Edition), February 23, 2004 (Factiva Database)

20. Everett Bauman, "Washington teme un efecto dominó," *El Universal*, December 29, 1998, http://www.eluniversal.com/1998/12/29/nac_art_29112CC.shtml (accessed March 4, 2006).

21. "FTAA, Frequently Asked Questions," Global Exchange.

22. Padgett, "Democrat or Demagogue?"

23. Bussey, "Venezuelan Candidate Has Image Problem Abroad."

24. "Election Watch, Venezuela (presidential)," CNN Web site, http://www.cnn.com/WORLD/election.watch/americas/venezuela.html (accessed February 26, 2006); Georgie Anne Geyer, "Poor Rich Venezuela: Miracle in Reverse," *The Washington Quarterly*, March 22, 1999 (Factiva Database).

25. Padgett, "Democrat or Demagogue?"; "Venezuelan Court Dismisses Corruption Case Against Ex-President," Associated Press, January 8, 1999 (Factiva Database); "Venezuelan Elite Wary of Leftist Election Victory," CNN Web site, November 9, 1998, http://edition.cnn.com/WORLD/americas/9811/09/venezuela.02/ (accessed March 25, 2006); "Court Orders Ex-President Arrested," Reuters, April 14, 1998 (Factiva Database); "Un tribunal dicta orden de arresto contra Carlos Andrés Pérez," *El Mundo*, April 15, 1998 (Factiva Database).

26. "Ex-Venezuelan Pres. Calls Corruption Allegations 'a Farce,'" Associated Press, December 19, 2001 (Factiva database); "Venezuela Insists that Plotting Underway in Dominican Republic," EFE, August 8, 2003 (Factiva Database); Becky Branford, "Analysis: Chávez at Eye of Storm," BBC News Online, August 13, 2004, http://news.bbc.co.uk/2/hi/americas/3559668.stm (accessed March 21, 2006); Ernesto Ecarri Hung, "Victoria aplastante en todas las regiones," *El Universal*, July 26, 1999, http://buscador.eluniversal.com/1999/07/26/pol_art_26104AA.shtml (accessed March 25, 2006); "Venezuela Ex-Chief Ordered Detained";"Ex-Venezuelan Pres. Calls Corruption Allegations 'a Farce,'" Dow Jones International News, December 19, 2001 (Factiva Database).

27. Anderson, "The Revolutionary." "Venezuela Rallies Behind a Reformer," Venezuela Analysis, August 19, 2004, reprinted from *Toronto Star*, http://www.venezuelanalysis.com/articles.php?artno=1255 (accessed March 4, 2006).

28. Tim McGirk, "Others Who Shaped 1999, Hugo Chávez Frías," *Time Europe* Web site, December 27, 1999, Vol. 154, No. 26, http://www.time.com/time/europe/magazine/1999/1227/Chávez.html (accessed February 27, 2006).

29. "History, the Uruguay Round," World Trade Organization Web site, "The 128 Countries that had Signed GATT by 1994," WTO Web site, http://www.wto.org/english/thewto_e/gattmem_e.htm (accessed February 27, 2006); "WTO, Globalization, and Alternatives, Pranjal Tiwari Interviews Michael Albert," *ZNet*, April 21, 2005, http://www.zmag.org/content/showarticle.cfm?SectionID=103&ItemID=7701 (accessed February 27, 2006); Naomi Koppel, "WTO Bolsters Free Trade," Associated Press, August 1, 2004, *Washington Times* Web site, http://www.washtimes.com/world/20040801-122536-7031r.htm (accessed February 27, 2006).

30. "World Trade Organization (WTO)," Public Citizen Web site, http://www.citizen.org/trade/wto/index.cfm (accessed February 27, 2006); "Top Reasons to Oppose the WTO," Global Exchange Web site, http://www.global-exchange.org/campaigns/wto/OpposeWTO.html, last updated September 16, 2005 (accessed February 27, 2006).

31. Fiona McGillivray, "Democratizing the World Trade Organization," Hoover Press, Essays in Public Policy, Hoover Institute, http://www.hoover.org/publications/epp/105/105b.html (accessed February 27, 2006).

32. "World Trade Organization (WTO)," Public Citizen.

33. "Seattle Mayor Declares Civil Emergency as WTO Unrest Grows, Pepper Spray Fired at Protesters," CNN Web site, November 30, 1999, http://www.cnn.com/US/9911/30/wto.03/ (accessed February 27, 2006); Norm Stamper, "Snookered in Seattle: The WTO Riots, an Exclusive Book Excerpt," *Seattle Weekly* Web site, June 1,2005 http://www.seattleweekly.com/news/0522/050601_news_stamper.php (accessed February 27, 2006); Geov Parrish, "Shutting Down Seattle," *Seattle Weekly* Web site, August 18, 1999, http://www.seattleweekly.com/news/9933/features-parrish.php (accessed February 27, 2006).

34. Jean Cho, Sarah Cooch, Phil Dur, Andrea Higuera, and Susan Ruskin, "Analysis of the WTO Talks in Seattle," Washington Council on International Trade, Web site, April 2000, http://www.wcit.org/resources/wto_archives/wto/post_ministerial/wto_student_andrea.htm (accessed February 27, 2006).

35. Geov Parrish, "WTO: Five Years After, is This What Failure Looks Like?" *Seattle Weekly*, November 24–30, 2004, http://www.seattleweekly.com/news/0447/041124_news_wtogeov.php (accessed March 4, 2006).

36. Churck Morse and Marina Sitrin, "The Life—or Death—of the Anti-Globalization Movement," Perspectives on Anarchist Theory, Spring 2004—Vol. 8, No. 1, Institute for Anarchist Studies, May 28, 2004, http://www.anarchist-studies.org/article/view/61/ (accessed February 27, 2006); Parrish, "WTO: Five Years After, is This What Failure Looks Like?"

37. Tamara Straus, "Protest in Prague," *The Nation*, October 23, 2000, http://www.thenation.com/doc/20001023/strauss (accessed March 4, 2006).

38. Greg Wilpert, "Mission Impossible? Venezuela's Mission to Fight Poverty," Venezuela Analysis, Nov 11, 2003, http://www.venezuelanalysis.com/articles.php?artno=1051, (accessed February 27, 2006).

39. Anderson, "The Revolutionary."

40. Robert Taylor, "The Chávez Revolution," *World Press Review*, September 1999 (Vol. 46, No. 09), http://www.worldpress.org/Americas/1521.cfm (accessed February 27, 2006); "Venezuela—A Critical Turning Point August 2003, Hugo Chávez Comes to Power, Chávez's Revolution: From Prison Cell to Presidential Palace," Frontline/World Fellows Project, PBS Web site, http://www.pbs.org/frontlineworld/fellows/venezuela0803/2.html (accessed February 27, 2006); C. P. Pandya and Justin Podur, "The Chávez Government's Economic Policies," ZNet, reprinted at Venezuela Analysis, January 22, 2004, http://www.venezuelanalysis.com/articles.php?artno=1092 (accessed February 27, 2006); "World Oil Market and Oil Price Chronologies: 1970–2004," EIA Web site, March 2005, http://www.eia.doe.gov/emeu/cabs/chron.html#a1999 (accessed February 27, 2006).

41. Anderson, "The Revolutionary."

42. Pandya and Podur, "The Chávez Government's Economic Policies."

43. Ellner, "The Radical Potential of Chavismo in Venezuela."

44. "Primer mandatario pasó 10 horas en Uruguay y anoche llegó a Argentina, Chávez califica de 'nefasto' al FMI y asegura que el ALCA 'no sirve,'" *El Universal*, August 17, 2003, http://www.eluniversal.com/2003/08/17/pol_art_17104EE.shtml (accessed March 4, 2006).

45. "El Fondo está despreocupado acerca de las opiniones del Presidente, FMI ironiza acerca de Chávez," *El Universal*, August 22, 2003, http://buscador.eluniversal.com/2003/08/22/eco_art_22110AA.shtml (accessed March 4, 2006).

46. Maitane Larrañaga, "IMF Flirts with Venezuela," Venezuela Analysis, December 17, 2004, http://www.venezuelanalysis.com/articles.php/articles.php?artno=1337 (accessed February 27, 2006).

47. "Worldbeaters."

48. "Enron, Who's Who, Robert Zoellick," BBC News Web site, http://news.bbc.co.uk/hi/english/static/in_depth/business/2002/enron/21c.stm (accessed February 27, 2006).

49. "United States Trade Representative, Ambassador Robert B. Zoellick," White House Web site.

50. Barry, "Profile, Robert Zoellick."

51. "Letter to President Clinton," Project for the New American Century Web Site, January 26, 1998, http://www.newamericancentury.org/iraqclintonletter.htm (accessed February 27, 2006); "Statement of Principles," Project for the New American Century Web Site, June 3, 1997, http://www.newamericancentury.org/statementofprinciples.htm (accessed February 27, 2006); Home Page of Project for the New American Century, http://www.newamericancentury.org/index.html (accessed February 27, 2006).

52. Barry, "Profile, Robert Zoellick."

53. Robert King, "Mom Calls Top U.S. Trade Adviser Home, the County GOP VIP Asks Her Son Robert Zoellick to Speak at Tonight's Lincoln Day Dinner in Brooksville," *St. Petersburg Times*, February 23, 2002. "Worldbeaters."

54. Eric Green, "Gore, Bush Campaigns Debate Policies for the Americas (Pastor speaks for Democrats, Diaz-Balart for Republicans)," *Washington File*, September 18, 2000, reprinted at United States Mission to Italy Web site, http://www.usembassy.it/file2000_09/alia/a009180h.htm (accessed March 4, 2006).

55. King, "Mom Calls Top U.S. Trade Adviser Home."

56. Barry, "Profile, Robert Zoellick"; King, "Mom Calls Top U.S. Trade Adviser Home."

57. Dana Milbank, "Protesters Disrupt Summit on Trade Demonstrations and Tear Gas Undercut 'Spirit of Civility' Called for by President," *Washington Post*, April 21, 2001, http://www.washingtonpost.com/ac2/wp-dyn?pagename=article&node=&contentId=A42089–2001Apr20 (accessed March 19, 2006).

58. Steve Early and Jeff Crosby, "Nervous in Québec City, Moving Beyond Seattle, Protesters Take Aim at "NAFTA on Steroids," *The Boston Globe*, April 15, 2001 (Factiva Database).

59. Milbank, "Protesters Disrupt Summit."

60. Steve Early and Jeff Crosby, "What's at Stake in Québec City—A Labor View" *The Independent*, reprinted at ZNet, http://www.zmag.org/CrisesCurEvts/Globalism/Québecearly.htm (accessed March 19, 2006).

61. Milbank, "Protesters Disrupt Summit on Trade Demonstrations."

62. Karen Hansen-Kuhn, "Free Trade Area of the Americas, the Development Gap," *Foreign Policy in Focus* 6, No. 12, April 2001, http://www.fpif.org/briefs/vol3/v3n6trad_body.html (accessed March 4, 2006).

63. Early and Crosby, "What's at Stake in Québec City"; Milbank, "Protesters Disrupt Summit on Trade Demonstrations."

64. Early and Crosby, "What's at Stake in Québec City."

65. Hansen-Kuhn, "Free Trade Area of the Americas, the Development Gap"; Early and Crosby, "What's at Stake in Québec City."

66. Milbank, "Protesters Disrupt Summit on Trade Demonstrations."

67. Hansen-Kuhn, "Free Trade Area of the Americas, the Development Gap."

68. "Cardoso y Chávez se reúnen en Brasilia," *El Universal*, April 3, 2001, http://buscador.eluniversal.com/2001/04/03/int_art_03107DD.shtml (accessed March 4, 2006).

69. International Centre for Trade and Sustainable Development, "Free Trade Area of the Americas Update, Draft Text of FTAA to Be Made Public Following Québec Summit," *Bridges Weekly News Digest* 5, No. 13, April 10, 2001, http://www.ictsd.org/html/weekly/10–04–01/story2.htm (accessed March 4, 2006).

70. Milbank, "Protesters Disrupt Summit on Trade Demonstrations."

71. Keefer, "Hugo Chávez Frías and the Sense of History."

72. Milbank, "Protesters Disrupt Summit on Trade Demonstrations."

73. "'Es una opción, no un destino,'" *El Universal*, April 24, 2001, http://buscador.eluniversal.com/2001/04/24/apo_art_24201II.shtml (accessed March 4, 2006).

74. "Chávez someterá el ALCA a referendo," *El Universal*, April 21, 2001, http://buscador.eluniversal.com/2001/04/21/pol_art_21102CC.shtml (accessed February 28, 2006).

75. Gina Rodríguez Vidal, "Cumbre de las Américas, Chávez se roba el show," *El Universal*, April 23, 2001, http://buscador.eluniversal.com/2001/04/23/int_art_23188DD.shtml (accessed March 4, 2006).

76. Gina Rodríguez Vidal, "George Bush aceptó invitación a Caracas," *El Universal* (Caracas, Venezuela), April 22, 2001, http://buscador.eluniversal.com/2001/04/22/int_art_22102HH.shtml (accessed March 4, 2006)

77. Steve Ellner, "Venezuela's 'Demonstration Effect': Defying Globalization's Logic," NACLA Report on the Americas, Sept–October 2005 issue, reprinted in Venezuela Analysis, October 17, 2005, http://www.venezuelanalysis.com/articles.php?artno=1579 (accessed March 4, 2006).

78. Parrish, "WTO: Five Years After, is This What Failure Looks Like?"

79. "September 2001 Mobilization! Mark Your Calendars Now! Washington, DC: September 28–October 4," Global Exchange Web site, http://www.globalexchange.org/campaigns/wbimf/wbimf032001.html (accessed February 28, 2006).

80. Parrish, "WTO: Five Years After, is This What Failure Looks Like?"

81. Barry, "Profile, Robert Zoellick."

82. Parrish, "WTO: Five Years After, is This What Failure Looks Like?"

83. Barry, "Profile, Robert Zoellick."

84. Parrish, "WTO: Five Years After, is This What Failure Looks Like?"; "Ecuador, Indigenous Protesters Reach Agreement, Indians Get Relief from High Fuel Costs," CNN, February 8, 2001, http://cnnstudentnews.cnn.com/2001/WORLD/americas/02/08/ecuador.agreement/ (accessed February 28, 2006).

85. "Profile: Hugo Chávez," BBC News, December 5, 2002, http://news.bbc.co.uk/2/hi/americas/3517106.stm (accessed February 28, 2006).

86. Wilpert, "Venezuela: Participatory Democracy or Government as Usual?"

87. Ellner, "Venezuela's 'Demonstration Effect.'"

88. "Durante su reunión en Texas, Estados Unidos Bush y Cisneros priorizan áreas de cooperación hemisférica," *El Universal*, October 24, 1999, http://buscador.eluniversal.com/1999/10/24/eco_art_24204FF.shtml (accessed March 4, 2006).

89. "Ex-presidente George Bush en el Ventuari," *El Universal*, February 1, 2001, http://buscador.eluniversal.com/2001/02/16/apo_art_16304CC.shtml (accessed March 4, 2006).

90. Cynthia Cotts, "Press Clips, Quid Pro Coup, The 'Times' Condones Censorship, Venezuelan Style," *Village Voice*, May 1–7, 2002, http://www.villagevoice.com/news/0218,cotts,34381,6.html (accessed March 4, 2006).

91. William Finnegan, "Castro's Shadow, America's Man in Latin America, and His Obsession," *New Yorker*, October 14–21, 2002, http://www.newyorker.com/fact/content/?021014fa_fact1 (accessed February 28, 2006).

92. Ed Vulliamy, "Venezuela Coup Linked to Bush team, Specialists in the 'Dirty Wars' of the Eighties Encouraged the Plotters who tried to Topple President

Chávez," *The Observer*, April 21, 2002, http://observer.guardian.co.uk/international/story/0,6903,688071,00.html (accessed February 28, 2006); Finnegan, "Castro's Shadow"; "Venezuelan Coup Leader Quizzed," BBC News Web site, May 2, 2002, http://news.bbc.co.uk/2/hi/americas/1965331.stm (accessed March 22, 2006); Cotts, "Press Clips, Quid Pro Coup."

93. "Analysis: Political Organization in Venezuela Being Charged with Treason for Allegedly Encouraging Citizens to Vote Against the Sitting President," Transcript of NPR: Morning Edition, December 30, 2004 (Factiva Database); "U.S. and Spain Knew of Chávez Coup Plot," *Latin American Weekly Report*, November 30, 2004 (Factiva Database); Bart Jones and Letta Tayler, "Venezuela Coup Plot Known, CIA Says," *Fort Wayne Journal Gazette*, November 24, 2004 (Factiva Database).

94. Nikolas Kozloff, "Chávez Launches Hemispheric, 'Anti-Hegemonic' Media Campaign in Response to Local TV Networks Anti-Government Bias," Memorandum to the Press 05.47, COHA, April 28, 2005, http://www.coha.org/NEW_PRESS_RELEASES/New_Press_Releases_2005/05.47_Telesur_%20the_one.htm (accessed February 28, 2006).

95. Cotts, "Press Clips, Quid Pro Coup."

96. Ibid.

97. Aram Rubén Aharonian, "Back, by Popular Demand? How Venezuela's Hugo Chávez Got a Second Chance, Hamburgers, Cured Ham, and Oil," Proceso, May 1, 2002, posted at Worldpress.org Web site, http://www.worldpress.org/Americas/581.cfm (accessed March 6, 2006)

98. "After the Coup, Venezuelan President Ponders Mystery of American Plane," Reuters, April 16, 2002, reprinted on *Guardian* Web site, http://www.guardian.co.uk/international/story/0,3604,685189,00.html (accessed March 4, 2006).

99. Brian Forrest, "The Revolution Will Not Be Televised; an Interview with Documentary Filmmakers Kim Bartley and Donnacha O'Briain," Z Net, November 2, 2003, http://www.zmag.org/content/showarticle.cfm?Section ID=45&ItemID=4442 (accessed March 4, 2006).

100. David Adams and Phil Gunson, "Media Accused in Failed Coup, Venezuelan News Executives Defend Themselves against Allegations that They Suppressed Facts as the Ousted President Returned," *St. Petersburg Times* (St. Petersburg, Florida), April 18, 2002, http://www.stpetersburgtimes.com/2002/04/18/Worldandnation/Media_accused_in_fail.shtml (accessed February 28, 2006).

101. Cotts, "Press Clips, Quid Pro Coup."

102. "Protagonistas," *El Universal*, July 11, 2002, http://buscador.eluniversal.com/2002/07/11/apo_art_11194BB.shtml (accessed March 4, 2006); Aharonian, "Hamburgers, Cured Ham, and Oil."

103. Cotts, "Press Clips, Quid Pro Coup."

104. David Corn, "Our Gang in Venezuela?" *The Nation*, August 5, 2002, http://www.thenation.com/doc/20020805/corn (accessed March 22, 2006).

105. Aharonian, "Hamburgers, Cured Ham, and Oil."

106. "FMI ofrece respaldo a Carmona Estanga," *El Universal*, April 13, 2002, http://buscador.eluniversal.com/2002/04/13/eco_art_13202GG.shtml (accessed March 4, 2006).

107. Alejandro J. Sucre, "Chávez versus Cisneros," *El Universal*, May 9, 2004, http://buscador.eluniversal.com/2004/05/09/opi_art_09491B.shtml (accessed March 4, 2006).

108. Iaian Bruce, "Venezuela to Seize 'Idle' Firms," BBC News Web site, last updated July 18, 2005, http://news.bbc.co.uk/2/hi/americas/4692165.stm (accessed February 29, 2006).

109. Juan Forero, "Chávez Restyles Venezuela With '21st-Century Socialism,'" *New York Times*, October 30, 2005, http://www.nytimes.com/2005/10/30/international/americas/30venezuela.html?ex=1288324800&en=d055b8491a6ddcb4&ei=5089&partner=rssyahoo&emc=rss (accessed February 29, 2006).

110. David Raby, "Venezuela's Subversive Example," Venezuela Analysis, May 6, 2004, http://www.venezuelanalysis.com/articles.php?artno=1171 (accessed March 1, 2006); Humberto Márquez, "State-Financed Experiments in Venezuela's Solidarity Economy," Inter Press Service, reprinted at Venezuela Analysis, November 28, 2005, http://www.venezuelanalysis.com/articles.php?artno=1614 (accessed March 1, 2006).

111. Forero, "Chávez Restyles Venezuela."

112. Greg Wilpert, "Venezuelan Authorities Seize Idle Heinz Ketchup Plant," Venezuela Analysis, September 9, 2005, http://www.venezuelanalysis.com/news.php?newsno=1751 (accessed March 4, 2006).

113. Ibid.

114. Bernardo Delgado, "Venezuela to Expropriate Idle Corn Processing Plant," Venezuela Analysis, September 28, 2005, http://www.venezuelanalysis.com/news.php?newsno=1770 (accessed March 4, 2006).

115. Forero, "Chávez Restyles Venezuela with 'Twenty-First-Century Socialism.'"

116. Wilpert, "Venezuelan Authorities Seize Idle Heinz Ketchup Plant."

117. Ellner, "Venezuela's 'Demonstration Effect.'"

118. "Biography: Robert B. Zoellick, Deputy Secretary of State," U.S. Department of State Web site, http://www.state.gov/r/pa/ei/biog/42449.htm (accessed March 1, 2006); "Zoellick Says Chávez Must Be Stopped," Associated Press, February 16, 2005; Patrick O'Donoghue, "Zoellick: Chávez Frías is the New Pied Piper of Populism in South America," Vheadline, February 16, 2005, http://www.vheadline.com/readnews.asp?id=25760 (accessed March 4, 2006).

119. Gerardo Young, Lucas Guagnini, and Alberto Amato, "Argentina's New Social Protagonists," *Clarín*, September 26, 2002, reprinted at World Press Review Web site, http://www.worldpress.org/Americas/789.cfm (March 1, 2006).

120. James Petras, "Road Warriors: Blocking Highways throughout Argentina, Unemployed Workers Lead a Promising Movement for Basic Change," Resource Center of the Americas Web site, February 2002, http://www.ameri-

cas.org/item_105 (accessed March 1, 2006); Petras biography, listed at James Petras, "The Granda Kidnapping Exposes the U.S./Colombia Plot Against Venezuela," Counterpunch Web site, January 25, 2005, http://www.counterpunch.org/petras01252005.html (accessed March 1, 2006).

121. Young, Guagnini, and Amato, "Argentina's New Social Protagonists."

122. Petras, "Road Warriors."

123. Young, Guagnini, and Amato, "Argentina's New Social Protagonists."

124. Petras, "Road Warriors."

125. Ibid.

126. "Mass March against Argentine Cuts," BBC News Web site, August 30, 2001, http://news.bbc.co.uk/2/hi/americas/1516142.stm (accessed March 1, 2006).

127. Petras, "Road Warriors"; Alfred Hopkins, "Running out of Patience," *World Press Review* Web site, February 27, 2002, http://www.worldpress.org/Americas/380.cfm (accessed March 1, 2006).

128. Hartford Campbell, "COHA Memorandum to the Press, Argentina's Néstor Kirchner: Peronism without the Tears," COHA Web site, January 27, 2006 http://www.coha.org/NEW_PRESS_RELEASES/New_Press_Releases_2006/06.08_Kirchner_distinct.html (accessed March 1, 2006).

129. "Primer mandatario pasó 10 horas en Uruguay y anoche llegó a Argentina, Chávez califica de 'nefasto' al FMI y asegura que el ALCA 'no sirve,'" *El Universal*, August 17, 2003, http://www.eluniversal.com/2003/08/17/pol_art_17104EE.shtml (accessed March 4, 2006).

130. Palast, "Chávez versus the Free Trade Zombies of the Americas."

131. Barry, "Profile, Robert Zoellick."

132. Jane Bussey, "U.S. Official Pushes Hard for FTAA, as the Summit to Forge a Free Trade Area of the Americas Nears, U.S. Trade Official Robert Zoellick Stresses the Need for All Proposed Member Nations to Find Common Ground," *Miami Herald*, November 15, 2003.

133. Keefer, "Hugo Chávez Frias and the Sense of History."

134. Deborah James, "Stopping the FTAA: Venezuela," Venezuela Analysis, February 23, 2004, http://www.venezuelanalysis.com/articles.php?artno=1110 (accessed March 4, 2006).

135. Ellner, "Venezuela's 'Demonstration Effect.'"

136. Keefer, "Hugo Chávez Frias and the Sense of History."

137. Teresa Arreaza, "ALBA: Bolivarian Alternative for Latin America and the Caribbean," Venezuela Analysis, January 30, 2004, http://www.venezuelanalysis.com/docs.php?dno=1010 (accessed March 4, 2006). Keefer, "Hugo Chávez Frias and the Sense of History."

138. Keefer, "Hugo Chávez Frias and the Sense of History."

139. Arreaza, "ALBA: Bolivarian Alternative for Latin America and the Caribbean."

140. "Anti-Bush Protesters Gather in Argentina," Associated Press, November 2, 2005, posted on ABC News Web site, http://abcnews.go.com/International/wireStory?id=1273530 (accessed March 1, 2006).

141. Joaquín Bustelo, "Mar del Plata Spin Cycle," Venezuela Analysis, November 7, 2005, http://www.venezuelanalysis.com/articles.php?artno=1597 (accessed March 1, 2006). "Anti-Bush Protesters Gather in Argentina," Associated Press, November 2, 2005, posted on ABC News Web site, http://abcnews.go.com/International/wireStory?id=1273530 (accessed March 1, 2006).

142. Cory Fischer-Hoffman, "Mar de Plata, Fighting the FTAA and Bush in Argentina," ZNet, November 11, 2005, http://www.zmag.org/content/showarticle.cfm?SectionID=13&ItemID=9097 (accessed March 2, 2006); Bill Cormier, "Chávez, Protesters Vow to Block U.S. Plan," Associated Press, November 4, 2005, reprinted at ABC News Web site, http://abcnews.go.com/International/wireStory?id=1281890&CMP=OTC-RSSFeeds0312 (accessed March 2, 2006).

143. Monte Reel and Michael Fletcher, "Violent Protests, Clashes Roil Start of Summit," Washington Post, November 5, 2005, reprinted at Boston Globe Web site, http://www.boston.com/news/world/latinamerica/articles/2005/11/05/violent_protests_clashes_roil_start_of_summit/?rss_id=Boston+Globe+—+World+News (accessed March 2, 2006).

144. Jordana Timerman, "Chávez and Maradona Lead Massive Rebuke of Bush," The Nation, November 6, 2005, http://www.thenation.com/doc/20051121/timerman (accessed March 4, 2006).

145. Timerman, "Chávez and Maradona"; Federico Fuentes, "A President, a Soccer Star and the Dreams of Millions"; Agencia Latinoamericana de Informacion y Analisis 2, 14 November 2005, http://www.alia2.net/article131017.html (accessed March 2, 2005).

146. Timerman, "Chávez and Maradona"; "No Trade Deal at Americas Summit," BBC Web site, November 6, 2005, http://news.bbc.co.uk/nolpda/ukfs_news/hi/newsid_4410000/4410190.stm (accessed March 2, 2006).

147. "Venezuela propondrá creación de Banco del Sur en reunión de G–77," El Universal, June 10, 2005, http://www.el-universal.com/movil/10A568309.html (accessed March 4, 2006).

148. Bernardo Delgado, "Venezuela Withdraws Foreign Reserves from U.S," Venezuela Analysis, October 1, 2005, http://www.venezuelanalysis.com/news.php?newsno=1773 (accessed March 4, 2006).

149. Ibid.

150. "Chávez Threatens to Send U.S. F–16s to Cuba, China," Associated Press, November 2, 2005.

151. Patrick O'Donoghue, "On Eve of Argentine Visit, Chávez Frias Calls for Regional Referendum on Foreign External Debt," Vheadline, August 17, 2003, http://www.vheadline.com/printer_news.asp?id=10383 (accessed March 4, 2006).

152. Kenneth Rapoza, "IMF on the Ropes in Brazil, Brazil's Decision to Cut Some Ties with the Fund is Indicative of Changing Times in Latin America," In These Times, April 11, 2005, http://www.inthesetimes.com/site/main/article/2063 (accessed March 4, 2006).

153. Ellner, "Venezuela's 'Demonstration Effect.'"

CHAPTER 5

1. Sarah Wagner, "U.S. General Says Venezuela is a Danger for the Hemisphere," Venezuela Analysis, June 14, 2005, http://www.venezuelanalysis.com/news.php?newsno=1662 (accessed March 2, 2006).

2. *South America, Central America and the Caribbean 2005* (London: Europa Publications, 2005), 866; Trinkunas, "Civil-Military Relations in Venezuela after 11 April"; Greg Wilpert, "Venezuela's Land Reform, Land for People Not for Profit in Venezuela," Venezuela Analysis, August 23, 2005, http://www.venezuelanalysis.com/articles.php?artno=1529 (accessed March 2, 2006); Raquel Barreiro, "Chávez agrega otro militar a la directiva de la empresa estatal Designado Guaicaipuro Lameda presidente de PdVSA," El Universal, October 16, 2000, http://www.eluniversal.com/2000/10/16/eco_art_16204DD.shtml (accessed March, 2006); Greg Wilpert, "Armed Forces Protect Venezuela's Oil Fields," Venezuela Analysis, May 4, 2005, http://www.venezuelanalysis.com/news.php?newsno=1611 (accessed March 2, 2006); Jonah Gindin, "Venezuela Signs Helicopter Deal with Russia, Boosts Border Security," Venezuela Analysis, March 11, 2005, http://www.venezuelanalysis.com/news.php?newsno=1543 (accessed March 2, 2006); Ewell, *Venezuela and the United States*, 156–57, 211.

3. "Juan Vicente Gómez," Encyclopedia Britannica Online, http://www.britannica.com/eb/article–9037322?tocId=9037322 (accessed March 5, 2006).

4. Ewell, *Venezuela and the United States*, 119.

5. International Committee for Political Prisoners, *Venezuela Land of Oil and Tyranny* (New York: International Committee For Political Prisoners, 1931), 4.

6. Wagner, "U.S. General Says Venezuela is a Danger."

7. Marta Harnecker, *Militares junto al pueblo* (Caracas: Vadell Hermanos, 2003), 13, 24–5.

8. Marta Harnecker, "The Venezuelan Military: the Making of an Anomaly," Venezuela Analysis, October 20, 2003, printed from *Monthly Review*, http://www.venezuelanalysis.com/articles.php?artno=1040 (accessed March 5, 2006).

9. Harnecker, *Militares junto al pueblo*, 13, 24.

10. Harnecker, "The Venezuelan Military."

11. Harnecker, *Militares junto al pueblo*, 25–27, 29.

12. Argenis Méndez Echenique, *Historia regional del estado apure* (Caracas: Academia Nacional de Historia, 1995), 20, 24, 26, 28.

13. Raymond Crist, "Along the Llanos," *Geographical Review*, vol. 46, no. 2 (April 1956), 191.

14. Harnecker, *Militares junto al pueblo*, 28.

15. Harnecker, "The Venezuelan Military."

16. Harnecker, *Militares junto al pueblo* 28.

17. Margarita López Maya, "Hugo Chávez Frías, su movimiento y presidencia," in Steve Ellner y Daniel Hellinger (eds.); *La política venezolana en la época de Chávez* (Caracas: Editorial Nueva Sociedad, 2003), 103.

18. Harnecker, *Militares junto al pueblo*, 63.

19. López Maya, "Hugo Chávez Frías."

20. Harnecker, "The Venezuelan Military"; School of Americas Watch, "Venezuelan Generals Backing Interim President are SOA Grads," April 12, 2002, http://www.soaw.org/new/print_article.php?id=335 (accessed March 5, 2006).

21. John R. Banister, "Columbus, Georgia," *Encyclopedia Americana*, Grolier Online 2006, Scholastic Library Publishing, http://go.grolier.com (accessed March 9, 2006).

22. Jim Houston, "Proud Protesters, Judge to Rule Today on School of Americas Challengers' Charges," Columbus, GA, *Ledger-Enquirer*, May 23, 2001, posted at Common Dreams Web site, http://www.commondreams.org/cgi-bin/print.cgi?file=/headlines01/0523–03.htm (accessed March 5, 2006).

23. "Western Hemisphere Institute for Security Cooperation (Successor to School of the Americas) Fort Benning, Georgia," Center for International Policy, http://www.ciponline.org/facts/soa.htm (accessed March 5, 2006).

24. George Monbiot, "Backyard Terrorism, the U.S. has been Training Terrorists at a Camp in Georgia for Years—and it's Still at it," *The Guardian*, October 30, 2001, http://www.guardian.co.uk/waronterror/story/0,1361,583254,00.html (accessed March 5, 2006).

25. "School of the Americas," Online Focus, a News Hour with Jim Lehrer Transcript, PBS Web site, September 21, 1999 (accessed March 5, 2006) http://www.pbs.org/newshour/bb/military/july-dec99/sotamericas_9–21.html; Monbiot, "Backyard Terrorism,"; "Efraín Ríos Montt," *New Internationalist*, September 2001, printed at Findarticles.com, http://www.findarticles.com/p/articles/mi_m0JQP/is_2001_Sept/ai_78900932 (accessed March 5, 2006).

26. "School of the Americas," Online Focus.

27. "More Than an Image Problem," *National Catholic Reporter*, February 18, 2005, http://ncronline.org/NCR_Online/archives2/2005a/021805/021805t.htm (accessed March 5, 2006).

28. School of the Americas Watch, "Venezuelan Generals Backing Interim President."

29. "Remembering the Martyrs of El Salvador," *National Catholic Reporter*, November 19, 1999, http://www.natcath.com/NCR_Online/archives/111999/111999d.htm (accessed March 5, 2006); Monbiot, "Backyard Terrorism"; "Critique of the Western Hemisphere Institute for Security Cooperation"; School of the Americas Watch, undated report, http://.www.soaw.org/new/article.php?id=260 (accessed April 2, 2006); "General Information," WHINSEC Web site, https://www.benning.army.mil/whinsex/about.asp?id=37 (accessed April 2, 2006); "Western Hemisphere for Security Cooperation (successor to the School of the Americas) Fort Benning, Georgia," Center for International Policy Web site, February 10, 2006, http://www.ciponline.org/facts/soa.htm (accessed April 2, 2006).

30. Harnecker, *Militares junto al pueblo*, 28, 29.

31. Harnecker, "The Venezuelan Military."

32. López Maya, "Hugo Chávez Frías," 104.

33. Harold A. Trinkunas, "Strategic Insight, 'Civil-Military Relations in Venezuela after 11 April: Beyond Repair?'" (Authored by analysts with the Center for Contemporary Conflict which analyzes threats to U.S. national Security, the Center is the research arm of the National Security Affairs Department and Naval Postgraduate School in Monterey, California) Center for Contemporary Conflict, May 3, 2002, http://www.ccc.nps.navy.mil/rsepResources/si/may02/latinAmerica.asp (accessed March 4, 2006).

34. *South America, Central America and the Caribbean 2005* (London: Europa Publications, 2005), 866; Trinkunas, "Civil-Military Relations in Venezuela after 11 April."

35. Marta Harnecker, "Interview with President Chávez: the Military in the Revolution and the Counter-Revolution," Venezuela Analysis, October 20, 2003, http://www.venezuelanalysis.com/articles.php?artno=1039 (accessed March 5, 2006).

36. Trinkunas, "Civil-Military Relations in Venezuela after 11 April."

37. Harnecker, "Interview with President Chávez."

38. Harnecker, *Militares junto al pueblo*, 29–32.

39. Harnecker, "The Venezuelan Military."

40. Harnecker, "Interview with President Chávez."

41. Harnecker, *Militares junto al pueblo*, 35.

42. Deborah Norden, "La democracia en uniforme: Chávez y las fuerzas armadas," in Ellner and Hellinger (eds.), *La política venezolana en la época de Chávez*, 131.

43. *South America, Central America and the Caribbean 2005*, 866.

44. Trinkunas, "Civil-Military Relations in Venezuela after 11 April."

45. Norden, "La democracia en uniforme," 137.

46. Trinkunas, "Civil-Military Relations in Venezuela after 11 April."

47. Harnecker, "The Venezuelan Military."

48. Greg Wilpert, "Mission Impossible? Venezuela's Mission to Fight Poverty," Venezuela Analysis, November 11, 2003, http://www.venezuelanalysis.com/articles.php?artno=1051 (accessed March 2, 2006).

49. Harnecker, "Interview with President Chávez,"; Wilpert, "Mission Impossible?"

50. Harnecker, "Interview with President Chávez."

51. Harnecker, "The Venezuelan Military."

52. Wilpert, "Mission Impossible?"

53. "El agregado militar de Cuba de paseo," *El Universal*, October 20, 2001, http://buscador.eluniversal.com/2001/10/20/apo_art_20112DD.shtml (accessed March 2, 2006).

54. Raquel Barreiro, "Chávez agrega otro militar a la directiva de la empresa estatal Designado Guaicaipuro Lameda presidente de PdVSA," *El Universal*, October 16, 2000, http://www.eluniversal.com/2000/10/16/eco_art_16204DD.shtml (accessed March 2, 2006).

55. "Appointment of Army General to Venezuela Oil Company Could Mean More Politics, Less Oil," CNN, October 16, 2000, http://archives.cnn.com/2000/WORLD/americas/10/16/venezuela.oil.reut (accessed March 4, 2006); Barreiro, "Chávez agrega otro militar."

56. "Semana petrolera, la globalización y los generales," *El Universal* (Caracas, Venezuela), October 23, 2000, http://buscador.eluniversal.com/2000/10/23/pet_art_23204AA.shtml (accessed March 2, 2006).

57. Trinkunas, "Civil-Military Relations in Venezuela after 11 April."

58. *South America, Central America and the Caribbean 2005*, 866.

59. Trinkunas, "Civil-Military Relations in Venezuela after 11 April."

60. Norden, "La democracia en uniforme," 137, 140–1–41.

61. "Transcripción del vídeo presentado por el Frente Institucional Militar (FIM) Luis García Morales," Venezuela Analitica, June 26, 2000.

62. "Aseguró que continuará en lucha por la democracia, García Morales exige protección al fiscal," *El Universal* (Caracas, Venezuela), July 28, 2000, http://buscador.eluniversal.com/2000/07/28/pol_art_28114CC.shtml (accessed March 2, 2006).

63. Alicia La Rotta Morán, "Un año después de su primer video, envía otro mensaje al presidente Chávez Capitán García llamó a la desobediencia civil," *El Universal*, June 16, 2001, http://buscador.eluniversal.com/2001/06/16/pol_art_16104GG.shtml (accessed March 2, 2006).

64. Norden, "La democracia en uniforme,"131; "Zulia State Governor Francisco Arias Cárdenas Mooted for Post of Vice-President of Venezuela," Vheadline, January 4, 2000, http://www.vheadline.com/0001/7553.asp (accessed March 6, 2006).

65. "Venezuela Leader's Foe Also Ex-Coup Plotter, but More Moderate," Associated Press, July 23, 2000, posted at CNN Web site, http://archives.cnn.com/2000/WORLD/americas/07/23/Chávez.schallenger.ap/ (accessed March 6, 2006).

66. "Venezuela Leader's Foe Also Ex-Coup Plotter," *South America, Central America and the Caribbean 2005*, 867.

67. Harnecker, "Interview with President Chávez."

68. Jorge Jorquera, "Venezuela's April 2002 Coup Revealed the Embryonic Development of a Counter-Power," Vheadline, July 10, 2003, http://www.vheadline.com/printer_news.asp?id=9410 (accessed March 6, 2006); Greg Morsbach, "Chávez Accused of Fostering Militia Links," BBC News Web site, June 12, 2002, http://news.bbc.co.uk/2/hi/americas/2038827.stm (accessed March 6, 2006).

69. Morsbach, "Chávez Accused of Fostering Militia Links."

70. Marta Harnecker, "After the Referendum: Venezuela Faces New Challenges," Venezuela Analysis, November 10, 2004, http://www.venezuelanalysis.com/articles.php?artno=1312 (accessed March 4, 2006).

71. Álvaro Sánchez, "Bolivarian Circles: a Grassroots Movement," Venezuela Analysis, September 30, 2003, http://www.venezuelanalysis.com/articles.php?artno=1026 (accessed March 2, 2006).

72. Morsbach, "Chávez Accused of Fostering Militia Links."

73. Sánchez, "Bolivarian Circles"; Michael Parenti, "Good Things Happening in Venezuela," ZNet Daily Commentary, April 4, 2005, http://www.zmag.org/Sustainers/Content/2005–04/02parenti.cfm (accessed March 6, 2006).

74. Morsbach, "Chávez Accused of Fostering Militia Links."

75. Jorge Rueda, "Military forces leader of Venezuela to resign" Associated Press, April 12, 2002 (Factiva Database)

76. Morsbach, "Chávez Accused of Fostering Militia Links."

77. Greg Wilpert, "Magazine's Reputation Seriously Damaged, U.S. News & World Report Spreads Disinformation about Chávez Government Support for Terrorism," Venezuela Analysis, October 2, 2003, http://www.venezuel-analysis.com/articles.php?artno=1027 (accessed March 2, 2006).

78. "Capitán García llamó a la desobediencia civil," *El Universal.*

79. Alicia La Rotta Morán, "El mandatario se reunió con los comandantes de Guarnición Presidente pasó revista al Plan Bolívar 2000," *El Universal,* June 3, 1999, http://buscador.eluniversal.com/1999/06/03/pol_art_03110DD.shtml (accessed March 2, 2006).

80. Gustavo Rodríguez, "Permanecen secuestrados 11 ganaderos venezolanos," *El Universal,* July 20, 2000, http://buscador.eluniversal.com/2000/07/20/ccs_art_20458CC.shtml (accessed March 2, 2006); "Niegan incursión de militares en Colombia," *El Universal,* March 25, 2000, http://buscador.eluniversal.com/2000/03/25/pol_art_25116FF.shtml (accessed March 2, 2006).

81. La Rotta Morán, "El mandatario se reunió con los comandantes de Guarnición"; "La provincia aguarda inicio del plan maestro del Gobierno," *El Universal* (Caracas, Venezuela), February 24, 1999, http://buscador.eluniversal.com/1999/02/24/pol_art_24103AA.shtml (accessed March 2, 2006).

82. La Rotta Morán, "Presidente pasó revista al Plan Bolívar 2000," *El Universal* (Caracas, Venezuela), June 3, 1999. http://buscador.eluniversal.com/1999/06/03/pol_art_03110DD.shtml (accessed March 2, 2006).

83. "SOA/WHINSEC Grads in the News, UPDATE 3/25/05: 'SOA Graduate Commands Brigade Accused of Massacre of Civilians in Colombia,'" School of the Americas Watch Web site, http://www.soaw.org/new/article.php?id=205 (accessed March 6, 2006); "Advierte el comandante general del Ejército, 'Aquí el único vocero soy yo,'" *El Universal* (Caracas, Venezuela), January 28, 2002, http://buscador.eluniversal.com/2002/01/28/pol_art_28110DD.shtml (accessed March 2, 2006).

84. School of the Americas Watch, "SOA Graduate Commands Brigade Accused of Massacre"; William Finnegan, "Castro's Shadow, America's Man in Latin America, and His Obsession," *The New Yorker,* October 14–21, 2002, http://www.newyorker.com/fact/content?021014fa_fact1 (accessed March 6, 2006); "Board of Visitors," WHISC Web site, https://www.benning.army.mil/WHINSEC/BOV.asp?id=27 (accessed March 6, 2006).

CHAPTER 6

1. "Anti-Government Terrorist Attacks Surface Once Again, Terror Attack in Venezuela Kills State Prosecutor Danilo Anderson," Venezuela Analysis,

November 19, 2004, http://www.venezuelanalysis.com/news.php?newsno= 1422 (accessed March 6, 2006).

2. Greg Wilpert, "Coup in Venezuela: An Eyewitness Report," Common Dreams, April 12, 2002, http://www.commondreams.org/views02/0412–08. htm (accessed March 4, 2006).

3. Eva Golinger, "Media War against the People: a Case Study of Media Concentration and Power in Venezuela," Venezuela Analysis, September 25, 2004, http://venezuelanalysis.com/articles.php?artno=1283 (accessed March 4, 2006).

4. Stuart Munckton, "Venezuela: Struggle for Power Intensifies," *Green Left Weekly*, October 2, 2002, http://www.greenleft.org.au/back/2002/511/ 511p18.htm (accessed March 4, 2006).

5. "Imputados de Llaguno," *El Universal*, May 24, 2002, http://buscador.eluniversal.com/2002/05/24/apo_art_24460GG.shtml (accessed March 2, 2006); "La mayoría de los imputados permanecen en fuga," *El Universal* (Caracas, Venezuela), June 11, 2002, http://buscador.eluniversal.com/2002/06/11/apo_art_11140CC.shtml (accessed March 2, 2006); Golinger, "Media War Against the People."

6. Golinger, "Media War Against the People."

7. Stuart Klawans, "A Documentary Coup," *The Nation*, November 23, 2003, http://www.thenation.com/doc/20031124/klawans (accessed March 6, 2006).

8. Golinger, "Media War Against the People."

9. Sarah Wagner, "Venezuelan Police Officers Accuse Police Chiefs of Ordering Them to Shoot at Demonstrators during Coup," Venezuela Analysis, December 14, 2004, http://venezuelanalysis.com/news.php?newsno=1445 (accessed March 2, 2006).

10. "Vásquez Velasco dijo que reaccionó contra el 'asesinato de inocentes,'" *El Universal* (Caracas, Venezuela), May 17, 2002, http://buscador.eluniversal. com/2002/05/17/pol_ava_17052002_30545.h.shtml (accessed March 2, 2006).

11. Roberto Giusti, "Rectificación/Relato de la entrega de Chávez a los generales, 'Si me dejan ir a Cuba renuncio,'" *El Universal*, April 18, 2002, http://buscador.eluniversal.com/2002/04/18/pol_art_18188AA.shtml (accessed March 2, 2006); "Días clave," *El Universal*, August 1, 2002, http://buscador.eluniversal.com/2002/08/01/apo_art_01102DD.shtml (accessed March 2, 2006).

12. Trinkunas, "Civil-Military Relations in Venezuela after 11 April"; Bridget Broderick, "Venezuela: Coup and Countercoup," *International Socialist Review* 23, May–June 2002.

13. Trinkunas, "Civil-Military Relations in Venezuela after 11 April."

14. "Vásquez Velasco dijo que reaccionó contra el 'asesinato de inocentes.'"

15. Giusti, "Rectificación."

16. "Los hechos," *El Universal*, July 27, 2002, http://buscador.eluniversal.com/ 2002/07/27/apo_art_27104EE.shtml (accessed March 2, 2006).

17. Harnecker, *Militares junto al pueblo*, 44.

18. Harnecker, "Interview with President Chávez."

19. Trinkunas, "Civil-Military Relations in Venezuela after 11 April."

20. "Anti-Government Terrorist Attacks Surface Once Again."

21. Kurt Nimmo, "Mission Accomplished in Haiti. Onward to Venezuela?" *Venezuela Analysis*, March 10, 2004, reprinted from Counterpunch, http://www.venezuelanalysis.com/articles.php?artno=1124 (accessed March 2, 2006).

22. Greg Wilpert, "The Economics, Culture, and Politics of Oil in Venezuela," *Venezuela Analysis*, August 30, 2003, http://www.venezuelanalysis.com/articles.php?artno=1000 (accessed March 2, 2006); Kurt Abraham, "Bravo for the General—a World of Oil—Guaicapuro Lameda Steps Down as Head of PdVSA," World Oil, April 2002, reprinted at Findarticles.com, http://www.findarticles.com/p/articles/mi_m3159/is_4_223/ai_84943627 (accessed March 6, 2006).

23. "Fiscalía presentará en diciembre acto conclusivo contra Guaicaipuro Lameda," *El Universal* (Caracas, Venezuela), October 25, 2005, http://buscador.eluniversal.com/2005/10/25/pol_ava_25A623203.shtml (accessed March 2, 2006).

24. Taynem Hernández, "Comisión militar negocia salida del Presidente," *El Universal* (Caracas, Venezuela), April 12, 2002, http://buscador.eluniversal.com/2002/04/12/pol_art_12106XX.shtml (accessed March 2, 2006).

25. "Altos oficiales desconocen autoridad del presidente Chávez," *El Universal*, April 12, 2002, http://buscador.eluniversal.com/2002/04/12/pol_art_12112BB.shtml (accessed March 2, 2006).

26. Harnecker, "Interview with President Chávez."

27. Broderick, "Venezuela: Coup and Countercoup"; Bart Jones, "Like Old Days, U.S. Role in Venezuela Coup Under Scrutiny," *National Catholic Reporter*, May 31, 2002, http://www.natcath.com/NCR_Online/archives/053102/053102j.htm (accessed March 6, 2006); Christopher Orlet, "At Large the New Quixote," *The American Spectator*, May 10, 2005, http://www.spectator.org/dsp_article.asp?art_id=8142 (accessed March 6, 2006).

28. Félix Carmona, "Jornada Decisiva/Visión nocturna, el ocaso de los Círculos," *El Universal*, April 12, 2002, http://buscador.eluniversal.com/2002/04/12/ccs_art_12402XX.shtml (accessed March 2, 2006).

29. Harnecker, *Militares junto al pueblo*, 45–46.

30. Aram Rubén Aharonian, "Back, by Popular Demand? How Venezuela's Hugo Chávez Got a Second Chance"; "Hamburgers, Cured Ham, and Oil," *Proceso*, May 1, 2002, posted at Worldpress.org Web site, http://www.worldpress.org/Americas/581.cfm (accessed March 6, 2006).

31. "Embassy Official: U.S. Personnel Not Involved in Coup," CNN, April 18, 2002, http://edition.cnn.com/2002/WORLD/americas/04/18/venezuela.us/ (accessed March 6, 2006).

32. Jack Sweeney, "Venezuela: Successful Counterstrike Unlikely, but Violence Possible Friday," Fox News, April 12, 2002.

33. Harnecker, "The Venezuelan Military."

34. Harnecker, "Interview with President Chávez."

35. Trinkunas, "Civil-Military Relations in Venezuela after 11 April."

36. Harnecker, *Militares junto al pueblo*, 46–47; Tom Haines, "The Power of Art, Venezuelans Use a Big Canvas for their Political Sentiments," *The Boston Globe*, December 28, 2003 (Factiva Database); Bart Jones, "Revolutionary Singer's Sons Stir Teen-Age Pandemonium," Associated Press, January 16, 1997 (Factiva Database).

37. Harnecker, *militares junto al pueblo*, 47.

38. Gonzalo Gómez, "Interview with Army Chief of Staff Gen. Raul Baduel, Energy Affairs, Technology and Security of the State," Venezuela Analysis, February 12, 2004, http://www.venezuelanalysis.com/articles.php?artno=1104 (accessed March 2, 2006).

39. Jorquera, "Venezuela's April 2002 Coup Revealed the Embryonic Development of a Counter-Power."

40. Harnecker, *Militares junto al pueblo*, 47.

41. Jorquera, "Venezuela's April 2002 Coup Revealed the Embryonic Development of a Counter-Power."

42. "Venezuelan Coup Leader Tries to Flee," BBC News Web site, May 24, 2002, http://news.bbc.co.uk/2/hi/americas/2005591.stm (accessed March 6, 2006); "Latin America, Venezuela Congress May Approve Constitution Change (Update2)," Bloomberg.com, September 15, 2004, http://quote.bloomberg.com/apps/news?pid=10000086&sid=aLEJ89FADDJM&refer=latin_america (accessed March 6, 2006); Sánchez, "Bolivarian Circles"; Scott Wilson, "Acting Leader of Venezuela Steps Down, Term Ends After One Day As Pro-Chávez Protests Grow," *Washington Post*, April 14, 2002, http://www.washingtonpost.com/ac2/wp-dyn/A44867–2002Apr13?language=printer (accessed March 6, 2006).

43. Jorquera, Venezuela's April 2002 Coup Revealed the Embryonic Development of a Counter-Power."

44. Harnecker, "Interview with President Chávez."

45. Jorquera, Venezuela's April 2002 Coup Revealed the Embryonic Development of a Counter-power."

46. Jon Beasley-Murray, "Venezuela Analysis: Media, The Revolution Will Not be Televised: Hugo Chávez's Return and the Venezuelan multitude," *NACLA*, July-August 2002, http://www.nacla.org/bodies/body20.php (accessed March 6, 2006).

47. Rachel Coen, "Spotlighting (Some) Venezuela Killings, Deaths During Pro-Chávez Protests Don't Interest *New York Times*," *Extra!*, July/August 2002, http://www.fair.org/extra/0207/venezuela.html (accessed March 6, 2006); Alexandra Olson, "Triumphant Chávez Returns to Power Two Days after Ouster; Stupefied Nation Seeks Answers," Associated Press, April 14, 2002 (Factiva Database).

48. Trinkunas, "Civil-Military Relations in Venezuela after 11 April."

49. Jorquera, Venezuela's April 2002 Coup Revealed the Embryonic Development of a Counter-Power."

50. Trinkunas, "Civil-Military Relations in Venezuela after 11 April."

51. Jorge Rueda, "Playoffs a Big Hit with Constituents," Associated Press, reprinted at *Boston Globe* Web site, May 26, 2004, http://www.boston.com/news/world/latinamerica/articles/2004/05/26/playoffs_a_big_hit_with_constituents/ (accessed March 6, 2006); Jorquera, "Venezuela's April 2002 Coup Revealed the Embryonic Development of a Counter-Power."

52. "Coup and Counter-Coup, Global Agenda," *The Economist*, April 15, 2002. "Vásquez Velasco dijo que reaccionó contra el 'asesinato de inocentes,'" "Vásquez Velasco: 'No reconocí a Carmona Estanga,'" *El Universal* (Caracas, Venezuela), May 17, 2002, http://buscador.eluniversal.com/2002/05/17/pol_ava_17052002_30539.h.shtml (accessed March 2, 2006)

53. Ken Dermota, "Investigation of Venezuelan Coup Finds Plotters Believed U.S. had a Role," Agence France-Presse, April 21, 2002 (Factiva Database).

54. Gómez, "Interview with Army Chief of Staff Gen. Raul Baduel."

55. Rodrigo Chaves and Tom Burke, "The Bolivarian Circles" ZNet, July 30, 2003, http://www.zmag.org/content/showarticle.cfm?SectionID=45&ItemID=3971 (accessed March 6, 2006); Jon Lee Anderson, "The Revolutionary," *The New Yorker,* September 10, 2001 issue (with short update on coup), http://www.newyorker.com/archive/content?020422fr_archive03 (accessed March 6, 2006).

56. "The Revolution Will Not Be Televised—Why is Amnesty Not Screening a New Documentary about the Failed 2002 Coup in Venezuela?," *Democracy Now!*, November 6, 2003, http://www.democracynow.org/article.pl?sid=03/11/06/1558221 (accessed March 6, 2006).

57. Jorquera, "Venezuela's April 2002 Coup Revealed the Embryonic Development of a Counter-Power."

58. Gómez, "Interview with Army Chief of Staff Gen. Raul Baduel."

59. Greg Wilpert, "Venezuela's Supreme Court Nullifies Sentence that Absolved Coup Organizers," Venezuela Analysis, March 12, 2005, http://www.venezuelanalysis.com/news.php?newsno=1544 (accessed March 2, 2006). "El Gobierno de EE UU se reunió con la oposición días antes del golpe," *El Pais* (newspaper in Madrid, Spain), April 16, 2002, http://www.elpais.es/articulo.html?d_date=20020416&xref=20020416elpepuint_2&type=Tes&anchor=elpepupor (accessed March 6, 2006), Pascal Fletcher, "Venezuela Appeals Coup Acquittals, Government Asks Court to Annul," Reuters, December 3, 2004, reprinted on *Boston Globe* Web site, http://www.boston.com/news/world/latinamerica/articles/2004/12/03/venezuela_appeals_coup_acquittals/ (accessed March 4, 2006)

60. "Colombia Denies Asylum to Venezuelans Wanted in 2002 Coup Attempt," Venezuela Analysis, September 21, 2005, http://www.venezuelanalysis.com/news.php?newsno=1761 (accessed March 2, 2005); José de Cordoba, "Venezuela's Chávez Becomes a New Foe for Little Havana," *Wall Street Journal*, January 29, 2003 (Factiva Database).

61. Cort Greene, "Open Letter to *El Nuevo Herald* and the *Miami Herald*," Venezuela Analysis, March 24, 2005, http://www.venezuelanalysis.com/articles.php?artno=1404 (accessed March 2, 2006).

62. Munckton, "Venezuela."

63. Morsbach, "Chávez Accused of Fostering Militia Links."

64. Phil Gunson, "Oil Factor Could Be Tipping Point in Venezuela," *The Christian Science Monitor,* December 10, 2002, http://www.csmonitor.com/2002/1210/p07s02-woam.html (accessed March 6, 2006).

65. Jorquera, "Venezuela's April 2002 Coup Revealed the Embryonic Development of a Counter-Power."

66. Chaves and Burke, "The Bolivarian Circles."

67. Gunson, "Oil Factor Could Be Tipping Point in Venezuela."

68. Gómez, "Interview with Army Chief of Staff Gen. Raul Baduel."

69. Gunson, "Oil Factor Could Be Tipping Point in Venezuela."

70. "López dice que se estudia toma militar de PdVSA para evitar sabotaje," *El Universal,* April 28, 2005, http://buscador.eluniversal.com/2005/04/28/pol_ava_28A555591.shtml (accessed March 2, 2006).

71. "Ministerio de la Defensa tomará medidas contra agentes norteamericanos, García Carneiro denunció infiltración de CIA en PdVSA," *El Universal,* April 29, 2005, http://buscador.eluniversal.com/2005/04/29/pol_art_29108E.shtml (accessed March 2, 2006).

72. Greg Wilpert, "Armed Forces Protect Venezuela's Oil Fields," Venezuela Analysis, May 4, 2005, http://www.venezuelanalysis.com/news.php?newsno=1611 (accessed March 2, 2006).

73. Monica Castro, "Están alerta ante sabotaje, López Hidalgo descarta militarización de PdVSA," *El Universal,* May 2, 2005, http://buscador.eluniversal.com/2005/05/02/pol_art_02198D.shtml (accessed March 2, 2006).

74. "Trabajadores de PdVSA manejarán unidad militar junto al Ejército," *El Universal,* June 4, 2005, http://buscador.eluniversal.com/2005/06/04/pol_art_04104D.shtml (accessed March 2, 2006).

75. U.S. Southern Command Web site, "Bantz J. Craddock, General, United States Army, Commander, U.S. Southern Command," http://www.southcom.mil/PA/Media/Media%20Relations/bios/southcom/bioCDR.htm (accessed March 7, 2006).

76. Ibid.

77. Frida Berrigan and Jonathan Wingo, "Arms Trade Resource Center, The Bush Effect, U.S. Military Involvement in Latin America Rises Development and Humanitarian Aid Fall," World Policy Institute, November 4, 2005, http://www.worldpolicy.org/projects/arms/reports/MilitaryAidLA110405.html (accessed May 13, 2006), Eric Schmitt and Tim Golden, "Force-Feeding at Guantánamo Is Now Acknowledged," New York Times, February 22, 2006, http://www.nytimes.com/2006/02/22/international/middleeast/22gitmo.html?ei=5088&en=bd3f5204abe66015&ex=1298264400&partner=rssnyt&emc=rss&pagewanted=print (accessed May 13, 2006)

78. "U.S. Southern Command (SouthCom) Struggles for a Role in the War on Latin American Terrorism," Council on Hemispheric Affairs, Memorandum to the Press 04.58, http://www.coha.org/NEW_PRESS_RELEASES/New_

Press_Releases_2004/04.58%20Terrorism%20FINAL%202.htm   (accessed March 7, 2006).

79. Larry Fine, "U.S. General Assails 'Shrill' Guantánamo Criticism," Reuters, May 27, 2005, reprinted on *Boston Globe* Web site, http://www.boston.com/news/nation/articles/2005/05/27/us_general_assails_shrill_guantanamo_criticism?mode=PF (accessed March 4, 2006); "U.S. Frees 18 Prisoners Held at Guantánamo Bay," *Washington Post*, March 27, 2003 (Factiva Database); "Bantz J. Craddock General, United States Army, Commander, U.S. Southern Command," Biography of Bantz Craddock, U.S. Southern Command Web site, http://www.southcom.mil/pa/Media/Media%20Relations/bios/southcom/bioCDR.htm (accessed March 25, 2006).

80. Nikolas Kozloff, "Miami South Com," *Z magazine*, December 1999, http://www.zmag.org/ZMag/articles/dec1999kozloff.htm (accessed March 7, 2006).

81. Council on Hemispheric Affairs, "U.S. Southern Command (SouthCom) Struggles."

82. Ibid.

83. Wagner, "U.S. General Says Venezuela is a Danger."

84. James Hodge and Linda Cooper, "Chávez to Withdraw Officers from U.S. Army Training School, SOA Watch Scores Victory in Venezuela," Venezuela Analysis, April 8, 2004, reprinted from *National Catholic Reporter,* http://www.venezuelanalysis.com/articles.php?artno=1154 (accessed March 2, 2006).

85. "Graduates Participated in 2002 Coup d état, Venezuela Ceases all Training of Soldiers at the School of the Americas," Venezuela Analysis, March 2, 2004, reprinted from SOA Watch/U.S. Newswire, http://www.venezuel-analysis.com/news.php?newsno=1210 (accessed March 4, 2006).

86. Hodge and Cooper, "Chávez to Withdraw Officers from U.S. Army Training School."

87. Sarah Wagner, "US-Venezuela Military Cooperation Indefinitely Suspended," Venezuela Analysis, April 25, 2005, http://www.venezuelanalysis.com/news.php?newsno=1599 (accessed March 2, 2006).

88. Trinkunas, "Civil-Military Relations in Venezuela after 11 April."

89. Wagner, "US-Venezuela Military Cooperation Indefinitely Suspended."

90. "Venezuela Might Send U.S. Fighter Jets to China or Cuba," Venezuela Analysis, November 04, 2005, http://www.venezuelanalysis.com/news.php?newsno=1805 (accessed March 8, 2006); Maria Daniela Espinoza, "Indican que traspaso de F16 requiere permiso de EEUU," *El Universal*, November 3, 2005, http://buscador.eluniversal.com/2005/11/03/pol_art_03106A.shtml (accessed March 2, 2006).

91. "Cuba considera 'legítimo' que Venezuela le ofrezca sus cazas F–16," *El Universal*, November 4, 2005, http://buscador.eluniversal.com/2005/11/04/pol_ava_04A628623.shtml (accessed March 2, 2006).

92. Espinoza, "Militar."

93. "Gobierno pretende intensificar cooperación con Cuba," *El Universal*, April 8, 2004, http://buscador.eluniversal.com/2004/04/08/eco_ava_08A445097.shtml (accessed March 2, 2006).

94. Richard Gott, *In the Shadow of the Liberator* (New York: Verso, 2000), 36, 60.

95. "Militares venezolanos observaron maniobras de los MIG–29 en Cuba," *El Universal*, August 11, 2005, http://buscador.eluniversal.com/2005/08/11/pol_ava_11A596627.shtml (accessed March 2, 2006).

96. Jonah Gindin, "Venezuela Signs Helicopter Deal with Russia, Boosts Border Security," Venezuela Analysis, March 11, 2005, http://www.venezuelanalysis.com/news.php?newsno=1543 (accessed March 2, 2006); "Militares venezolanos observaron maniobras de los MIG–29 en Cuba."

97. U.S. Department of Defense Web site, Office of the Assistant Secretary of Defense (Public Affairs), News Transcript, Secretary Rumsfeld Interview with Andres Oppenheimer of the *Miami Herald*, April 5, 2005, http://www.defenselink.mil/transcripts/2005/tr20050405-secdef2461.html (accessed March 8, 2006).

98. Romeo Langlois, "Chávez Defies Bush and Buys Arms from Spain," *Le Figaro*, November 30, 2005, reprinted at truthout.org, http://www.truthout.org/docs_2005/113005H.shtml (accessed March 8, 2006).

99. Gindin, "Venezuela Signs Helicopter Deal with Russia."

100. Sarah Wagner, "Colombia's Uribe Said Cooperation with Venezuela is Improving Every Day; Venezuela to Create Military Reserve Force of 1.5 Million," Venezuela Analysis, April 4, 2005, http://www.venezuelanalysis.com/news.php?newsno=1572 (accessed March 2, 2006).

101. Jane Monahan, "Venezuela Looks to Boost Social Spending," BBC News Web site, December 16, 2005, http://news.bbc.co.uk/2/hi/business/4400052.stm (accessed March 8, 2006); "Presidente Chávez reiteró llamado a la unidad del país," *El Universal*, August 28, 2004, http://buscador.eluniversal.com/2004/08/28/pol_ava_28A487475.shtml (accessed March 8, 2006); Robin Nieto, "Civic-Military Parade Celebrates Venezuela's Social Programs," Venezuela Analysis, August 30, 2004, http://venezuelanalysis.com/news.php?newsno=1352 (accessed March 2, 2006).

102. Greg Wilpert, "Venezuela's Land Reform, Land for People Not for Profit in Venezuela," Venezuela Analysis, August 23, 2005, http://www.venezuelanalysis.com/articles.php?artno=1529 (accessed March 2, 2006).

103. Jorge Martín, "Venezuela Announces War Against 'Latifundios,'" Venezuela Analysis, January 14, 2005, http://www.venezuelanalysis.com/articles.php?artno=1351 (accessed March 2, 2006).

104. Greg Wilpert, "Venezuelan Authorities Seize Idle Heinz Ketchup Plant," Venezuela Analysis, September 9, 2005, http://www.venezuelanalysis.com/news.php?newsno=1751 (accessed March 2, 2006).

105. "Delegación militar venezolana se reunió con Fidel Castro," *El Universal*, June 17, 2005, http://buscador.eluniversal.com/2005/06/17/pol_art_17106E.shtml (accessed March 2, 2006).

106. Wagner, "Colombia's Uribe Said Cooperation with Venezuela is Improving"; "La reserva no debe ser utilizada con fines políticos," *El Universal*, March 25, 2005, http://buscador.eluniversal.com/2005/03/25/pol_art_25A5 44829.shtml (accessed March 8, 2006); Andrés Oppenheimer "Venezuela's

Leader Mixing Military and Politics," *Philadelphia Inquirer,* July 17, 2005, http://www.philly.com/mld/inquirer/news/editorial/12150200.htm (accessed March 8, 2006).

107. Humberto Márquez, "Venezuela's Chávez Consolidates His Power, as Opposition Weakens," Inter Press Service, April 19, 2005, http://www.ipsnews.net/africa/interna.asp?idnews=28321 (accessed March 8, 2006).

108. "García Carneiro defiende plan de defensa integral de la nación," *El Universal* (Caracas, Venezuela), May 24, 2004, http://buscador.eluniversal.com/2004/05/24/pol_ava_24A463423.shtml (accessed March 2, 2006).

CHAPTER 7

1. Natalie Obiko Pearson, "U.S. Denies Role in Venezuela Vote Boycott," Associated Press, December 3, 2005, reprinted on Common Dreams, http://www.commondreams.org/cgi-bin/print.cgi?file=/headlines05/1203–05.htm (accessed March 4, 2006).

2. "Petrobrás y PdVSA firman acta de nacimiento de Petroamérica," *El Universal,* June 30,1999, http://buscador.eluniversal.com/1999/06/30/apo_art_30102CC.shtml (accessed March 8, 2006).

3. Jonah Gindin, "Venezuela and the 'New Democracy,'" *Canadian Dimension,* http://canadiandimension.com/articles/2005/07/01/15/ (accessed March 23, 2006).

4. Néstor Sánchez, "Brazil, Argentina and Venezuela Announce the Birth of PetroSur," Vheadline, May 12, 2005, http://www.vheadline.com/printer_news.asp?id=33937 (accessed March 8, 2006).

5. Gindin, "Venezuela and the 'New Democracy.'"

6. "Online Focus, Slick Deal?" a News Hour with Jim Lehrer Transcript, December 1, 1998, PBS Web site, http://www.pbs.org/newshour/bb/business/july-dec98/oil_12–1.html (accessed March 8, 2006), "BP, Amoco Aim is Growth," CNN Money Web site, August 12, 1998, http://money.cnn.com/1998/08/12/deals/intv_oil/ (accessed March 8, 2006); "The Chevron Texaco Merger," *San Francisco Chronicle,* October 10, 2001, http://www.sfgate.com/cgi-bin/article.cgi?file=/chronicle/archive/2001/10/10/BU159305.DTL&type=business&nl=biz (accessed March 8, 2006).

7. Geri Smith, "Is Venezuela's Chávez Killing the Golden Goose?" *Business Week,* March 14, 2005, http://www.businessweek.com/print/magazine/content/05_11/b3924086_mz058.htm?chan=gb& (accessed March 8, 2006).

8. Jonah Gindin, "Venezuela and the 'New Democracy,'" Venezuela Analysis, October 11, 2005, http://www.venezuelanalysis.com/articles.php?artno=1575 (accessed April 18, 2006).

9. "Brazil and Venezuela Looking Again at Uniting their Oil Companies," Alexander's Gas and Oil Connections, October 5, 1999, http://www.gasandoil.com/goc/news/ntl92419.htm (accessed March 8, 2006).

10. Santiago Fittipaldi, Anita Hawser, and Laurence Neville, "World's Best Companies 2004," *Global Finance,* reprinted at Findarticles.com, http://www.

findarticles.com/p/articles/mi_qa3715/is_200411/ai_n9470032/pg_11 (accessed March 8, 2006); "Latin America: Petrobrás 4th-Qtr Net Soars on Prices, Lower Costs (Update1)," Bloomberg.com, February 17, 2006 (accessed March 8, 2006).

11. Humberto Márquez, "Oil: Venezuela Forges Ahead towards Regional Energy Integration," Inter Press Service, October 22, 2004, http://ipsnews.net/interna.asp?idnews=25977 (accessed March 8, 2006).

12. Greg Wilpert, "Venezuela to Invest in Refineries in Brazil and Argentina," Venezuela Analysis, October 3, 2005, http://www.venezuelanalysis.com/news.php?newsno=1774 (accessed March 4, 2006).

13. Gindin, "Venezuela and the 'New Democracy.'"

14. "Brazil and Venezuela Looking Again at Uniting their Oil Companies," Alexander's Gas and Oil Connections, May 5, 1999, http://www.gasandoil.com/goc/news/ntl92419.htm (accessed March 8, 2006).

15. Ibid.

16. Ibid.

17. "Chávez Promotes Creation of Petro-America Energy Enterprise," Alexander's Gas and Oil Connections, March 14, 2002, http://www.gasandoil.com/goc/news/ntl21525.htm (accessed March 8, 2006).

18. "Chávez quiere crear una OPEP sudamericana" Reuters—Noticias Latinoamericanas, July 26, 2002 (Factiva Database).

19. Michael Astor, "Haves and Have Nots Clash Over Plan to Divert River for Drought Relief," Associated Press, January 11, 2006 (Factiva Database); Jack Epstein, "Brazil Rushes Food to Stem Peasants' Looting Their Crops Parched, Their Beasts Dead or Dying of Thirst, the Starving People of the Nation's Northeast are Stealing Whatever They Can to Survive a Water Shortage for which Many Blame the Landowner-politicians," *Globe and Mail*, May 20, 1998 (Factiva Database).

20. "Pernambuco," *Encyclopedia Americana*, Grolier Online 2006, Scholastic Library Publishing, http://go.grolier.com/ (accessed March 8, 2006).

21. Kempton Webb, "Brazil >> 1. The Land and Natural Resources," *Encyclopedia Americana*, Grolier Online 2006, Scholastic Library Publishing, http://go.grolier.com/ (accessed March 8, 2006); Jack Epstein, "Brazil Rushes Food."

22. Epstein, "Brazil Rushes Food."

23. Alan Riding, "In Brazil's Northeast, Misery Molded by Man and Nature," *New York Times*, May 3, 1988 (Factiva Database).

24. Manuel Martínez, "Brazil Study Highlights Extensive Child Prostitution in Cities," EFE News Service, January 26, 2005 (Factiva Database).

25. "Lula da Silva, Luiz Inácio," *Encyclopedia Americana*, Grolier Online 2006, Scholastic Library Publishing, http://go.grolier.com/ (accessed March 8, 2006).

26. "Luiz Inácio da Silva," OSCE Consulta Database, Diccionario de Biografías, Editorial Oceano 2001, (accessed March 19, 2006).

27. "Lula: Fourth Time Lucky," BBC News Web site, October 28, 2002, http://news.bbc.co.uk/2/hi/americas/2367851.stm (accessed March 9, 2006).

28. Alan Riding, "In Brazil's Northeast, Misery Molded by Man and Nature," *New York Times*, May 3, 1988 (Factiva Database).

29. Simon Romero, "São Paulo Becomes the Kidnapping Capital of Brazil," *New York Times*, February 13, 2002, *New York Times and New York Post (2000-present)*; Thomson Gale, New York Public Library, March 19, 2006, http://find. galegroup.com/itx/infomark.do?&contentSet=IAC-Documents&type=retrieve&tabID=T003&prodId=SPN.SP00&docId=A82836307&source=gale &srcprod=SP00&userGroupName=nypl&version=1.0.

30. Kempton Webb, "São Paulo," Encyclopedia Americana, Grolier Online, 2006, Scholastic Library Publishing, http://go.groiler.com (accessed March 10, 2006).

31. "Lula da Silva, Luiz Inácio," *Encyclopedia Americana*.

32. "Lula: Fourth Time Lucky," BBC News.

33. Robert Alexander, "Brazil >> History >> 11. Contemporary Brazil," *Encyclopedia Americana*, Grolier Online, 2006, Scholastic Library Publishing, http:// go.grolier.com, (accessed March 10, 2006); Stephen Rabe, "The Johnson Doctrine," March 1, 2006, *Presidential Studies Quarterly* 48, Vol. 36; Issue 1 (Factiva database).

34. "Lula da Silva, Luiz Inácio," *Encyclopedia Americana*; "Lula: Fourth Time Lucky," BBC News.

35. Andrew Downie, "The Evolution of Brazil's 'Lula,' Brazilians Go to the Polls Sunday, and a Former Socialist Appears Ready to Become the Next President," *Christian Science Monitor*, October 4, 2002, http://www.csmonitor.com/ 2002/1004/p06s01-woam.html (accessed March 4, 2006).

36. Michael Astor, "Brazil Calls Out Military to Fight Unconventional Enemies," Associated Press, July 19, 2004 (Factiva database).

37. "Lula da Silva, Luiz Inácio," *Encyclopedia Americana*.

38. Roger Burbach, "Commentary, Brazil, Another World is Possible," *Z Magazine*, October 2002, http://zmagsite.zmag.org/Oct2002/Commentary/burbach1002.htm (accessed March 10, 2006).

39. "Petrobrás CEO Dutra Boosts Profits, Expands Across Region," Bloomberg.com, November 13, 2003, http://quote.bloomberg.com/apps/ news?pid=10000086&sid=a83b7InH4cD8&refer=latin_america (accessed March 10, 2006).

40. "Petrobrás Offers 20.9 Percent Raise; Workers Reluctant," Dow Jones News Service August 23, 1995 (Factiva Database).

41. "Brazil: Oil Strike Ends as Government Moves Forward with Privatization Policies," June 9, 1995, NotiSur-Latin American Political Affairs, Latin American Database/Latin American Institute (Factiva Database).

42. "Brazil's Petrobrás Workers Protest Alleged Punitive Measures," Dow Jones Emerging Markets Report, August 16, 1995 (Factiva Database).

43. "Brazil: Oil Strike Ends."

44. "Brazil's Senate Approves New Petroleum Investment Law," *The Oil and Gas Journal* 37, Vol. 95, No. 30, July 28, 1997 (Factiva Database).

45. "Brazil/Petrobrás–3: Strike Cost Petrobrás $186 Million in May," Dow Jones International News, August 23, 1995 (Factiva Database); Mario Osava, "Brazil-Oil: Joint Ventures to End State Monopoly," Inter Press Service, July 24, 1997 (Factiva Database); "Brazil: Oil Strike Ends."

46. "Brazil's Senate Approves New Petroleum Investment Law."

47. "Brazil—Fiscal Analysis," *World of Information Country Report* 25, January 8, 2001 (Factiva Database).

48. Immanuel Wallerstein, "Brazil and the World-System: The Era of Lula," Fernand Braudel Center, Binghamton University, Commentary No. 120, September 1, 2003, http://fbc.binghamton.edu/120en.htm (accessed March 10, 2006).

49. "Korea Targets Brazil in Bid to Diversify Trade and Investment," Alexander's Gas and Oil Connections, November 17, 2004, http://www.gasandoil.com/goc/news/ntl44978.htm (accessed March 10, 2006); "Brazil Now Latin America's Largest Economy," Associated Press, September 30, 2005, reprinted at MSNBC Web site, http://www.msnbc.msn.com/id/9548374 (accessed March 10, 2006).

50. "Lula da Silva, Luiz Inácio," *Encyclopedia Americana.*

51. "Chávez ofreció su corazón a Brasil," *El Universal,* January 2, 2003, http://buscador.eluniversal.com/2003/01/02/int_art_02207DD.shtml.

52. "Para Lula es un 'chiste de mal gusto' bloque con Chávez," *El Universal* (Caracas, Venezuela), October 10, 2002, http://www.eluniversal.com/2002/10/10/pol_art_10109EE.shtml (accessed March 4, 2006).

53. Ibid.

54. Peter O. Wacker, "Brazil," *The New Book of Knowledge Encyclopedia,* Scholastic Library Publishing, 2006, http://nbk.grolier.com (accessed March 10, 2006); Kenneth Maxwell, "Western Hemisphere"; Book review of *Trandsotming Brazil: A Reform Era in Perspective* by Mauricio A. Font; *Foreign Affairs,* September/October 2003, http://www.foreignaffairs.org/20030901fa-book82543/mauricio-a-font/trandsotming-brazil-a-reform-era-in-perspective.html?mode=print (accessed March 10, 2006); Geisa María Rocha, "Neo-Dependency in Brazil," *New Left Review* 16, July–August 2002, http://www.newleftreview.net/NLR25001.shtml (accessed March 10, 2006).

55. Rocha, "Neo-Dependency in Brazil"; Paul Blustein and Sandra Sugawara, "Japan's Woes Hurt Markets Worldwide," *Washington Post,* August 12, 1998, http://www.washingtonpost.com/wp-srv/business/longterm/asiaecon/stories/woes081298.htm (accessed March 10, 2006); "Brazil Unveils Crisis Plan," CNN Money Web site, October 27, 1998, http://money.cnn.com/1998/10/27/emerging_markets/brazil/ (accessed March 10, 2006).

56. "Asian Markets Wary, but not Panicked by Brazil Crisis," January 14, 1999, CNN Web site, http://www.cnn.com/WORLD/americas/9901/14/brazil.03/ (accessed March 10, 2006); "Business: the Economy, Brazil—a Catastrophe in the Making?," BBC News Web site, January 22, 1999, http://news.bbc.co.uk/2/hi/business/260777.stm (accessed March 10, 2006).

57. Rocha, "Neo-Dependency in Brazil."

58. Emir Sader, "Taking Lula's Measure," *New Left Review* 33, May–June 2005, http://www.newleftreview.net/NLR26706.shtml (accessed March 4, 2006).

59. Joseph Contreras, "Energy Crunch, is Latin America too Protective of its Power Sector?" *Newsweek International*, May 31, 2006, reprinted on MSNBC Web site, http://www.msnbc.msn.com/id/5040781 (accessed March 10, 2006).

60. "Brazil Min: No Decision on Fuel-Price Hikes Yet," Dow Jones International News, May 17, 2004 (Factiva Database); "Brazil's Lula Names Dilma Rousseff as Cabinet Chief (Update1)," Bloomberg.com, June 20, 2005, http://www.bloomberg.com/apps/news?pid=10000086&sid=abX84SSi7mlE&refer=latin_america (accessed March 10, 2006).

61. Andrei Khalip, "Newsmaker-Brazil's Iron Lady Rousseff Gets Key Cabinet Job," Reuters, June 21, 2005 (Factiva Database); "Brazil's Lula Names Dilma Rousseff."

62. Khalip, "Newsmaker-Brazil's Iron Lady."

63. Contreras, "Energy Crunch."

64. Bradley Brooks, "Feature: Brazil's Oil Giant under Scrutiny," United Press International, February 10, 2003, http://www.upi.com/inc/view.php?StoryID=20030210–040730–7776r (accessed March 10, 2006).

65. "Profitable but Political (Petroleo Brasileiro S.A.)," *LatinFinance* 54, Issue 155, March 1, 2004 (Factiva database).

66. "Petrobrás CEO Dutra Boosts Profits."

67. Brian Ellsworth, "The Oil Company as Social Worker," *New York Times*, March 11, 2004, http://www.nytimes.com/2004/03/11/business/worldbusiness/11pdvsa.html?ex=1394427600&en=179f03b724d3dcc9&ei=5007&partner=USERLAND (accessed March 11, 2006); "Petrobrás CEO Dutra Boosts Profits."

68. Downie, "The Evolution of Brazil's 'Lula.'"

69. Roger Burbach, "Has Lula Sold Out? With New Friends, Brazil's Leading Leftist is Finally Poised to Win the Presidency," Resource Center of the Americas, October 2002, http://www.americas.org/item_93 (accessed March 11, 2006).

70. James Petras, "Latin America: the Empire Changes Gears," Counterpunch, December 7, 2004, http://www.counterpunch.org/petras12072004.html (accessed March 4, 2006); Ben Terrall, "Lula's Troops in Haiti," ZNet, November 18, 2004, http://www.zmag.org/content/showarticle.cfm?SectionID=55&ItemID=6691 (accessed March 11, 2006).

71. "U.S. Snubbed over Aristide Ouster," Al Jazeera, March 17, 2004, http://english.aljazeera.net/NR/exeres/661958CF-CE04–4E47–91B7–1736624C5AFC.htm (accessed March 9, 2006).

72. "Chávez y Lula se reunirán para superar fricciones," *El Universal* (Caracas, Venezuela), December 10, 2004, http://www.el-universal.com/2004/12/10/imp_pol_ava_10A515103.shtml (accessed March 4, 2006); "U.S. Snubbed over Aristide Ouster."

73. Claudia Jardim and Jonah Gindin, "Interview with Tariq Ali, Venezuela: Changing the World by Taking Power," Venezuela Analysis, July 22, 2004, http://www.venezuelanalysis.com/articles.php?artno=1223 (accessed March 4, 2006); Wallerstein, "Brazil and the World-System."

74. James Petras, "Lula's 'Workers' Regime' Plummets in Stew of Corruption," Counterpunch, July 30–31, 2005, http://www.counterpunch.org/petras 08012005.html (accessed March 4, 2006).

75. William Greider and Kenneth Rapoza, "Lula Raises the Stakes," *The Nation*, December 1, 2003, http://www.thenation.com/doc/20031201/greider (accessed March 4, 2006).

76. "Should Developing Countries Demand Fairer Trade?" BBC News Web site, June 21, 2004, http://news.bbc.co.uk/2/hi/talking_point/3805231.stm (accessed March 11, 2006); Carmen Gentile, "Paraguay: Lula Defends Mercosur," United Press International, June 20, 2005, reprinted at *Washington Times* Web site, http://www.washtimes.com/upi/20050620–071327–6196r. htm (accessed March 11, 2006).

77. Greider and Rapoza, "Lula Raises the Stakes."

78. Claudio Katz, "The Center-Left, Nationalism, and Socialism," *International Socialist Review*, 41, May–June 2005, http://www.isreview.org/issues/41/katz. shtml (accessed March 4, 2006); Tom Lewis, "Brazil: Lula, the IMF, and the Left," *International Socialist Review* Issue 39, January–February 2005, http://www.isreview.org/issues/38/report_Brazil.shtml (accessed March 11, 2006).

79. "Chávez y Lula se reunirán para superar fricciones."

80. "World Social Forum: 'Globalising' Porto Alegre," Inter Press Service, February 1, 2005, http://www.ipsnews.net/africa/Radio/interna.asp?idnews=2582 (accessed March 11, 2006).

81. Juan Forero, "Opposition to U.S. Makes Chávez a Hero to Many," *New York Times*, June 1, 2005, http://www.nytimes.com/2005/06/01/international/ americas/01letter.html?ei=5088&en=d2adb41fda4813c8&ex=1275278400& adxnnl=1&partner=rssnyt&emc=rss&adxnnlx=1134038198-D/YA+TiZ3eb6 G6GyK2Cpog (accessed March 4, 2006).

82. Roger Burbach, "The WSF and the Tale of Two Presidents: Chávez of Venezuela and Lula of Brazil," Venezuela Analysis, February 3, 2005, http:// www.venezuelanalysis.com/articles.php?artno=1367 (accessed March 4, 2006).

83. Cleto Sojo, "'Imperialism is Not Invincible,' Venezuela's Chávez Closes World Social Forum with Call to Transcend Capitalism," Venezuela Analysis, January 31, 2005, http://www.venezuelanalysis.com/news.php?newsno=1486 (accessed March 4, 2006).

84. Burbach, "The WSF and the Tale of Two Presidents."

85. Sojo, "'Imperialism is Not Invincible.'"

86. "Venezuela's Economy Shows Strong Signs of Recovery after Lock-out/ Strike," Venezuela Analysis, September 27, 2003, http://www.venezuelanalysis.com/news.php?newsno=1042 (accessed March 11, 2006).

87. Greg Wilpert, "Venezuela's Oil Company Presents Audited Finances of Industry Shutdown Year," Venezuela Analysis, July 26, 2005, http://www. venezuelanalysis.com/news.php?newsno=1700 (accessed March 11, 2006).

88. "Venezuela Begins Importing Oil," BBC News Web site, December 27, 2002, http://news.bbc.co.uk/2/hi/americas/2607909.stm (accessed March 11, 2006).

89. "Mandatario electo rechaza críticas opositoras," *El Universal*, December 27, 2002, http://buscador.eluniversal.com/2002/12/27/int_art_27107FF.shtml (accessed March 11, 2006).

90. Larry Rohter, "Venezuela Gets Fuel Aid, Brazil Ships Gasoline to Show Support for Chávez," *New York Times*, December 27, 2002, reprinted at *San Francisco Chronicle* Web site, http://www.sfgate.com/cgi-bin/article.cgi?file=/chronicle/archive/2002/12/27/MN130218.DTL.

91. "Lula teme efecto dominó con Chávez," *El Universal*, January 30, 2003, http://www.eluniversal.com/2003/01/30/pol_art_30107DD.shtml (accessed March 4, 2006).

92. Alan Clendenning, "'Axis of Good' for Brazil, Cuba and Venezuela?" Associated Press, January 3, 2003, reprinted at Common Dreams Website, http://www.commondreams.org/cgi-bin/print.cgi?file=/headlines03/0103–01.htm (accessed March 11, 2006).

93. "Venezuela Begins Importing Oil."

94. "Roundup—Brazilian Tanker Arrives in Venezuela," December 29, 2002, Xinhua News Agency (Factiva Database); "Fuel Shipment Arrives in Venezuela," BBC News Web site, December 29, 2002, http://news.bbc.co.uk/2/hi/americas/2611747.stm (accessed March 11, 2006).

95. "Brazil's Oil Union: Against Sending Workers to Venezuela," Dow Jones International News, January 6, 2003 (Factiva Database).

96. "Brazil Petrobrás:Venezuela Requests are Commercial Matter," Dow Jones International News, January 7, 2003 (Factiva Database).

97. According to diplomats, however, the oil strike ended before the technicians were ever sent. Personal email from Cultural Attache at Brazilian Embassy in Washington, D.C., Murilo Fernandes Gabrielli, May 18, 2006.

98. "Factbox-Recovery of Venezuela Oil Industry," Reuters, April 7, 2003 (Factiva Database).

99. "Brazil and Venezuela Looking Again at Uniting their Oil Companies," Alexander's Gas and Oil Connections, May 10, 1999, http://www.gasandoil.com/goc/news/ntl92419.htm (accessed March 11, 2006).

100. Marla Dickerson, "Close-up, Brazil's Ethanol Effort Helping Lead to Oil Self-sufficiency," *Los Angeles Times*, June 17, 2005, reprinted at *Seattle Times* Web site, http://seattletimes.nwsource.com/html/nationworld/2002339093_brazilfuel17.html (accessed March 11, 2006); Humberto Márquez, "Oil: Venezuela Seeks to Diversify Markets," Inter Press Service, February 17, 2005, http://www.ipsnews.net/africa/interna.asp?idnews=27479 (accessed March 11, 2006).

101. Kenneth Rapoza, "World Briefings," *Washington Times*, July 19, 2005, http://www.washtimes.com/world/20050718–101343–7079r_page2.htm (accessed March 4, 2006).

102. "Venezuela's Economy Shows Strong Signs of Recovery"; Wilpert, "Venezuela to Invest in Refineries in Brazil and Argentina"; "Brazil, Venezuela

Companies to Build Refinery," Associated Press, July 20, 2005, reprinted at *Forbes* Web site, http://www.forbes.com/business/businesstech/feeds/ap/2005/07/20/ap2148870.html (accessed March 11, 2006).

103. Harold Olmos, "Chávez, in Brazil to Discuss Refinery Construction, says Foreign Powers Should Get Hands off Iraqi Oil," Associated Press, April 25, 2003 (Factiva Database).

104. Ibid.

105. "Presidente Chávez ofrece ayuda financiera a uruguayos," *El Universal*, December 9, 2005, http://www.eud.com/2005/12/09/eco_art_09201E.shtml (accessed March 4, 2006).

106. Wilpert, "Venezuela to Invest in Refineries in Brazil and Argentina."

107. "Venezuela's Chávez Strengthens Cooperation in Uruguay, Argentina, and Brazil," Venezuela Analysis, August 12, 2005, http://www.venezuelanalysis.com/news.php?newsno=1714 (accessed March 12, 2006).

108. Wilpert, "Venezuela to Invest in Refineries in Brazil and Argentina."

109. Márquez, "Venezuela Seeks to Diversify Markets."

110. "Venezuela's Oil Company Promotes Latin American Integration."

111. Iain Bruce, "Lula and Chávez to Boost Alliance," BBC News Web site, February 14, 2005, http://news.bbc.co.uk/1/hi/world/americas/4263025.stm (accessed March 11, 2006).

112. "Chávez, Lula Da Silva Sign Trade Pacts," Associated Press, February 14, 2005, reprinted at MSNBC Web site, http://msnbc.msn.com/id/6968837 (accessed March 4, 2006).

113. E-mail from Martin Castro to author, January 1, 2006.

114. Hartford Campbell, "COHA Memorandum to the Press, Argentina's Néstor Kirchner: Peronism Without the Tears," COHA Web site, January 27, 2006 http://www.coha.org/NEW_PRESS_RELEASES/New_Press_Releases_2006/06.08_Kirchner_distinct.html (accessed March 1, 2006).

115. Katz, "The Center-Left, Nationalism, and Socialism."

116. James Petras, "Latin America: Political Re-Alignment and Empire," Venezuela Analysis, November 26, 2004, http://www.venezuelanalysis.com/articles.php?artno=1324 (accessed March 11, 2006).

117. Ibid.

118. All of the information is based on 2005 figures. Central Intelligence Agency World Factbook, "Ecuador," http://www.odci.gov/cia/publications/factbook/geos/ec.html, "Brazil," http://www.odci.gov/cia/publications/factbook/geos/br.html, "Venezuela," http://www.odci.gov/cia/publications/factbook/geos/ve.html, "Argentina," http://www.odci.gov/cia/publications/factbook/geos/ar.html, "Mexico," http://www.odci.gov/cia/publications/factbook/geos/mx.html (all Web pages updated May 16, 2006 and accessed May 17, 2006).

119. "Argentina, Natural Gas," Country Analysis Brief, EIA, February 2006, http://www.eia.doe.gov/emeu/cabs/Argentina/NaturalGas.html (accessed March 11, 2006).

120. "Argentina," in Latin American Petroleum Privatization (Chapter three of *Privatization and the Globalization of Energy Markets*), EIA, undated, http://www.eia.doe.gov/emeu/pgem/ch3a.html (accessed March 11, 2006).

121. Carl Solberg, "Entrepreneurship in Public Enterprise: General Enrique Mosconi and The Argentine Petroleum Industry," Business History Review, Vol. 56, No. 3 (autumn, 1982), 7, Pablo Pozzi, "Popular Upheaval and Capitalist Transformation in Argentina," Latin American Perspectives, Issue 114, Vol. 27 No. 5, September 2000, 64

122. "Argentina Leaps Back into the Energy Business," Alexander's Gas and Oil Connections, October 25, 2004, http://www.gasandoil.com/goc/company/cnl44564.htm (accessed March 11, 2006).

123. "Argentina," in Latin American Petroleum Privatization.

124. "Argentina Leaps Back into the Energy Business."

125. "Argentina," in Latin American Petroleum Privatization

126. "Repsol May Bid for First Calgary to Boost Reserves (Update3)," Bloomberg.com, March 16, 2005, http://www.bloomberg.com/apps/news?pid=10000082&refer=canada&sid=aRpI6NpGufTk (accessed March 11, 2006); "Repsol Bids $13B for YPF," CNN Money, April 30, 1999, http://money.cnn.com/1999/04/30/worldbiz/repsol/ (accessed March 11, 2006).

127. Katz, "The Center-Left, Nationalism, and Socialism."

128. "Argentina," Country Analysis Brief, EIA, January 2005, http://www.eia.doe.gov/emeu/cabs/argentna.html (accessed March 11, 2006).

129. "Argentina Leaps Back into the Energy Business."

130. Elliott Gotkine, "Argentina's Threadbare Recovery," BBC News Web site, December 19, 2003, http://news.bbc.co.uk/2/hi/business/3328723.stm (accessed March 11, 2006).

131. Marcela Valente, "Argentina: Energy Crisis—Gov't Upbeat, Experts Still Worried," Inter Press Service, June 10, 2004, http://www.ipsnews.net/africa/interna.asp?idnews=24142 (accessed March 11, 2006).

132. "Argentina Leaps Back into the Energy Business."

133. Ibid.

134. Modesto Emilio Guerrero, "Venezuela Fuel Shipment Warmly Welcomed in Argentina," Venezuela Analysis, May 13, 2004 (accessed March 11, 2006).

135. Humberto Márquez, "Oil: Venezuela Forges Ahead."

136. Humberto Márquez, "Venezuela Seeks to Diversify Markets," Inter Press Service, February 17, 2005, http://www.ipsnews.net/africa/interna.asp?idnews=27479 (accessed March 11, 2006).

137. "Swapping Oil for Influence," USA Today, August 28, 2005, http://www.usatoday.com/printedition/news/20050829/a_Chávezbox29.art.htm (accessed March 4, 2006); Márquez, "Oil: Venezuela Forges Ahead."

138. "Venezuela's Chávez Strengthens Cooperation in Uruguay, Argentina, and Brazil."

139. Steve Ellner, "Venezuela's 'Demonstration Effect' Defying Globalization's Logic," Venezuela Analysis, October 17, 2005, http://www.venezuelanalysis.com/articles.php?artno=1579 (accessed March 11, 2006).

140. Márquez, "Venezuela Seeks to Diversify Markets."

141. Forero, "Opposition to U.S. Makes Chávez a Hero to Many."

142. "Venezuela Cambia Socios Estratégicos," El Universal, March 14, 2005, http://www.eud.com/2005/03/14/eco_art_14120C.shtml (accessed March 4, 2006).

143. Wilpert, "Venezuela to Invest in Refineries in Brazil and Argentina."
144. "Uruguay Profile," EIA Country Analysis Brief, November 2005, http://www.eia.doe.gov/emeu/cabs/Uruguay/Profile.html (accessed March 11, 2006).

CHAPTER 8

1. Carlos Caillabet, "Uruguay: con el senador tupamaro José Mujica, 'Estoy más cerca de Marx que de Lenin,'" *La Insignia* (independent Spanish newspaper based in Madrid), July 4, 2004, http://www.lainsignia.org/2004/julio/ibe_010.htm (accessed March 11, 2006).
2. Martin Weinstein, "Uruguay," *Grolier Multimedia Encyclopedia*, Scholastic Library Publishing, 2006, http://gme.grolier.com (accessed March 12, 2006); George Thomas Kurian, "Uruguay," *Encyclopedia of the World's Nations* (New York: Facts on File, Inc., 2002), Facts on File, Inc., *World History Online*, www.factsonfile.com (accessed March 12, 2006).
3. Robert Alexander, "Uruguay," Encyclopedia Americana, Grolier Online, 2003, http://go.grolier.com (accessed March 11, 2006); "Tupamaros," *La Nueva Enciclopedia Cumbre*, Scholastic Library Publishing, http://nec.grolier.com, (accessed March 9, 2006); Carl Sifakis, "Mitrione, Daniel A.," *Encyclopedia of Assassinations*, Revised Edition (New York: Facts on File, Inc., 2001), Facts on File, Inc., *World History Online*. www.factsonfile.com (accessed March 9, 2006).
4. Cindy C. Combs and Martin Slann, "Tupamaros," *Encyclopedia of Terrorism* (New York: Facts on File, Inc., 2002) Facts on File, Inc., *World History Online*, www.factsonfile.com (accessed March 12, 2006).
5. Caillabet, "Uruguay."
6. A. J. Langguth, *Hidden Terrors* (New York: Pantheon Books, 1978), 235, 251.
7. Sifakis, "Mitrione, Daniel A."; Rick Nathanson, "International Man of Security," *Albuquerque Journal*, November 15, 2002 (Factiva Database); "Intriguing Past of Ex-FBI Agent in Drug Case," United Press, *San Francisco Chronicle*, March 16, 1985, (Factiva Database).
8. Sifakis, "Mitrione, Daniel A."
9. Langguth, *Hidden Terrors*, 251, 286.
10. "En Primera Plana," *Diario 16*, September 19, 2001 (Factiva Database).
11. Sifakis, "Mitrione, Daniel A."
12. Ibid.
13. Felicity Arbuthnot, "Crimes in Iraq, As American as Apple Pie," Centre For Research on Globalisation, May 14, 2004, http://globalresearch.ca/articles/ARB405A.html (accessed April 4, 2006).
14. Alexander, "Uruguay."
15. Caillabet, "Uruguay."
16. "Tupamaros," *La Nueva Enciclopedia Cumbre;* Caillabet, "Uruguay."
17. "Tupamaros," *La Nueva Enciclopedia Cumbre;* "Ex-Rebel to Chair Uruguay Senate," BBC News Web site, February 16, 2005, http://news.bbc.co.uk/2/

hi/americas/4269219.stm (accessed March 12, 2006); Diana Cariboni, "Elections-Uruguay: Historic Triumph by the Left," Inter Press Service, October 31, 2004, http://www.ipsnews.net/africa/interna.asp?idnews=26084 (accessed March 12, 2006); "Se instaló el nuevo parlamento con la impronta del FA," *El Observador* (newspaper based in Montevideo, Uruguay), February 15, 2005, http://www.observador.com.uy/Osecciones/especiales2/nota.aspx?id=28792 (accessed March 12, 2006).

18. "Tupamaros," *La Nueva Enciclopedia Cumbre;* Alexander, "Uruguay"; Cariboni, "Elections-Uruguay."

19. "Uruguay's Vázquez Pledges to Pay Debts, Boost Tax (Update3)," Bloomberg.com, March 1, 2005, http://www.bloomberg.com/apps/news?pid=10000086&sid=a8Rwnp6gaEjA&refer=latin_america (accessed March 12, 2006).

20. "Uruguay Goes Left," *Multinational Monitor,* November 2004, http://multinationalmonitor.org/mm2004/112004/behind-the-lines.html (accessed March 12, 2006); Raúl Pierri, "Uruguay: Economic and Social Rights on the Decline," Inter Press Service, http://www.ipsnews.net/interna.asp?idnews=26671 (accessed March 12, 2006).

21. Pierri, "Uruguay: Economic and Social Rights."

22. "Banking Crisis Grips Uruguay," BBC News Web site, July 30, 2002, http://news.bbc.co.uk/2/hi/business/2162050.stm (accessed March 12, 2006).

23. "Uruguay Receives $1.13 Billion in IMF Loan Accord (Update1)," Bloomberg.com, June 8, 2005, http://www.bloomberg.com/apps/news?pid=10000086&refer=latin_america&sid=aKlxG8WJaVSY (accessed March 12, 2006); Tom Hennigan, "Uruguay: Little Kid on the Block," *Christian Science Monitor,* August 29, 2003, http://www.csmonitor.com/2003/0829/p09s01-woam.htm (accessed March 12, 2006).

24. Alexander, "Uruguay."

25. "South America, Uruguay Rejects Oil Privatization Bid," Reuters, December 8, 2003, reprinted at *Latin Petroleum,* http://www.latinpetroleum.com/printer_2634.shtml (accessed March 12, 2006); "Uruguay, Oil," Energy Information Administration (EIA) Country Analysis Brief, November 2005, http://www.eia.doe.gov/emeu/cabs/Uruguay/Oil.html (accessed March 12, 2006).

26. "Former Guerrillas Take Helm of Uruguay's Congress," Reuters, February 16, 2005, reprinted at *Boston Globe* Web site, http://www.boston.com/news/world/latinamerica/articles/2005/02/16/former_guerrillas_take_helm_of_uruguays_congress/ (accessed March 4, 2006).

27. Darío Montero, "Politics-Mercosur: The Lost Generation's Turn," Inter Press Service, March 2, 2005, http://www.ipsnews.net/africa/interna.asp?idnews=27692 (accessed March 12, 2006).

28. Héctor Tobar, "Socialist Favored to Win in Uruguay Country Hit Hard by Recession Votes Today for President," *Los Angeles Times,* October 31, 2004, reprinted at *San Francisco Chronicle* Web site, http://www.sfgate.com/cgi-bin/article.cgi?file=/chronicle/archive/2004/10/31/MNGVC9JFHI1.DTL (accessed March 12, 2006); Kevin Gray, "Uruguayans Cast Ballots in Election that Could

Chose First Leftist President," Associated Press, October 31, 2004, reprinted at *San Diego Union Tribune* Web site, http://www.signonsandiego.com/news/world/20041031–1201-uruguay-election.html (accessed March 12, 2006); Marcelo Jelen, "Elections-Uruguay: President-Elect Brings Healing Touch to New Job," Inter Press Service, November 1, 2004, http://www.ipsnews.net/africa/sendnews.asp?idnews=26093 (accessed March 12, 2006).

29. Kevin Gray, "Uruguay Inaugurates First Leftist Leader," Associated Press, March 1, 2005, reprinted at *Boston Globe* Web site, http://www.boston.com/news/world/europe/articles/2005/03/01/uruguay_to_inaugurate_leftist_president?pg=full (accessed March 4, 2006); Tobar, "Socialist Favored to Win."

30. Jelen, "Elections-Uruguay."

31. "Leftist Candidate for President Wins Uruguay Election," *New York Times* News Service and Associated Press, November 1, 2004, reprinted at *San Diego Union Tribune* Web site, http://www.signonsandiego.com/uniontrib/20041101/news_1n1uruguay.html (accessed March 12, 2006).

32. Gray, "Uruguay Inaugurates First Leftist Leader."

33. "Headlines for March 2, 2005, Uruguay Swears in Nation's First Leftist Leader," *Democracy Now!* Web site, March 2, 2005, http://www.democracynow.org/article.pl?sid=05/03/02/154203 (accessed March 12, 2006).

34. "Uruguay's Vázquez Pledges to Pay Debts."

35. Katz, "The Center-Left, Nationalism, and Socialism."

36. "Uruguay," EIA Country Analysis Brief, December 2004, http://www.eia.doe.gov/emeu/cabs/uruguay.pdf (accessed March 12, 2006); "Uruguay y Venezuela suscriben acuerdos de cooperación."

37. "Uruguay y Venezuela suscriben acuerdos de cooperación."

38. "Chávez resalta trascendencia de mandato," *El Universal*, March 2, 2005, http://www.el-universal.com/2005/03/02/imp_int_art_02144C.shtml (accessed March 4, 2006).

39. "Swapping Oil for Influence"; "Chávez resalta trascendencia de mandato."

40. "Uruguay y Venezuela suscriben acuerdos de cooperación"; "Venezuela's Chávez Strengthens Cooperation in Uruguay, Argentina, and Brazil."

41. "Venezuela's Chávez Strengthens Cooperation in Uruguay, Argentina, and Brazil."

42. "Suscribieron acuerdo petrolero, convenio Telesur y declaración conjunta Venezuela y Uruguay afianzan relación energética," *El Universal*, March 3, 2005, http://internacional.eluniversal.com/2005/03/03/pol_art_03106A.shtml (accessed March 4, 2006).

43. "Suscribieron acuerdo petrolero."

44. Néstor Sánchez, "Brazil, Argentina, and Venezuela Announce the Birth of PetroSur," Vheadline, May 12, 2005, http://www.vheadline.com/printer_news.asp?id=33937 (accessed March 12, 2006).

45. Sánchez, "Brazil, Argentina and Venezuela Announce the Birth of PetroSur."

46. Márquez, "Oil: Venezuela Forges Ahead."

47. "Swapping Oil for Influence."

48. Márquez, "Oil: Venezuela Forges Ahead."

49. Danna Harman, "Chávez Seeks Influence with Oil Diplomacy," *Christian Science Monitor,* August 25, 2005, http://www.csmonitor.com/2005/0825/p01s04-woam.html (accessed March 4, 2006).

50. Pedro Pablo Peñaloza, "Análisis/Presidente pretende exportar las misiones junto con los acuerdos energéticos" *El Universal,* July 24, 2005, http://www.eluniversal.com/2005/07/24/pol_art_25186A.shtml (accessed March 4, 2006).

51. "Chávez Promotes Creation of Petro-America Energy Enterprise," Alexander's Oil and Gas Connections 7, No. 7, March 14, 2002, http://www.gasandoil.com/goc/news/ntl21525.htm (accessed March 4, 2006).

52. "Chávez atribuye deterioro de relación con EEUU a pugna energética," *El Universal,* July 24, 2005, http://www.eluniversal.com/2005/07/24/pol_ava_24A581649.shtml (accessed March 4, 2006).

53. Humberto Márquez, "Energía-America Latina: Venezuela y Ecuador camino a Petroamérica," Inter Press Service, July 28, 2003.

54. Peñaloza, "Análisis"; "Ecuador y Venezuela crearán 'Petroamérica,'" EFE, July 10, 2003, reprinted at *La Prensa* Web site, http://mensual.prensa.com/mensual/contenido/2003/07/14/hoy/negocios/1130453.html (accessed March 12, 2006).

55. Yolanda Pincay, "Correa da como hechos acuerdos con Venezuela," *El Universo,* July 19, 2005, http://www.eluniverso.com/2005/07/19/8/64f9ebf48af14c0f956b784aab3bad4e.html?EUID (accessed March 4, 2006).

56. Peñaloza, "Análisis."

57. Ángel Páez, "Peru: Pro-Indigenous Retired Colonel Sees Meteoric Rise in the Polls," Inter Press Service, December 13, 2005.

58. Juan Forero, "Elections Could Tilt Latin America Further to the Left," *New York Times,* December 10, 2005, http://www.nytimes.com/2005/12/10/international/americas/10bolivia.html?ex=1291870800&en=3a7c6492214e82f2&ei=5089&partner=rssyahoo&emc=rss (accessed March 4, 2006); Páez, "Peru."

59. Juan Forero, "Venezuela Pushes to Lead Regional Oil Economy," *New York Times,* August 13, 2004, http://www.nytimes.com/2004/08/13/business/worldbusiness/13diplo.html?ex=1250136000&en=63f5d2ee16698391&ei=5090&partner=rssuserland (accessed March 4, 2006).

60. EIA Report, Colombia Oil, July 2005, http://www.eia.doe.gov/emeu/cabs/Colombia/Oil.html (accessed April 15, 2006)

61. DeLong, "South American Unity."

62. Gindin, "Venezuela and the 'New Democracy.'"

63. David Gaddis Smith, "Mexico City Mayor Looking like Successor to Fox," *San Diego Union Tribune,* February 16, 2003, http://www.signonsandiego.com/news/mexico/20030216–9999_1n16mexleft.html (accessed March 12, 2006); Seth DeLong, "Venezuela and the Latin American New Left: to Washington's Chagrin, Chávez's Influence Continues to Spread Throughout the Continent," Memorandum to the Press 05.26, Council on Hemispheric Affairs, March 8, 2005, http://www.coha.org/NEW_PRESS_RELEASES/New_Press_Releases_2005/05.26%20Venezuela%20and%20the%20New%20Left%20the%20one.htm (accessed March 12, 2006).

64. "LA Times: Venezuela Out to Give Latin Americans a Better Picture of Their World," Vheadline, June 19, 2005, http://www.vheadline.com/read-news.asp?id=38196 (accessed March 12, 2006); Gary Marx, "Government-Backed Channel Raises Concerns about Propaganda," *Chicago Tribune*, July 17, 2005.

65. "LA Times: Venezuela Out to Give Latin Americans a Better Picture."

66. "Concepto," Telesur Web site, http://www.telesurtv.net/concepto.php (accessed March 12, 2006); Marx, "Government-Backed Channel Raises Concerns"; "LA Times: Venezuela Out to Give Latin Americans a Better Picture."

67. Marx, "Government-Backed Channel Raises Concerns."

68. Nikolas Kozloff, "Chávez Launches Hemispheric, 'Anti-Hegemonic' Media Campaign in Response to Local TV Networks Anti-Government Bias," Memorandum to the Press 05.47, Council on Hemispheric Affairs, April 28, 2005, http://www.coha.org/NEW_PRESS_RELEASES/New_Press_Releases_2005/05.47_Telesur_%20the_one.htm (accessed March 12, 2006); Aram Aharonian, "Venezuela, referendum y después, RR: retórica o realidad," *Question*, October 20, 2004, http://www.voltairenet.org/article122452.html (accessed March 12, 2006); Aram Aharonian, "Hacia dónde va la nueva Venezuela," La Agencia Latinoamericana de Información y Análisis-dos, December 9, 2004, http://www.voltairenet.org/article123131.html (accessed March 12, 2006).

69. Emiliano Cotelo, "Telesur, un proyecto de informatión 'anti-hegemónica,'" Espectador.com (Montevideo, Uruguay radio station that can be accessed on the internet and which provides radio transcripts), March 31, 2005, http://www.espectador.com/nota.php?idNota=39397 (accessed March 4, 2006).

70. Aram Aharonian, "Intervención de Aram Aharonian, presidente de la asociación Latinoamericana para la comunicación social, en el ateneo de Caracas, el 30 de Octubre de 2001, en el foro gobiernos y libertad de expresión," Venezuela Analítica, November 2, 2001, http://www.analitica.com/va/sociedad/documentos/1786863.asp (accessed March 12, 2006); "Si me ayudas te ayudo, Arrimado a buen arbor," *El Universal* (Caracas, Venezuela), March 20, 2005, http://buscador.eluniversal.com/2005/03/20/pol_apo_20161C.shtml (accessed March 4, 2006).

71. Cotelo, "Telesur"; José Alejandro Sánchez, "Telesur de Chávez, con un pie en México," *La Crónica de Hoy*, August 29, 2005, http://www.cronica.com.mx/nota.php?idc=199443 (accessed March 13, 2006); "Si me ayudas te ayudo, Arrimado a buen arbor."

72. http://www.deepdishtv.org/ (accessed March 13, 2006).

73. Kozloff, "Chávez Launches Hemispheric, 'Anti-Hegemonic' Media Campaign."

74. Marx, "Government-Backed Channel Raises Concerns."

75. Thais Leon, New Latin-focused TV Station Transmitting with Venezuela's support," Associated Press, July 25, 2005, reprinted on *Seattle Times* Web site, http://seattletimes.nwsource.com/html/nationworld/2002400494_ventv25.html (accessed March 13, 2006).

76. Kozloff, "Chávez Launches Hemispheric, 'Anti-Hegemonic' Media Campaign"; David Adams, "Latin America's Balanced/Biased Voice," *St. Petersburg Times* (St. Petersburg, Florida), August 8, 2005, http://www.sptimes.com/2005/08/08/State/Latin_America_s_balan.shtml (accessed March 13, 2006).

77. Kozloff, "Chávez Launches Hemispheric, 'Anti-Hegemonic' Media Campaign."

78. Adams, "Latin America's Balanced/Biased Voice."

79. Kozloff, "Chávez Launches Hemispheric, 'Anti-Hegemonic' Media Campaign."

80. William Fisher, "Anti-Chávez Broadcasts May Be Hot Air," Inter Press Service, July 29, 2005, http://www.ipsnews.net/news.asp?idnews=29695 (accessed March 23, 2006).

81. Kozloff, "Chávez Launches Hemispheric, 'Anti-Hegemonic' Media Campaign"; Florencia Copley, "Telesur is Constructing Another View," Venezuela Analysis, December 14, 2000, http://www.venezuelanalysis.com/articles.php?artno=1630 (accessed March 4, 2006).

82. Kozloff, "Chávez Launches Hemispheric, 'Anti-Hegemonic' Media Campaign."

83. "Analysis: Venezuela Starts Test Transmissions of Regional TV Service Telesur," BBC Monitoring Media, May 25, 2005 (Factiva Database); DeNeen L. Brown, "In Canada, Exceptions are Rule for Al-Jazeera," *Washington Post*, July 26, 2004, http://www.washingtonpost.com/wp-dyn/articles/A14009–2004Jul25.html (accessed March 13, 2006).

84. "Un canal para la integración," Telesur Web site, http://www.telesurtv.net/cobertura.php (accessed March 13, 2006).

85. "Telesur: A Counter-Hegemonic Project to Compete with CNN and Univisión," Venezuela Analysis, reprinted from *La Jornada*, March 2, 2005, http://www.venezuelanalysis.com/articles.php?artno=1388 (accessed March 13, 2006).

86. Jeremy Scahill, "Did Bush Really Want to Bomb Al Jazeera?" *The Nation*, November 23, 2005, http://www.thenation.com/doc/20051212/scahill (accessed March 4, 2006).

87. Kozloff, "Chávez Launches Hemispheric, 'Anti-Hegemonic' Media Campaign."

88. "Look Out *Telenovelas, Telesur* is in Town," Council on Hemispheric Affairs Memorandum to the Press, August 21, 2005, http://www.coha.org/NEW_PRESS_RELEASES/New_Press_Releases_2005/05.98_Look_out_Telenovelas_Telesur_is_in_Town.htm (accessed March 13, 2006).

89. Copley, "Telesur is Constructing Another View."

90. "Look Out *Telenovelas*."

91. Fisher, "Anti-Chávez Broadcasts May Be Hot Air"; Nancy San Martín, "House Members Approve Broadcasts to Venezuela," *Miami Herald*, July 21, 2005.

92. "Look Out *Telenovelas*."

93. Patrick O'Donoghue, "U.S. Congress Caves in to Miami-Cuban Lobby; Will Launch Radio/TV Bolívar vs. Telesur," Vheadline, July 21, 2005, http://www.

vheadline.com/readnews.asp?id=42474 (accessed March 13, 2006); Fisher, "Anti-Chávez Broadcasts May Be Hot Air."

94. O'Donoghue, "U.S. Congress Caves in to Miami-Cuban Lobby."
95. "Look Out *Telenovelas.*"
96. Casto Ocando, "Planean campaña continental contra el canal Telesur," *El Nuevo Herald*, July 29, 2005, reprinted in Venezuela Analítica, http://www.analitica.com/va/vpi/3955838.asp (accessed March 13, 2006).
97. Fisher, "Anti-Chávez Broadcasts May Be Hot Air."
98. San Martín, "House Members Approve Broadcasts to Venezuela."
99. Fisher, "Anti-Chávez Broadcasts May Be Hot Air"; O'Donoghue, "U.S. Congress Caves in to Miami-Cuban Lobby."
100. Copley, "Telesur is Constructing Another View."
101. Seth DeLong, "South American Unity May No Longer Be a Distant Dream: The Region's Left-leaning Governments Strive for Integration as Washington's Plan to Isolate Venezuela's Chávez Fails," Council On Hemispheric Affairs, Memorandum to the Press, 05.41, April 11, 2005, http://www.coha.org/NEW_PRESS_RELEASES/New_Press_Releases_2005/05.41%20South%20American%20Unity%20the%20one.htm (accessed March 13, 2006).
102. Rapoza, "World Briefings."
103. DeLong, "South American Unity."
104. Seth DeLong, "Venezuela and the Latin American New Left: To Washington's Chagrin, Chávez's Influence Continues to Spread throughout the Continent," Council on Hemispheric Affairs Memorandum to the Press 05.26, March 8, 2005, http://www.coha.org/NEW_PRESS_RELEASES/New_Press_Releases_2005/05.26%20Venezuela%20and%20the%20New%20Left%20the%20one.htm (accessed March 13, 2006).
105. "Chávez Promotes Creation of Petro-America Energy Enterprise."
106. Patrick K. O'Brien, gen. ed. "Sucre, Antonio José de.," *Encyclopedia of World History*, Copyright George Philip Limited (New York: Facts on File, Inc., 2000), Facts on File, Inc. *World History Online*, www.factsonfile.com (accessed March 13, 2006); "Sucre, Antonio José de.," *Grolier Multimedia Encyclopedia*, Scholastic Library Publishing, 2006, http://gme.grolier.com (accessed March 13, 2006).
107. DeLong, "South American Unity."
108. Ibid.
109. Ibid.
110. Ibid.
111. Harman, "Chávez Seeks Influence with Oil Diplomacy."
112. "Chávez resalta trascendencia de mandato."

CHAPTER 9

1. *South America, Central America and the Caribbean 2005* (London: Europa Publications, 2005), 864.

2. Patrick K. O'Brien, gen. ed. "Viceroyalty of New Granada." *Encyclopedia of World History*, Copyright George Philip Limited (New York: Facts on File, Inc., 2000), Facts on File, Inc., *World History Online*. www.factsonfile.com (accessed March 13, 2006).

3. *South America, Central America and the Caribbean 2005*, 864.

4. "Chávez Promotes Creation of Petro-America Energy Enterprise," Alexander's Gas and Oil Connections, 7, No. 7, April 2002, http://www.gasandoil. com/goc/news/ntl21525.htm (accessed March 4, 2006).

5. Gustavo González, "Latin America: 'War on Terror' Has Indigenous People in its Sights," Inter Press Service, June 6, 2005, http://www.ipsnews.net/interna.asp?idnews=28962 (accessed March 13, 2006); "Mapping the Global Future," National Intelligence Council Web site, http://www.cia.gov/nic/ NIC_globaltrend2020.html (accessed March 13, 2006).

6. Nikolas Kozloff, "Hugo Chávez and the Politics of Race," Counterpunch, October 14, 2005 (http://www.counterpunch.org/kozloff10142005.html (accessed March 13, 2006).

7. Winthrop Wright, *Race, Class and National Image in Venezuela* (Austin: University of Texas Press, 1990), 23.

8. Kozloff, "Hugo Chávez and the Politics of Race."

9. Jon Lee Anderson, "The Revolutionary," *The New Yorker*, September 10, 2001, http://www.newyorker.com/archive/content?020422fr_archive03 (accessed March 13, 2006).

10. Nikolas Kozloff, "Hugo Chávez and the Politics of Race," *Counterpunch*.

11. Global Exchange, "Venezuela and Indigenous Rights," Venezuela Analysis, February 25, 2004, http://www.venezuelanalysis.com/articles.php?artno=1112 (accessed March 4, 2006).

12. Kozloff, "Hugo Chávez and the Politics of Race."

13. Carol Williams, "In Venezuela, Words Spread Far and Wide," Venezuela Analysis, June 14, 2004, reprinted from *Los Angeles Times*, http://www.venezuelanalysis.com/articles.php/print.php?artno=1196 (accessed March 13, 2006).

14. Ibid.

15. Ibid.

16. Constanza Vieira, "Rights-Colombia: Nasa Indians Demand Urgent Action from UN," Inter Press Service, May 26, 2005, http://www.ipsnews.net/interna.asp?idnews=28836 (accessed March 13, 2006).

17. "Bogotá," Human Rights Watch Report, 1994, http://www.hrw.org/reports/ 1994/colombia/gener1.htm (accessed March 13, 2006).

18. Ibid.

19. Justin Podur, "The Battle for Colombia," *Frontline* (political magazine in India), 21, No. 8, April 2004, http://www.flonnet.com/fl2108/stories/ 20040423001406100.htm (accessed March 4, 2006).

20. "Report, Civil Conflict and Indigenous Peoples in Colombia," Amazon Watch Report, March 1, 2002, http://www.amazonwatch.org/newsroom/ view_news.php?id=538 (accessed March 13, 2006).

21. James Parsons, "Colombia," *The New Book of Knowledge Encyclopedia*, Scholastic Library Publishing, 2006 http://nbk.grolier.com (accessed March 13, 2006).

22. "Civil Conflict and Indigenous Peoples in Colombia."

23. Constanza Viera, "Indigenous Women in Colombia," Inter Press Service, July 30, 2005 reprinted on ZNet, http://www.zmag.org/content/showarticle.cfm? SectionID=9&ItemID=8406 (accessed March 13, 2006); Bill Weinberg, "Cauca: Autonomy Under the Gun, Colombia's Nasa Indians Caught in the Crossfire in Uribe's New Counter-Guerilla Offensive," World War 4 Report, September 16, 2003, http://ww3report.com/nasa.html (accessed March 13, 2006).

24. "Civil Conflict and Indigenous Peoples in Colombia."

25. Luis Jaime Acosta, "Colombian Police Back Off as Indians Grab Land," Reuters, December 9, 2005, reprinted *at Boston Globe* Web site, http://www. boston.com/news/world/latinamerica/articles/2005/12/09/colombian_ police_back_off_as_indians_grab_land/ (accessed March 4, 2006).

26. Weinberg, "Cauca: Autonomy Under the Gun."

27. Nikolas Kozloff, "The Struggle for Control of the Land," *Colombian Post* (Bogotá, Colombia), November 18–25, 1993.

28. Viera, "Indigenous Women in Colombia."

29. Nikolas Kozloff, "Venezuela's War of Religion," Venezuela Analysis, October 24, 2005, http://www.venezuelanalysis.com/articles.php?artno=1584 (accessed March 4, 2006).

30. Marta Harnecker, *Hugo Chávez Frías, un hombre, un pueblo* (Havana: Editorial de Ciencias Sociales, 2002), 68.

31. Ian James, "Missionaries Ordered to Leave Venezuela," Associated Press, October 12, 2005, reprinted on *Boston Globe* Web site, http://www.boston. com/news/world/latinamerica/articles/2005/10/12/missionaries_ordered_to_ leave_venezuela?mode=PF (accessed March 14, 2006); Nikolas Kozloff, "Venezuela's War of Religion," Venezuela Analysis, October 24, 2005, http:// www.venezuelanalysis.com/articles.php?artno=1584 (accessed March 4, 2006).

32. Kozloff, "Venezuela's War of Religion"; Thais Leon, "Venezuela's Chávez Presents Land Titles to Indigenous Groups," Associated Press, August 9, 2005, reprinted at *San Diego Union Tribune* Web site, http://www.signon-sandiego.com/news/world/20050809–1857-venezuela-indigenouslands.html (accessed March 14, 2006).

33. Kozloff, "Venezuela's War of Religion."

34. David Pallister, Sibylla Brodzinksy, and Owen Bowcott, "Secret Aid Poured into Colombian Drug War," *The Guardian*, July 9, 2003, http:// www.guardian.co.uk/print/0,4708406–103681,00.html (accessed March 14, 2006).

35. Scott Wilson, "Colombian Frontrunner Looks to War, Candidate Favors Force in Battle Against Rebels," *Washington Post*, May 20, 2002, http:// www.washingtonpost.com/ac2/wp-dyn/A42625–2002May19?language= printer (accessed March 14, 2006); John C. Fredriksen, "Uribe, Álvaro," *Biographical Dictionary of Modern World Leaders: 1992 to the Present* (New York:

Facts on File, Inc., 2003), Facts on File, Inc., *World History Online*, www.factsonfile.com (accessed March 10, 2006).

36. Jeremy McDermott, "Profile: Álvaro Uribe Vélez," BBC News Web site, August 7, 2002, http://news.bbc.co.uk/2/hi/americas/1996976.stm (accessed March 14, 2006).

37. Fredriksen, "Uribe, Álvaro"; Pallister, Brodzinksy, and Bowcott, "Secret Aid"; Wilson, "Colombian Frontrunner Looks to War."

38. "Medellín," *Grolier Multimedia Encyclopedia*, Scholastic Library Publishing, 2006, http://gme.grolier.com (accessed March 14, 2006); Wilson, "Colombian Frontrunner Looks to War."

39. Fredriksen, "Uribe, Álvaro"; "Medellín," *Grolier Multimedia Encyclopedia.*

40. "Medellín," *Grolier Multimedia Encyclopedia.*

41. "Medellín," *Encyclopedia Americana*, Grolier Online, 2006, Scholastic Library Publishing, http://go.grolier.com (accessed March 14, 2006).

42. "Señor Presidente de la República de Colombia, Álvaro Uribe Vélez," Presidency of Colombia Web site, http://www.presidencia.gov.co/presidente/perfilingles.htm (accessed March 14, 2006).

43. "Señor Presidente de la República"; Pallister, Brodzinksy, and Bowcott, "Secret Aid"; Juan Forero, "'91 U.S. Report Calls Colombian Leader Ally of Drug Lords [Corrected]," *New York Times*, August 2, 2004 (Factiva Database).

44. "Señor Presidente de la República."

45. Pallister, Brodzinksy, and Bowcott, "Secret Aid."

46. McDermott, "Profile: Álvaro Uribe Vélez."

47. Juan Forero, "'91 U.S. Report Calls Colombian Leader Ally of Drug Lords [Corrected]," *New York Times*, August 2, 2004 (Factiva Database).

48. "Señor Presidente de la República."

49. Forero, "'91 U.S. Report Calls Colombian Leader Ally of Drug Lords."

50. Rebecca Milzoff, "Mano Firme, Corazón Grande," *Harvard Crimson*, April 25, 2002, http://www.thecrimson.com/article.aspx?ref=205287 (accessed March 14, 2006); "Señor Presidente de la República."

51. McDermott, "Profile: Álvaro Uribe Vélez."

52. Fredriksen, "Uribe, Álvaro."

53. Podur, "The Battle for Colombia."

54. Ibid.

55. Hector Mondragón, "Of Agro Industrialists, Godfathers, and Hangmen," ZNet, June 07, 2003, http://www.zmag.org/sustainers/content/2003–06/07mondragon.cfm (accessed March 14, 2006).

56. Héctor Latorre, "Protesta Indígena," BBC Mundo Web site, September 12, 2004, http://news.bbc.co.uk/hi/spanish/latin_america/newsid_3650000/3650260.stm (accessed March 14, 2006).

57. Weinberg, "Cauca: Autonomy Under the Gun."

58. Ibid.

59. "Breves Política, 'Chávez instala encuentro indígena,'" *El Universal*, October 12, 2002, http://buscador.eluniversal.com/2003/10/12/pol_art_12108E.shtml (accessed March 4, 2006).

60. "Breves Política, 'Reunión en la UBV,'" *El Universal*, August 29, 2003.
61. Secretaría de Organización del CBP, "Que es el CBP, Para Volver al Espíritu de Ayacucho," Congreso Bolivariano de Los Pueblos (CBP) Web site, http://www.congresoBolívariano.org/modules.php?name=Content&pa=showpage&pid=28 (accessed March 14, 2006).
62. CBP Web site, "Proclama Bolivariana de Caracas II Congreso Bolívariano de Los Pueblos," December 9, 2004, http://www.congresoBolívariano.org/IIcongreso/index_congreso.htm (accessed March 14, 2006).
63. Pilar Díaz, "Análisis/Aversión a EEUU incrementa nacionalismos latinoamericanos Internacional Bolivariana es una 'colcha de retazos,'" *El Universal*, June 5, 2005, http://buscador.eluniversal.com/2005/06/05/int_art_05142A.shtml (accessed March 4, 2006).
64. "Proclama Bolivariana de Caracas II."
65. Weinberg, "Cauca: Autonomy Under the Gun"; "Civil Conflict and Indigenous Peoples in Colombia."
66. Bruce Bagley, "Drug Trafficking, Political Violence and U.S. Policy in Colombia in the 1990s," paper presented at "Colombia in Context" conference, Center for Latin American Studies, University of California, Berkeley, March 2, 2001, http://ist-socrates.berkeley.edu:7001/Events/conferences/Colombia/workingpapers/working_paper_bagley.html (accessed March 14, 2006).
67. "Feature: Venezuela Throws out DEA, Washington Threatens Decertification," Stop the Drug War Web site, August 12, 2005, http://stopthedrugwar.org/chronicle/399/venezuela.shtml (accessed March 20, 2006).
68. Bagley, "Drug Trafficking, Political Violence, and U.S. Policy."
69. "Civil Conflict and Indigenous Peoples in Colombia."
70. Scott Wilson, "Coca Invades Colombia's Coffee Fields, Falling Prices Push Farmers to Plant Illegal Crops, Threatening U.S. Drug War," *Washington Post*, October 30, 2001 (Factiva Database).
71. Jon Lottman, "Colombia in Crisis," transcript of program in TV series *America's Defense Monitor* (formerly aired on PBS), Center for Defense Information, December 19, 1999, http://www.cdi.org/adm/1315/index.html (accessed March 14, 2006).
72. "Civil Conflict and Indigenous Peoples in Colombia."
73. Al Gedicks, "Indigenous Colombians Bear Brunt of Drugs War," Reuters Foundation Alert Net (humanitarian news network based in London, United Kingdom) Web site, November 15, 2002, http://www.alertnet.org/thefacts/reliefresources/550440.htm (accessed March 14, 2006).
74. "Civil Conflict and Indigenous Peoples in Colombia."
75. Gedicks, "Indigenous Colombians Bear Brunt of Drugs War."
76. "Civil Conflict and Indigenous Peoples in Colombia."
77. "Bush Hails Colombia's Efforts against Drug Trade," CNN Web site, November 22, 2004, http://www.cnn.com/2004/WORLD/americas/11/22/colombia.bush/ (accessed March 15, 2006).
78. Gedicks, "Indigenous Colombians Bear Brunt of Drugs War."

79. "Challenging U.S. Military Aid to Colombia," Amazon Watch Report, undated, http://amazonwatch.org/amazon/CO/plancol/index.php?page_number=99 (accessed March 14, 2006); "Civil Conflict and Indigenous Peoples in Colombia."

80. "Civil Conflict and Indigenous Peoples in Colombia."

81. "Ecopetrol's Siriri Oil Project, What the U'wa Want," Amazon Watch Report, undated, http://amazonwatch.org/amazon/CO/uwa/index.php?page_number=5 (accessed March 14, 2006).

82. "Civil Conflict and Indigenous Peoples in Colombia."

83. Gedicks, "Indigenous Colombians Bear Brunt of Drugs War."

84. Garry Leech, "Is a Redistributive Political Project Viable in Colombia?" Colombia Journal, October 3, 2005, http://www.colombiajournal.org/colombia218.htm (accessed March 14, 2006).

85. Gedicks, "Indigenous Colombians Bear Brunt of Drugs War."

86. Gedicks, "Indigenous Colombians Bear Brunt of Drugs War"; "Colombian Right-Wing Warlord Quits," BBC News Web site, June 6, 2001, http://news.bbc.co.uk/2/hi/americas/1373994.stm (accessed March 22, 2006); Juan Forero, "Loss of Leader Gives Colombia Militias Leverage," New York Times, May 21, 2004 (Factiva database).

87. Bill Weinberg "Oil Makes U.S. Raise Military Stakes in Colombia," New York Newsday, November 26, 2004, reprinted at Common Dreams Web site, http://www.commondreams.org/cgi-bin/print.cgi?file=/views04/1126–05.htm (accessed March 4, 2006).

88. "Venezuela and the United States, and Now it's Drugs," The Economist, September 22, 2005, http://www.economist.com/displayStory.cfm?story_id=4424181 (accessed March 4, 2006); "Feature: Venezuela Throws Out DEA, Washington Threatens Decertification," report by Drug Reform Coordination Network, August 12, 2005, Stop the Drug War Web site, http://stopthedrugwar.org/chronicle/399/venezuela.shtml (accessed March 15, 2006).

89. "Rangel reitera rechazo contra programa militar, 'Chávez no es vocero de la política anti Plan Colombia,'" El Universal, January 5, 2001, http://buscador.eluniversal.com/2001/01/05/int_art_05109BB.shtml (accessed March 4, 2006).

90. Juan Forero, "Opposition to U.S. Makes Chávez a Hero to Many," New York Times, June 1, 2005, http://www.nytimes.com/2005/06/01/international/americas/01letter.html?ei=5088&en=d2adb41fda4813c8&ex=1275278400&adxnnl=1&partner=rssnyt&emc=rss&adxnnlx=1134038198-D/YA+TiZ3eb6?G6GyK2Cpog (accessed March 4, 2006).

91. "Bula defiende a capa y espada Plan Colombia," El Universal, December 16, 2000, http://buscador.eluniversal.com/2000/12/16/int_art_16112BB.shtml (accessed March 4, 2006).

92. "'Sobrevuelos se basan en razones simplistas," El Universal, March 25, 2000, http://www.eluniversal.com/2000/03/25/pol_art_25116AA.shtml (accessed March 3, 2006).

93. Steven Dudley and Pablo Bachelet, "U.S. Says Venezuela No Longer Ally in War on Drugs / Bush Stops Short of Cutting Aid to the Nation Because

Money Helps Fund Democracy Efforts," *Miami Herald*, September 16, 2005 (Factiva Database).

94. Dudley and Bachelet, "U.S. Says Venezuela No Longer Ally in War on Drugs"; "Feature: Venezuela Throws Out DEA."

95. Dudley and Bachelet, "U.S. says Venezuela No Longer Ally in War on Drugs"; "Feature: Venezuela Throws Out DEA."

96. Juan Forero, "Colombia War Spills into Indians' Peaceful World," *New York Times*, May 2, 2005, http://www.nytimes.com/2005/05/02/international/americas/02indians.html?ex=1272686400&en=1fa4db6e125e5a12&ei=5088&partner=rssnyt&emc=rss (accessed March 4, 2006).

97. Gustavo González, "Latin America: 'War on Terror' Has Indigenous People in its Sights," Inter Press Service, June 6, 2005, http://www.ipsnews.net/interna.asp?idnews=28962 (accessed March 15, 2006).

98. Acosta, "Colombian Police Back Off."

99. "Colombia: Indigenous Mobilize, Despite State Terror, Indigenous Hold Nationwide 'Minga,' Two Die," *Weekly News Update on the Americas*, October 23, 2005, reprinted on World War 4 Report Web site, http://www.ww4report.com/node/1241/print (accessed March 15, 2006).

100. Leech, "Is a Redistributive Political Project Viable in Colombia?"

101. "Colombia: Indigenous Mobilize."

102. David Coddon, "Colombia's Democratic Left," Center for International Policy, May 16, 2005, http://www.ciponline.org/colombia/050516codd.htm (accessed March 15, 2006).

103. "Colombia: Indigenous Mobilize."

104. Viera, "Indigenous Women in Colombia."

105. Coddon, "Colombia's Democratic Left"; Andrew Selsky, "Leftists Win in Bogotá Mayor Race Seen as Dawn of a New Political Era in Colombia," Associated Press, October 27, 2003, reprinted at *San Diego Union Tribune* Web site, http://www.signonsandiego.com/news/world/20031027–1409-colombia-leftistvictory.html (accessed March 15, 2006).

106. "Leftist Legalizer Elected Mayor of Bogotá in Voter Rebuke of Colombian President," Drug Reform Coordination Network report, October 31, 2003, Stop the Drug War Website, http://stopthedrugwar.org/chronicle/309/lucho.shtml (accessed March 15, 2006); "Otros caceroleados," *El Universal*, January 15, 2003, http://www.eluniversal.com/2003/01/15/apo_art_15103CC.shtml (accessed March 4, 2006).

107. Leech, "Is a Redistributive Political Project Viable in Colombia?"; Coddon, "Colombia's Democratic Left."

108. Hugh Bronstein, "Colombia's Uribe Announces 2006 Re-Election Bid," Reuters, November 27, 2005, http://today.reuters.com/news/CrisesArticle.aspx?storyId=N27211148 (accessed March 4, 2006).

109. Coddon, "Colombia's Democratic Left."

110. Leech, "Colombia's Challenge from the Left," Colombia Journal, June 6, 2005.

CHAPTER 10

1. Acosta, "Colombian Police Back Off as Indians Grab Land."
2. González, "Latin America: 'War on Terror.'"
3. Ehuenguime Enqueri, Luis Macas, Alicia Cahueya, Efrén Caladucha, and Moi Enomenga, "Huaorani Letter to the President of Ecuador," Save America's Forests, Web site, July 12, 2005, http://www.saveamericasforests.org/Yasuni/Indigenous/Documents/7.12.05%20Huaorani%20Letter%20to%20 Presidente%20of%20Ecuador.htm (accessed May15,2006).
4. Brandon Yoder, "Indigenous People and Oil Production in Ecuador's Oriente," *Fourth World Journal* (Center for World Indigenous Studies) 5, No. 1, (2002), http://www.cwis.org/fwj/51/b_yoder.html (accessed March 4, 2006).
5. Perkins, *Confessions of an Economic Hit Man*, 166.
6. "Interview with John Perkins," Democracy Now! Web site, November 9, 2004, http://www.democracynow.org/article.pl?sid=04/11/09/1526251 (accessed March 15, 2006).
7. Perkins, *Confessions of an Economic Hit Man*, 166.
8. "Facts on File, SIL Responds to Errors in *Confessions of an Economic Hit Man*," Summer Institute of Linguistics Web site, November 2005, http://www.sil. org/sil/facts/JPerkins.htm (accessed March 15, 2006).
9. Frances Rivers, "Making Waves: Christian Broadcasters Beam their Messages to the World," *The Progressive*, November 1993, reprinted at Findarticles. com, http://www.findarticles.com/p/articles/mi_m1295/is_n11_v57/ai_14233513 (accessed March 4, 2006).
10. Humberto Márquez, "Religion: Venezuela to Expel U.S. Evangelical Group," Inter Press Service, October 12, 2005, http://www.ipsnews.net/ news.asp?idnews=30610 (accessed March 15, 2006); Kozloff, "Venezuela's War of Religion."
11. Kozloff, "Venezuela's War of Religion."
12. Nikolas Kozloff, "Evangelicals in Venezuela: Robertson Only the Latest Controversy in a Long and Bizarre History," Council on Hemispheric Affairs Memorandum to the Press, September 21, 2005, http://www.coha.org/ NEW_PRESS_RELEASES/New_Press_Releases_2005/05.103_Venezuelan_Evangelicals_and_Robertson.html (accessed March 15, 2006).
13. Ibid.
14. Ibid.
15. Alexander Luzardo, *Amazonas, el negocio de este mundo* (Caracas: Ediciones Centauro, 1988), 125–26.
16. Kozloff, "Evangelicals in Venezuela."
17. Kozloff, "Venezuela's War of Religion"; "Venezuela Orders U.S. Missionary Group Out, Chávez Alleges New Tribes Mission has Links to CIA," Associated Press, October 13, 2005, reprinted at MSNBC Web site, http://www. msnbc.msn.com/id/9680023 (accessed March 15, 2006).

18. Kozloff, "Venezuela's War of Religion"; Márquez, "Religion: Venezuela to Expel U.S. Evangelical Group"; "Venezuela Orders U.S. Missionary Group Out"; "Chávez ordena salida del país de las 'nuevas tribus,'" *El Universal*, October 12, 2005, http://buscador.eluniversal.com/2005/10/12/pol_ava_12A619173.shtml (accessed March 15, 2006).

19. Kozloff, "Venezuela's War of Religion."

20. "Surprise Announcement in Venezuela," New Tribes Mission Web site, October 13, 2005, http://www.ntm.org/news/news_details.php?news_id=2461 (accessed March 15, 2006).

21. "Brownfield espera que diálogo aclare situación de misioneros," *El Universal*, October 15, 2005, http://buscador.eluniversal.com/2005/10/15/pol_art_15107E.shtml (accessed March 15, 2006).

22. Kozloff, "Venezuela's War of Religion."

23. "Rangel: Expulsión de Nuevas Tribus defiende la soberanía," *El Universal*, October 13, 2005, http://buscador.eluniversal.com/2005/10/13/pol_ava_13A619417.shtml (accessed March 15, 2006).

24. "Chávez ordena salida del país."

25. Kozloff, "Venezuela's War of Religion."

26. "Huaorani Letter to the President of Ecuador."

27. "Fueling Destruction in the Amazon, Interview Between the *Multinational Monitor* and Dr. Luis Macas, President of the Confederation of Indigenous Nationalities of Ecuador (CONAIE)," *Multinational Monitor*, April 1994, reprinted at Center for World Indigenous Studies Web site, http://www.cwis.org/fwdp/Americas/macas.txt (accessed March 15, 2006).

28. "Who is Luis Macas?" Latin American Intelligence Service (provided by *Latin American Newsletters*, based in London, United Kingdom, www.latin-news.com, January 11, 2005

29. José Luis Bedón, "El pensamiento de Luis Macas," Ecuarunari (Confederacion de los Pueblos de Nacionalidad Kichua del Ecuador) Website, December 23, 2004, http://www.ecuarunari.org/conaie/23dic04b.html (accessed April 4, 2006)

30. Norman Haard, S.A. Odunfa, Cherl Ho-Lee, R. Quintero Ramirez, et al., Fermented Cereals. A Global Perspective, FAO Services Bulletin No. 138, "Chapter 4. Cereal Fermentation in Latin American Countries," Food and Agriculture Organization of the United Nations, http://www.fao.org/docrep/x2184e/x2184e10.htm (accessed April 4, 2006)

31. Bedón, "El pensamiento de Luis Macas"

32. Luis Angel Saavedra, "Growing from the Grassroots—Latin America: Ecuador—Indigenous Movements," *New Internationalist*, May 2003, http://www.newint.org/ (accessed March 15, 2006).

33. Bedón, "El Pensamiento de Luis Macas," "Hoja de vida de Luis Alberto Macas Ambuludí," Ecuarunari web site, http://www.ecuarunari.org/conaie/macas.html (accessed May 15, 2006)

34. "Brief Profiles of Pachakutik's Nominees for Cabinet Published," BBC Monitoring Americas, December 17, 2002 (Factiva Database).

35. "Who is Luis Macas?" profile.
36. Bedón, "El Pensamíento de Luis Macas"
37. Marcos Almeida, "Ecuador: Beyond the Dollar Coup," *Unesco Courier,* September 1, 2000 (Factiva Database), 27.
38. Saavedra, "Growing from the Grassroots."
39. Ibid
40. Bedón, "El Pensamíento de Luis Macas"
41. "Who is Luis Macas?" profile.
42. Perkins, Confessions of an Economic Hit Man, 183, New York Times, May 31, 1981, "Quito Ratifies Break in Ties With Linguistics Institute," (ProQuest Historical Newspapers Database)
43. Jeanne Hey, "Ecuadoran Foreign Policy Since 1979: Ideological Cycles or a Trend Towards Neoliberalism?" *Journal of Interamerican Studies and World Affairs,* Winter 1995, reprinted at Findarticles.com, http://www.findarticles.com/p/articles/mi_qa3688/is_199501/ai_n8717693/pg_3 (accessed March 4, 2006).
44. Saavedra, "Growing from the Grassroots."
45. *Democracy Now!* interview with John Perkins.
46. Perkins, *Confessions of an Economic Hitman,* 184
47. Saavedra, "Growing from the Grassroots"
48. "Who is Luis Macas?" profile.
49. Ibid.
50. Ibid.
51. "Chronology for Lowland Indigenous Peoples in Ecuador."
52. Ibid.
53. "Historia de rebelión nativa," *El Universal,* September 5, 2000, http://buscador.eluniversal.com/2000/09/05/apo_art_05106CC.shtml (accessed March 4, 2006).
54. "Chronology for Lowland Indigenous Peoples in Ecuador."
55. "Ecuadorean Indigenous vs. FTA," Prensa Latina, November 17, 2005; Luis Macas, "La CONAIE establece como únicos puntos de su agenda la Lucha Contra el TLC, La Occidental y El Plan Colombia," Congreso Bolivariano de Los Pueblos Web site, undated, http://www.congresobolivariano.org/modules.php?name=News&file=article&sid=1398#4 (accessed March 15, 2006).
56. "Ecuador: Ten Thousand Protest Trade Pact," *Weekly News Update on the Americas,* November 20, 2005, reprinted on WW4 Web site, http://www.ww4report.com/node/1345 (accessed March 15, 2006).
57. Luis Macas, "Asaltan nuevamente oficinas de la CONAIE," November 24, 2005, Congreso Bolivariano de Los Pueblos Web site, http://www.congresobolivariano.org/modules.php?name=News&file=article&sid=1431 (accessed March 15, 2006).
58. Rivers, "Making Waves."
59. "Civil Conflict and Indigenous Peoples in Colombia."
60. "Activists Protest U.S. Base," Resource Center of the Americas Report, http://www.americas.org/item_6149 (accessed March 16, 2006).

61. "Indígenas ven en Palacio gobierno de transición," *El Universal,* April 23, 2005, http://buscador.eluniversal.com/2005/04/23/int_art_23104C.shtml (accessed March 4, 2006); Macas, "La CONAIE establece como Únicos Puntos."

62. "Programa del II Congreso," Congreso Bolivariano de Los Pueblos Web site, "Programa," list of invited persons, December 6, 2004, http://www.congresobolivariano.org/IIcongreso/index_congreso.htm# (accessed March 16, 2006).

63. "MESA 3: Movimiento Indígena de Nuestra América," Second Congress of Bolivarian Peoples Web site, December 14, 2004, Maracaibo, http://www.congresobolivariano.org/modules.php?name=Content&pa=showpage&pid=60 (accessed March 16, 2006).

64. Humberto Cholango, "El Movimiento Indígena del Ecuador apoya al gobierno bolivariano de Hugo Chávez," Second Congress of Bolivarian Peoples Web site, December 5, 2004, http://www.congresobolivariano.org/modules.php?name=News&file=article&sid=1508 (accessed March 16, 2006).

65. José Luis Bedón, "Triunfo del NO debe respetarse, La CONAIE rechaza la intromisión del Imperio en el referendo venezolano," ANPE (Agencia Plurinacional del Ecuador), reprinted at Voltaire net, August 12, 2004, http://www.voltairenet.org/article121780.html#article121780 (accessed March 16, 2006).

66. Boletín de Prensa Pachakutik, "Pachakutik felicita a quinta república por triunfo en Venezuela," Congreso Bolivariano de Los Pueblos Web site, December 12, 2004, http://www.congresobolivariano.org/modules.php?name=News&file=article&sid=1538 (accessed March 16, 2006); Chris Strunk, "Ecuador President's Plight: Gutiérrez's Future in Doubt after Break with Indigenous Ally," Memorandum to the Press 03.54, August 14, 2003, http://www.coha.org/NEW_PRESS_RELEASES/New_Press_Releases_2003/03.54_Ecuador_President's_Plight.htm (accessed March 16, 2006).

67. Raúl Zibechi, "A Panorama of Social Movements in South America, Dangerous Liaisons: Center-Left Governments & the Grassroots," Americas Program, Interhemispheric Resource Center, December 7, 2004, http://americas.irc-online.org/reports/2004/0412movements.html (accessed March 4, 2006).

68. "Who is Luis Macas?" profile.

69. "Ecuador/elecciones: ex coronel sorprende," BBC Mundo, November 21, 2002, http://news.bbc.co.uk/hi/spanish/specials/elecciones_en_ecuador/newsid_2345000/2345471.stm (accessed March 16, 2006); Iain Haddow, "Ecuador Indians Confront Government," BBC News Web site, January 19, 2000, http://news.bbc.co.uk/2/hi/americas/609661.stm (accessed March 16, 2006).

70. "Gutiérrez, el presidente de uniforme" BBC Mundo, November 25, 2002, http://news.bbc.co.uk/hi/spanish/specials/elecciones_en_ecuador/newsid_2335000/2335879.stm (accessed March 16, 2006).

71. "Gutiérrez, Lucio Edwin," *La Nueva Enciclopedia Cumbre,* Scholastic Library Publishing, http://nec.grolier.com (accessed March 9, 2006).

72. Chris Strunk, "Ecuador President's Plight: Gutiérrez's Future in Doubt after Break with Indigenous Ally," Council on Hemispheric Affairs, Memorandum to the Press 03.54, August 14, 2003, http://www.coha.org/NEW_PRESS_RELEASES/New_Press_Releases_2003/03.54_Ecuador_President's_Plight.htm (accessed March 16, 2006).

73. Saavedra, "Growing from the Grassroots," "Ex-Coup Leader Wins Ecuador Election," BBC News Web site, November 25, 2002, http://news.bbc.co.uk/2/hi/americas/2509463.stm (accessed March 16, 2006).

74. Monte Reel, "Long Fall in Ecuador: Populist to Pariah," *Washington Post*, April 23, 2005, http://www.washingtonpost.com/wp-dyn/articles/A10416–2005Apr22.html (accessed March 4, 2006).

75. Saavedra, "Growing from the Grassroots."

76. "Who is Luis Macas?" profile.

77. Reel, "Long Fall in Ecuador."

78. "Ecuador: New President Seeks Fragile Balance among Complex Web of Political, Social Pressures," Inter Press Service, April 29, 2005, http://www.ips-news.net/africa/interna.asp?idnews=28509 (accessed March 16, 2006).

79. Reel, "Long Fall in Ecuador."

80. "Who Is Luis Macas?" profile

81. Peel, "Long Fall in Ecuador"

82. "Ecuador: 9 años, 9 presidentes," BBC Mundo, April 21, 2005, http://news.bbc.co.uk/hi/spanish/latin_america/newsid_4469000/4469621.stm (accessed March 16, 2006); "Ecuador Congress Sacks President," BBC News Web site, April 20, 2005, http://news.bbc.co.uk/2/hi/americas/4466697.stm (accessed March 16, 2006); Karl Penhaul, "Ecuador's Ousted President Arrives in Brazil," CNN Web site, April 24, 2005, http://www.cnn.com/2005/WORLD/americas/04/24/ecuador/ (accessed March 16, 2006).

83. "Ecuador: New President Seeks Fragile Balance."

84. Zibechi, "A Panorama of Social Movements."

85. "Who Is Luis Macas?" profile.

86. "Ecuador: Ten Thousand Protest Trade Pact."

87. Dan Glaister, "Triumph for Bolivia's Candidate of Poor," *The Guardian*, December 20, 2005, http://www.guardian.co.uk/international/story/0,3604,1671000,00.html (accessed March 16, 2006); Kevin Gray, "Anti-U.S. Leftist Clinches Bolivia Election," Reuters, December 18, 2005, reprinted at ABC News Web site, http://abcnews.go.com/US/wireStory?id=1419748 (accessed March 4, 2006).

88. Jimmy Langman, "A Man for the People, Indigenous Leader Evo Morales is a Rising Political Star," *Newsweek International*, 2005, reprinted on MSNBC Web site, http://www.msnbc.msn.com/id/4825405/site/newsweek/from/RL.2/ (accessed March 16, 2006).

89. "Evo Morales cree que Chávez, Castro y Lula integran red antiglobalización," *El Universal*, April 21, 2003, http://www.eluniversal.com/2003/04/21/int_art_21112FF.shtml (accessed March 4, 2006).

90. Glaister, "Triumph for Bolivia's Candidate of Poor"; Joel Brinkley, "U.S. Keeps a Wary Eye on the Next Bolivian President," *New York Times*, December 21,

2005,   http://www.nytimes.com/2005/12/21/international/americas/21latin.
html?ex=1292821200&en=1c955e325980e4a6&ei=5090&partner=rssuser-
land&emc=rss (accessed March 16, 2006).

91. Harnecker, *Hugo Chávez Frías, un hombre, un pueblo*, (Havana: Editorial de
Ciencias Sociales, 2002), 120; Tom Hennigan, "Gas Wealth Fuels Populist
Experiment in Bolivia," *Christian Science Monitor*, July 16, 2004, http://
www.csmonitor.com/2004/0716/p01s03-woam.html (accessed March 16,
2006); Glaister, "Triumph for Bolivia's Candidate of Poor."

92. Edymar Ablan Pacheco, "Análisis/Contactos de Chávez con indígenas
suramericanos 'forman parte de su política exterior,'" *El Universal*, February
8, 2003, http://buscador.eluniversal.com/2003/02/08/pol_art_08158AA.shtml
(accessed March 4, 2006).

93. Ibid.

94. Ibid.

95. "Hugo Chávez ayudará a indígenas bolivianos," *El Universal*, August 12,
2002, http://buscador.eluniversal.com/2002/08/12/int_art_12110FF.shtml (accessed March 4, 2006).

96. Pacheco, "Analisis / Contactos de Chávez con indígenas suramericanos,"
Alexander, Robert J., "Bolivia," *Grolier Multimedia Encyclopedia*, Scholastic Library Publishing, 2006 http://gme.grolier.com (March 16, 2006).

97. "Evo cargado de misiles," *El Universal*, October 3, 2004, http://buscador.elu-
niversal.com/2004/10/03/apo_art_03152B.shtml (accessed March 16, 2006);
Alex Contreras Baspineiro, "Globalizing the Bolivarian Revolution, Hugo
Chávez's Proposal for Our América," Narco News, April 24, 2003. http://
www.narconews.com/Issue29/article746.html (accessed March 16, 2006).

98. John Hunt, "Evo Morales Elected Bolivian President in Landslide Victory,"
Toward Freedom, December 19, 2005, http://towardfreedom.com/home/con-
tent/view/708/ (accessed March 16, 2006); Forrest Hylton and Sinclair
Thomson, "The Chequered Rainbow," *New Left Review* 35, September–
October 2005, http://www.newleftreview.net/NLR26903.shtml (accessed
March 16, 2006).

99. Ibid.

100. Ibid.

101. Daphne Eviatar, "Bolivia's Home-Grown President," *The Nation*, December
21, 2005 (web only), http://www.thenation.com/doc/20060109/eviatar (accessed March 4, 2006).

102. Diego Cevallos, "Indigenous Leaders Celebrate Morales Victory," Inter
Press Service, December 19, 2005, http://www.ipsnews.net/news.asp?id-
news=31494 (accessed March 4, 2006).

103. "Bolivia: Tiny Nation, Big Troubles," *Christian Science Monitor*, June 9, 2005,
http://www.csmonitor.com/2005/0609/p08s01-comv.html (accessed March
4, 2006).

104. Daniel Howden, "In the Footsteps of Che Guevara: Democracy in South
America," *The Independent*, December 16, 2005, http://news.independent.co.
uk/world/americas/article333457.ece (accessed March 16, 2006).

105. "Bolivia: Tiny Nation, Big Troubles," *Christian Science Monitor*, June 9, 2005.

106. Hunt, "Evo Morales Elected."

107. Howden, "In the Footsteps of Che Guevara."

108. Hunt, "Evo Morales Elected."

109. Glaister, "Triumph for Bolivia's Candidate."

110. Gray, "Anti-U.S. Leftist Clinches Bolivia Election."

111. Glaister, "Triumph for Bolivia's Candidate"; Danna Harman, "In Bolivia, a Setback for U.S. Coca Drive," *Christian Science Monitor*, December 22, 2005, http://www.csmonitor.com/2005/1222/p04s02-woam.html (accessed March 4, 2006).

112. Glaister, "Triumph for Bolivia's Candidate."

113. Eviatar, "Bolivia's Home-Grown President"; Jerry Eisner, "Folk Medicine," *Encyclopedia Americana* (Grolier Online, 2003), http://go.grolier.com (accessed March 16, 2006); Varro E. Tyler, "Coca," *Encyclopedia Americana* (Grolier Online, 2003), http://go.grolier.com (accessed March 16, 2006).

114. David Mercado, "Bolivian Coca Farmers Less Hostile to Eradication," Reuters, reprinted on *Boston Globe* Web site, September 20, 2005, http://www.boston.com/news/world/latinamerica/articles/2005/09/20/bolivian_coca_farmers_less_hostile_to_eradication?mode=PF (accessed March 16, 2006).

115. Howden, "In the Footsteps of Che Guevara."

116. Mercado, "Bolivian Coca Farmers"; "New Government, Same Old Coca War," BBC News Web site, September 7, 2002, http://news.bbc.co.uk/2/hi/americas/2242739.stm (accessed March 16, 2006); Martín Arostegui, "Coca Wars Flare up Again in Bolivia," United Press International, reprinted on *Washington Times* Web site, June 28, 2004, http://www.washtimes.com/upi-breaking/20040628–011252–6155r.htm (accessed March 16, 2006).

117. Benjamin Dangl, "An Interview with Evo Morales, Legalizing the Colonization of the Americas," Counterpunch, December 2, 2003, http://www.counterpunch.org/dangl12022003.html (accessed March 4, 2006).

118. Ibid.

119. Tim Padgett, "Taking the Side of the Coca Farmer," *Time*, August 5, 2002, http://www.time.com/time/archive/preview/0,10987,1002983,00.html (accessed March 4, 2006).

120. Dangl, "An Interview with Evo Morales."

121. Jessica Holzer, "Dispatches From Bolivia," Slate.com, February 5, 2004, http://www.slate.com/id/2094899/entry/2094904 (accessed March 16, 2006); "Facts About Bolivian Candidate Morales," Associated Press, December 17, 2005, reprinted at *Boston Globe* Web site, http://www.boston.com/news/world/latinamerica/articles/2005/12/17/facts_about_bolivian_candidate_morales/ (accessed March 16, 2006).

122. Hugh O'Shaughnessy, "NS Profile—Evo Morales," *New Statesman*, January 23, 2006, http://www.newstatesman.com/200601230022 (accessed March 16, 2006); Danna Harman, "Bolivian Scores with Anti-U.S., Pro-Coca Stance," *USA Today*, December 15, 2005, http://www.usatoday.com/news/world/2005–12–15-morales-bolivia_x.htm?csp=34 (accessed March 17, 2006).

123. Juan Forero, "Elections Could Tilt Latin America Further to the Left," *New York Times*, December 10, 2005, http://www.nytimes.com/2005/12/10/international/americas/10bolivia.html?ex=1291870800&en=3a7c6491214e8332&ei=5088&partner=rssnyt&emc=rss (accessed March 4, 2006).

124. Langman, "A Man for the People."

125. Fernando Dias de Ávila Pires, "Llama," *Encyclopedia Americana* (Grolier Online, 2006), http://go.grolier.com (accessed March 16, 2006).

126. "Profile: Evo Morales," BBC News Web site, December 14, 2005, http://news.bbc.co.uk/2/hi/americas/3203752.stm (accessed March 16, 2006); "'Mesa quiere eliminarnos con racismo,' dice el líder cocalero de Bolivia Evo Morales," *El Tiempo*, March 22, 2005, http://eltiempo.terra.com.co/inte/latin/noticias/ARTICULO-WEB-_NOTA_INTERIOR-2016537.html (accessed March 17, 2006).

127. Langman, "A Man for the People."

128. Harman, "Bolivian Scores"; O'Shaughnessy, "NS Profile—Evo Morales"; Forero, "Elections Could Tilt Latin America,"

129. O'Shaughnessy, "NS Profile—Evo Morales"; "Morales: Fight Traffickers, Not Growers," Associated Press, January 28, 2006, reprinted at *Boston Globe* Web site, http://www.boston.com/news/world/latinamerica/articles/2006/01/28/morales_fight_traffickers_not_growers/?rss_id=Boston.com+%2F+News (accessed March 16, 2006).

130. "Facts about Bolivian Candidate Morales."

131. Hunt, "Evo Morales Elected Bolivian President."

132. Gray, "Anti-U.S. Leftist Clinches Bolivia Election"; Glaister, "Triumph for Bolivia's Candidate."

133. Padgett, "Taking the Side of the Coca Farmer."

134. Ibid.

135. Howden, "In the Footsteps of Che Guevara."

136. Dangl, "An Interview with Evo Morales."

137. Howden, "In the Footsteps of Che Guevara."

138. Cevallos, "Indigenous Leaders Celebrate."

139. Padgett, "Taking the Side of the Coca Farmer."

140. "Coca: ¿patrimonio o demonio?" June 23, 2005, BBC Mundo, http://news.bbc.co.uk/hi/spanish/forums/newsid_4115000/4115076.stm (accessed March 17, 2006).

141. "Tragedia Boliviana demuestra cinismo del sistema internacional," *El Universal*, October 20, 2003, http://buscador.eluniversal.com/2003/10/20/pol_art_20108C.shtml (accessed March 17, 2006).

142. Eviatar, "Bolivia's Home-Grown President."

143. Nick Buxton, "Trying to Reverse the Tide," ZNet, June 7, 2005, http://www.zmag.org/content/showarticle.cfm?SectionID=52&ItemID=8025 (accessed March 17, 2006).

144. Greg Wilpert, "Venezuela to Aid Bolivia's New President Morales," Venezuela Analysis, January 4, 2006, http://www.venezuelanalysis.com/news.php?newsno=1859 (accessed March 17, 2006).

145. Eviatar, "Bolivia's Home-Grown President."

146. Howden, "In the Footsteps of Che Guevara."

147. Gray, "Anti-U.S. Leftist Clinches Bolivia Election"; Ray Henkel, "Cochabamba," *Grolier Multimedia Encyclopedia*. Scholastic Library Publishing, 2006 http://gme.grolier.com (accessed March 17, 2006).

148. Cevallos, "Indigenous Leaders Celebrate"; Hunt, "Evo Morales Elected Bolivian President."

149. Howden, "In the Footsteps of Che Guevara."

150. Cevallos, "Indigenous Leaders Celebrate."

151. "Chávez vaticina refundación de Bolivia," *El Universal*, December 22, 2005, http://www.eluniversal.com/2005/12/22/int_art_22111C.shtml (accessed March 4, 2006).

152. Wilpert, "Venezuela to Aid Bolivia's New President."

153. "Buenos amigos," *El Universal*, June 8, 2005, http://buscador.eluniversal.com/2005/06/08/int_apo_08105C.shtml (accessed March 4, 2006).

154. Ibid.

155. "Jefe militar de EEUU asegura que Chávez financia a Evo Morales," *El Universal* (Caracas, Venezuela), January 21, 2005, http://buscador.eluniversal.com/2005/01/21/pol_art_21186E.shtml (accessed March 4, 2006); "U.S. Southern Command (SouthCom) Struggles for a Role in the War on Latin American Terrorism," Council on Hemispheric Affairs, Memorandum to the Press 04.58, September 2, 2004, http://www.coha.org/NEW_PRESS_RELEASES/New_Press_Releases_2004/04.58%20Terrorism%20FINAL%202.htm (accessed March 17, 2006); "Jefe militar de EEUU asegura que Chávez financia a Evo Morales"; "Evo Morales niega financiamiento desde Venezuela y Libia," *El Universal*, October 16, 2003, http://buscador.eluniversal.com/2003/10/16/int_art_16110D.shtml (accessed March 4, 2006).

156. "Evo Morales expresa su admiración por Hugo Chávez," *El Universal* (Caracas, Venezuela) June 4, 2004, http://buscador.eluniversal.com/2004/06/04/pol_ava_04A466047.shtml (accessed March 4, 2006).

157. "Evo Morales niega financiamiento desde Venezuela y Libia."

158. "Evo Morales expresa su admiración por Hugo Chávez."

159. Buxton, "Trying to Reverse the Tide."

160. "Natural Gas," Bolivia Country Analysis Brief, Energy Information Administration, October 2005, http://www.eia.doe.gov/emeu/cabs/Bolivia/NaturalGas.html (accessed March 17, 2006).

161. Buxton, "Trying to Reverse the Tide"; Eviatar, "Bolivia's Home-Grown President"; "Bolivia Candidate Morales Embraces Chávez to Battle Exxon, BG," Bloomberg.com, December 16, 2005, http://www.bloomberg.com/apps/news?pid=10000086&refer=latin_america&sid=aDd_2jJNqnQ4 (accessed March 17, 2006).

162. Eviatar, "Bolivia's Home-Grown President."

163. Howden, "In the Footsteps of Che Guevara"; Eviatar, "Bolivia's Home-Grown President."

164. Buxton, "Trying to Reverse the Tide."

165. Eviatar, "Bolivia's Home-Grown President."
166. "Bolivia: Morales habla de insurrección," BBC Mundo, July 12, 2002, http://news.bbc.co.uk/hi/spanish/latin_america/newsid_2125000/2125158.stm (accessed March 17, 2006).
167. "Chávez Makes Waves Again in Latin America," El Universal, January 7, 2006, http://english.eluniversal.com/2006/01/07/en_pol_art_07A651627.shtml (accessed March 17, 2006).
168. "Evo Morales cree que Chávez, Castro y Lula integran red antiglobalización."
169. Dangl, "An Interview with Evo Morales."
170. "Concluyó reunión entre Chávez y Evo Morales," El Universal, March 30, 2004, http://buscador.eluniversal.com/2004/03/30/pol_ava_30A443153.shtml (accessed March 4, 2006).
171. Howden, "In the Footsteps of Che Guevara."
172. Ibid.
173. Eviatar, "Bolivia's Home-Grown President."
174. Wilpert, "Venezuela to Aid Bolivia's New President."
175. Alan Clendenning, "Gas Reserves Could Ease Bolivia's Poverty," Associated Press, reprinted at ABC News Web site, http://abcnews.go.com/International/wireStory?id=1435833&page=2 (accessed March 17, 2006).
176. Jorge García, "Petrosur: Argentina y Venezuela quieren a Bolivia en la alianza," InfoBae (Argentine newspaper), July 22, 2004, http://www.infobae.com/notas/nota.php?Idx=127439&IdxSeccion=100442.
177. Alberto Garrido, "Tiempo Real, La andinización," El Universal, October 21, 2003, http://buscador.eluniversal.com/2003/10/21/opi_art_21106M.shtml (accessed March 4, 2006).
178. Barrios de Pie, "Evo Morales respaldó a Petroamérica," Clausura del II Congreso Bolivariano de los Pueblos, CBP Web site, December 13, 2004.

EPILOGUE

1. "Puerto Rico Profile: José Serrano," Puerto Rico Herald, July 28, 2000, http://www.puertorico-herald.org/issues/vol4n30/ProfileSerrano-en.shtml (accessed March 4, 2006)/
2. "New York's 16th District," Web site of Congressman José Serrano, undated, http://www.house.gov/serrano/district.shtml (accessed March 17, 2006).
3. "Puerto Rico Profile: José Serrano"; "Mayagüez," Encyclopedia Americana (Grolier Online, 2006), Scholastic Library Publishing, http://go.grolier.com (March 17, 2006).
4. "Serrano Named Most Liberal House Member," José Serrano Web site, February 15, 2001, http://www.house.gov/serrano/pressarchive/pr_010215_rating2.html (accessed March 17, 2006).
5. "Puerto Rico Profile: José Serrano."
6. José Serrano, "End the Embargo, for Cubans' Sake!" José Serrano Web site, May 25, 1999, http://www.house.gov/serrano/pressarchive/pr_990525_em-

bargo.html (accessed March 17, 2006); Pablo Bechelet, "U.N. Summit, Chávez Gets a Cheer in the Bronx," *Miami Herald,* September 18, 2005.

7. "Rep. José Serrano: One of Three Congress Members to Vote for Immediate U.S. Troop Withdrawal from Iraq, One of Two to Accept Venezuelan President Chávez' Offer of Cheap Oil to Poor U.S. Communities," *Democracy Now!* Web site, introduction to segment with José Serrano, December 1st, 2005.

8. "U.S. Congressman Blasts Bush Administration for Handling of Venezuela Coup; Seeks NED Accountability," Venezuela Analysis, December 8, 2004, http://www.venezuelanalysis.com/news.php?newsno=1440 (accessed March 4, 2006).

9. Backelet, "U.N. Summit, Chávez Gets a Cheer in the Bronx."

10. Diego Santos, "Chávez Criticizes U.N. Reforms in Speech," Associated Press, September 17, 2005, reprinted at *Boston Globe* Web site, http://www. boston.com/news/world/latinamerica/articles/2005/09/17/Chávez_criticizes_un_reforms_in_speech?mode=PF (accessed March 4, 2006); Bernardo Delgado, "Supporters Celebrate President Chávez's Return to Venezuela from New York," Venezuela Analysis, September 21, 2005, http://www. venezuelanalysis.com/news.php?newsno=1760 (accessed March 17, 2006).

11. Juan González, "Oil for Bronx Poor is a Foreign Gift Santa Claus, Make Way for Santa Chávez," New York *Daily News,* November 22, 2005, http://www. nydailynews.com/news/col/story/368051p–313135c.html (accessed March 4, 2006).

12. González, "Oil for Bronx Poor"; Jonathan Hicks, "Venezuela's Leader to Send Heating Oil to South Bronx," *New York Times,* November 26, 2005, http://www.nytimes.com/2005/11/26/nyregion/26oil.html?ex=1290661200&en=8d297d65b42bff17&ei=5089&partner=rssyahoo&emc=rss (accessed March 4, 2006).

13. González, "Oil for Bronx Poor is a Foreign Gift Santa Claus."

14. Nikolas Kozloff, "A Real Racial Democracy? Hugo Chávez and the Politics of Race," Counterpunch, October 14, 2005, http://www.counterpunch.org/kozloff10142005.html (accessed March 4, 2006).

15. Juan González, "Oil for Bronx Poor is a Foreign Gift Santa Claus."

16. Kozloff, "A Real Racial Democracy?"; Bernardo Delgado, "Venezuela to Provide Discounted Heating Oil and Free Eye Operations to U.S. Poor," Venezuela Analysis, August 28, 2005, http://www.venezuelanalysis.com/news.php?newsno=1736 (accessed March 17, 2006).

17. Kozloff, "A Real Racial Democracy?"

18. Matthew Robinson, "Venezuela Touts Cheap Fuel to U.S. as Bush Takes Heat," Reuters, December 2, 2005, reprinted at *Boston Globe* Web site, http://www.boston.com/news/nation/articles/2005/12/01/venezuela_touts_cheap_fuel_to_us_as_bush_takes_heat?mode=PF (accessed March 17, 2006).

19. Kozloff, "A Real Racial Democracy?"; "Outspoken Glover Under Fire," *Houston Chronicle,* May 14, 2005 (Factiva Database).

20. Ibid.
21. Ibid.
22. Ibid.
23. Ibid.
24. Ibid.

INDEX

AD (Acción Democrática), 19–20, 27,
    41–42, 53–55, 61
African Americans, Chávez's ties to,
    175, 177
Agrarian Reform Institute, 144
agrarian reforms, 20, 66, 111, 144, 148,
    160–61
Aharonian, Aram, 124–27
Al Jazeera, 30, 127–28, 130
Alaby, Michel, 130
ALBA (Bolivarian Aternative for the
    Americas), 73–74, 145
Alcántara, Pedro Pablo, 68
Alfonzo, Juan Pablo Pérez, 24
Alegría, Rafael, 165
Almeida, Beto, 127
Aló, Presidente, 3, 26, 100, 136, 169, 172,
    177
Amaru, Túpac, 119
ANCAP (Administración Nacional de
    Combustibles, Alcohol, y
    Portland), 121
Angarita, Medina, 17, 43
anti-Chavista campaign, 29–30, 57, 68,
    91–93, 129–30
antiglobalization movement, 44, 58,
    60–61, 63, 67, 171
Apertura party, 56
Argentina
    Mercosur and, 131–32
    Petrosur and, 105, 122–23, 172
    piqueteros in, 71–72
    Summit of the Americas and, 114–18
    Telesur and, 127–28
Aristide, Jean Bertrand, 33, 110
Asencio, Diego, 55
Aymara, 164, 166–67, 169
Azpurua, Carlos, 156

Baduel, José, 30, 94, 96
Baker, James, 13, 38, 63
Barranco Yopal, 84, 141–42, 157–58
Barry, Tom, 39
Betancourt, Rómulo, 19–20, 43
Blair, Tony, 128
Bolívar, Simón, symbolic importance of,
    3–4, 34, 39–40, 46, 51, 73, 83–91,
    93–97, 109, 122, 131, 159, 162,
    164–65, 170–72
Bolivarian Circles, 88–89, 91, 94–97
Bolivarian Revolution, 4, 34, 88
Bolton, John, 62
Borges, Esteban Gil, 15
Botero, Jorge Enrique, 127
Bourgeois, Ray, 100
Brazil
    oil diplomacy and, 105–18
    opposition to U.S. trade policies, 65,
        74
    Petrosur and, 122
    political movements in, 4, 72, 132
    Telesur and, 127–28
    trade with Venezuela, 33
Broad Front, 120–21
Broadcasting Board of Governors
    (BBG), 130
Bronx, NY, 173–75, 177
Brownfield, William, 100, 158
Bush, George H.W., 13, 38–39
Bush, George W., 155, 160, 170, 172,
    174–77
    Carlyle and, 13–14
    Chávez and, 1–2, 5, 8, 105, 107,
        109–10, 155, 160, 170, 172,
        174–77
    FTAA and, 63–68, 72–73
    oil trade and, 26–27, 124

protests against, 73–74, 114
Telesur and, 127–28
Venezuelan arms purchases and,
    101–2
war on drugs and, 145–49
Buxton, Julia, 176

Cabrera, Ovidio, 127
cacerolazos, 53, 72, 94
Caldera, Rafael, 54, 62
Campins, Luis Herrera, 42–43
Caño Limón pipeline, 148
CAP. *See* Pérez, Carlos Andres
capitalism, 38, 43, 65, 70, 111, 144–45,
    171
Cárdenas, Arias, 88
Cardona, Sergio, 87
Cardoso, Fernando Henrique, 65, 106,
    108–12
Carlyle Group, 13–14
Carmona, Pedro, 28–30, 68–69, 93–96,
    146
Carneiro, Jorge Luis García, 78–82,
    84–85, 90, 92–95, 98, 103
Carrara, Antonio, 112–13
Castro, Fidel, 14, 18, 25, 30, 32, 40–41,
    62, 88, 101, 105, 130, 137, 170,
    174
Cauca, 139–40, 144, 146, 150–51, 164
Central Intelligence Agency. *See* CIA
Chancoso, Blanca, 165
Cheney, Dick, 13, 172, 177
China, 35–36, 101, 116
Cholango, Humberto, 162
CIA (Central Intelligence Agency) 2,
    12, 32, 98, 100, 134, 154–55, 158,
    160
Ciciliano, Pedro, 135
Cisneros, Gustavo, 50–52, 54–55, 57,
    68–69, 127, 129
Cisneros, Patricia Phelps de, 51
CITGO, 35, 87, 174–76
civil-military relations, 82, 91, 94,
    102–3
Clinton, Bill, 13, 26, 39–40, 50, 55,
    62–63, 65, 139
coca, farming of, 51, 138, 140, 143,
    146–51, 162, 164–70
Coddon, David, 151

Cofán Indians, 161
COHA (Council on Hemispheric
    Affairs), 4
Colombia
    Chávez and, 30
    FARC and, 99, 101–2
    indigenous peoples and, 136–42,
        144
    kidnapping of Venezuelan ranchers
        and, 89–90
    PdVSA and, 35
    U.S. drug war and, 146–54, 161–62,
        168–69
    Venezuela and, 123–24
Convergencia party, 54
CONAIE (Confederation of
    Ecuadorian Indigenous
    Nationalities), 154–55, 158–64
CONVIVIR, 144
COPEI (Social Christian Party), 42,
    54–55, 61
coup d'etat, against Chávez, 2, 4, 27,
    29–30, 33–34, 41, 43, 46–47, 53,
    55, 67–69, 72, 74, 78, 82, 88,
    92–98, 100, 103, 108–9, 114, 163,
    169, 174
Craddock, John, 77–78, 98–99, 103, 170
Creole Petroleum Corporation, 12, 14,
    16–17, 57, 162
CTV (Venezuelan Workers
    Confederation), 27
Cuba, 170, 174
    Chávez and, 3, 14, 40–41, 54, 62
    media and, 126–28, 136–37
    military ties to Venezuela, 77, 86–87,
        89, 97–98, 101–3
    oil trade and, 25, 29–32, 73

De la Rúa, Fernando, 72
de Lozada, Sánchez, 165
de Sucre, Antonio José, 131, 141, 170
De Vida, Julio, 122
Defense Intelligence Agency, 143
DeLong, Seth, 124, 130–32
Díaz, Ricardo, 134
drugs, war on, 3, 89, 99, 101, 123–24,
    134, 139, 143, 146–51, 161, 163,
    167–68, 170
Dutra, José Eduardo, 110, 113

Eagle Plan, 92
Ecuador, 4, 35, 67, 106, 123, 131,
    133–34, 148, 151, 153–54,
    158–65, 169–70
ejidos, 48
Ellner, Steve, 46, 54, 62, 70, 75, 117
Enarsa (Energía Argentina Sociedad
    Anónima), 116–18
energy integration, 106, 113, 117, 130,
    172
environmental issues, 15–16, 38, 40,
    58–59, 63–65, 67, 154, 174
Escobar, Pablo, 142–43
Exxon-Mobil, 34

FARC (Revolutionary Armed Forces of
    Colombia), 101, 139–41, 143,
    148–52
FBI, 17, 119
Fedepetrol, 27
Fletcher, Bill, 178
FMLN (Farabundo Martí National
    Liberation Front), 44
foreign debt, 154, 163, 169
    ALBA and, 74–75
    Argentina and, 71–72
    Brazil and, 109, 111, 113
    Uruguay and, 120–23
    Venezuela and, 24, 42–43, 54–56, 62
foreign investment, 37, 40, 54, 108–9
Foreign Relations Reauthorization Bill,
    130
Frank, Andre Gunder, 65
free trade, 37, 39–40, 51–52, 55, 57–58,
    67, 72–73, 114–15, 123, 131, 144,
    149–51, 161, 164
FTAA (Free Trade Area of the
    Americas) 39–41, 55, 63–68,
    72–74, 115, 131–32, 144–46,
    149–50, 171
    Québec summit, 63–67, 75

GAO (Government Accountability
    Office), 36
Garrido, Alberto, 146
Garzón, Luis Eduardo, 151
Gas del Estado, 116
GATT (General Agreement on Tariffs
    and Trade), 57

Gedicks, Al, 148
Giusti, Luis, 8–11, 13–14, 17, 24–28,
    34, 89
globalization, 5, 37, 44, 49–52, 57–61,
    63, 65, 67, 72, 106, 111, 171
Glover, Danny, 127, 176–77
Gómez, Juan Vicente, 14–17, 77–78
Gómez, María Luz, 168
Gran Colombia federation, 131, 133
Gulf War, 24, 46
Gutiérrez, Lucio, 163–64

Haiti, 33, 110, 115
Hill, James, 170
Humala, Ollanta, 123–24
Hurricane Katrina, 175–76
hydrocarbon industry, 25–26, 34,
    116–17, 122, 170–71
Hydrocarbons Law, 25–26, 34, 117

I Speak to Caracas, 156
IESA (Instituto de Estudios Superiores
    de Administración) 27–28, 43, 46,
    63
IMF (International Monetary Fund),
    37, 43–44, 53–55, 58–60, 62, 67,
    69, 72, 74, 109, 111, 121, 136,
    151, 169
indigenous peoples, 4, 49, 51, 67, 84,
    89, 126, 128, 134–37, 139–42,
    144–51, 153–67, 169–72, 177
information war, 119–31
    See also media
International Military Front, 87, 89
International Relations Center, 39
internationalism, 39, 63, 125, 159–60
INTESA (Informática, Negocios, y
    Tecnología), 12, 32, 34
Iraq, 3, 11, 13, 27, 98, 125, 128, 174,
    177
Izarra, Andrés, 127
Izarra, William, 127

Jersey Standard, 14
Jiménez, Julio, 155
Jiménez, Marcos Pérez, 19–20, 78

Keller, Alfredo, 132
Kichwa Confederation of Ecuador, 162

Kirchner, Nestor, 72–74, 115–17, 131
Kiwa, Ati, 128
Koppel, Ted, 1, 18

La Causa R, 24
Labio, Luis, 140–41
Laird, Melvin, 12
Lake Maracaibo, oil production in, 8–9, 12, 14–16, 23, 32, 57, 66, 77, 90, 129, 136
Lameda, Guaicaipuro, 26, 29, 87, 89, 92–93
land reform, 3, 20, 102–3, 160–61, 163
Leahy, Patrick, 147
Leech, Garry, 151–52
Llaguno Bridge, battle at, 91–92
Los Barrosos–2, 15
Lugar, Richard, 36
Lula da Silva, Luiz Inácio, 72, 74, 106–15, 170
Lusinchi, Jaime, 42–43
Luzardo, Alexander, 158

Macas, Luis, 158–64, 170
Mack, Connie, 129–30
Mahuad, Jamil, 163
Maisto, John, 61–62
Mar del Plata, 73–74, 114–15
maracuchos, 16
Maradona, Diego, 74
Maraven, 9–10
Marcos, Subcomandante, 49–50, 78
Mariño, Antonio, 156
MAS (Moviemento al Socialismo), 54, 157, 165, 171–72
MBR 200 (Movimiento Bolivariano Revolucionario 200) 46, 53, 80, 82, 94
McCormack, Sean, 1
media, 4–5, 8, 15, 27, 45, 51, 55, 58–59, 63, 67, 69, 72, 85–86, 91–93, 125–27, 129, 157, 160, 174, 176–77
Mexico, 7, 25, 38–40, 48–50, 54, 57, 60, 116, 124, 128, 135
Ministry of Energy and Mines, 10, 12
Miraflores, 27, 45, 47, 55, 80, 83, 90–93, 95, 102
Mission Robinson, 137

Mission Guaicaipuro, 26, 29, 87, 141
missionaries, 154–60
Mitrione, Dan, 119–20
Mommer, Bernard, 10–11, 18, 25
Morales, Cipriano Martínez, 87
Morales, Evo, 74, 164–72
Morales, Luis Eduardo García, 87
Movimento dos Trabalhadores Rurais Sem Terra. *See* MST
MPP (Movement of Popular Participation), 120
MST (Movimento dos Trabalhadores Rurais Sem Terra), 4, 111
Mujica, José, 119–21
MVR (Movimiento Quinta República), 31, 41, 46, 54, 61, 162

Nasa, 139–41, 144–45, 147, 150–51, 154, 164
National Endowment for Democracy, 2, 4, 27
nationalization, 9, 42–43, 116, 124, 170, 172
Navarro Wolf, Antonio, 151
neoconservatism, 38, 62, 86, 98
neoliberalism, 31, 37–41, 43–46, 48–50, 53–57, 59, 61–63, 65, 67, 69, 71–75, 109, 114–15, 134, 136, 139, 145, 148, 151, 171–72
New Tribes Mission, 155–58
"Nojolivud," 126

Obrador, Andrés Manuel López, 124
Occidental, 148
oil companies, foreign, 9–10, 17, 24, 34
OPEC (Organization of Petroleum Exporting Countries) 3, 7, 11, 24–26, 30–31, 41, 62, 106
OPIC (U.S. Overseas Private Investment Corporation), 34
Orchila, imprisonment of Chávez at, 69, 93
Organization of Petroleum Exporting Countries. *See* OPEC
Oriente oil field, 46, 154
Orinoco Oil Belt, 7, 34, 113, 122, 137, 142, 157

Pachakutik Movement, 162

Palacio, Alfredo, 123, 163–64
Palast, Greg, 40
pardos, 23, 41, 54, 135
Parrish, Geov, 66–67
Patriotic Junta, 87, 92
PdVSA (Petróleos de Venezuela
    Sociedad Anónima) 7–14, 24–29,
    31–35, 37, 77, 87, 89, 91–92,
    97–98, 105, 110, 112–13, 116–18,
    122, 128
Pérez Alfonzo, Isaac, 28
Pérez, Carlos Andrés (CAP), 42–48,
    53–54, 56, 62, 68–69, 82, 85, 87,
    121
Pérez Recao, Isaac Rafael, 28–30
Perkins, John, 154, 160
Petras, James, 71, 111, 115
Petroamérica, 105–7, 112–13, 123–24,
    172
Petrobrás (Petróleo Brasileiro), 105–6,
    108–10, 112–13, 116
petroleum, exports of, 3, 7–9, 11–12, 14,
    17–18, 24, 28, 32, 34–35, 41–42,
    54, 57, 60, 66, 97, 106, 108, 113,
    116–17, 122–23, 127, 154
Petroleum Investment Law, 108
Petrosur, 3, 105, 116, 122, 124, 172
piqueteros, 71–73, 114–15
Pittier, Henri, 15
Plan Bolívar, 83–88, 90
Plan Colombia, 146–49, 162–64
    See also drugs, war on
Pocaterra, Nohelí, 177
Podur, Justin, 144
Powell, Colin, 110
PPT (Patria Para Todos), 24, 31
PRD (Party of the Democratic
    Revolution), 124
PRI (Institutional Revolutionary Party),
    48–49
privatization, 11, 13, 25, 37, 48, 54–55,
    62, 67, 72–73, 108, 110, 115–16,
    121, 144, 161, 171
PT (Partido dos Trabalhadores), 72, 108
Punto Fijo Pact, 47, 61
Putumayo, 147–49

Quijada, Ramón, 20–21
Quinn, Tom, 138

Quiroga, Jorge, 170
Quispe, Felipe, 164

Radio Martí, 130
Ramírez, Rafael, 10, 12, 122
Ramos, Jorge, 128
Rangel, José Vicente, 100, 149, 156–58
Reagan, Ronald, 38, 51, 160
Reed, Curtis, 130
Reich, Otto, 50, 68–69, 90
*Resource Rebels: Native Challenges to
    Mining and Oil Corporations*
    (Gedicks), 148
Richardson, Bill, 26
Robertson, Pat, 1, 155, 158, 177
Rodríguez, Alí, 1, 17–18, 21, 23–27,
    30–34, 74, 78, 85, 110, 113, 172,
    174
Rodríguez, Félix, 2, 174
Rodríguez, Simón, 137
Rojas, Alberto Müller, 155
Roldós, Jaime, 159–60
Romer, Henrique Salas, 55, 69
Rousseff, Dilma, 110, 122
Rumsfeld, Donald, 1, 62, 98–99, 101,
    103
Russell, A. Lewis, 17

SAIC (Science Applications
    International Corporation),
    11–12, 32, 34
Salinas de Gortari, Carlos, 39, 48–49
Sandinistas, 160
School of the Americas, 81, 89, 92, 96,
    99
Selsky, Andrew, 95
September 11, 2001, effects on U.S.-
    Venezuelan relations, 13, 67, 134,
    149
Serrano, José, 173
Shell Oil, 9, 13–14, 43
Simer, Jeremy, 66
Southern Command, 77, 99, 170
Stiglitz, Joseph, 37
student protests, 45
Summit of the Americas, 51, 55, 73, 114

taxes, 3, 31, 35, 172
Telesur, 3, 125–30, 177

Texaco, 106, 154
torture, allegations of, 78, 98, 100, 110,
    119
TransAfrica Forum, 176–78
Tupamaros, 119–20, 122, 126

United States, 1–2, 13, 26, 38, 62–63,
    96, 100, 102, 105–106, 110, 120,
    124–125, 130, 134, 164, 172, 177
    2000 election, 63
    Drug Enforcement Agency, 149, 167
    State Department, 1, 15, 30, 38, 90,
        149, 158, 164, 170, 174
Univisión, 50, 57, 127–28
Uribe, Alváro, 124, 142–44, 148–52
Uruguay, 38, 72, 74, 105, 118–23,
    125–28, 132
U.S. AID (United States Agency for
    International Development), 4
U'wa Indians, 148

Vásquez, Efraín, 81, 89, 91–97, 121
Vázquez, Tabaré, 121–22
Venevisíon, 47, 50–51, 68–69
Venezuelan military, 5, 15, 41, 70,
    77–79, 81, 86, 99–101, 103, 131,
    156–57
Venezuelan Peasants Federations, 20

Venoco, 28
"Vuelvan Caras" ("Turning Lives
    Around") program, 102

Walters, John, 149
Washington Consensus, 37–38, 41, 43,
    46, 48, 50, 57, 109, 115, 134, 146,
    160–61
WHISC (Western Hemisphere
    Institute for Security
    Coorperation), 81–82, 90, 99–100
Wilhelm, Charles, 99
Wilpert, Greg, 32, 67, 70, 89, 103, 129
Wolfowitz, Paul, 62
World Bank, 37, 59–60, 67, 166, 169
World Social Forum, 111
WTO (World Trade Organization), 38,
    57–58, 66, 74
    Seattle convention, protests at,
        57–60, 64, 66

Yavari, Barne, 156
YPF (Yacimientos Petrolíferos Fiscales),
    116, 172

Zapatistas, 49–50, 60, 71
Zoellick, Robert, 38–39, 62–65, 67,
    71–73, 111